Yesterday

Yesterday

A NEW HISTORY OF
NOSTALGIA

Tobias Becker

Harvard University Press

Cambridge, Massachusetts | London, England   2023

Library of Congress Cataloging-in-Publication Data

Names: Becker, Tobias, author.

Title: Yesterday : a new history of nostalgia / Tobias Becker.

Description: Cambridge, Massachusetts ; London, England : Harvard University Press, 2023.

Identifiers: LCCN 2023002237 | ISBN 9780674251755 (hardcover)

Subjects: LCSH: Nostalgia—History. | Nostalgia—Political aspects. | Collective memory. | Progress. | Popular culture.

Classification: LCC BF575.N6 B435 2023 | DDC 155.9/2—dc23/eng/20230501

LC record available at https://lccn.loc.gov/2023002237

To Josie and Len

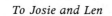

Contents

Then one day the violent need is there: Get off the train! Jump clear! A homesickness, a longing to be stopped, to cease evolving, to stay put, to return to the point before the thrown switch put us on the wrong track.

—Robert Musil, *The Man without Qualities*

Longing on a large scale is what makes history.

—Don DeLillo, *Underworld*

The place I love best is a sweet memory.

—Bob Dylan, "Workingman's Blues #2"

Introduction

Yesterday
All my troubles seemed so far away
Now it looks as though they're here to stay
Oh, I believe in yesterday

—The Beatles, "Yesterday"

hances are, when you read these lyrics, you also start to hear the music in your head. "Yesterday" is one of the most recorded songs of all time. A wide range of artists have covered it, including Count Basie, Ray Charles, Aretha Franklin, Frank Sinatra, Elvis Presley, Bob Dylan, Joan Baez, the Royal Philharmonic Orchestra, and Boyz II Men.[1] It has been on the radio countless times, been strummed around campfires. It has been played at weddings and at funerals. In a way, it was a classic from the moment it came to Paul McCartney in a dream one morning in 1964. He was so convinced he had heard the melody before, he went around for a month asking anyone he came across if they knew it. When no one did, he wrote it down. Coming up with the lyrics took longer. Certainly, the song would have been less successful with the lines the Beatles used as a placeholder: "Scrambled eggs / Oh my baby how I love your legs."[2]

"Yesterday" is a lover's lament, but the sentiment the song expresses—and perhaps also evokes for many listeners—is a more general one, commonly known as nostalgia. The word is more than three centuries old, but it did not always have the meaning that it has for us today. When it was coined in 1688 (and not 1678, as some accounts claim) by the Alsatian (often wrongly described as Swiss) physician Johannes Hofer, it was used to describe what Hofer saw as a new, pathological, and, in some cases, even lethal form of homesickness. Hofer sought a scientific term and so cobbled together the ancient Greek words for "return" (*nostos*) and "pain" (*algos*) from Homer's *Odyssey*. That *nostalgia* was truly just a fancy synonym for the German *Heimweh* (homesickness) is already apparent from the title of his medical dissertation: "De Nostalgia, Oder Heimwehe."[3] Neither Hofer's dissertation nor the considerable medical literature expanding on it over the course of the next two hundred years helps to explain how nostalgia shed its spatial connotation as yearning for home to take on a temporal one as yearning for the past.[4]

For some scholars, Hofer's original interpretation implicitly contained a temporal dimension; for others, homesickness and nostalgia began to overlap—or to drift apart, depending on the perspective—during the nineteenth century; for a third group, this shift began in the early twentieth century.[5] But it has hardly been noticed that the word *nostalgia*—in its new, temporal connotation—first appeared in dictionaries in the 1960s and only gained widespread usage in intellectual thought and everyday language in the 1970s. In fact, it was in the very same year that McCartney came up with the melody for "Yesterday" that *The Concise Oxford English Dictionary* first listed the new definition: "sentimental yearning for (some period of) the past."[6] On the surface, the meaning has not changed much since then. Now online, the latest version of *The Oxford English Dictionary* defines *nostalgia* as a "sentimental longing for or regretful memory of a period of the past."[7]

That broad definition does not capture the full meaning of nostalgia. In particular, it neglects the ideological subtexts and often negative connotations that are involved in how we understand and use the concept. *Yesterday* argues that those connotations are essential for explaining the timing of nostalgia's reappearance in a new meaning that was anything but coincidental. In the era of the Vietnam War, the countercultural movement, economic downturn, domestic terrorism, the fear of nuclear holocaust, environmental destruction, and the depletion of natural resources, as well as what many felt to be accelerated social and cultural change, the very idea of progress began to appear more suspect and contested than ever before.[8] As a result of a troubled present and uncertain future, more and more people sought refuge in an allegedly better past—or so it seemed to many contemporary observers. One of them was the American futurologist Alvin Toffler, who did much to popularize this theory. He also coined the phrase "nostalgia wave," which quickly caught on with the media and intellectuals alike.[9] The meaning it adopted was a negative one, denoting misguided attitudes toward or improper uses of the past. Despite—or perhaps exactly because of—such connotations, *nostalgia* became a key term of intellectual as well as public discourse.

For its critics, nostalgia was a new phenomenon: a symptom of and a response to what they saw as a crisis of Western modernity. Yet neither longing for the past nor believing it to be superior to the present was an invention of modernity. What postwar modernity—postmodernity—produced was not what it called nostalgia, *Yesterday* argues, but the nostalgia critique as a veiled defense of the modern idea of progress that had come under threat. The historical context of its origins has determined the meanings of nostalgia to this day: try as one might, it is almost impossible to apply it in a neutral or analytical manner due to the overwhelmingly pejorative connotations it carries in intellectual thought. The way we think about nostalgia today remains deeply rooted in these older debates. That is why it is important to explore the concept's genesis, to reconstruct how it has evolved, and to examine how it still informs today's thinking—in short, to historicize it.

With some notable exceptions, however, historians have been reluctant to engage with nostalgia, more reluctant still to historicize it. The reasons for this are not hard to find: among the nostalgia critics, historians are the fiercest. As the British historian Raphael Samuel has observed, historians generally treat nostalgia "as a contemporary equivalent of what Marxists used to call 'false consciousness' and existentialists 'bad faith.'"[10] The most common charge is that it distorts the past: by redesigning it "as a comfortable refuge," it makes the past "better and simpler than the present."[11] For the historian Charles Maier, for instance, nostalgia is not at all the same as longing but a debased version of it at best: "Nostalgia is to longing as kitsch is to art," he declares.[12] Christopher Lasch, another historian, insists that nostalgia "does not entail the exercise of memory at all."[13] Through the very act of rendering the past an object of sentimental reminiscence, nostalgia disfigures it, making it the very opposite of history; and taken together, these remarks fundamentally call into question the *Oxford English Dictionary* definition. "Nostalgia

Tells It Like It Wasn't," the title of one article succinctly puts it.[14] Whereas history explores the past to better *understand* it and, through it, the present, nostalgia, or "history without guilt," falsifies the past to *feel* better in the present and, to that end, forgets, downplays, and ignores its horrors.[15] It is considered, at the very least, "dangerous," and the historian Dipesh Chakrabarty has even called it—winkingly—"the sin of sins."[16]

Yet if we historians are so adamant in our rejection of nostalgia, we should at the very least be clear about what it is we are rejecting. If we accuse others of it, what is it exactly that we are accusing them of? And what are we defending? Asking these questions is especially important because, all too often, the urge to dismiss nostalgia offhandedly seems to be rooted in an unacknowledged belief in progress and the felt need to preserve it. At other times, historians evoke nostalgia to dispose more easily of the experiential and emotional engagement with the past that is characteristic of popular history and, thereby, to uphold their interpretative authority over the past and their own approach as the only legitimate one. If nostalgia is so problematic for us historians, that should be all the more reason for us to investigate it and what makes it appear so problematic. Paying more attention to what we hold to be the "opposite of history" may end up telling us a lot about how we understand and create history and the unquestioned assumptions involved in such processes.

Studies of nostalgia alternate between not defining the word at all, because its meaning is taken for granted, and losing themselves in ever more nuanced definitions, often by distinguishing between different forms such as reflexive and interpreted nostalgia, reflective and restorative nostalgia, or nostalgic mood and nostalgia mode, to name but a few.[17] *Yesterday* chooses a different approach. Instead of coming up with yet another definition to add to the growing list of existing ones, it investigates the history of the term and the concept itself, the meanings and connotations attached to it.

Terminology, and changes in terminology specifically, says a lot about societies. In an article from 1966, the first historical study on nostalgia, the Swiss historian of medicine and ideas Jean Starobinski applied "historical semantics" to the subject of nostalgia.[18] Starobinski, focusing on nostalgia in its old, medical meaning, concluded by highlighting that it had recently taken on a "poetic meaning," now denoting a "useless yearning for a world or for a way of life from which one has been irrevocably severed," but did not investigate it further.[19] *Yesterday* picks up exactly where Starobinski left off: in the 1960s, as one meaning ceased and another came into vogue, charting the career of the concept over the following decades, by studying closely who used it; how, why, and in what contexts they used it; and how it acquired, through its usage, meaning and meanings far beyond the dictionary definition. At the same time, the book concentrates on what it holds to be the dominant understanding of nostalgia since the middle of the twentieth century—as counterpart or antithesis to progress. Such a history is the prerequisite for employing the concept in a more meaningful and reflective way than is often the case, even in specialist literature. The conceptual approach is closely wedded to three other approaches and fields: the study of memory, emotions, and temporality.

Except perhaps for Lasch, few would doubt that nostalgia has something to do with memory. What this something may be, however, is less clear. Is nostalgia a certain kind or form of memory? Or is it, by contrast, a memory deficiency, not rendering the past as it was (does memory ever?) but distorting it? When the French sociologist Maurice Halbwachs discovered the social foundations of memory in the 1920s, he devoted a chapter on nostalgia, marveling at the "incomprehensible attraction" it bestows on the past.[20] Yet when researchers rediscovered his texts in the 1980s as a cornerstone for the then-emerging field of memory studies, they were initially slow to include nostalgia in their deliberations. Even now, there is no comprehensive theory of nostalgia as memory. As a work of history, *Yesterday* cannot provide such a theory either. Rather, it shows how central the issue of nostalgia was to the thinking about memory and particularly how it was used to discredit memory as a subject of investigation, by emphasizing its unreliability. In other words, the present book is more interested in the thinking about memory than its workings.

One reason why memory studies came rather late to the topic of nostalgia may have to do with its emotional quality. After all, nostalgia can be understood as a "historical emotion," as scholar Svetlana Boym has termed it.[21] In his work on nostalgia, Starobinski already proposed "historical semantics" as an indispensable tool for a "history of emotions."[22] When it emerged as a field in its own right, the history of emotions—though likely unaware of Starobinski's remark—took up his idea.[23] Still a relatively young field, it has already produced considerable research on nostalgia, if mainly in its old guise as homesickness.[24] It also provides a set of questions and tools to historicize emotions—for instance, by asking how they are communicated through language and performed through expressions, habits, or rituals. Are, for instance, practices like preserving, collecting, restoring, or reenacting inherently nostalgic? Is there something like an emotional style of nostalgia, a certain way in which it is experienced, fostered, and displayed? Is nostalgia part of the emotional regime, the normative order of emotions, in the twentieth century, or does it, in contrast, act as an emotional refuge, as a niche of deliberate slowness and intentional backwardness in societies emphasizing speed and progress?[25] Again, however, this book is primarily concerned with a more fundamental point: how emotions are employed as an accusation; in this case, how characterizing someone or something as nostalgic and therefore as emotional and, by implication, irrational dismisses their engagement with the past. *Yesterday* argues that nostalgia cannot be studied divorced from the emotional quality attributed to it because it was this quality that determined so much of how it was understood.

A lot of the writing on nostalgia also operates with—often implicit—assumptions about time; namely that nostalgia is predicated on the modern understanding of time as linear, dynamic, and homogeneous. According to this line of thought, change was too slow and gradual in premodern societies to allow for a nostalgic view of the past. It only emerged thanks to a fundamental break with the past around 1800—the time of the French and the Industrial Revolutions—that triggered an acceleration of history to which nostalgia was result, reaction, and antidote all in one.[26] What could be called the "standard theory of nostalgia," however, not only underestimates the extent of change in past societies, it also overlooks that many of them conceived of the past exactly in the way the twentieth century came to call nostalgic: viewing it as better than the present, a lost golden age. Indeed, neither longing for the past nor extolling it was inherently modern, but, on the contrary, each was a common mode by which most premodern societies made sense of time. What modernity pioneered was not nostalgia but the idea of universal progress.[27] As the traditional past orientation did not fit in with the new view of time, contradicted it even, it had to be contained and excluded, and this was done by pathologizing it—resurrecting an antiquated medical term for an outmoded sickness—as nostalgia, thereby affirming the modern idea of homogeneous, uniform, linear, teleological time. Here *Yesterday* builds on and adds to the history of temporalities by corroborating its findings that the modern understanding of time came to be contested in the second half of the twentieth century by the realization that even within Western (let alone other) societies, people experienced and perceived time in different ways, as well as by the emergence of postmodern theories about time.[28]

Commonly understood as a phenomenon of Western modernity, it is not surprising that nostalgia has been studied mostly for Western societies, particularly the United States and Europe—in a revealing distinction, Eastern Europe was only included after it became part of Western, capitalist modernity following the fall of communism. Little research has been conducted on other regions of the world, although nostalgia is sometimes applied to them without an awareness of the implications of imposing a Western concept on non-Western cultures. Psychologists even go a step further when they argue that nostalgia is a "pancultural emotion" that can be found across the globe.[29] Similarly, the historian David Lowenthal has claimed that "nostalgia is worldwide."[30] Is it really? Given that even the variations of Hofer's neologism across European languages carry slightly different connotations, it is more than likely that differences between cultures are even more pronounced. For the Japanese language—which has two concepts for nostalgia, the English loanword *nosutarujia* and the much older but confusingly similar-sounding indigenous word *natsukashisa*—historian Makoto Harris Takao has shown how implicit and explicit Anglocentric concepts have come to overwhelm and sideline local understanding.[31]

While a comparison of related concepts across cultures promises fascinating results, this would still presuppose a better knowledge of what the concept means in the Western context in which it originated—especially because it has so often been understood as inherently Western and modern. It is not out of a disregard for other cultures, then, that *Yesterday* focuses on the modernized West, but because a clearer understanding of nostalgia in this context is the basis for any comparison. Boym argues that many European nations like to invoke some form of nostalgia as a marker rendering them unique and different from anyone else: the Portuguese have *saudade,* the Czech *litost,* the Germans *Sehnsucht,* the Russians *toska,* and so on. For Boym, all these allegedly untranslatable words are "in fact synonyms."[32] But are they really? Writing in English and using the English word *nostalgia,* Boym takes this for granted, and so have most studies on nostalgia, thereby neglecting local meanings and differences between languages.

Studying nostalgia exclusively in a national framework, on the other hand, would be too narrow, particularly because, as Boym has rightly criticized, it has so often been framed as nation specific. Such an approach would neglect the transnational nature of the nostalgia discourse and of the phenomena and practices it sought to explain. Ideas know no borders and neither do fashions, intellectual and otherwise. Whereas the diagnosis of a "nostalgia wave" spread to Europe almost as soon as it emerged, the word *retro* was taken up so quickly and widely that most people were not even aware that it derived from a specifically French debate about the afterlife of the German occupation.[33] Given such border crossings, it would be not only shortsighted but also misleading to explore the history of nostalgia merely in a national context, especially as that would also further substantiate existing national readings. *Yesterday* therefore takes a transnational perspective focusing mainly on the United States and the United Kingdom, where the new definition originated and where nostalgia was debated most heatedly, occasionally bringing in Germany—West Germany for most of the period in question—and France as points of comparison. Sometimes it follows transnational movements, sometimes it compares examples from different countries, and sometimes it uses one case to make a general point that pertains to all of them. But in all these instances it tries to keep the balance between viewing nostalgia in both specific local and wider transnational contexts.

The ambivalent meanings of nostalgia and how they developed and changed over time, as well as how nostalgia was theorized and used depending on different historical contexts, are the subject of Chapter 1. It begins with Toffler's diagnosis of nostalgia as a response to "future shock" before examining the roots of this theory in the preceding decades and returning to its reception and the 1970s discussion of the nostalgia wave. From there, it traces the nostalgia discourse through the following decades, focusing particularly on its role in debates about heritage, postmodernism, memory, and presentism. The chapter concludes by discussing the problems of the existing theories of nostalgia. Such a conceptual and discursive history of the term *nostalgia* is essential for employing it more analytically. It also provides the narrative thread for the following chapters, which examine the issues raised by the nostalgia discourse in more detail, confronting it with the phenomena and practices it tries to explain in order to come to a better understanding of both.

Chapter 2 looks at the "politics of nostalgia," a term that emerged as part of the liberal critique of "New Conservatism" and conservative politicians like Barry Goldwater in the 1950s and 1960s. After examining these debates, the chapter jumps to the 1980s when the phrase—and the charge it contained—was attached to Ronald Reagan, Margaret Thatcher, and, to a lesser degree, Helmut Kohl. It picks up again in the recent past when the nostalgia argument resurfaced to explain the outcome of the British European Union membership referendum and the election of Donald Trump as American president. While the Left has also on occasion been accused of nostalgia, conservative politicians, programs, and political projects have been the primary aims of the charge, which is why the chapter concentrates on them. More even than in other respects, nostalgia carries overwhelmingly pejorative and polemical connotations when it comes to politics, which renders it virtually unsuitable for political analysis, the chapter argues. Insofar as speech and rhetoric are acts, the book here moves from discourse (what is said about nostalgia) to practices (how the concept is used).

The most often cited manifestations of the successive nostalgia waves, however, were not in politics but in popular culture—no book on nostalgia in the twentieth century can avoid this topic. The interpretation *Yesterday* puts forward in Chapter 3 differs from existing ones in three ways. First, it argues that retro was an invention not, as has often been claimed, of the nostalgia wave of the 1970s but in fact of the countercultural 1960s. In doing so, it relativizes the popular dichotomy of the optimistic, future-looking, progressive 1960s and the gloomy, backward-looking, nostalgic 1970s. Second, while nostalgia can be understood with the music critic Simon Reynolds as "one of the great pop emotions," the chapter emphasizes the need to differentiate between retro practices and nostalgia as one motivation or mode to experience them.[34] Finally, it argues that turning to the past for inspiration is neither evidence of a lack of originality nor a sign of cultural decline but, on the contrary, a source of creative innovation.

Chapter 4 makes a similar point with regard to popular history. Many academic historians have traditionally dismissed practices such as preserving and collecting, presenting and exhibiting, reviving and reenacting as nostalgic, as improper engagements with and uses of the past. But as both the voices of people participating in the practices and the research carried out in other disciplines suggest, many different reasons and motivations are, in fact, at play here. Gradually, historians have come around to this view and have begun to study these practices and sometimes even to engage in them themselves. By juxtaposing discourses and practices, this chapter not only questions whether nostalgia should be applied to such phenomena but also contributes to the underexplored history of public history.[35]

This book draws throughout on a tradition of earlier studies of nostalgia. Yet instead of simply building on this tradition as one would normally do, it tries to examine it from outside by considering all texts on nostalgia, no matter when they appeared, as primary sources that need to be scrutinized by placing them in their original historical context and by charting how the ideas they put forward developed over time. In this way, it seeks to contribute to a more cautious and careful understanding and use of nostalgia. While the indiscriminate application of nostalgia to so many different phenomena has rendered the concept both broad and vague, this simultaneously allows us to examine a variety of issues in a fresh light and to make connections where at first none seemed to exist. This approach is what makes this book a *new* history of nostalgia, one that simultaneously aims to provide the emerging field of "nostalgia studies" with a sounder theoretical and historical basis.[36]

Nostalgia is a notoriously vast subject. No book can do justice to its complexity and diversity. Limiting itself to the concept, how it is used, and how it is predominantly theorized and understood—a limited region and period of time—*Yesterday* still paints a broad canvas, encompassing not only the history of ideas, politics, popular culture, and popular history but also how people have tried to make sense of history itself, of time and change, modernity and postmodernity. As a history, it may be more *about* the present as well as rooted *in* the present than even contemporary histories usually are. The debates about nostalgia that began in the 1950s, 1960s, and 1970s are still very much with us today. This makes it both hard and all the more necessary to put them into perspective. If our arguments about nostalgia are to continue, as *Yesterday* suggests they are, it is important that we come to a clearer understanding of what the concept means for us.

One

Revisiting

The Meanings of Nostalgia

> In the course of my work, which takes me to just about every corner
> of the globe, I see many aspects of a phenomenon which I'm just be-
> ginning to understand. Our modern technologies have achieved a
> degree of sophistication beyond our wildest dreams. But this tech-
> nology has exacted a pretty heavy price. We live in an age of anx-
> iety, a time of stress, and with all our sophistication we all are in fact
> the victims of our own technological strength. We are the victims of
> shock—of future shock![1]

Orson Welles delivers these words, having just landed at an international
airport and while standing on a moving sidewalk, at the beginning of the
1972 documentary *Future Shock*. A moment later, we meet him again, this
time in the wood-paneled interior of a comfortable country house, extolling

the qualities of old things—old houses—that give us "the feeling that some things, at least, stay the same."[2] Like the short drive connecting the two scenes, the shock of the future and the comfort of the past are, the scene implies, interrelated: two sides of the same coin.

Like the term *future shock,* this idea stems from the book on which the documentary was based, futurologist Alvin Toffler's 1970 nonfiction bestseller *Future Shock.* The title is not meant metaphorically: Toffler understood "future shock" as an actual "disease," triggered by the "acceleration of change in our time."[3] Just as people who, traveling to faraway countries, can feel disoriented, people in modern societies experience "future shock" because the world around them is altering so profoundly and rapidly that they, no longer able to make sense of it, feel similarly adrift: "It is culture shock in one's own society."[4] Presenting itself as a wake-up call, *Future Shock* diagnoses the sickness, describes its symptoms, and offers, if not cures, then at least ways to deal with it. According to Toffler, even though change is unstoppable, it is still possible to cope with and adapt to it.

Whatever else it may have been, *Future Shock* was a good example of the increasing skepticism about progress in the 1960s. If Toffler used the term at all, he did so mainly as a descriptive adjective or in a very limited way—as in "material progress," for instance—not to describe a belief in universal improvement. "The moment is right," he wrote in the last chapter, "for total self-review, a public self-examination aimed at broadening and defining in social, as well as merely economic, terms, the goals of 'progress.'"[5] Progress, in a larger sense, had to be put in scare quotes. If *Future Shock* conveyed anything, it was that the future was no longer imagined as a promised land but as a threat.

Due to its focus on the future and the present, it is easy to overlook the fact that *Future Shock* also had important things to say about the past: the past before and different from the future-shocked present, as well as the meaning of the past for this present, particularly its function as escape or what Toffler diagnosed, with another phrase soon to be widely adopted, as a "wave of nostalgia."[6] The two concepts were not unconnected.

The malaise Toffler described in his book, although it had become obvious and acute by 1970, had roots reaching further back in history. "Western society for the past 300 years has been caught up in a fire storm of change."[7] This storm left nothing unaffected in its wake, not even the understanding and experience of time, or the "time-bias" of a society, as Toffler called it.[8]

When premodern "stagnant societies," where "the past crept forwards into the present and repeated itself in the future," were swept away by accelerated change, a fundamental "break with the past" occurred: "We no longer 'feel' life as men did in the past. And this is the ultimate difference, the distinction that separates the truly contemporary man from all others."[9] People in modern societies may be alienated from each other and perhaps also from themselves, but they are certainly alienated from all preceding generations, stranded and thrown back on themselves in a present changing ever more rapidly thanks to the introduction of ever-newer technologies.

One effect of accelerated change and the transformed time-bias is nostalgia. Toffler first touches on nostalgia when discussing the "victims of future shock": in addition to those who simply denied the scale of change, there are the "Reversionists," politicians and people on the political right first and foremost who advocate the "politics of nostalgia," demanding a "return to the glories of yesteryear."[10] Because of its prevalence, however, Toffler judges the general "reversion to pre-scientific attitudes," as borne out and accompanied by a "tremendous wave of nostalgia in society," to be more dangerous. The examples Toffler invokes, the revival of older fashions and the return of "faded pop-cult celebrities," all come from pop culture.[11] The *Future Shock* documentary, showing pictures of countercultural communes in the countryside, adds "young people" seeking "escape from the hectic over-stimulation of a high-speed society" and rejecting "today by returning to yesterday."[12] Apparently, "reversionism" could be found across the whole of society and the entire political spectrum.

Related to nostalgia—and equally problematic—is what Toffler calls "presentism," a term that would later play a much more central role in the thinking about nostalgia and that he defines as the "philosophy of nowness": a celebration of the moment without consideration for past and future. People who "plunge backwards into irrationality, anti-scientific attitudes, a kind of sick nostalgia, and an exaltation of now-ness . . . are not only wrong, but dangerous," Toffler decrees: "Nothing could be more dangerously maladaptive."[13] Given the concerns expressed in his book, it is hardly surprising that Toffler rejects nostalgia: whether it appears as a longing to bring back the past or a longing to cowardly escape the present, it is not just futile, it is counterproductive, a dangerous distraction from solving the problems posed by the future.

However, despite Toffler's impassioned critique of nostalgia, some passages in *Future Shock* can also be read as defending it. Discussing strategies for "coping with tomorrow," Toffler writes, "No society racing through the turbulence of the next several decades will be able to do without specialized centers in which the rate of change is artificially depressed." In such "enclaves of the past"—Amish villages and living museums are his examples—"people faced with future shock can escape the pressures of overstimulation for weeks, months, even years."[14] Here, "men and women who want a slower life" could be "living, eating, sleeping" as people had in the past.[15] But how are these enclaves different from the hippie communes in the documentary? And why did Toffler not include them under nostalgia, given that other observers would categorize them as such?

Toffler, then, already applied the term *nostalgia* in a vague and tendentious way, using it for engagements with the past he held in low esteem but not for those he valued more highly. He thereby revealed an underlying worldview in which change, if not positive, was at the very least inevitable, in which the future was of primary concern and the past, not providing any useful model or knowledge for the present, was a state to be overcome, not something to cling to, let alone to esteem. Against this background, *Future Shock* put forth a theory of nostalgia that would remain surprisingly consistent over the following decades: both a product of and a response to modernity, dependent on the modern understanding of time and caused by accelerated change, nostalgia was simultaneously opposed to modernity.

This theory, though influential, was not entirely original. It was already circulating in the 1950s and 1960s, the decade in which *Future Shock,* often seen wrongly as a book of the 1970s, originated. This is why this chapter begins by going back to that period, before turning to the impact of *Future Shock* and the wider debate of a "nostalgia wave" in the 1970s. From there it tracks the nostalgia discourse across the decades, focusing on its role in the debates about heritage, postmodernity, and memory in the 1980s and 1990s, as well as the diagnosis of presentism in the 2000s. As this discourse is so closely bound up with notions of time, temporality is a primary focus of this chapter.

The chapter presents a combination of a conceptual and an intellectual history of nostalgia, reconstructing how the concept and its meanings, as well the ideas surrounding it, changed over the course of the second half of the twentieth and the beginning of the twenty-first centuries. Instead of offering a comprehensive history of nostalgia, it constructs a genealogy of how nostalgia came to mean what it means today. *Future Shock* makes for an ideal

starting point—not because it was so innovative but rather because it summarized and consolidated the contemporary thinking about nostalgia, because
it presented it in a catchy, concise, and convincing way and thereby popularized it. The chapter focuses on this theory of nostalgia because it became so
dominant and enduring, determining nostalgia's negative reputation to this
day. Only by scrutinizing and criticizing it is it possible to come to a fuller
understanding of what nostalgia meant and, to a large extent, still means.

Nostalgia before *Future Shock*

In many ways, and this may have been part of its success, *Future Shock* was
more a work of synthesis and emphasis than originality. Toffler himself
stressed the countless books and the "literally hundreds of experts on different aspects of change" he and his wife, Heidi, had consulted in writing
it, their names liberally peppering the pages of his work.[16] When it came to
nostalgia, critical remarks on the subject could be found as early as the beginning of the postwar era—the historian Richard Hoftstadter lamented
the "overpowering nostalgia of the last fifteen years" in 1948.[17] The idea at
the heart of *Future Shock,* that the rapid pace of change was increasingly af-
fecting both individuals and societies, had already been frequently voiced
in the 1950s and 1960s as well. "During all human history until this century,"
the British writer C. P. Snow argued in his 1959 lecture on "the two cultures,"
"the rate of social change has been very slow. So slow, that it would pass un-
noticed in one person's lifetime. That is no longer so. The rate of change has
increased so much that our imagination can't keep up."[18] Toffler quoted both
Snow and the Dutch social scientist Egbert de Vries, who also stressed the
impact of rapid social change, identifying the "glorification of the past" as
one of the most common "defence mechanisms," which does not appear to be
so different from Toffler's "enclaves of the past."[19]

　One of the first to understand nostalgia as the flipside of modernity was
the media theorist Marshall McLuhan, whose influence on the thinking of
the postwar era can hardly be overestimated—in *Future Shock* the "prophet
of the electric age" is characterized slightly irreverently as an example of
intellectual faddism.[20] In his first book, *The Mechanical Bride,* from 1951,
McLuhan already noted, in passing, "the deep nostalgia of an industrial society, a nostalgia bred by rapid change."[21] A decade and a half later, in his

best-known book, *The Medium Is the Massage,* McLuhan returned to the theme, writing, "When faced with a totally new situation, we tend always to attach ourselves to the objects, to the flavor of the most recent past. We look at the present through a rear-view mirror. We march backwards into the future."[22]

In the 1960s comments on these themes picked up significantly. In 1965 Toffler published "The Future as a Way of Life," the first kernel of *Future Shock* and the first time he used this term.[23] In 1968 the psychiatrist and psychohistorian Robert J. Lifton set out his theory of "protean man," which, like *future shock,* would become a key term for the 1970s. For Lifton, modern human beings are protean—that is, complex and multidimensional, full of conflicting aims, ambitions, and attitudes, among them nostalgia, the "longing for a 'Golden Age' of absolute oneness": "midst the extraordinarily rapid change . . . the nostalgia is pervasive, and can be one of his most explosive and dangerous emotions."[24] As it was for McLuhan and Toffler, for Lifton nostalgia was tied to accelerated change, the backward longing an effect of a culture charging forward, an emotion as ubiquitous as it was perilous—though he, unlike Toffler, did not specify where exactly its dangers lay.

Some historians shared this view, among them the Cambridge don J. H. Plumb, who was, incidentally, a friend of Snow. In a set of wide-ranging lectures held at the City College of New York in 1968 and later published as *The Death of the Past,* he drew a sharp distinction between history and the past, the latter of which, as the title implies, he saw as dying, if not already dead. Complicit in its death were historians themselves, who had "helped to weaken the past" by turning it into history.[25] Unlike older cultures, Plumb argued, industrial societies were oriented toward "change rather than conservation" and thus did not need the past. "The new methods, new processes, new forms of living of scientific and industrial society," he continued, "have no sanction in the past and no roots in it. The past becomes, therefore, a matter of curiosity, of nostalgia, a sentimentality."[26] In Plumb's understanding, industrialization marked a watershed, the beginning of an entirely new kind of society, as well as a new way of thinking, completely divorced from that which had come before, which, no longer reaching into the present or helping to solve its problems, was reduced to an object of nostalgia.

Neither McLuhan nor Plumb aimed to historicize nostalgia but nevertheless did so indirectly by portraying it as a phenomenon of industrial modernity. Arthur P. Dudden, one of the first historians to take an interest in nostalgia—which he defined as "a preference for things as they are believed to have been"—came to a different conclusion. In an article published in 1961, Dudden portrayed nostalgia as a "continuous undercurrent of American life" since the eighteenth century at least.[27] He linked it less to industrialization than to progress because, for him, "the bright belief in progress" and "the despair of nostalgia," or "the optimistic faith in progress" and "the poignant pessimism of nostalgia," were both equally dominant in American thought, constantly contradicting and balancing each other: two sides of the same coin, they both portrayed the present as a "transitory stage between past and future."[28] Dudden was one of the first to overtly conceptualize nostalgia as the counterpart of progress, a term earlier (as well as later) texts tended to avoid even though many of them understood nostalgia in the same way. Nevertheless, Dudden's contribution to the debate, as well as his injunction to recognize the "historic importance of nostalgia for understanding the moods and motives of Americans," largely fell on deaf ears.[29]

Like Dudden, the Swiss historian Jean Starobinski placed nostalgia within a longer—though an entirely different—historical trajectory. Trained both as a physician and as a historian of literature and ideas, Starobinski had the perfect background to track its changing meanings. He was the first to reconstruct its career in medical and philosophical discourse, following it from Johannes Hofer via Jean-Jacques Rousseau, Immanuel Kant, and the Romantics all the way to the twentieth century. Unlike Dudden, Starobinski focused on *nostalgia*'s earlier meaning as "homesickness," a meaning, he added, that it had, by this time, the mid-1960s, largely lost. "In current usage, its acquired poetic meaning has little by little taken on a pejorative connotation: the word implies the useless yearning for a world or for a way of life from which one has been irrevocably severed."[30]

This raises the question of when exactly *nostalgia* ceased to mean "homesickness" and took on a temporal meaning. The current *Oxford English Dictionary* locates the first examples for *nostalgia* as "sentimental longing for or regretful memory of a period of the past" in the early 1900s.[31] However, in the interwar period the term was still quite uncommon and used more often in its old sense. The US Army told its doctors to watch out for cases of nostalgia well into the Second World War.[32] As this suggests, the semantic shift from a spatial to a temporal longing occurred slowly and gradually, an impression reinforced by a look at dictionaries of the time. *Webster's* still defined *nostalgia* solely as "homesickness" in 1957, adding a second definition in 1961: "a wistful or excessively sentimental sometimes abnormal yearning for return to or return of some real or romanticized period or irrecoverable condition or setting in the past."[33] Similarly, *The Concise Oxford Dictionary of Current English* featured "sentimental yearning for (some period of the past)" for the first time in 1964.[34] By this time, *nostalgia* was rarely used in its old, medical sense anymore and also vanished from medical dictionaries, while the usage of its new meaning dramatically increased.

In the case of the French equivalent, historian Thomas Dodman recently argued that *nostalgie* had already come to signify a longing for the past in the nineteenth century.[35] However, when Maurice Halbwachs wrote about nostalgia in the 1920s, he used the term "nostalgie du passé," which suggests that *nostalgie* alone signified mere yearning.[36] This is supported by the 1958 *Dictionnaire de la langue française,* which defined *nostalgia* simply as "mal du pays" still.[37] The 1966 *Dictionnaire du français contemporain* was one of the first dictionaries to include, "a vague sadness caused by distance from what one has known, a feeling for a bygone past, an unfulfilled desire."[38] Hence, *nostalgie* retained an even greater ambiguity than its English equivalent, allowing for all kinds of yearnings, including but not limited to one for the past, and these multiple meanings have remained to this day.[39] By comparison, the German word *Nostalgie* was hardly known at all outside medical discourse before the 1970s. Commenting on a 1920s revival in 1962, Theodor W. Adorno once used the English word in quotation marks instead, which suggests that *Nostalgie* did not yet have the same meaning as *nostalgia* in English.[40] This is also evident from the German translation of Halbwachs's work, where "nostalgie du passé" became "homesickness for the past."[41]

Although, as Starobinski noted, *nostalgia* already carried a pejorative connotation by the mid-1960s, it was not uniformly condemned. Some authors took an ambivalent stance, among them the British writer Stephen Spender. Primarily concerned with its role in literature and art, he portrayed nostalgia as burying "the contemporary world under the heaped-up memories of the past," as well as "one of the most productive and even progressive forces in modern literature."[42] Whether nostalgia could have both harmful and beneficial effects or whether it could be productive precisely because it, by celebrating aspects of the past, drew attention to deficiencies of the present, it was predicated on an "irreparable break . . . between the past and the present" and the realization that the "dubious material gains of progress have been made at the price of stupendous spiritual loss."[43] In short, nostalgia was progressive inasmuch as it drew attention to the costs of progress.

Spiritual loss was also a concern for Ralph Harper, an American theologian influenced by European existentialist thought. In a book published in 1966, he set out to rescue nostalgia from those who conceived of it—mistakenly, in his view—as "a remnant of shallow optimism, as sickly, illusory, unprogressive."[44] Because nostalgia allows us to recognize "what we hold most dear," without it we "would have no way of telling . . . what life ought to be like."[45] Harper cherished nostalgia as a guiding light, illuminating that which is important in life.

Spender's and Harper's interpretations of nostalgia differ from other authors' insofar as they are less interested in its social than its individual, spiritual, and artistic dimensions, as is also evident from their prose. In nostalgia, Spender writes, the present appears as "a torn fabric through whose rents the past burns with illumined clarity."[46] "In nostalgia," Harper rhapsodizes, "one smells and tastes, one responds from the darkest corners of oneself, as a renewed whole, to some reality one loves, a person or a place or even an idea."[47] Where others dismiss nostalgia as a futile longing, the poet and the theologian find beauty in the articulation of absence. Like other commentators, however, they, too, see nostalgia in direct relation to progress.

Given the existence of such defenses, it does not seem as if the "denunciation of nostalgia had become a ritual, performed, like all rituals, with a minimum of critical reflection" by the 1960s, as Christopher Lasch later opined.[48] Clearly, however, nostalgia had by this time cast off its connection with homesickness and come to relate almost entirely to the past. It entered the critical vocabulary, and here it is hard to contradict Lasch, without being accompanied by a lot of critical reflection—its dialectical relationship to progress and modernity went largely unquestioned. If it had not yet been ritually invoked, this is certainly what occurred with the publication of *Future Shock*.

The "Nostalgia Wave"

Despite its densely printed five hundred pages, *Future Shock*, with its snappy title, its urgency, and its mixture of popular science, sermon, and self-help book, was a runaway hit. Lingering for months on the *New York Times* best-seller list, translated into other languages, and reprinted well into the 1980s and 1990s, it sold over ten million copies worldwide.[49] Many of the intellectual eminences cited in its pages endorsed the book on its cover: Snow called it "remarkable," the professional visionary Buckminster Fuller and the feminist activist Betty Friedan described it as "brilliant," and McLuhan praised it by saying, "*Future Shock* . . . is 'where it's at,'" despite its irreverent characterization of himself.[50]

Among the book's catchphrases that soon cropped up across intellectual thought, popular culture, and everyday language, including "future shock," "instant society," and "information overload," was also "nostalgia wave." At first the term was quoted with reference to Toffler, for example, in a *Newsweek* article from 1970, according to which nostalgia was "sweeping the country like a Kansas twister."[51] Soon, however, the term and the diagnosis connected to it developed lives of their own. Articles in 1971 framed nostalgia as a "protection against future shock" or talked about "nostalgia shock" without mentioning Toffler.[52] The same year a piece in *Time* wondered, "How much more nostalgia can America take?"[53]

The answer was, apparently, a lot. Warnings that American—but not only American—society was slowly succumbing to a wave of nostalgia (whether derived from *Future Shock* or seemingly independent of it) were a constant part of social commentary and academic analysis throughout the 1970s. For the anthropologist Howard F. Stein, nostalgia occurred "when the felt continuity between past and present experience and the expectation of the future is broken," and he was convinced this was precisely what had happened in the United States.[54] Milton Singer, another anthropologist, agreed: "Americans had lost their nerve and their zest for progress and innovation, and had been so disturbed by 'future shock'" that they longed to escape into the past.[55] According to the writer Jim Hougan, the present was "suffused with nostalgia, albeit of a false and wistful kind," from which he distinguished a positive "radical nostalgia" as displayed by the counterculture movements.[56] In his influential analysis of "value change," the political scientist Ronald Inglehart also spoke of a "recent wave of nostalgia" that signaled a "retreat into the past for the population at large."[57] In short, nostalgia had "become so widespread, so common" in the 1970s "that it is difficult not to be nostalgic"—or at the very least it had become an inescapable stereotype for cultural criticism to target.[58] Rather than trying to explain nostalgia, most indicted it as a sign of a culture that, ill at ease in the present and with little hope for the future, turned to the past.

Fred Davis's sociological study *Yearning for Yesterday,* published in 1979, offered a more substantial contribution to the debate. Although Davis made some attempts toward a more general theory of nostalgia—surveying its history, its relation to the life cycle and the arts—as a sociologist he was primarily interested in its role in contemporary society, or what he called the "nostalgia wave" or "nostalgia orgy of the nineteen-seventies," which, to him, was not so much a general reaction to the acceleration of change as it was "intimately related . . . to the massive identity dislocation of the sixties."[59] Rarely "in modern history," he argued, "has the common man had his fundamental taken-for-granted convictions about man, woman, habits, manners, law, society, and God . . . so challenged, disrupted, and shaken," resulting in stress and disorientation.[60]

While the change to which nostalgia was a reaction had often remained rather abstract, general, and vague in earlier works, Davis was more specific. In his account the revolutionary 1960s, by challenging traditional norms, values, and ways of life, had left many people feeling unsettled, disoriented, and yearning for the past, before things had changed so radically. Ultimately, however, Davis found the roots of what he, like many, saw as an abundance of nostalgia in contemporary society somewhere else: "Nostalgia exists of the media, by the media, and for the media," he concluded.[61] Not enough that the media propagated nostalgia, the objects people longed for were themselves created by the media. In the end, however, it was Davis's remarks on nostalgia as a reaction to rapid social change that would become influential, affirming as they did the existing theory. What is more, by making nostalgia an object of sociological research, Davis turned it from a subject of cultural criticism into one of academic research. Despite focusing on nostalgia in a particular context—the United States in the 1970s—his study was soon applied to other eras and regions, thereby shaping the perception of nostalgia in general.[62] If *Future Shock* had invented and popularized the notion of the nostalgia wave, *Yearning for Yesterday* turned it into a scientific and historical fact.

But what was nostalgia a longing for? As the discussion moved from the abstract to the concrete, its object became more specific: the 1970s longed for the 1950s, which, following the upheavals of the 1960s, retrospectively appeared as stable, solid, and secure, Davis and many others argued. Contemporaries and historians could remind the public of Cold War fears, Communist witch hunts, and conservative morals as much as they wanted, but this did not diminish the craze for 1950s films, fashions, and fads in the least. Because these trends also had the benefit of providing fodder for colorful illustrations, the illustrated press jumped at the opportunity with articles, often little more than photo spreads, on the 1950s and their contemporary return, such as "The Nifty Fifties" (*Life*), "Back to the '50s" (*Newsweek*), or "Back to the Unfabulous '50s" (*Time*).[63] "Must we be nostalgic about the fifties?" asked writer Thomas Meehan. Obviously, many Americans had to be, as "an enormous number" of them were "looking back on the decade as a shimmeringly serene and happy time."[64]

But it was not just Americans. Neither the nostalgia wave nor its association with the 1950s revival was specific to the United States. "What are we to make of the rampant, ubiquitous, unashamed nostalgia which leers at us these days whichever way we turn?" wondered the British critic Michael Wood, noting how "popular music has simply become haunted by the 50s"—the "fascinating '50s" had Britain just as much in their grip as they did the United States.[65]

With the 1950s revival, the nostalgia wave finally washed up in West Germany, too. In January 1973, *Der Spiegel*, the country's foremost news magazine, published a cover story on nostalgia that painted a picture of a rampant "passion for the passé" (see Figure 1.1).[66] During the 1960s, dictionaries had still only defined it as "homesickness."[67] The 1971 *Brockhaus* encyclopedia was the first to add, "also: yearning for the past."[68] The preposed "also:" makes it seem as if the new definition had been added shortly before publication to account for a recent change in meaning. This impression is further confirmed by the *Der Spiegel* article, according to which *nostalgia* was "the very latest fashionable term of the cultural scene," while the anthropologist Ina-Maria Greverus credited the article itself with acquainting Germans with the term.[69] When the new, completely revised edition of the *Brockhaus* came out in 1979, it featured a much extended article on nostalgia, tracing its history back to Hofer.[70] The newest edition of the *Meyers* encyclopedia went even further: not only did it include a new article on nostalgia—complete with a reference to the "so-called nostalgia wave"—the issue was deemed so important as to warrant the inclusion of a four-page essay.[71] Usage of the term downright exploded in the early 1970s, probably because it did not undergo a protracted transformation but was adopted directly from the American discourse.[72]

Figure 1.1   "The business with yearning." This 1973 issue of *Der Spiegel* on nostalgia popularized
the term in West Germany. © Der Spiegel

As in other countries, the shift in meaning was both accompanied and driven by comments from intellectuals and the media. The historian Wolfgang Schivelbusch and the educationalist Dieter Baacke both understood the "nostalgic wave" in terms of a "collective regression" by which people shielded themselves from the "exhaustion of coping with capitalist realities," or, put more simply, from the pressure of constantly having to buy new things, as well as a "diffuse discontent" with the present.[73] While its manifestations were "everywhere"—in music, pop culture, fashion, the hippie and the environmental movements, the new appreciation for nature and hiking, and the rediscovery of Romanticism—Baacke, probably not surprising for an expert on youth culture, was convinced that nostalgia primarily affected young people.[74] The leftist author Gerhard Zwerenz even believed that the "majority of young people" displayed acute symptoms of nostalgia, a view shared by many American writers. Like Davis, Zwerenz perceived the nostalgia wave as a backlash to the preceding "wave of activism," but, in his view, driven not so much by the disoriented bystanders as by the disillusioned former revolutionaries.[75]

More conservative commentators had a different take on nostalgia. The philosopher and sociologist Arnold Gehlen saw nostalgia as rooted in the "repulsive effect of contemporary conditions, a repulsion that opens us up for the magnetic appeal of the past," and a repulsion he unquestionably shared. Convinced that the past was less frenzied and fearful than the present, he insisted on the "right to seek out more humane worlds, if only in fantasy."[76]

This point could well have come from the philosopher Hermann Lübbe. Starting in the late 1970s, Lübbe began to think about the function of the past in the modern world, which inevitably led him to also consider nostalgia. Like Toffler, Lübbe understood it as rooted in the acceleration of change. His analysis relied heavily on the work of the historian Reinhart Koselleck, according to whom the "space of experience" (or the past) and the "horizon of expectation" (or the future) had been drifting further and further apart since the 1800s, resulting in what Lübbe later would call a "contraction of the present."[77] As the future arrived with increasing speed, the present turned into the past ever more rapidly. Despite writing about the eighteenth and nineteenth centuries, Koselleck rooted his theory in his own time, as he unwittingly revealed when he observed in passing that "today, thanks to the population explosion, development of technological powers, and the consequent frequent changes of regime, acceleration belongs to everyday experience."[78] In all likelihood it was the other way around: the experience of an accelerated present and its continued discussion sent Koselleck looking for its origins in the past.

It was only logical, then, that Lübbe applied Koselleck's theory to the contemporary world, where, he argued, acceleration had reached a point where the present no longer recognized itself in the past.[79] Paradoxically, this did not result in indifference but instead in a heightened interest in the past, as a host of phenomena Lübbe summarized under the terms "nostalgic exaltations" and "nostalgia obsession" bore out.[80] While these engagements with the past could not provide orientation, they offered something equally important, a "cultural compensation for the acceleration-induced loss of the sense of familiarity."[81] And similarly, "nostalgia as a relief through a retreat into old-fashionedness provides a mental resting place in the restless movement."[82] Nostalgia cannot stop, cannot even pause, the ticking of the clock, but it provides a space where it cannot be heard as a sort of refuge. While Lübbe's explanation of nostalgia was not so different from Plumb's, his conclusion was closer to Davis's insofar as he saw nostalgia as beneficial and as an inescapable effect of modernity.

Although not all conservative intellectuals regarded nostalgia more sympathetically than progressive ones, the most vicious attacks on nostalgia doubtless came, as Davis noted, from radical and liberal authors.[83] At the same time, some observers pointed out that nostalgia was also to be found on the left, with Toffler noting a "strange coalition of right wingers and New Leftists."[84] Others, Baacke for one, perceived it as apolitical, a withdrawal from politics into the private sphere.[85]

In general, however, politics were a marginal part of the nostalgia discourse, especially when compared with pop culture. This is all the more surprising because, as we will see in Chapter 2, the term frequently cropped up in political rhetoric and political contexts during the 1970s. While the Federal Republic of Germany experienced a debate about a wave of "Nazi nostalgia," French intellectuals discussed *la mode rétro,* the resurfacing of the resistance and collaboration in popular culture that, sometimes translated as the "forties revival," introduced the term *retro* for styles inspired by the past. As these debates were hardly reflected in the writings on nostalgia, we will come back to them when discussing politics and popular culture proper.[86] It is necessary to mention them here, however, as they show how wide the discussion of nostalgia was becoming, resulting in a corresponding broadening of the term: right after dictionaries took account of the shift in meaning from homesickness to a "sentimental yearning for the past," this definition already was too limited.

But not only politics was missing from contemporary accounts of nostalgia. The crises of the 1970s—Vietnam and Watergate, civil unrest and domestic terrorism, energy crises and economic downturn, fear of nuclear annihilation and environmental collapse—which are retrospectively invoked to explain the alleged nostalgia of the decade, may have played a role in the background but were otherwise absent from the nostalgia discourse at the time.[87] It is equally noteworthy that hardly anyone rejected the diagnosis—apart, that is, from the duke of dissent, Gore Vidal, who, consulted by *Time* on nostalgia in 1971, shrugged it off with customary assertiveness: "It's all made up by the media. It's this year's thing to write about."[88] Vidal's remained a lone voice. Whatever their take on nostalgia, those writing about it all agreed that it was a central feature of the age. His prediction also turned out to be incorrect: nostalgia proved to be next year's thing, too.

Past Shock

"The British national disease is not going on strike. Nor is it indulging in periodic fits of public morality. It is being nostalgic."[89] There can be no doubt about it: the historian Douglas Johnson was fed up with the "nostalgia boom" and what, for him, was its most obvious manifestation: the conservation movement. Written in 1978, Johnson's article touched on an issue that would occupy British historians—and not just them—throughout the 1980s: the country's obsession with the past in general and historic preservation in particular, or what would eventually be subsumed under the term *heritage*. Future shock was followed by past shock.

One year later, shortly after Margaret Thatcher had been elected prime minister, the writer and historian Patrick Wright returned to Britain after five years in Canada. He felt as if he "had stumbled inadvertently into some sort of anthropological museum." It seemed to him "as if the whole of British society was frozen over in an arresting display of the past."[90] In an attempt to account for this impression, he began to investigate the place of the past in contemporary Britain, culminating in the publication of his book *On Living in an Old Country* in 1985.

Wright was far from the only person wondering about Britain's relationship to its past. In 1979 the historians David Lowenthal and Marcus Binney organized a symposium in London to examine the growth of the conservation movement.[91] Binney was a key player in the movement. In comparison, Lowenthal was much more skeptical. His book *The Past Is a Foreign Country* is closer in spirit to Wright's—it came out in the same year—if not in much else: whereas *On Living in an Old Country* is heavy on theory with succinct case studies, *The Past Is a Foreign Country* is encyclopedic and meandering, drawing on countless examples and sources.

If Wright felt like he was living in a museum, the rate at which museums were growing in number had the journalist and historian Robert Hewison wondering, "How long would it be before the United Kingdom became one vast museum?"[92] Hewison explored this and related questions in various radio and TV documentaries, as well as his 1987 book *The Heritage Industry*.[93] Writing at the same time and examining the same territory, all three, Wright, Lowenthal, and Hewison, became key protagonists of what would retrospectively be called the "heritage debate" or even the "heritage panic."[94] For all three, the growth of heritage—borne out by the popularity of historic preservation, museums, period films, historical reenactments, and family history—was rooted in a deep sense of nostalgia: "the universal catchword for looking back" and "a sickness that has reached fever point."[95]

Given that, in principle, they all agreed with one another—as did a number of other historians and journalists—the existence of much of a debate at all can be doubted.[96] One of the few dissenting voices belonged to Raphael Samuel, Marxist, Oxford historian, and founder of the History Workshop movement. Not that Samuel did not also observe a lot of nostalgia, but he considered "heritage-baiting," as he called it, and how it treated nostalgia to be patronizing and condescending.[97] To him the "new version of the national past" then emerging was "not only more democratic than earlier ones but also more feminine and domestic."[98]

What exactly *heritage*—which, like *nostalgia,* was an old term rapidly soaking up new meaning—actually meant was highly contested.[99] Perhaps it eluded conventional definition entirely, as the conservative member of Parliament and conservation activist Patrick Cormack implied in his 1976 book *Heritage in Danger.* "When I am asked to define our heritage I do not think in dictionary terms," Cormack wrote, "but instead reflect on certain sights and sounds. I think of a morning mist on the Tweed at Dryburgh where the magic of Turner and the romance of Scott both come fleetingly to life; of a celebration of the Eucharist in a quiet Norfolk church with the medieval glass filtering the colours, and the early noise of the harvesting coming through the open door; of standing at any time before the Wilton Diptych. Each scene recalls aspects of an indivisible heritage and is part of the fabric and expression of our civilization."[100]

For its critics, this passage encapsulated everything that was wrong with heritage. Wright, Lowenthal, and Hewison all quoted it at length, deriding its "language of vague and evocative gesture," its "sub-lyrical vagueness," and its "pastoral, romantic and religiose evocation."[101] They had a point: Cormack's definition could, as he admitted, hardly have featured in a dictionary, it *was* sublyrical, evocative, and vague. All the same, Cormack captured an essential truth: heritage was subjective and charged with emotion. In the eyes of its critics, heritage was conceptualized as overwhelmingly male, white, Anglo-Saxon, Christian, and conservative—reproducing existing social hierarchies rather than challenging them—though there were, as Samuel emphasized, other strands pointing toward a more inclusive vision.

Given his evocative style and his emotional concept of heritage, Cormack opened himself up to accusations of nostalgia especially because he portrayed the national heritage as, if not already lost, then in the process of being lost. He also contrasted scenes of rural tranquility and past beauty with the forces threatening them: the "devastation of mining and quarrying, the urban sprawl spawned to house a growing and consuming population, the march of the pylon bringing electricity to the Highlands, the swathe cut by the motorway," or, in short, "the menaces of twentieth-century civilization."[102] The defense of heritage here turned into a wholesale critique of modernity.

Ignored by his critics, *this* passage was harder to discount: Cormack clearly had a point—a point, moreover, that an increasing number of people began to share. The time when planners designed motorways and demolished old houses or even whole streets under the banner of modernization while a puny preservation movement looked on, its protests falling on deaf ears, had come to an end. As modernity's costs for the environment—natural and urban—became obvious, conservation gained support among the public and politicians. Nothing showed this more than the 1975 European Architectural Heritage Year, which acknowledged its importance and blew wind in its sails by putting heritage center stage, in addition to making it a household term.[103]

In fact, when *Heritage in Danger* came out the following year, heritage was most likely less in danger than it had ever been. A historian of conservation in 1979 declared confidently that the "strife is o'er, the battle won—we are all on the side of virtue now, with preservation taking precedence over destruction."[104] The early 1980s brought more good news for conservationists, when the British Parliament passed the National Heritage Act, establishing the National Heritage Memorial Fund, followed by another act establishing the Historic Buildings and Monuments Commission, thereby recognizing the government's responsibility for the preservation of historic structures and enshrining the term *heritage* in national legislation: the ethics of conservation had replaced the ethics of modernity.

If the postwar conservation movement was a reaction to an excess of modernist planning and destruction, the heritage critique was a reaction to what it saw as an excess of preservation. While conservationists perceived the heritage year and the new legislation as progress, for their critics they were signs of decline, a concept that played a central role in their thinking. For Wright and Hewison, nostalgia was directly connected to a widespread perception of national decline: heritage articulated a "sense of history as entropic decline" gathering momentum "in the sharpening of the British crisis"; it was indicative of a country "gripped by the perception that it is in decline."[105]

Decline was an almost inescapable topic in Britain during the 1970s and the early 1980s, its relevance increasing among economic and financial turmoil, the energy crisis, and the miners' strikes. The British establishment obsessed over Britain's economic decline, and no one more so than Thatcher.[106] Such fears gained further legitimacy with the publication of historian Martin Wiener's *English Culture and the Decline of the Industrialist Spirit* in 1981, which diagnosed a deep-set nostalgia and anti-industrial attitude in British culture as responsible for the country's economic problems.[107] Widely acclaimed, the book quickly became "part of the received wisdom in interpreting recent British history and our prospects for the future," especially for the masterminds of Thatcherism.[108]

The heritage critics all quoted the book, albeit in a spirit of critique.[109] If Wiener attacked nostalgia from the right, they did so from the left. Not least thanks to the Heritage Acts, Wright and Hewison equated conservation with conservatism.[110] Hewison intended his attack on heritage as an intervention in the 1987 election campaign, through which he hoped to alert the public to Thatcherism's impact on culture.[111] Viewing the "heritage industry" as another Thatcherite experiment in privatization, he, like many historians, took offense to what he held to be an increasing commodification of the past. This view may have been accurate, but he also chose to overlook the public money and the voluntary work involved in heritage. For Samuel, by contrast, it made the past more accessible to a greater number of people, and not just as passive consumers.

But perhaps this was the problem. Precisely because heritage was the work of many people—few, if any, of them trained historians—professional historians regarded it with a degree of condescension. Not that the critics, most of them belonging to the left, would have admitted to this attitude—it took an ardent advocate of "history from below" like Samuel to point it out. Whatever else it may have been, the heritage critique was a knee-jerk reaction to the "history boom" of the 1970s and, as a result, used nostalgia not as an analytical category but as a rhetorical tool to dismiss popular history and to defend historians' interpretative authority over the past.

Although the heritage critics constantly claimed that the past was growing, that it was "everywhere," they—or at least Lowenthal—also saw it as simultaneously being "swallowed up by the ever-expanding present."[112] At first, this may seem paradoxical: How could the past and the present expand simultaneously? How could nostalgia be both escapist *and,* to use a term that would become much more central in the 2000s, presentist? Yet this dual meaning seems to have been exactly Lowenthal's point: the present was obsessed with the past not as distinctive from but as part of itself, as a self-projection. Rooted in the present, nostalgia gave preeminence to it, distorting the past in its image, thereby devaluing both the present and the past. What was decreasing, by comparison, was the future: "While future perspectives seem to shrink, the past is steadily growing."[113] Once lauded as the promised land, the future—or rather the belief in a better or just malleable future—had also been reduced to a "nostalgic memory."[114] Or as Lowenthal would phrase it in 1989 in the sequel to *The Past Is a Foreign Country,* "Nostalgia for things old and outworn supplants dreams of progress and development."[115]

Operating within the modern understanding of time, in which the past was a stage to be overcome on the way to a better future, the heritage critics somehow had to account for the fact that the past not only seemed to not be past but also was given a second lease on life in conservation—as well as conservatism. One reviewer of *On Living in an Old Country* picked up on this, noting that when Wright had left the country, "campus radicalism was still flourishing, and Tony Benn was preparing to hoist the red flag over the ruins of capitalism," while upon his return Wright found Thatcher in power.[116] Lowenthal even accused Wright of "left-wing nostalgia."[117] Coming from Lowenthal this might sound disingenuous, but he nevertheless had a point. While the heritage critics denounced heritage for its nostalgic take on the past, they were themselves—Lowenthal included—looking back to, in their view, more progressive, less nostalgic times, which gives their critique a hypocritical tint.

By the end of the 1980s, some of them began to nurse doubts about their portrayal of nostalgia. Again, Lowenthal led the charge, now condemning the critics who "misconceive nostalgia and exaggerate its evils"; he even considered it a "good antidote" against those trying to instrumentalize the past for their own ends.[118] "A lot of the talk of 'nostalgia' is hopelessly general," Wright, too, conceded in an interview in 1989: "It conflates any number of different impulses, and it also seems to assume that the desirable state for a society is to be untroubled by any sort of historical awareness at all."[119] Indeed, by focusing so much on nostalgia as an explanation for the heritage boom, its critics had never bothered to examine more closely why and how people engaged with the past.

Of course, it was all very well and good to voice these doubts now that, as Lowenthal proclaimed—in an astonishingly nostalgic turn of phrase— nostalgia had "lost its innocence and become a social pariah."[120] Johnson's observation from the beginning of the decade had become a commonplace complaint by its end, as judgments like "no society has dabbled so thoroughly in nostalgia as Britain" were frequently evoked: the "omnipresence of 'nostalgia'" had become "the prime focus of educated concern."[121]

Heritage, by comparison, emerged strengthened, though the debate dragged on into the 1990s, when, incidentally, Hewison's fear of Britain turning into a vast outdoor museum finally came true—if only in fiction. In Julian Barnes's novel *England, England,* an entrepreneur acquires the Isle of Wight and converts it into a heritage theme park replica of England, complete with its own Big Ben, Sherwood Forest, Stonehenge, and White Cliffs of Dover as well as, in a particularly shrewd move, the real royal family. The point of the park, as the entrepreneur reminds his underlings, is not to educate its visitors about the past but to make them "feel better" by letting them "enjoy what they already know."[122] This was the heritage critique as novel. Yet while the heritage debate was as long lived as it was wide ranging, it was in another sense surprisingly narrow.

Heritage, *Patrimoine, Heimat*

"Naturally one realizes that this is not a purely British phenomenon," Johnson corrected himself as soon as he had claimed nostalgia as a national disease.[123]

For Samuel as well, the "notion that nostalgia is a peculiarly British disease, and that the rise of 'heritage' in the late 1970s and 1980s represented a recrudescence of 'Little Englandism' is not one which could survive comparative analysis intact."[124] Still, neither of them—nor anyone else—took it upon themselves to analyze heritage in a comparative perspective, least of all the heritage critics, probably because admitting that similar developments were in evidence elsewhere would have undermined their arguments about national decline and Thatcherism. Later historians, too, have done little to put the heritage debate in a broader context, thereby feeding into the notion that it, and, by extension, the rise of heritage, was a British peculiarity.

An exception of sorts was Lowenthal, who, perhaps because he was born in the United States, perceived what he termed "creeping heritage" to be as much an American as a British phenomenon.[125] While the British debate did not seem to resonate in the United States, the American historian Michael Kammen shared some of its concerns. Despite defining heritage neutrally as "that portion of the past perceived by a segment of society as significant at any given moment in time," Kammen saw the "heritage syndrome"—a term already implying a pathological component—in a predominantly critical way. By selecting what they deemed significant, societies tended to "remember what is attractive or glittering and to ignore all the rest."[126] As this characterization suggests, nostalgia was as central to Kammen's argument as it was to that of the British heritage critics. He believed that nostalgia had become "pervasive" in the United States since the 1970s in response to social and cultural change and a growing "sense of discontinuity with its past."[127]

More in line with Samuel, Kammen conceded that heritage also had positive aspects, indicating a "popularization and democratization of history."[128] Nevertheless, he remained skeptical; distinguishing between heritage and history, he clearly privileged the latter. This does not seem to have been the universal view among American historians, or at least the United States experienced nothing amounting to a heritage debate. Most of them viewed heritage as benign if not beneficial—perhaps they were generally more accommodating toward public history, which began to establish itself as a distinctive field in the late 1970s with the foundation of the journal the *Public Historian* in 1978 and the National Council on Public History in 1979.[129]

If continental Europe played any role in the discussion of heritage, it was more on the side of its proponents than its detractors. *Heritage in Danger,* for instance, not only included a chapter comparing preservation provisions and programs across continental Europe, it also noted that there was "hardly a notable expression of our civilization that does not betray, if not portray, its European roots," regretting "how little work has been done of a comparative nature."[130] Such a comparison would have been all the more fitting given the cross-border cooperation in the European Architectural Heritage Year and in international bodies such as the International Council on Monuments and Sites.

France, for instance, would have provided an ideal case for comparison as it, too, suffered from "past shock": the "object of desire" was no longer "the future but the past," as Annie Ernaux noted, looking back on the 1980s in her masterpiece *Les Années* (published 2007 in French, 2018 in English).[131] Indeed, France witnessed a "comparable obsession with the nation's heritage" in the 1980s, here revolving around the term *patrimoine*.[132] Like *heritage*, *patrimoine* originally signified inheritance but took on a much wider meaning in the 1980s. Similarly vague, the two terms roughly meant the same thing, as the "French intellectual" in *England, England* notes: "We in our country have a certain idea of *le patrimoine*, and you in your country have a certain idea of '*Eritage*.'"[133]

Initially limited to historic buildings and sites, by the end of the 1970s *patrimoine* no longer meant "cold stones or the glass separating us from exhibits in a museum. It is also the village *lavoir*, the little country church, local dialects, the charm of family photos, skills and techniques, language, written and oral tradition, humble architecture," as Jean-Philippe Lecat, minister for culture and communication, put it at the inaugural event for the 1980 *l'année du patrimoine* (inspired by the European Architectural Heritage Year).[134] The fact that it was a minister who set out to define *patrimoine* shows the much greater involvement of the state compared with Britain. Still, the "impetus came from the grass roots, from the provinces," Pierre Nora emphasized, and it was here that *patrimoine* resonated most, as thousands of local associations for the defense of heritage and promotion of rural culture demonstrated.[135]

Like heritage, *patrimoine* met with critique among French historians, if a more muted one. Nora, who might have been expected to welcome such an endeavor, derided the *année du patrimoine* as the "May '68 of provincials and peasants" and criticized the lack of concern for the future.[136] Another critic called it "a real curiosity shop," alluding to the economic motives behind the government's promotion of *patrimoine*: what Lecat praised in poetic phrases to critics seemed primarily aimed at attracting tourists to the French countryside.[137]

As its counterparts had in the United Kingdom and the United States, *patrimoine* also attracted accusations of nostalgia: if it acted as "a nostalgic and anachronistic" mirror, the *année du patrimoine* laid out "the landscape of effective nostalgia."[138] Like here, *nostalgia* generally figured more as a descriptive term in the French debate; the "pain regarding the pastness of the past" was evoked less often to explain the conserving urge in general.[139] The reason for this may be twofold. First, *nostalgie* was not as common in French critical discourse as it was in the English; second, French intellectuals seemed, by and large, not as negatively inclined toward *patrimoine* as the British ones were to heritage.

Juxtaposing the two countries, the British historian Tony Judt detected in the heritage industry "an obsession with the way things weren't—the cultivation, as it were, of genuine nostalgia for a fake past," whereas "the French fascination with its spiritual *patrimoine* has a certain cultural authenticity."[140] Since the reasons why *patrimoine* should be more authentic than heritage remain unclear—as the concepts and subjects they described overlapped so much and particularly as *patrimoine* was much more state driven and therefore more in danger of being put in the service of the government and national politics than heritage was in Britain—Judt's remark seems to have been based less on an in-depth comparison than on what historians in the two countries had written on the matter, or perhaps his Francophile sensibilities distorted his judgment.

The question of what *patrimoine* was a longing for, on the other hand, seems to have been easier to answer in the French case: France pined for its peasant past. With the mechanization and industrialization of farming and the exodus of people from the countryside into cities—which had begun in the nineteenth century but accelerated enormously after the Second World War—living and working in the city had become the norm. As the peasantry vanished, it was reconstructed as the core of the nation, as evident, for instance, in its musealization in the form of the *ecomusée,* open-air museums devoted to rural life.[141] It was even more evident in the success of memoirs of rural life such as *Le cheval d'orgueil* (1975) by Pêr-Jakez Helias—adapted into a film by Claude Chabrol in 1980 and only one of many films set in the countryside in the past that were coming out at that time—and *Une soupe aux herbes sauvages* (1977) by the teacher Émilie Carles.[142] Britain saw something similar with the success of Edith Holden's *The Country Diary of an Edwardian Lady* (written in 1906, published in 1977)—much mocked by heritage critics—and films like *Akenfield* (1974) and *Requiem for a Village* (1975) about the vanishing of the rural world.[143] Finally, it was borne out by the amount of ethnographic research focusing on peasants both contemporary and historical, including Emanuel Le Roy Ladurie's study *Montaillou* (1975), about a small village in the Pyrenees in the early fourteenth century.[144] In spite of, or perhaps because of, its success—*Montaillou* sold more than a quarter of a million copies in France and was translated into many languages—the book polarized historians: some hailed it as a masterpiece of microhistory and the *histoire des mentalités,* while others scorned it as a nostalgic evocation of the past.[145]

Montaillou fits into another trend originating in the 1970s and continuing well into the 1980s: a surge of interest in the Middle Ages. In West Germany, a 1977 exhibition about the medieval dynasty of the Staufer—soon followed by a number of blockbuster shows on historical themes—attracted more than double the three hundred thousand visitors expected, astonishing both the organizers and the media.[146] The same year, a biography of medieval poet Oswald von Wolkenstein by German novelist Dieter Kühn also found a wide audience, which had one critic speculate that the nostalgia wave now also encompassed the Middle Ages.[147] One medievalist saw the public appeal of both the exhibition and the biography as rooted in a desire to escape a present characterized by social misery and environmental collapse.[148]

Successful as they were, none of these books came even remotely close to Umberto Eco's novel *The Name of the Rose* (1980), which sold over fifty million copies worldwide, making it one of the best-selling books of all time.[149] If there was no wave of medievalism before it, there certainly was one afterward. Though Eco would later claim to have triggered it, in 1984 he also noted how a "few minutes in an American bookstore allow you to discover many interesting specimens of this neo-medieval wave."[150] One example he did not mention was the Society for Creative Anachronism, though given his fascination with some of the more eccentric ways in which American society engaged with the European past, he probably would have thought it compelling. The Society for Creative Anachronism had been founded by members of the Berkeley counterculture movement in 1966 to reenact a fictionalized version of the Middle Ages as a "protest against the 20th century."[151] Bringing all these different examples together, the journalist Cullen Murphy observed a "nostalgia for the Dark Ages" in 1984.[152] Whether or not the popularity of books, films, exhibitions, and reenactments really reflected a widespread yearning for the Middle Ages, its characterization in these terms demonstrated how wide-ranging the nostalgia diagnosis had become by the 1980s: there was nothing that could not be brought under that label.

In addition to participating in the wave of medievalism, West Germany also witnessed its own heritage debate. As they were everywhere else, the advances made by the conservation movement and a growing "musealization" were sources of concern for intellectuals.[153] Unlike its parallel debates, however, the one in Germany did not so much revolve around heritage—*Kulturerbe* in German, an old-fashioned, technocratic, and awkward-sounding term— but around *Heimat,* an even more cloudy, charged, and contested concept than either heritage or *patrimoine.* Literally meaning "home" or "homeland," it was first invoked as a reaction to and against industrialization and urbanization in the nineteenth and early twentieth centuries and, as such, came to be associated with the political Right, especially after the Second World War.[154] From the late 1970s, however, the term was gradually adopted and adapted by the Left, acquiring new meaning and new importance. In 1978 a German writer noted how "in the wake of nostalgia" and the European Architectural Heritage Year, it had become possible to "say 'Heimat' without fear of being suspected of fascist affinities."[155] The same year, the writer Siegfried Lenz published his novel *Heimatmuseum,* later titled *The Heritage* in the United States.[156]

As *Heimat* was less a real than an imaginary place, something either lost or in the process of being lost and, thus, an object of yearning, it was hardly surprising that it was closely associated with nostalgia. In one of the first academic studies on *Heimat,* Ina-Maria Greverus devoted an entire chapter to it. Unlike other writers, Greverus stressed the painful aspect of nostalgia and downplayed regressive and reactionary tendencies.[157] In a review of the book, *Der Spiegel* also linked *Heimat* to nostalgia, observing how it had shifted politically: it was no longer conservatives who were concerned with *Heimat* but the members of the conservation, environmental, and antinuclear movements—in short, the leftist-alternative milieu.[158]

The biggest outing for *Heimat* came in 1984 with the ambitious elevenpart television series *Heimat,* which made the cover of *Der Spiegel* in 1984 (see Figure 1.2.). Cowritten and directed by Edgar Reitz, it chronicled the life of one woman and one village in the Hunsrück—a wind- and rain-swept region in the westernmost part of Germany—from the end of the First World War to the present. Like the French and British films about the countryside,

Figure 1.2 "Yearning for *Heimat*," 1984 cover of *Der Spiegel.* © Der Spiegel

it dealt with ordinary people and rural life. Despite relying heavily on amateur actors speaking in their regional dialect, the series was a remarkable success both nationally and internationally. It also divided opinions especially for its depiction—or rather nondepiction—of the Holocaust.[159] Because Reitz portrayed *Heimat* and its inhabitants not—or not primarily—as bigoted, prejudiced, and small-minded but rather as victims of a modernity that made their lifestyle obsolete and whose effects they struggled to navigate, much less to control, critics also homed in on the "often nostalgic descriptions of everyday life in the village" in a series "full of nostalgic craving for a lost world."[160]

Among historians, *Heimat*—the series as well as the concept—did not meet with much interest at the time. One exception was Celia Applegate, whose study *A Nation of Provincials,* while mainly about the nineteenth century and the first half of the twentieth, was clearly informed by the resurgence of the concept in the present. In a description reminiscent of Greverus, Applegate characterized *Heimat* as "tinged with nostalgia for a past that never was."[161] The book came out in 1990, the year of German reunification and, hence, the beginning of a new chapter in the history of the Germans' uneasy and complicated relationship to nation and *Heimat.*

As the discussions of *patrimoine* and *Heimat* illustrate, the heritage debate was far from unique and, while all three concepts are difficult to translate into other languages, they share a lot of common ground: they all came to the fore during the 1980s, signaling a new reflection about the place of the past in the present, framed everywhere, if with varying emphasis, as nostalgic. None of these debates pondered nostalgia as such, and yet, in applying the term so profusely, they contributed to how it was understood, thereby further expanding its scope. Whereas in the 1970s the discussion of nostalgia had fixated on the most recent past, mainly relying on pop culture for its examples, a decade later, this was still the case, in addition to which there was now a debate about popular engagements with the past through historic preservation and museums that were also framed as nostalgic. Because they extended to times as far back as the Middle Ages if not further still, nostalgia, no longer limited to periods within memory, now was seen as embracing "the whole length of the past."[162] What did not change and, if anything, became even more pronounced, were nostalgia's negative, pejorative connotations: the term was used almost exclusively by those aiming to criticize certain engagements with the past that in their eyes were backward-looking as well as approaching the past in an emotional key, both of which rendered them the opposite of history—and this was, mainly, what nostalgia was to imply.

Postmodern Nostalgia

The "French intellectual" in *England, England* has no name, nor does he need one. He is there only for four pages to provide intellectual legitimacy for the theme park and a short essayistic interlude for the readers. He also does not need to be named because "the French intellectual" already says it all. What it said, at the time Barnes wrote the novel, was "postmodernism." Although the intellectual quotes Guy Debord, his speech sounds more like genuine Jean Baudrillard: "It is important to understand that in the modern world we prefer the replica to the original because it gives us the greater *frisson*."[163]

Nostalgia and postmodernity are so frequently associated with one another that some have interpreted the "whole experience of postmodernity as a kind of macro-nostalgia."[164] Others have claimed that an "elective affinity between nostalgia and the postmodernist attitude towards the past" exists and that "postmodernists rehabilitated nostalgia."[165] As we will see, this is more than doubtful, but nostalgia certainly occupies an important role in postmodernist thought. In Baudrillard's best-known book, *Simulacra and Simulation* (1981), it is closely linked to the simulacrum, the copy of the copy that, no longer referring to any original, has come to replace it, much as the "hyperreal" has replaced the real.[166] It is from this open wound that nostalgia, the pain of loss, emanates. Jean-François Lyotard may well have believed that "most people have lost the nostalgia for the lost narrative," but then Lyotard celebrated the death of the grand narratives.[167] Baudrillard did not. "When the real is no longer what it was," he writes, "nostalgia assumes its full meaning."[168] *Nostalgia* here means "nostalgia for a lost referential," a longing for something that provides meaning to signs, narratives, and history beyond and outside themselves. When such "a controlling idea no longer selects, nostalgia endlessly accumulates."[169] Once the old metanarratives are gone, may they be religious, philosophical, or political, nothing remains into which the past can be organized so that it, consequently, threatens to disintegrate into individual episodes, all equally important and interesting, the *lavoir* as much as the Louvre. "Our entire linear and accumulative culture collapses if we cannot stockpile the past in plain view," Baudrillard warned, and collapsed it had. What took its place was a sort of metanostalgia: not for a specific period or a specific aspect of the past—though that also happened as, Baudrillard believed, "the fetishized history will preferably be the one immediately preceding our 'irreferential' era"—but for a time when history still made sense, in the double sense of having and providing meaning.[170]

Another major postmodern thinker, the American literary critic Fredric Jameson—while thinking it not "an altogether satisfactory word"—frequently commented on nostalgia.[171] He first noticed a "crisis in historicity" in the mid-1980s, which then turned into the "ultimate historicist breakdown" as the decade wore on.[172] No longer able to "imagine the future at all," postmodernity was tantamount to a "perpetual present," in which the past disintegrated into "a series of pure and unrelated presents in time."[173] Propelled by "an omnipresent and indiscriminate appetite for dead styles and fashions" that knew no distinctions, no deeper meaning, no historical continuity, what this present yearned for was not the past but "pastness," the veneer of historicity instead of the real thing—whatever that may have been.[174] For Jameson the postmodern approach—or understanding—of the past was inferior to the modern one to a degree that Linda Hutcheon has called his view of postmodernity "strangely nostalgic."[175] Similarly, cultural historian Elizabeth Wilson has argued that behind the "lament for the loss of norms" lay "a romantic longing for some past that is never made explicit."[176]

An important context for the debate was technological change and television especially. Baudrillard referred to it throughout his book; Jameson dedicated a whole chapter to video.[177] Of course, television had become a mass medium in the 1950s—McLuhan's work at the time had revolved around it—but the innovations of the 1980s revolutionized the medium. With cable television, relying as it did on reruns of older programs, and video recording technology, the televisual past reappeared in spectacular fashion. "Never before have people had nearly unlimited access to what has gone before, been able to call it up and play it back and relive it again and again," the American television critic Tom Shales observed in 1986. Television was a "national time machine," fueling the nostalgia cycle as "yesterday's topicality might be today's nostalgia."[178] The 1980s were the "Re Decade," Shales declared, "the decade of replay, recycle, recall, retrieve, reprocess, and rerun." Switching between programs from many different periods, he reported, profoundly disrupted his sense of time: "We are all time shifters now. Or time shiftees. Time is for shifting."[179] What better illustrates the postmodern understanding of time as a simultaneity of equivalent, disorganized pasts and presents than randomly flying from one decade to another at the push of a button?

Drawing primarily on popular culture, postmodern critics of nostalgia did not comment on other manifestations of the past, though Baudrillard mentioned "museumification" in passing, noting how the "museum, instead of being circumscribed as a geometric site, is everywhere now."[180] If this is reminiscent of the heritage critique, heritage and postmodern critics were, indeed, not far apart from one another. Samuel even suspected that "it is not the traditionalism but the modernism and more specifically the postmodernism of heritage" that offended its critics.[181] While starting from different vantage points, critics of heritage and critics of postmodernity concurred insofar as they perceived contemporary engagements with the past as nostalgic *and* presentist: the reasons to seek out the past as well as the ways of doing so were rooted in the present. In this way, the heritage debate could be understood as a uniquely British contribution to the discussion of postmodernity.

If anyone brought the two critiques together, it was the geographer and anthropologist David Harvey, whose *Condition of Postmodernity* (1989) drew on film and heritage, Jameson and Hewison.[182] Postmodernity, eschewing the idea of progress as well as the sense of historical continuity, amounted to nothing less than a "breakdown of the temporal order."[183] As "time horizons shorten to the point where the present is all there is," future and past disappear.[184] The predominance of the present over all other times was the conclusion at which both the critics of heritage and the critics of postmodernity arrived. Where Plumb had diagnosed the "death of the past" in the 1960s, they diagnosed the death of history—not of the discipline but of the thinking underlying it, the capacity to see the past as different from the present. Even when they viewed it as inevitable, many critics mourned the loss of the modern, historical understanding of time.

But what if it had been false in the first place? This was the thesis of Bruno Latour's book *We Have Never Been Modern,* published in 1991 in French (1992 in English), the same year as Jameson's magnum opus. Whether or not the title's claim that we have never been modern—which can only mean that we have never been postmodern either—was just another postmodern sleight of hand, Latour's attack on the modern understanding of time can be helpful to capture it more clearly. "The moderns," he contends, "have a peculiar propensity for understanding time that passes as if it were really abolishing the past behind it."[185]

Because they perceive time as an "irreversible arrow, as capitalization, as progress," they feel compelled to conserve it: "They want to keep everything, date everything, because they think they have definitively broken with their past. The more they accumulate revolutions, the more they save. . . . Maniacal destruction is counterbalanced by an equally maniacal conservation."[186]

For Latour, destroying and conserving are two sides of the same coin; putting the past behind glass in a museum is as much a way to get rid of it, to rob it of life, as destroying it—"extermination by museumification," Baudrillard had called it—and both are indicative of a modern view of time.[187] Against this understanding of time, Latour insists that "the past is not surpassed but revisited, repeated, surrounded, protected, recombined, reinterpreted and reshuffled." To the moderns, in Latour's analysis, this was incomprehensible: "Thus they treat it as the return of the repressed. They view it as an archaism." Time's arrow could only point up or down, never back: "Progress and decadence are their two great resources."[188] Not so for Latour, for whom time—or times, rather—resembled a "plate of spaghetti."[189] Latour's autopsy of the modern understanding of time helps to reveal the modernist bias of the nostalgia critique, which rejected nostalgia because it perceived it not only as backward-looking but as constantly resurrecting and reviving the past, which to them was a sign of cultural decline.

Whereas Latour mounted an attack on the idea of progress from a postmodern perspective, the American historian Christopher Lasch presented his from a conservative one in *The True and Only Heaven,* which incidentally came out the same year as Latour's book. If, until that point, the nostalgia critique had been dominated by voices from the left, with conservative thinkers appearing to be more forgiving, Lasch was anything but. He saw nostalgia as progress's "ideological twin" and "mirror image," and the same, for him, applied to the nostalgia critique, which shared with its object "an eagerness to proclaim the death of the past and to deny history's hold over the present."[190] Nostalgia may be the wrong attitude toward the past, but most who criticized it were wrong, too, as their critique was based on a belief in progress.

Still, his own critique of nostalgia was not so far removed from what had come before. Like the critics of heritage and postmodernity, Lasch believed that nostalgia did not establish a connection with the past. Rather, "a sense of continuity is exactly what nostalgia fails to cultivate. . . . It not only misrepresents the past but it diminishes the past," evoking it "only to bury it alive."[191] Nostalgia misrepresents the past by denying its complexity, by rendering it timeless and unchanging, and thus devaluing it, subordinating it to the present: "By exaggerating the naive simplicity of earlier times, it implicitly celebrated the maturity and worldly wisdom from which we look back on them," or, in other words, the present.[192] Thus nostalgia's presentism seems to have been what irked Lasch most, as it had earlier critics as well.

This was not the case for the postmodernist historian Frank Ankersmit, whose more sympathetic appraisal reveals a lot about the nostalgia critics, especially because he is attracted by precisely those attributes that appall them. At first, his claim in *History and Tropology* (1994) that nostalgia offers "the most intense and the most authentic experience of the past" may sound as if Ankersmit, contrary to other theorists, proposes that nostalgia does indeed establish a connection with the past.[193] Quickly, however, things become more complicated. What, according to Ankersmit, "we experience historically in nostalgia is not 'the past itself' . . . but the difference or the distance between the present and the past."[194] As all experience can only take place in the present, it is not possible to experience the past, at least not as anything other than absent, and, for Ankersmit, that is exactly what nostalgia is the experience of: the realization that the past does not exist in an ontological sense, that it cannot be recovered, that it can only ever be remembered and reconstructed in the present. Although Ankersmit did not discuss time overtly, he largely seems, despite his postmodern credentials, to have understood it in the modern sense as Latour characterized it. If this made him a modernist, he was a postmodernist at least insofar as he welcomed nostalgia for questioning "historist and positivist assumptions" about the nature of the past.[195]

Whatever one may think about Ankersmit's contribution to the debate about nostalgia, it certainly was an original take—so original, in fact, that the literature on nostalgia has virtually ignored it. If, as some have claimed, postmodernist thought rehabilitated nostalgia—and given Baudrillard's and Jameson's remarks, that seems like an exaggeration—Ankersmit came closest to it. Conceiving of nostalgia primarily on a collective level—the representation of the past in popular culture and popular history—its critics saw it as sentimentalizing and distorting and, thus, as negative. Ankersmit, by contrast, sought to purge nostalgia of its "associations with sentimentalism" by emphasizing the individual experience, the sudden remembrance of a (usually happy) moment in the past and the simultaneous, painful recognition that it is irretrievably lost, which, taken together, constitute what is often described as its bittersweet character.[196]

Understood in this way, nostalgia, for Ankersmit, was a "most useful and welcome instrument for clarifying our understanding of the past and how we experience it."[197] Useful because it challenged what he sees as traditional historians' often unquestioned "reification of the past," whose flipside was their—and here Ankersmit referred explicitly to Lasch—"verdict for nostalgia."[198] If Ankersmit was right, that could also explain why traditional historians were so opposed to nostalgia: not so much because it distorted the past but because it threatened to undermine the foundations of their discipline as they conceived of it. If the past was not recoverable in the way historist historians—in Ankersmit's view—believed it to be, where would that leave history? In short, Ankersmit welcomed nostalgia exactly for those reasons Lasch rejected it. Nostalgia here became a feature separating traditional historist and postmodernist history.

Of course, it was far from the only one. In the larger debate between traditionalist and postmodernist historians, other issues took a much more important role, including the questioning of scholarly objectivity, of metanarratives, and of concepts such as, crucially, progress. As history threatened to disintegrate into stories like so much ancient paper in the archive crumbling to dust, some historians began to look for new ways to approach the past, a transfusion of fresh blood to keep Clio's aged body alive. One likely donor was memory.

The Memory Boom

The discovery of memory as a subject for the humanities in the 1980s was actually a rediscovery. The sociologist Maurice Halbwachs published a sociology of memory, *Les cadres sociaux de la mémoire,* in 1925, leaving the manuscript for a second book behind when he perished in a Nazi concentration camp in 1944. It took almost another four decades for his work to have its full impact. Halbwachs dedicated a chapter of *Les cadres sociaux de la mémoire* to nostalgia, portraying it as an anthropological phenomenon primarily, but by no means exclusively, found in older people, a "kind of retrospective mirage by which a great number of us persuade ourselves that the world of today has less color and is less interesting than it was in the past, in particular regarding our childhood and youth."[199] For Halbwachs nostalgia was not only a common experience, to which a "great majority of people more or less frequently are given," but also a potentially positive one, a temporary escape from the pressures of society that helped people to better cope with them, and certainly an integral aspect of memory.[200]

However, it was not Halbwachs's remarks on nostalgia that drew attention in the 1980s—in fact, they did not catch on at all—but rather his idea of memory as socially grounded or, in short, as "collective memory." When the French historian Pierre Nora published his first article on the subject in 1978, it bore the title "La memoire collective."[201] The text was the prelude to a much larger, almost encyclopedic undertaking, the seven-volume *Les lieux de mémoire* that Nora edited between 1984 and 1992. A sensation at home and abroad, the project defined what soon came to be called the "memory boom."[202] It is less well known as an example for how historians engage with nostalgia, and perhaps its inclusion here is a bit surprising because Nora did not discuss nostalgia at all, at least not overtly. In his programmatic introduction, he only used the term once and in a conventional manner, when noting how traditional institutions of memory such as museums, archives, and cemeteries have become "relics" or "exercises in nostalgia."[203] On a deeper, subconscious level, however, the whole project could be said, and indeed has been said, to advance a nostalgic reading of the past.

The phrase "acceleration of history" opens Nora's introduction, and though he does not refer to Koselleck, he offers a strikingly similar interpretation. Due to the "acceleration of history," Nora argues, "things tumble with increasing rapidity into an irretrievable past"; the more rapid the change, the more rapidly things fall out of fashion, use, and experience. But this acceleration affects more than just things. Like those who, one or two decades earlier, warned that the built heritage was in danger of being lost, Nora also saw something as being under threat—memory itself: "Memory is constantly on our lips because it no longer exists."[204] He was not the only one to think so. "The bond with the past was fading. Only the present was imparted now," Ernaux would confirm later.[205]

While rapid change destroyed memory, it also wreaked havoc on society's sense of temporality. Like the critics of heritage and postmodernity, Nora perceived the future to be in retreat: "once a visible, predictable, manipulable, well-marked extension of the present," it "has come to seem invisible," and with it the past, once "firmly rooted," has become "a world from which we are fundamentally cut off," following a "radical break in continuity."[206] In the process, memory and history grew apart from one another.[207] Furthermore, history, the way "modern societies organize a past they are condemned to forget because they are driven by change," contributed to memory's demise, much as Plumb had seen it contributing to the death of the past.[208]

Another factor was technology, and television in particular.[209] When everything is instantly recorded and preserved, archived, and stored, there is no need to remember anything anymore, rendering memory as such superfluous.[210] Again Ernaux made the same point.[211] As did Lasch: "Our collective understanding of the past has faltered at the very moment when our technical ability to re-create the past has reached an unprecedented level of development."[212] For Nora, the latter was responsible for the former: video had not only killed the radio star, it had also murdered memory.

If Nora's lament for the loss of memory already implied a degree of yearning for a time when it still was in good health, other passages were even more suggestive. "Never have we longed more," Nora writes, "for the feel of mud on our boots, for the terror that the devil inspired in the year 1000, or for the stench of an eighteenth-century city. . . . We study the everyday life of the past because we want to return to a slower-paced, more savory existence."[213] Or conversely, our fast-paced present instills in us a desire to plunge back into what we perceive as a more tranquil and authentic past. This was similar to the heritage critique, only that Nora seems to include himself in the longing as well, thus provoking accusations of nostalgia that were not long in coming.[214]

Nora therefore represents a third approach between and beyond the historist school represented by Lasch and the postmodernist school represented by Ankersmit. Like Lasch, Nora values historical continuity, but he is convinced that the bond between past and present has been severed. As the fading of memory cannot be prevented, Nora (somewhat paradoxically given his reservation vis-à-vis preservation) sets out to conserve its last vestiges with (in a similarly paradoxical way) the means of history, the accomplice in its demise. Accepting the past as distant, Nora made this distance the subject of his project, thereby, in a way, fulfilling the potential Ankersmit had seen in nostalgia. In this, however, he did not go nearly far enough for Ankersmit, who, while applauding his project generally, criticized Nora for forsaking historical experience "for the safe and so reassuring position of the historical."[215]

As he brought the seventh volume over the finish line, Nora began to have second thoughts himself. A decade earlier he had begun his work by reading memory its last rites only to find out now that "commemoration has over-taken it." Commemoration? "Commemorative bulimia"! If, back then, memory had been in danger of being superseded by history, now it was the other way around. In the process, the "solidarity of past and future has been replaced by the solidarity of memory with the present."[216] Instead of linking past and present, memory was put to the service of the here and now. As had the critics of heritage and postmodernity before him, Nora thereby arrived at a diagnosis of presentism.

Nora's critical remarks at the conclusion of *Les lieux de mémoire* did not garner nearly the same level of attention as his earlier programmatic text, which had almost single-handedly triggered a memory boom in academia that, with the rise of commemoration, soon turned into a fruitful field of study. It did not include, however, nostalgia, despite Halbwachs's early inclusion of it and the role it played—albeit subliminally—in *Les lieux de mémoire*.[217] Given nostalgia's reputation and the fact that some held the whole memory boom to be "nostalgic, a yearning for a vanished or rapidly vanishing world," perhaps memory studies preferred not to touch on the subject.[218]

This said, by the early 2000s, some historians engaged in memory studies did turn their attention to nostalgia, most notably Peter Fritzsche. "Nostalgia stalks modernity as an unwelcome double," Fritzsche wrote pointedly. It was a "fundamentally modern phenomenon"—modernity understood as the pe-riod since the late eighteenth century.[219] Borrowing from Koselleck the idea of a "deep rupture in remembered experience" that had occurred in the decades around the 1800s and resulted in "a fundamental break with the past," and from Davis the idea of nostalgia as a "symptom of erratic cultural stress" and a "by-product of rapid change," Fritzsche conceptualized nostalgia as both a result of and a reaction to the upheavals preceding and following the French Revolution, the prime manifestation of which was Romanticism and its ideal-ization of the Middle Ages, the ur-nostalgia wave, so to speak.[220] Only the destruction of the old, ordered, stable temporality made nostalgia possible; only thanks to the ensuing "sense of discontinuity, in which past, present, and future were imagined as ontologically distinct places, could nostalgia articu-late itself"—or in short, no nostalgia without modernity.[221] All later nos-talgia waves were just subsequent manifestations of the same fundamental response to the one constant of modernity: constant change.

Unlike many earlier authors, Fritzsche did not aim to criticize but to his-toricize nostalgia. If he nevertheless ended on a rather bleak note, this was because he saw nostalgia not as a threat but as threatened. In his view, the growing commodification and medialization of the past was not indicative of a growing sense of nostalgia but, if anything, made nostalgia obsolete. If "the past is no longer a different place," how can it inspire longing? Together with historical consciousness more generally, nostalgia was in danger of vanishing in a "nightmare of an eternal present."[222] In this way, Fritzsche's account also begins with nostalgia and arrives at presentism—with the crucial difference that he, unlike earlier authors, saw the two as antithetical.

It is probably no coincidence that Fritzsche is a historian of modern Germany.[223] Even though his study was about the early nineteenth century, his interest in change and the reaction to it in the age of the French Revolution was in all likelihood not unaffected by the transformations occurring in contemporary Germany following the fall of the Berlin Wall and reunification— especially as they led to a heated debate about a specific East German nostalgia for the former German Democratic Republic.[224] While demonstrating that nostalgia had lost nothing of its polemical, accusatory potential, the debate was rather unproductive in theoretical terms because it seldom put nostalgia in a larger historical and geographical perspective.

This is all the more surprising because phenomena similar to those discussed regarding East Germany could be found all over Eastern Europe, as Svetlana Boym's *Future of Nostalgia* (2001) demonstrated. Inspired by her visits to cities in former communist countries such as Saint Petersburg, Moscow, Berlin, and Prague, the book offered a more general theoretical probing into nostalgia. Like Fritzsche—and also building on Koselleck— Boym conceptualized nostalgia as an "incurable modern condition" rooted in the "modern conception of unrepeatable and irreversible time" and simultaneously opposing it, as a "rebellion against the modern idea of time, the time of history and progress." "Nostalgia and progress are like Jekyll and Hyde," two contradictory personalities inextricably tied to each other.[225] Similarly, Boym differentiated between two types of nostalgia: a collective and potentially aggressive restorative (or reactionary) nostalgia that aimed to bring back the past and a more personal and melancholic reflective nostalgia that confined itself to reflecting on and mourning the passing of time.[226] While this already allowed for a more positive view on nostalgia, Boym went even further when she characterized it, in line with Davis and Lübbe, as a "defense mechanism in a time of accelerated life and historical upheavals."[227]

Far from dismissing it, as so many critics before them had done, Boym and Fritzsche—in the context of the new research on memory and contemporary debates about nostalgia following the end of communism in Eastern Europe— painted a more nuanced portrait of nostalgia, accentuating its function as a coping mechanism. Apart from this, however, their overall understanding of nostalgia as bound to modernity stayed largely true to the established inter- pretation. For them, as for earlier authors, nostalgia was a quintessentially modern phenomenon that had not existed before the 1800s but was both a reaction and response to profound, prolonged accelerated change or, in other words, to modernity. While Fritzsche was more interested in the 1800s, Boym more in the present, this is where their two analyses met. Which leaves one question yet to be explored: What would happen to Hyde if Jekyll died, if modernity itself came to an end? With that, it is finally time to examine the idea of presentism more closely.

Present Shock

Books as iconic as *Future Shock* rarely disappear for good—Lowenthal, Jameson, Harvey, and Lasch, among others, all referred to it.[228] Forty and fifty years after its publication, people took stock of how accurate Toffler's pre- dictions had been, with a group of futurologists who viewed themselves as his heirs publishing *After Shock* as a tribute.[229] For others, however, change had accelerated to a degree that the future—and "future shock" with it—was a thing of the past, replaced by "present shock." "Our society has reoriented itself to the present moment. Everything is live, real time, and always-on," wrote media theorist Douglas Rushkoff in his 2013 book *Present Shock*. "It is not a mere speeding up, however much our lifestyles and technologies have accelerated the rate at which we attempt to do things. It's more of a dimin- ishment of anything that isn't happening right now—and the onslaught of everything that supposedly is."[230]

Following *Future Shock* and especially during his youth in the 1990s, Rush- koff continued, "everything and everyone was leaning toward the future."[231] That was no longer the case in the 2010s: "If the end of the twentieth cen- tury can be characterized by futurism, the twenty-first can be defined by presentism."[232] Misreading Toffler, for whom, after all, future shock was a contemporary and not a future phenomenon, *Present Shock* embodied what it diagnosed—saying little about the past beyond the 1990s and little about the future beyond the idea of imminent apocalypse, it reveled in the description of the cultural moment.[233] But if Rushkoff was right and everything was about now, where did that leave the past and any longing for it?

Present Shock was part of a new crop of books about acceleration, as well as its effects and dangers, that came out at the beginning of the new millennium.[234] The most comprehensive and ambitious was *Social Acceleration* by the German sociologist Hartmut Rosa, promising nothing less than, as the subtitle of the English edition announced, "a new theory of modernity" (published 2005 in German, 2013 in English).[235] Given that it reads like a more succinct, sophisticated, and scholarly version of *Future Shock,* it is remarkable that Toffler only appears in a single footnote.[236] In the tradition of Lübbe—together with Koselleck an indispensable influence—Rosa saw acceleration as the prime mover of modernity, if not identical to it: "the experience of modernity," he asserted, "is an experience of acceleration."[237] Leaving no area of human life—politics, economics, work, leisure, social relations—unaffected, acceleration had first and foremost altered the perception and experience of time, resulting in a "contraction of the present," a term he borrowed from Lübbe; a future perceived as contingent, uncertain, and threatening; and a "detemporalization of history."[238] No longer a "directed, dynamic process," history came to be seen as "an almost 'static' space of juxtaposed and successively unfolding histories" that "exist alongside one another simultaneously."[239] Although Rosa did not use the term *presentism,* this was what it amounted to: history had lost its meaning and with it its coherence, giving way to an "orderless *simultaneity of historical fragments.*"[240]

This understanding of time apparently did not preclude nostalgia in Rosa's view, as "almost every surge of acceleration is followed by a discourse of acceleration and deceleration in which, as a rule, the call for deceleration and the nostalgic desire for the lost 'slow world,' whose slowness first becomes a distinct quality in retrospect." As an effect of acceleration, "territorial and social niches or oases of deceleration that have until now been partly or entirely left out of the accelerating processes of modernisation . . . gain 'nostalgic' value and make more enticing promises the rarer they become."[241] Not only are Rosa's "islands of deceleration" reminiscent of Toffler's "enclaves of the past" (even more so as he, too, mentions the Amish as an example), but his account of nostalgia as a reaction to change also stays true to how Toffler,

Davis, Lübbe, and others had explained it.[242] In contrast to them, however, Rosa sets little stock on such phenomena: if they may temporarily relieve the pain of living in a high-speed society, they cannot prevent the unpreventable disaster of a world racing—ever more quickly—toward the abyss.

If presentism is secondary to acceleration in Rosa's book, the reverse is true for François Hartog's investigation into the changing understanding of time and history in *Regimes of Historicity* (published 2003 in French, 2015 in English). In many ways closer in spirit to Lübbe, Hartog builds on the work of Koselleck as well.[243] He distinguishes between three successive "regimes of historicity"—that is, modes in which past, present, and future are related to one another: whereas traditional societies are characterized by an orientation toward the past, modern societies after the Enlightenment adhered to a "futurist regime of historicity" that, oriented toward the future, presented "itself as constantly accelerating," until, in turn, this order also underwent a crisis in the second half of the twentieth century, giving way to a "presentist regime of historicity" centered on a "permanent, elusive, and almost immobile present" that has "*extended* both into the future and into the past."[244] For Hartog, the altered understanding of time is also due to both a "momentous acceleration of time" and a "crisis of the future": as the future goes from utopia to dystopia in the wake of environmental and nuclear fears, the past becomes an "extension of the present."[245]

As a historian, Hartog is less concerned with the effects of presentism on the understanding of the future than its effects on the past, which, he believes, were nowhere more conspicuous than in the memory boom and its "alter ego," heritage.[246] While he faults the commemorative overkill for, quoting Nora, making "the present present to itself," his critique of heritage is reminiscent of the British heritage critics of the 1980s, to whom, however, he seems oblivious save for a single reference to *The Heritage Industry*.[247] In contrast to them, however, Hartog has little use for nostalgia. Although he wonders whether the "taste for the past, for everything old," emerged as a "kind of nostalgia for an older regime of historicity," to him the real issue is presentism.[248] If anyone is longing for the past in Hartog's account, it might very well be himself, as he obviously prefers the futurist over the presentist regime: despite, or precisely because of, his assurance to his readers that his "position is neither nostalgic . . . nor accusatory," it definitely appears to be both.[249]

A third theorist of presentism, the literary critic Hans Ulrich Gumbrecht, has no such qualms: people accusing him of nostalgia are "certainly accurate, and I do not care to defend myself against them."[250] What Gumbrecht called the "chronotope" of "historical consciousness"—the idea of linear time with a closed past and an open future—is largely identical to Hartog's futurist regime and, like Hartog, he understands it as in the process of vanishing, if not already gone, and being supplanted by the "broad present": "Between the pasts that engulf us and the menacing future, the present has turned into a dimension of expanding simultaneities. All the pasts of recent memory form part of this spreading present; it is increasingly difficult for us to exclude any kind of fashion or music that originated in recent decades from the time now."[251] Employing the opposite image of Rosa's—the present is expanding rather than contracting—Gumbrecht and Hartog nevertheless arrive at the same conclusion: linearity has given way to simultaneity. As does Aleida Assmann in *Is Time Out of Joint? On the Rise and Fall of the Modern Time Regime* (published 2013 in German, 2020 in English), which gives an overview of the discourse from Koselleck and Lübbe to Gumbrecht and Hartog.[252]

As Hartog's critique of heritage brought to mind the heritage critique of the 1980s, the very same simultaneously experienced a comeback with the reissue of *On Living in an Old Country* in 2009, followed by a revised version of *The Past Is a Foreign Country* in 2015.[253] Although they did not yet have the same terms available, Wright's and Lowenthal's discussion of nostalgia had, as we have seen, led them to a critique of presentism. In their rereleases, doubtless feeling validated by Hartog's and Gumbrecht's books—Wright quotes the former, Lowenthal the latter—they reinforce it.[254] "Rather than a foreign country," Lowenthal concludes, "the past becomes our sanitized own."[255] Making a case for the foreignness of the past, the title of his book now took on a new and heightened meaning.

The simultaneity of pasts seemed nowhere more conspicuous than in relation to media technologies and popular culture—it was no coincidence that Gumbrecht mentioned fashion and music as examples—at least if one believed the music critic Simon Reynolds. In his 2011 book *Retromania,* he takes the pop culture of the first decade of the new millennium to task for wallowing in its own past, as a stream of "revivals, reissues, remakes, re-enactments" testified.[256] "Is nostalgia stopping our culture's ability to surge forward," Reynolds asks, "or are we nostalgic precisely because our culture has stopped moving forward and so we inevitably look back to more momentous and dynamic times?" Whatever the answer, whether it was cause, effect, or merely a symptom, nostalgia found itself once again in the dock, as "time itself seemed to become sluggish" and progress and innovation gave way to "a simultaneity of pop time that abolishes history."[257] Reynolds was not alone in making this point. Fellow critics Mark Fisher and Owen Hatherley, too, noted that "the very distinction between past and present is breaking down," a "failure to articulate the differences between the past and the present" in pop culture.[258] Mixing and merging different pasts without differentiating between them— or even seeing them as past at all—pop, "putting history into shuffle mode," has not simply become presentist, it embodies presentism.[259] Taking its cue from pop culture, the critique of pop thus also arrived at a critique of presentism—unaware, it seems, that critics like Jameson and Baudrillard had already made the same point in the 1980s.

"Shuffle mode" was a telling metaphor. Much like the nostalgia critique of the 1980s, Shales's most notably, had revolved around new media technology like cable television, the VCR, and the Walkman, the critique of the 2000s was a way to come to grips with the arrival of such innovations as shuffling, streaming, and sampling in the early to mid-2000s. The iPod Shuffle not only made music even more conveniently portable, it also replaced the linear form of the album—still a characteristic of both the cassette tape and the CD—with a nonlinear approach by playing songs at random. These could be downloaded from iTunes, which, together with streaming services, made an ever-growing library of music available at a click of a mouse or the tap of a button. Never before had it been so easy to access the music of the past, jumping at will from one artist, band, genre, and, thereby, period to another. The critics were quick to realize this and to analyze its impact. To some extent, the whole retro critique of the 2000s and 2010s really was a critique—or a way to make sense—of this new technology and its effects on culture. *Retromania,* for instance, is littered with copious references to YouTube, iTunes, Spotify, and sampling culture.[260] Innovations in pop no longer came so much from new bands, styles, or genres as they did from new technologies, futurist technologies that, incidentally, also acted as time machines. The same was true for the internet in general. "The web was the royal road for the remembrance of things past," Ernaux observes. "Archives and all the old things that we'd never even imagined being able to find again arrived with no delay. Memory became inexhaustible, but the depth of time, its sensation conveyed through the odour and yellowing of paper, bent-back pages, paragraphs underscored in an unknown hand, had disappeared. Here we dwelled in the infinite present."[261]

If the switching between TV channels disrupted the sense of temporal continuity, as Shales reported in the 1980s, surfing and shuffling did even more so. Just as shuffling dissolves the linear unity of the music album, giving way to a randomized mix of songs from different artists and eras, so do bits and pieces from the pop-cultural past resurface—or are resurrected—freed from their original context. Although specific artifacts might trigger memories in recipients for whom they have a personal meaning, for listeners unschooled in the history of pop, the impression is one of a simultaneity of musical styles independent of their place in historical chronology, resulting in the dehistoricization of pop. Just as new media technologies inspired postmodern theory in the 1980s and 1990s, so too did they provoke the critique of presentism in the 2000s and 2010s.

The same year *Retromania* came out, the historian Daniel T. Rodgers published *Age of Fracture,* a history of ideas in the last quarter of the twentieth century. His chapter on time begins with a quote from Lowenthal, "Nostalgia was everywhere," followed by a reference to Toffler.[262] In this way, Rodgers both adopts and affirms interpretations from the time, turning them into historical fact. A sense of "living within fragmenting and accelerating time," he continues, has made history since the 1970s "a point of acute importance" and nostalgia pervasive.[263] It has also dissolved the "boundary between past and present" in a "perfect storm of simultaneity": "One might reach nostalgically for a fragment of the past, but the time that dominated late-twentieth-century social thought was now"—and not only social thought, one might add with a view to a larger cultural landscape.[264] For Rodgers, as for Rosa and Reynolds, nostalgia and presentism are not mutually exclusive, though the latter is certainly the more dominant and dangerous trend.

Despite hailing from different disciplinary backgrounds as well as starting from different vantage points, Rosa, Hartog, Gumbrecht, Reynolds, and Rogers all arrived at the same conclusion: that the modern, historical understanding of time as linear, chronological, and homogeneous had given way to a postmodern one of simultaneity. In itself this was not a new claim, as the critics of heritage and postmodernism had already made this point, but with *presentism* there now was a term for it (although this term was not new either).

Historians have long used *presentism* as "a term of abuse conventionally deployed to describe an interpretation of history that is biased towards and coloured by present-day concerns, preoccupations and values."[265] Together with anachronism and nostalgia, presentism is one of the major criticisms that can be leveled at how the past is presented or approached.[266] Indeed, the three terms are related insofar as they all denote misrepresenting the past based on an inability to imagine it as distinct from the present. This also applies to *nostalgia,* which, though on the face of it denoting a preference for the past, is here understood as establishing the present as superior to it. Consequently, the critique of nostalgia more and more culminated in a critique of presentism, with Hartog elevating presentism to the level of a "regime of historicity," where any other view of the past apart from the presentist one has become impossible.

Like the critics of nostalgia, the critics of presentism operate within the modern, historical understanding of time on which their critique is based and which they, by critiquing presentism, defend. At the same time, however, they could be said to be presentist themselves insofar as most of them perceive the 1970s and 1980s not as past but as part of an ongoing present— or what else could it mean that Rosa treats the analysis of Lübbe and Koselleck, Hartog that of Nora and the heritage critique, Reynolds that of Shales, and Rodgers that of Toffler and Lowenthal not in their respective historical contexts but as contemporaneous, as providing explanations and answers for the contemporary world? In this regard, the critique of presentism could be said to be complicit in exactly what it criticizes—or to find itself caught between two temporal regimes, the modernist and the presentist one. While preferring the former, they themselves are subject to the effects of the latter. The question is, where does this leave nostalgia?

Conclusion

One of the surprising aspects of the nostalgia discourse is how uncontested and durable it proved to be. Since the beginning of the 1970s, there has been no period when nostalgia has not been pervasive according to some observer. Apart from Gore Vidal and Christopher Lasch, there was hardly anyone who, in the face of such debates, claimed that the attention heaped on nostalgia was out of proportion. Indeed, nostalgia has featured in almost every major intellectual trend since the middle of the twentieth century, as this chapter has shown.

Given the long series of debates on the subject, as well as the diversity of voices, it is equally surprising how consistent the discourse on nostalgia has been. It is true that, once the word arrived in the public domain, its meanings and connotations, as well as the objects it was applied to, started to multiply rapidly. And still, among those writing about nostalgia from a theoretical and historical perspective, one reading was dominant. From McLuhan in the 1950s, Toffler and Lifton in the 1960s, Davis and Lübbe in the 1970s, and the debates about heritage, postmodernity, and memory in the 1980s and 1990s to the discussion of presentism since the 2000s, theorists of nostalgia almost uniformly conceived of it as both a product of and a reaction to accelerated change in modernity.

According to this theory, modernity first made nostalgia possible by establishing a new understanding of time, one in which the past was closed off from the present. Then it resulted in nostalgia becoming pervasive as an increasing number of people, suffering from the stress of acceleration, sought refuge from it in a past they retrospectively imagined to be slower. Some thinkers saw nostalgia as an unavoidable outcome of modernity, crediting it for providing a coping mechanism, something to cling to in the whirlwind of change. Most, however, even when they shared this view, saw it as not only futile but also outright dangerous: a flight from the challenges of the present and the future, it distorted the past in the bargain.

On closer consideration, the idea that nostalgia was a specifically modern phenomenon is, paradoxically, both wrong and right. It is wrong because what modernity came to call nostalgia—looking back to the past, longing for it, conceiving of it as superior to the present and so on—was not specific to modernity. Rather, an orientation toward the past was particular to premodern societies; indeed, it was the default mode in which they made sense of time. They generally regarded innovations—change of any kind really—as so suspect that, far from proclaiming novelty or a bright future, they were framed as a return to a former state, as is indicated by terms like *renaissance, reformation,* and *revolution.*[267] That does, however, mean precisely that the modern concept of nostalgia cannot be applied to premodern times. Doing so would not only be anachronistic because the word did not exist then (or, once Hofer had coined it in 1688, meant something else); it would mean conferring a modern concept on premodern eras.

Because what *was* modern was the concept of nostalgia. Since the six-teenth century and particularly since the eighteenth century and the era of Enlightenment, Europe (and its extensions) had witnessed the emergence of the modern understanding of time as homogeneous and linear that imagined the future as open and superior to a past now reduced to a state that needed to be overcome and history as a process of continual improve-ment.[268] While this new, future-oriented understanding of time gradually became more dominant, it did not replace the older, past-oriented under-standing of time. Except for the occasional clash, the two coexisted and to some degree even complemented each other, as when the nineteenth century housed modern institutions in buildings that looked like Roman temples or Gothic churches.

Given the catastrophes of the twentieth century, not few of which were committed in the name of modernity and progress, the idea of progress found itself under more pressure than at any time before.[269] For those who wanted to retain the hope of the possibility of progress, looking back now took on a sinister veneer. When, after Plumb had pronounced the past dead in the 1960s, it seemed to resurface spectacularly in the 1970s in the form of a wide-spread popular interest in it, this seemed at the time not just a quirky new old-fashionedness but a rejection of progress, a notion Plumb himself fought tooth and nail for because, for him, there was, in 1964, only "one certain judgement of value that can be made about history, and that is *the idea of progress.*"[270] Without the notion of progress, history was meaningless.

It was in this historical constellation that the modern concept of nostalgia finally fully emerged as an antonym to progress. For the adherents of pro-gress, an interest in the past not as a state to be overcome but as something of value, something worthy of conservation or providing a model, could only be irrational and pathological, and so they pathologized it by resurrecting an old medical term that was looking for a new use. In this way, modernity did, after all, invent nostalgia—in the sense that it invented the concept of nostalgia. By giving a name to what previously had been nameless, it was able to articulate and engage with it in new, primarily critical ways.

So self-evident was the modern concept of time in the eyes of the critics of nostalgia, they rarely commented on it or clarified their own positions. They did not even notice that by condemning what they called nostalgia, they could be said to reinforce it—not just by making it a talking point but by articulating it: Did their repeated claims that nostalgia had never been more present, more pervasive, not also suggest that there was a previous time when progress prevailed and nostalgia was negligible? And was this not what they otherwise would classify as a nostalgic narrative? In the end, all nostalgia critics were "nostalgic for a time when we were not nostalgic," though only Boym, whose book closes with that confession, had the self-awareness to admit it.[271]

The nostalgia critique carried with it its own contradiction, which also pertains to the understanding of time. If nostalgia was only conceivable under the regime of modernity, then how could it survive it? If, as the critics of heritage and postmodernity, and later those of presentism, argued, the death of the past is followed by a death of history, does this not spell the end of nostalgia, too? If the temporal boundaries are blurred, simultaneity reigns, and the past is included in the present, how can anyone long for it any longer? Fritzsche provided a kind of answer by expecting us to wake up from our bittersweet dream of nostalgia to "the nightmare of an eternal present." However, not only has this awakening not happened—at least not so far— what is more, most theorists of presentism do not even see the two as mutually exclusive; rather, they see them as interrelated to the extent that some of them even use the two terms, *nostalgia* and *presentism,* as interchangeable.

In the end, the different critical strands discussed in this chapter all arrive at a cul-de-sac. While they recognize that the modern understanding of time no longer applies and perhaps even that it never really applied, they remain so rooted in it that they can conceive of its disappearance only in terms of decline. Instead of acknowledging that time was never homogeneous, given that not only different societies but also different groups and people within a society perceive and experience it differently, nor linear, given that the past is not closed off but remains, constantly resurfacing and resurrected, they lament its demise. In the end, *presentism* is as much a term of abuse as *nostalgia,* and that makes them both unsuitable for analytical purposes.

With *pluritemporality,* the German historian and theorist of history Achim Landwehr has provided us with a preferable alternative.[272] Not only is this term more neutral, but it also captures the availability of different times, different temporal possibilities and references. It allows for the sort of history the German philosopher Walter Benjamin called for, shortly before his suicide during his flight from the Nazis in 1940, in his "Theses on the Philosophy of History." Arguing against a history that narrated "the sequence of events like the beads of a rosary," Benjamin instead advocated for grasping "the constellation" that any given present "has formed with a definite earlier one."[273] The concept of pluritemporality allows us to bring such constellations into view, by conceiving of simultaneities not only as inevitable but also as opportunities. Rather than condemning the past for swallowing up the present, or the present for swallowing up the past, it enables us to investigate temporal interconnections and elective affinities between different moments in time.

Far from rendering them superfluous, these objections make the theories discussed in this chapter even more important. They are essential for understanding how nostalgia is perceived and conceptualized today, as these theories continue to be influential. By ignoring this genealogy and using nostalgia in an uncritical, unhistorical—presentist—fashion, as much of the literature on the topic has done, we run the risk of perpetuating these concepts, thereby limiting our understanding of nostalgia. If it is to mean more than an accusation of backward-lookingness and an implicit defense of progress, we must be aware that nostalgia, since acquiring its current meaning, has usually been understood in exactly this way.

Two

Regressing

The Politics of Nostalgia

When intellectuals began to think about nostalgia, politics played a marginal role at best. As we have seen, Alvin Toffler and Robert J. Lifton touched on the "politics of nostalgia" only in passing, equating it by and large with right-wing politics and politicians.[1] Like them, most writers, when they mentioned politics at all, associated nostalgia with a conservative, or even reactionary, mind-set. Most nostalgia critics were, as Fred Davis observed, "liberals and radicals" criticizing nostalgia "for being conservative, if not outright reactionary, for turning peoples' heads away from the 'important issues of the day.'"[2] As common as the equation of nostalgia and conservatism was, that did not prevent conservatives from challenging it. No one challenged it more than the self-proclaimed conservative Christopher Lasch. A fierce critic of nostalgia, as noted, he firmly rejected the "prevalent confusion of nostalgia with conservatism."[3] For him there was nothing conservative about nostalgia: he saw it as a mirror image of the belief in progress and so, indirectly at least, laid the blame for it at the feet of liberalism. That, however, did not keep other conservatives like Arnold Gehlen and Hermann Lübbe from viewing nostalgia in a kinder light, as a coping mechanism to survive the constant onslaught of change in modernity.

A third group of commentators were undecided whether nostalgia was right, left, both, or neither: simply apolitical. Robert Hewison, for instance, saw it as "profoundly conservative," yet quickly added that "nostalgia is a vital element in the myths of the Left as well as of the Right."[4] If nostalgia was political at all, Dieter Baacke concluded, it was an escape from politics, driven by the wish to carve out "a private sphere free of the grasp of public control" and therefore able to unite "conservative preservers and left-wing critics of the system." As a critique of modernity, however, he saw it as "ultra-conservative."[5]

More interested in philosophical discussions of nostalgia, few of these writers discussed it with real-life politics in mind, although they hovered in the background, of course. None of them seemed aware that nostalgia had already begun to figure in a political context before intellectuals turned their attention to it and even before its new meaning entered the dictionaries. The phrase "the politics of nostalgia," which would become a recurring slogan in political rhetoric, commentary, and analysis over the course of the second half of the twentieth century, began its career in the 1950s as an indictment of conservatism. The first to use it was the liberal American historian Arthur M. Schlesinger Jr. in a 1955 article titled "The New Conservatism."[6] The conservative intellectuals to whom the phrase referred also used nostalgia to distinguish themselves and their various brands of conservatism from one another.

In the following decades, the phrase "the politics of nostalgia" returned without fail whenever conservatism and conservative politicians were gaining support. It first became part of political and partisan rhetoric when Barry Goldwater ran as a Republican candidate for US president in 1964. Following his defeat, it vanished almost as quickly as it had appeared, only to reappear a decade and a half later, when Ronald Reagan ran for and won the presidency in 1980. His British counterpart Margaret Thatcher, who had been elected prime minister the year before, was also frequently linked to nostalgia, as was the chancellor of the Federal Republic of Germany, Helmut Kohl.

Now a well-established rhetorical tool, the phrase "politics of nostalgia" has never been more prominent than in the years following the British European

Union membership referendum and the election of Donald Trump as the forty-fifth president of the United States of America. Up to that point it had been employed primarily to characterize politicians and their politics. Now it was more often employed to describe voters who, according to this argument, voted the way they did not due to their own interests or convictions but because of a sentimental attachment to a past that Brexit and Trump promised to restore. At first appearing in the media coverage, this explanation for the outcome of the referendum and the election was soon taken up in a number of studies by political scientists, sociologists, and historians.[7]

Using Schlesinger as a starting point, this chapter examines the use of the term *nostalgia* in political language from the 1950s through the 1980s to the most recent past. As the foregoing quotes may have already suggested, and as the chapter will show, nostalgia in politics rarely appears as anything other than an insult. It takes on the function of an accusation that, in the words of political scientist Michael Kenny, "serves to delegitimize a rival argument by associating it both with the retrospective, rather than prospective, gaze, and with forms of sentiment and affect that are taken to provide unsafe guides to action and argument in the present."[8] Kenny already draws attention to two main features that make nostalgia such a useful accusation: first, it implies emotional rather than rational behavior, and second, it insinuates that something or someone—an idea, a person, or a group—is backward-looking and therefore unable to provide solutions for the problems of the present and the future. Because its meaning is based on an—often unconscious—understanding of emotions and temporality in politics, nostalgia has to be viewed in this context.

Studies on nostalgia have rarely done this, as most of them conceive of nostalgia primarily as a cultural phenomenon. The study of emotions in politics, whether by historians or political scientists, is still a relatively new field and has, thus far, focused largely on more visceral and passionate emotions such as fear, anger, resentment, and hate. Similarly, the relationship between politics and time has only become an object of research recently.[9] Finally, political analyses drawing on the term *nostalgia* have often not sufficiently defined and conceptualized their understanding of it. Some of them have built on Svetlana Boym's distinction between reflective and restorative nostalgia, which is far from unproblematic because it often merely reproduces the distinction between progressive and conservative. Worse still, many of these studies either have not been aware of or have overlooked its partisan use to delegitimize rival politics, which tinges their political analysis—if it does not devalue it altogether.

To avoid such pitfalls, this chapter follows a different approach along the lines of the one employed in Chapter 1. Instead of starting with a preconceived notion of nostalgia or aiming to conceptualize it as an analytical category, it historicizes it and thereby scrutinizes it by reconstructing who used the term, how and for whom they used it, for what reasons and in what historical contexts, and how, in the process, the meanings and connotations of *nostalgia* were shaped and how they changed or did not change over time. In doing so, it also contributes to the history of conservatism and the history of emotions and temporality in politics. It concludes by arguing that *nostalgia,* because of its ideological connotations, and its use in partisan rhetoric, is not a suitable term for analyzing politics, especially not when its underlying meanings are not acknowledged, and should therefore be dropped from the vocabulary of political analysis altogether.

A Rootless Nostalgia for Roots in 1950s America

"In the United States at this time," the literary critic Lionel Trilling wrote in 1950, "liberalism is not only the dominant but even the sole intellectual tradition. For it is the plain fact that nowadays there are no conservative or reactionary ideas in general circulation."[10] In the postwar United States, liberals could hardly have been more self-confident: the country, they were convinced, was staunchly liberal and would remain so. Even the few scattered intellectuals describing themselves as "conservative" admitted that this term "is among the most unpopular words in the American vocabulary."[11] And though many liberals were shocked when, after two decades of Democratic presidents, Republican candidate Dwight D. Eisenhower triumphed over Adlai Stevenson in the 1953 presidential election, they were not really worried about the future. Even more so because the conservatives in his own party did not consider Eisenhower to be one of them: as a moderate, he compromised with liberalism and did not roll back the liberal reforms of the New Deal era that continued to incense hardcore conservatives.[12]

All the same, the mid-1950s were a time of soul-searching for liberal intellectuals and particularly for the historian—and sometime speechwriter for

Stevenson—Arthur M. Schlesinger Jr.[13] Son of the renowned social historian Arthur M. Schlesinger Sr.—whose own father had emigrated from Prussia, subsequently converted from the Jewish faith to Protestantism, and married a *Mayflower* descendant—Arthur Jr. had a good start in life, studying at Harvard and graduating summa cum laude. Still only in his late twenties, he published *The Age of Jackson,* which became a best seller and gained him the Pulitzer Prize. The book turned Schlesinger into one of the best-known historians and public intellectuals in the United States. While history was his profession, politics was his passion. Looking for answers for Stevenson's defeat, Schlesinger laid the blame squarely at his own camp's door. Liberalism, he admitted in a 1953 essay, had become "bogged down in the ruts of old issues and old debates."[14]

In an article in the *New York Times* in 1950, Schlesinger lauded the benefits of a strong opposition, wondering, "Is American conservatism dead beyond recall?"[15] He should have been careful what he wished for: just three years later, he was forced to take note of a "resurgence of political conservatism," noticing, in passing, how "European conservatism is to this day permeated by a kind of feudal nostalgia."[16] It was the first time Schlesinger—or anyone else, for that matter—brought the two concepts of conservatism and nostalgia together and used the latter to attack the former. In this instance, it served merely as a pointed aside against European conservatism. When Schlesinger returned to the topic of New Conservatism, as it came to be called, in 1955, nostalgia was so central to his argument, it even featured in the subtitle: "The Politics of Nostalgia."[17] "No intellectual phenomenon has been more surprising in recent years than the revival in the United States of conservatism as a respectable social philosophy. For decades liberalism seemed to have everything its way. The bright young men were always liberals; the thoughtful professors were generally liberals," observed Schlesinger, only five years after Trilling had pronounced conservatism dead and buried. "But in the last year or two, it has all seemed to change. Fashionable intellectual circles now dismiss liberalism as naive, ritualistic, sentimental, shallow. . . . Today, we are told, the bright young men are conservatives; the thoughtful professors are conservatives."[18]

Had conservatism returned from the dead? Schlesinger would not go quite that far. For him, conservatism was not so much alive as undead—a zombie, an anachronism—and this was what the term *nostalgia* was meant to convey in this context. When the "bright young men" and the "thoughtful professors" turned to conservative philosophy, they did not do so out of concern for current political issues. Rather, they were driven by a purely theoretical "romantic nostalgia" for the great tradition of conservative thought. Schlesinger quoted the conservative critique of the "liberal reformer who wishes to remake society by imposing on it abstract ideological schemes" and directed it against the conservatives themselves.[19] In his eyes, conservatism was European and, as such, alien to the United States. Implementing it in the United States, Schlesinger implied, not only amounted to something like philosophical high treason, it would also profoundly transform the politics of the country and would, therefore, be anything but conservative. As the United States was founded on liberal principles, a conservatism worthy of the name could only mean liberalism. Schlesinger ended his text by reassuring his readers— as well as himself—that the New Conservatism was just a temporary fad and that it did not rise to the challenges of the present. "For the New Conservatism is essentially the politics of nostalgia," he concluded.[20]

Did Schlesinger have a point? And who were the "thoughtful professors" he was attacking? Never one to dodge an argument, Schlesinger did not shy away from naming names. The names he did name were those of Russell Kirk, Peter Viereck, and Clinton Rossiter—all historians teaching at universities in New England; in short, people not unlike Schlesinger himself, which might have made their conservatism all the more irksome to him. Like Schlesinger, Viereck was partly of German origin and had been to Harvard, graduating summa cum laude in 1937, one year before Schlesinger. Viereck's father, George Sylvester Viereck—whose own father, legend had it, was an illegitimate son of Kaiser Wilhelm I and an actress—had immigrated to the United States in 1896. A successful poet, he was better known as a defender of Hitler. Between 1942 and 1947, he was imprisoned for violating the Foreign Agents Registration Act. Peter Viereck followed in his father's footsteps in becoming a poet, but forcefully rejected his politics. Yet unlike so many of his peers, in the face of fascism he did not opt for the Left: Viereck embraced conservatism.

In 1949, Viereck was awarded the Pulitzer Prize for Poetry and published *Conservatism Revisited,* a mixture of manifesto and history book.[21] The first major work on conservatism after the Second World War, it popularized the term *conservatism* in the United States and gave the "nascent movement a label."[22] So important was Viereck for a short while, he has been called "the first conservative."[23] However, Viereck was a highly unusual conservative: he neither embraced laissez-faire capitalism nor denounced the New

Deal; he was anticommunist but hated Joseph McCarthy; he also voted for Stevenson in 1956.[24] As one confused reviewer of his book noted, Viereck's "conservative 'principles' are as often characteristic of liberals as of conservatives."[25]

Ambiguous as they may have been, Viereck's conservative principles are interesting in our context because they also included nostalgia. "The conservative principles par excellence," Viereck declared, "are proportion and measure; self-expression through self-restraint; preservation through reform; humanism and classical balance; a fruitful nostalgia for the permanent beneath the flux; and a fruitful obsession for unbroken historic continuity."[26] Viereck thus elevated nostalgia to a conservative principle—provided that it was "fruitful" and directed toward stability in a changing world. As this qualification already implied, nostalgia could also be a negative force, and this was how Viereck would increasingly come to see it.

As something of a contrarian, the young Viereck was attracted to conservatism precisely because it was so unfashionable. Once the New Conservatism, to whose birth Viereck had contributed, caught on, he quickly felt estranged from it. After attacking liberalism in *Conservatism Revisited* in the 1940s, from the mid-1950s he took New Conservatism to task. Simultaneously, nostalgia turned from a principle of conservatism to one of New Conservatism's principal faults: "The main defect of the new conservatism," Viereck wrote, "threatening to make it a transient fad irrelevant to real needs, is its rootless nostalgia for roots."[27] The rootlessness of New Conservatism so agitated Viereck that he kept on attacking it from various angles. In contrast to the conservatism he had propagated, "today's conservatism of yearning is based on roots either never existent or no longer existent." The "conservatism of nostalgia," as he called it, lacked "the living roots of genuine conservatism."[28] It was driven by "romantic nostalgia."[29] What Viereck meant by "rootless nostalgia for roots" or "traditionless worship of tradition" was chiefly a conservatism that looked for roots not in America itself but abroad, particularly in the philosophy of Edmund Burke.[30]

Viereck's critique was odd, and for two reasons: first, because the conservatism he had in mind would have conserved the New Deal and "the Kennedy program," the two most important liberal projects.[31] And second, because he himself had looked for conservative roots abroad, when he made Metternich the center of his book, a figure much more foreign to American politics than Burke, who had spoken out on behalf of the American colonists in the

1770s. It seems as if Viereck had adopted Schlesinger's critique from seven years earlier to the extent that he even used Schlesinger's phrase "romantic nostalgia." Whereas in 1949 Viereck had mentioned nostalgia only once and in a positive way, thirteen years later it was a term of abuse. "Nostalgia," "yearning," and "rootlessness" had become synonymous with one another and synonymous with what was wrong with the New Conservatism. Even for conservatives—or at least for "the first conservative," Viereck—nostalgia now carried a negative connotation.

In contrast to Schlesinger, Viereck did not go into detail about who aroused his anger—apart from one exception: Russell Kirk, a thinker Schlesinger had also mentioned (see Figure 2.1). In many ways, Kirk was the quintessential conservative. Quitting his university career in 1959 because of what he saw as declining standards, Kirk moved to Mecosta, a small village in Michigan, where he had grown up and where his family had lived for five generations in a house called Piety Hill. There he devoted himself entirely to writing. In 1963, he converted to Catholicism and married.[32] Cultivating a deliberately old-fashioned persona, Kirk rejected many aspects of modernity to the point of eccentricity. He despised automobiles as "mechanical Jacobins," and he preferred to write his books on his great-uncle's typewriter because it filled him with a "profound sense of continuity."[33] He wrote ghost stories on the side and claimed to possess a "Gothic mind, medieval in its temper and structure."[34]

Disliking Kirk was easy. His quirkiness invited satirical commentary. No conservative was accused of nostalgia more often than he was. "A third handful of men," wrote Clinton Rossiter, another pioneer of conservative thought, in *Conservatism in America,* "are taking special delight in another aspect of the present climate: nostalgia. There are the pure traditionalists, the sentimental reactionaries, the men who are sick, in Thomas Cook's phrase, with 'political necrophilia.'"[35] "Political necrophilia" neatly captured what nostalgia meant for its critics: a love for dead political ideas. The remark was aimed directly at Kirk, who, Rossiter quipped, sounded "like a man born one hundred and fifty years too late and in the wrong country."[36] Viereck could not have agreed more. Indeed, he liked the phrase so much, he quoted it in the 1962 revised edition of *Conservatism Revisited.*[37] Similarly, the constitutional scholar Walter Berns spoke of "Mr. Kirk's hatred for the present and his yearning for a verdant and innocent and . . . integral past."[38] All of these commentators were fellow conservatives. With friends like these, who needed enemies?

Figure 2.1 A Gothic mind at home: Russell Kirk posing as a country gentleman in front of Piety Hill, in Michigan. Jay McNally/picture alliance

Less surprisingly, Kirk's liberal critics of the mid-1950s also drew on what they perceived as his nostalgia. For the legal scholar Francis Biddle, Kirk embodied "the nostalgic unreality of so much of contemporary American conservatism."[39] Gordon K. Lewis accused Kirk of an "impassioned nostalgia for a dead society," and the journalist William V. Shannon accused him of harboring a "hopeless yearning and a barren nostalgia for the irretrievable past of small shops and craft guilds."[40] Whether liberals or conservatives, nostalgia had become a common political insult.

Of course, these critics were not referring to Kirk's personal eccentricities. Their comments concerned his magnum opus, *The Conservative Mind* (1953), after Viereck's *Conservatism Revisited* the most important book in bringing forth a conservative intellectual movement in the United States. Unlike Viereck or Rossiter, Kirk himself practically never used the term *nostalgia,* in either a positive or negative sense. He characterized the liberal as "a man in love with constant change," as someone who "tended to despise the lessons of the past and to look forward confidently to a vista of endless material progress."[41] But he did not categorically oppose change, admitting that "society must alter, for slow change is the means of its conservation."[42]

Certainly, his conservatism was skeptical about the chances for improvement and advocated the conservation of traditional institutions. But such sentiments, hardly controversial, were conservative core beliefs. His six principles—Kirk called them canons—of conservative thought were not fundamentally different from those Viereck had drawn up: if anything, they were more concrete.[43] It is certainly true that Kirk's thinking was rooted in the thought of the Tory and, worse still, foreigner Burke, but it is hard to see how this alone warranted the charge of nostalgia—writing about conservative thought without mentioning Burke would be like writing about Marxism and ignoring the person whose name the movement bears.

One passage in Kirk's follow-up book *A Program for Conservatives* (1954), however, was more suggestive. In the last chapter, on tradition, Kirk wrote,

> When I was a very small boy, I used to lie under an oak on the hillside above the millpond, in the town where I was born, and look beyond the great willows in the hollow to a curious and handsome house. . . . This was an octagonal house, its roof crowned with a glass dome—a dignified building, for all its oddity. Well, the country planners have chopped down the willows and converted the land round about the old mill-pond into what the traffic-engineers and professional town-planners think a "recreational area" should look like. . . . And the octagon-house was bought by a man with more money than he knew how to spend, who knocked the house down . . . and built upon its site a silly "ranch-type" dwelling. . . . The old genius is departed out of the town and the country about it.[44]

With passages like these, Kirk was doomed to being accused of nostalgia. Here, his childhood in the countryside—a nostalgic trope if ever there was one—merges with the past of the country in a distant golden age before the fall that occurs when planners and capitalists arrive to destroy both nature and the human dwellings in harmony with it to replace them with modern facilities.

If Kirk hated anyone, it was planners: they, and not the ghostly spirits often turning out to be rather good-natured, are the true villains of many of his ghost stories. "Ex Tenebris," for instance, a story he published a year before *A Program for Conservatives,* is set in England and features a "Planning Officer," described as "a thick-chested, hairy man, forever carrying a dispatch case, stooping and heavy of tread, rather like a large earnest ape."[45] Obviously not a likeable person, he has decided to transplant an old lady from her small and unsanitary but beloved cottage to a council flat—despite the objections of the local lord who acts as Kirk's mouthpiece: "Why do you whirl her off to your desolation of concrete roadways that you designed, so far as I can see, to make it difficult for people to get about on foot? Why do you have to make her live under the glare of mercury-vapour lamps and listen to other people's wireless sets when she wants quiet?"[46] When nothing can dissuade the zealous Planning Officer, the ghost of the local vicar long deceased takes matters into his own hands and kills him. A conservative genre in general, where the past haunts the present, the ghost story served Kirk as another means of critiquing modernity.

"Ex Tenebris" and the passage in *A Program for Conservatives* about the loss of his childhood paradise—probably the Mecosta to which he later returned—are also parables about the modern world. The destruction of the willows and the octagonal house symbolizes "a larger revolutionary movement calculated to efface the Past and establish a new society Utilitarian in its principles."[47] For Kirk, the past was something he remembered fondly and the loss of which he mourned sincerely. But remembering and conserving were not ends in themselves. On the contrary, Kirk clarified, the past mattered because it served the interests of the present and future generations: "If we retain any degree of concern for the future of our race, we need urgently to re-examine the idea of an eternal contract that joins the dead, the living, and those yet unborn. Even if we have lost most of that solicitude for posterity, still we may need to return to the principle of continuity out of simple anxiety for self-preservation."[48] This could just as well have been written by a spokesperson for the environmentalist movement.

Idiosyncratic he might have been, but Kirk was not as unworldly as he appeared to many—or as he liked to make himself appear. After the success of *The Conservative Mind* and *A Program for Conservatives,* Kirk left the ivory tower and became involved with practical politics. Not exactly an intellectual himself, presidential hopeful Barry Goldwater asked for Kirk's advice and acknowledged his influence, writing that he "gave the conservative viewpoint an intellectual foundation and respectability it had not attained in modern society."[49] For a while in the 1960s Kirk joined the Goldwater campaign.[50] He even proudly claimed to have been "the first writer to suggest Mr. Goldwater as a serious claimant for the presidential office."[51] His new worldliness, however, did not endear him to his critics: Viereck harshly criticized Kirk for his involvement with Goldwater, calling him "the senator's mouthpiece and court philosopher."[52]

Like Kirk, Goldwater and his supporters were occasionally accused of nostalgia. The liberal historian Richard Hofstadter, for instance, saw the "Goldwater movement" as a "revolt against the whole modern condition as the old-fashioned America sees it" and doubted the sincerity of its conservatism: "Though they can find very little that they want to conserve, the word conservatism is precious to them because it conceals the wild utopianism that emerges out of their nostalgia."[53] Similarly, Irving Howe, the leftist editor of *Dissent,* wrote, "A good part of the feeling behind the Goldwater movement does stem from a nostalgia for the days when Negroes knew their place, cities had not swamped the landscape, income taxes were not so oppressive, and little countries crossing the US could be handled with gunboats."[54] Both of these quotes date from 1964, when Goldwater ran as the Republican candidate against President Lyndon B. Johnson—and lost by a landslide. Goldwater's defeat seemed to prove beyond all doubt that conservatism, far from coming back, was a sure way to lose elections.

In *Future Shock* Toffler mentions Goldwater together with George Wallace, the Democratic governor of Alabama, as examples of a "reversionist"—that is, someone unable and, more to the point, unwilling to adapt to the challenges of the present and the future: "The middle-aged, right-wing reversionist yearns for the simple, ordered society of the small town—the slow-paced social environment in which his old routines were appropriate."[55] By lumping Goldwater together with the staunch antisegregationist Wallace, Toffler implied that he—and, by extension, the reversionist type—was also racist. That was not entirely fair to Goldwater, who had been an early supporter of civil rights and desegregation but nevertheless voted against the 1964 Civil Right Act. While not a racist himself, Goldwater certainly articulated a "philosophy which gives aid and comfort to the racists," as Martin Luther King Jr. said about him.[56]

At the time, Goldwater and Wallace may have seemed like reversionists, especially after the former's spectacular defeat by Johnson. In the long run, however, the—sometimes subtle, sometimes open—appeal to racist prejudice in white voters in the South of the United States paved the way to the presidency for both Richard Nixon and Ronald Reagan as the "Southern Strategy."[57] By calling them "nostalgic" or "reversionist," the liberal critique could itself be said not to have taken racism seriously enough, pretending that it was a thing of the past, when, in reality, it was an integral part of contemporary politics.

"Ten years ago, who could have predicted the rise of a new conservatism in American life?" asked the writer Joseph Epstein in 1973.[58] Yet the "new conservatism" Epstein had in mind was not that of Viereck and Kirk, but what became more widely known as neoconservatism. The "neocons," most of whom were lapsed liberals and socialists, distanced themselves from both old-school conservatism and the New Conservatism of the 1950s and 1960s, and they did so by drawing on the language of nostalgia.[59] "What is 'neo' ('new') about this conservatism," their ideological godfather Irving Kristol wrote retrospectively in 1983, "is that it is resolutely free of nostalgia."[60] "Neocons feel at home in today's America to a degree that more traditional conservatives do not," Kristol insisted. "Though they find much to be critical about, they tend to seek intellectual guidance in the democratic wisdom of Tocqueville rather than in the Tory nostalgia of, say, Russell Kirk."[61] Coming from a completely different direction, Kristol effectively echoed what Viereck had already written in the mid-1950s. Again, Kirk—and nostalgia with him—served as the strawman of what and how conservatism was not supposed to be.

Kirk remained a divisive figure for conservatism well into the 1980s. At the same time, with the election of Ronald Reagan in 1979, he could pride himself on the fact that the seeds he and other "thoughtful professors" had sown in the mid-1950s had finally borne fruit. Although Kirk did not agree with Reagan's entire program and did not involve himself with Reagan's campaign as he had with Goldwater's, he nevertheless supported him.[62] Like Goldwater, Reagan acknowledged Kirk as an important intellectual figure for conservatism. At a dinner in Kirk's honor in 1981, he credited him with helping to "renew a generation's interest and knowledge of 'permanent things,' which are the underpinnings and the intellectual infrastructure of

Figure 2.2 Ronald Reagan shaking hands with Russell Kirk in the Oval Office. The Russell Kirk Center

the conservative revival of our nation."[63] Shortly before the end of his second administration, he bestowed the Presidential Citizens Medal on him (see Figure 2.2).

Although Kirk made it easy for his liberal as well as conservative detractors to portray him as a nostalgic figure, it must mean something that both Goldwater and Reagan, who between the two of them managed to turn the Republican Party into a conservative party, paid him their respect. One of Kirk's conservative defenders, the political scientist Donald Atwell Zoll, dismissed the nostalgia charge as "essentially silly": "If Kirk is a 'nostalgic romantic' then so must be all who revere anything else than the immediate utilitarian conveniences," he declared.[64] Indeed, Kirk's conservatism was not mere antimodernism, his interest not confined to the past and his work not without influence on his present. While Figure 2.1 shows Kirk as he wanted to be seen and as many of his critics saw him—posing as the American idea of an English aristocrat in front of his home reminiscent of an English country house—Figure 2.2, with Reagan in the Oval Office, shows a different but equally important Kirk: if his ideas had not helped to win the presidency for Reagan directly, they had prepared the ground and helped to legitimize conservatism as an American ideology.

Clearly, however, *nostalgia,* from the moment it surfaced in a political context, was nothing if not a polemical term, figuring at first in liberal attacks on conservatism and then also in the turf wars within the conservative movement. Starting off as one of Viereck's defining features of conservatism, it almost instantly became a feature against which conservatives defined themselves. By contrast, the meanings of *nostalgia,* which itself was never defined, much less conceptualized in detail, remained opaque at best in these discussions, describing an exaggerated—sentimental, romantic—attachment to the past and, even more so, an attachment to a wrong past, the wrong roots. In the end, one thing was obvious: no one defended nostalgia. From a polite invective that "thoughtful professors" threw at each other's heads in scholarly journals, nostalgia gradually became part of the broader political language, no longer attached only to ideas or thinkers but to politicians as well. There is no better example of this than Ronald Reagan.

An Engulfing Flood of Nostalgia in Reaganite America

If Kirk and his fellow New Conservatives pioneered the "politics of nostalgia" as an ideology, Reagan was the quintessential politician of nostalgia—at least if we believe the historical commentary. According to James Combs, Reagan "made nostalgia into a political art."[65] Not only did he "articulate and embody the political nostalgia of the conservative movement," writes Daniel Marcus, as president he "put conservative nostalgia into action within economic, social, and foreign policies."[66] "Reaganism was nostalgic in the literal and original sense of the term," is also Sean Wilentz's position.[67]

Such assessments of Reagan and his politics as nostalgic build on how he was perceived at the time. When Governor Bob Graham of Florida nominated Jimmy Carter at the 1980 Democratic Party Convention, he described the leader of his party as practicing "the politics of reality in a complex world where there are no easy answers," in contrast to Reagan, who "proposes to practice the politics of nostalgia, in a make-believe world whose problems are those of a small town in the 1920s."[68] Having descended from the lofty heights of intellectual discourse, Schlesinger's phrase now entered the vocabulary of election campaigning.

Democrats were not the only ones characterizing Reagan in such terms. Many journalists covering the 1980 elections also saw the Republican contender as a representative of the "politics of nostalgia."[69] Richard Reeves, editor of *Esquire,* rated Reagan's chance of being elected as very slim because he had nothing new to say or offer: "Reagan seems to be a nostalgia figure whose time has passed; he looks like the past, he talks like the past."[70] Writing on Reagan's campaign in the *New Yorker,* Elizabeth Drew used the same term.[71] And Lou Cannon from the *Washington Post,* who knew Reagan better than any other journalist because he had covered him as governor of California, thought him an "unlikely leader of the nation," whose "suits were as out of date as his metaphors."[72]

To some extent, Reagan's persona and bearing invited such characterizations. At sixty-nine, he was past retirement age when he won the Republican nomination; he went on to become the oldest person to be elected president (until Donald Trump and Joe Biden). Though he had retained his boyish good looks, the wrinkles time had carved into them were hard to ignore. But it was not his age alone: Reagan reminded Americans of the 1950s, when he had first appeared on their cinema and television screens. Reagan himself added to this impression, enjoying nothing more than entertaining audiences with anecdotes about his childhood in the Midwest and his years in Hollywood.

His politics did the rest: Reagan came with impeccable conservative credentials, rejecting the welfare state in favor of laissez-faire capitalism, the détente with the Soviet Union in favor of a ramped-up anticommunist rhetoric, and liberal values in favor of conservative ones such as family and religion. For many people this harked back to the days of Goldwater. Indeed, Reagan had first appeared on the national political stage as an ardent Goldwater supporter.[73] Predictably, Reagan's politics triggered staunch liberal opposition and renewed ideological confrontation. It was in this context that the term *nostalgia* became common currency in the political vocabulary and with Reagan as its target.

The first thing that should be noted about the relationship between Reagan and nostalgia is something that the existing literature, despite its emphasis on the matter, has ignored: Reagan himself used the term frequently and also in relation to himself. He had been governor of California for less than nine months when he took time out of his busy schedule to travel to the small town of Eureka, Illinois, to speak at the dedication of a new library building at the local college where he had gone to university. For Reagan, the visit was both a labor of love and a trip down memory lane. He began his speech with, "It must be evident to most of you that only a thin wall of wavering willpower stands between you and an engulfing flood of nostalgia."[74] It had been ten years, he recounted, since he had stood in the same place to receive an honorary degree, thirty-five since he was awarded his first. Reagan fondly remembered his time as a student in Eureka, as he did his youth in small-town Tampico, a hundred miles north of Eureka, describing it in his autobiography as "one of those rare Huck Finn-Tom Sawyer idylls"—not dissimilar to how Kirk had portrayed his youth in the countryside.[75]

The Eureka speech was an early example of what would come to characterize Reagan's rhetoric during his presidency. Delivering an address at the University of Notre Dame in 1981, he had to keep his nostalgia in check once again: "Now, if I don't watch out, this may turn out to be less of a commencement than a warm bath in nostalgic memories."[76] At a rally in 1984, he threatened his audience with: "I may just bathe all of you in warm nostalgia."[77] Speaking at a reception for the performing arts in 1988, Reagan pronounced "this night . . . a time for reflection and nostalgia."[78]

And these were no one-offs; Reagan regularly used the term *nostalgia* in his speeches, usually at the very beginning.[79] Even when he did not mention it explicitly, he often started a speech by reminding his audience of when he had last spoken to them or treating them to one of his anecdotes relating to a shared past. For instance, he began a talk at a dinner of the Conservative Political Action Conference in 1982 by saying, "Coming here tonight has been a sentimental journey for me, as I'm sure it has been for many of you."[80] Frequently he included his audience in his nostalgia, thereby inviting everyone to partake in the same feeling ("I know everyone here must have been bathed in nostalgia").[81] In addition to his words, his body language and facial expression—his head slightly slanted, his eyes gazing above the heads of the audience into the distant past—aimed to convey and instill emotion.[82]

Reagan—not for nothing nicknamed the "Great Communicator"—was far too skilled an orator for this to be spontaneous.[83] Not only was he a trained actor, as a motivational speaker for General Electric he had also given an estimated nine thousand speeches across the country.[84] According to one ecstatic GE representative, their spokesman had an "almost mystical ability to achieve an empathy with almost any audience."[85] Reagan himself was not only aware of this ability, he lived for it. In his autobiography he recalled how, when he gave his first public speech at university, he "discovered . . . that an audience has a feel to it and . . . that audience and I were together."[86] Reagan actively sought this feeling of togetherness—to the extent that at least one commentator has described it as the driving force behind his whole career.[87]

Conjuring up a shared past was one way of creating this feeling of oneness between Reagan and his audience. By referring to a previous occasion when he had spoken to a given audience, by drawing on his own past in such a general way that everyone could relate to it, or by invoking a national past all Americans allegedly had in common—or indeed by using all three strategies at once—Reagan underscored the fact that they were all part of the same memory community.[88] By infusing the act of remembering with an emotional quality, Reagan simultaneously created an emotional bond between himself and his audience, an emotional community.[89] In that feeling Reagan called nostalgia, these two strands, the memory community and the emotional community, intersected and reinforced each other. Although Reagan, in reaching out to his audiences, drew on other emotions as well—the hatred of communism or the love for one's country, the fear of national decline or the desire for success and wealth—psychologists have argued that nostalgia is a particularly effective emotion in producing a sense of community.[90] Whether by experience or by intuition, Reagan certainly seems to have been aware that what he called nostalgia, the mixture of shared memories and shared emotions, was a sure way to capture his audiences, as underscored by his habit of opening his speeches by referring to it.

Reagan saw nostalgia predominantly in positive terms: he freely admitted to indulging in it, and he often used the term with the adjective *warm,* as in, "great pleasure and warm nostalgia."[91] Like any pleasure, however, nostalgia called for moderation. "Nostalgia has its time and place," but, Reagan added, "nostalgia isn't enough. The challenge is now. It's time we stopped looking backward at how we got here."[92] This cautionary tone was present as early as his speech at Eureka College, in which he elaborated on his view of history. When he advised students to turn to the "accumulated knowledge of the past," Reagan did not suggest "that we turn back the clock or retreat into some dim yesterday that we remember only with nostalgia." Rather, "we must learn from yesterday to have a better tomorrow."[93] Here Reagan distinguished between nostalgia, which was pleasurable but ultimately gratuitous, and history, which was instructive and useful.

For many of his critics, however, it was exactly Reagan's historical excursions that constituted his "politics of nostalgia." Reagan's speeches were liberally riddled with references to figures, events, and episodes from the American past. "The past matters. We need to rely on it for our guidance as we approach the future," Paul Erickson summarized Reagan's idea of history in a 1985 study of his rhetoric, concluding, "This position, the most basic premise of Anglo-American conservatism, underlies all of Reagan's politics."[94] However, that did not mean that Reagan represented the past faithfully or accurately. As Erickson admitted, Regan's "interpretation of history" was based not on fact "but on metaphor, on acting and on story treatments"; it was "not history, but consciously crafted mythology."[95]

Unsurprisingly, the historical profession was not pleased by what one contemporary historian called "Reaganscribing history."[96] Not only were Reagan's improvisations on past themes often factually unsound, "Reagan offered a past that was stable, comforting, and complimentary."[97] "Visiting Reaganland," as Garry Wills has described it, "is very much like taking the children to Disneyland. . . . It is a safe past, with no sharp edges to stumble against."[98] Indeed, Reagan often idealized the national past or concentrated on its more favorable chapters. If he touched on darker episodes, he stressed the American ability to overcome them, thus portraying the past as both instructive and reassuring.

There was one chapter in American history, however, whose edges Reagan did not round off but emphasized instead, and that was "the sorry story of the sixties and seventies."[99] Whether government expansion and taxation ("the overtaxing, overspending, overregulating binge of the sixties and seventies"), education ("Somehow in the sixties and seventies, people decided that discipline was old fashioned and high standards unnecessary"), drugs ("Back in the 1960s and 1970s, America crossed a deadly line"), criminality ("the crime epidemic that spread across our country in the sixties and seventies"), or morality in general ("We're still paying for the permissiveness of the 1960s and 1970s"), everything that Reagan hated somehow had its origins or had come to fruition in that period.[100]

Historians have therefore argued that Reagan contributed to and tapped into a broader idealization of the 1950s. Indeed, compared with the gloomy picture Reagan drew of the 1960s and 1970s, the 1950s automatically looked much brighter, but that was almost the extent of Reagan's references to them. Apart from an occasional nod to "the boom years of the fifties . . . when America's self-confidence and optimism were almost palpable," Reagan said surprisingly little about that decade.[101] An allegedly better past was of far less interest to him than fixing the "bad past" of the 1960s.

In the end, the narrative Reagan employed was not so much one of nostalgia as one of decline and projected revival, in which America had peaked in the 1950s, declined since the mid-1960s, and now awaited reawakening— by none other, of course, than Reagan himself. Reagan repeatedly spoke about "the decline of America's economic strength" and "the decline of America's defenses," particularly during his campaign and the first year of his administration.[102] Never loath to contradict himself, he attacked the declinist narrative at the same time. "We're not," he reassured his audience in his first inaugural address, "as some would have us believe, doomed to an inevitable decline."[103] The idea of decline went hand in hand with one of a return to greatness. When he campaigned for the presidency in 1980, Reagan's slogans were "Let's make America great again" and "Renew America's strength with great American values" (see Figure 2.3).[104] At his acceptance speech at the Republican Convention in 1980, he spoke about his aim to "renew the American spirit," spur a "rebirth of the American tradition," and "recapture our destiny."[105] If America wanted to be the proud nation it once was, Reagan declared, it had to leave the road it had taken in the mid-1960s and return—not to a better past, but to the right path.

Despite its frequent references to the past, Reagan's rhetoric was ultimately present-centered and forward-looking. History and future were intertwined. "He does not want to return to the past," wrote columnist and Reagan ally George Will, "he wants to return to the past's way of facing the future," alluding to an optimism about the future that Americans allegedly had lost.[106] Similarly, Lou Cannon held that Reagan "spoke of the future in the accents of the past"; he was "at once old-fashioned and forward-looking . . . [he] frequently sounded as if he wanted to go back to the future."[107] "Reagan not

Figure 2.3   "Let's make America great again,"
the motto of Ronald Reagan's 1980 presidential
campaign. Wikimedia Commons

only represents the past," Garry Wills also emphasized, "but resurrects it as
a promise of the future."[108] All three commentators stressed Reagan's habit of
looking to the past to formulate a vision for the future. Indeed, Reagan used
the term *future* more often than *past, god, peace,* and even *freedom;* the only
term he used more often was *America*.[109]

The declinist narrative itself had a future component: decline was not unstoppable. If only Americans elected Reagan and followed his politics,
decline would be reversed. That was his promise and that was what he delivered—at least rhetorically. Once he had been president for a while, it was
no longer the economy or military power that was in decline, but unemployment, inflation, and even terrorist attacks.[110] At the same time, his snide remarks against the "false prophets of decline" became louder.[111] When his
second term as president drew to a close, Reagan openly attacked the "liberal ideology of decline" and "the liberal pundits," who droned on about
"America's inevitable decline."[112]

Not satisfied with blaming America's decline on the liberal reforms of the
1960s and the 1970s, Reagan also blamed liberals for the declinist narrative—
conveniently forgetting that he had employed it himself. Taken together, decline and renewal made for a powerful political narrative and one that,

moreover, was deeply embedded in the American rhetorical tradition, known as the "American jeremiad."[113] Ever the accomplished orator, Reagan used it skillfully to promote and legitimize his politics, portraying American history as fundamentally positive except for that one wrong turn in the 1960s when it strayed from the right path. Over the course of his career, Reagan himself first promised to steer the nation back to this path and then claimed to have successfully done so.

In terms of his rhetoric, the future increasingly brightened up as Reagan's time in power wore on. Whereas his first inaugural address had rejected the idea of national decline, his second did not even mention it. Instead, he now chastened those who thought about the past at all, reminding his audience that when he had been elected, "voices were raised saying that we had to look to our past for the greatness and glory." Second-term Reagan, however, would tolerate none of this because "we, the present-day Americans, are not given to looking backward. In this blessed land, there is always a better tomorrow."[114]

This was an odd remark from a politician who, from his earliest speeches to his farewell address, drew on the past and praised the past as a guiding star of the present. At least Reagan was consistent in his inconsistency. Of course, he was neither a philosopher nor a historian; he was a politician and his rhetoric served political ends: to get himself elected and to keep him in power. This Reagan achieved—not least by reassuring Americans that they could be proud of their past and confident about their future.

So much for Reagan the orator, but what about Reagan the political actor: Did his practical politics amount to a "politics of nostalgia"? Was he "turning back the clock" as his liberal adversaries complained and his hard-core conservative cheerleaders demanded?[115] If there was one particular issue where Reagan was accused of this, it was civil rights, because Reagan was certainly no champion of them.[116] Like Goldwater, he had opposed the 1964 Civil Rights Act, the Voting Rights Act of 1965, and, initially at least, the 1988 Civil Rights Restoration Act. However, conservative hardliners in the Republican Party and Reagan's cabinet failed to get a majority of their colleagues to agree to roll back minority preference policies. In the end, a turnaround in civil rights policy did not occur, mainly because civil rights were not as high up on Reagan's agenda as other issues. Still, Reagan's rhetoric made the Republican Party into an almost entirely white party, and, in the field of the federal judiciary, his legacy endured through his appointment of many conservative judges.[117]

When it came to welfare spending, Reagan had rhetorically committed himself to radical reductions as well. He was rather reluctant to put them into practice, however, fearing that it could endanger his reelection. Therefore, he cut programs aimed at the poorest and neediest but spared the middle classes, so that, in the end, overall welfare spending actually increased during his tenure.[118] Finally, Reagan did little on conservative pet issues such as restoring school prayers or abolishing abortion because they were too divisive.[119]

Reagan's foreign policy also struck some observers as nostalgic. "Ronald Reagan's view of the world is a perfectly preserved image of international relations circa 1948. In its broadest manifestations it is the 'politics of nostalgia'; one of its subsidiary parts is the 'diplomacy of nostalgia,'" criticized the political scientist Ross K. Baker in 1982.[120] The "second Cold War" that resulted from Reagan's rejection of the détente with Soviet Russia—which he famously called an "evil empire"—and the military buildup he initiated must indeed have felt like a throwback to the time of McCarthy, Goldwater, and the Cuban missile crisis. However, the second Cold War was not only somewhat farcical—Reagan was surprised to learn that the Russians saw the United States as the aggressor—it was also rather short-lived. Once Mikhail Gorbachev had become general secretary and Reagan converted to the policy of détente, it was over. Turning from hawk to dove, Reagan alienated many of his neoconservative supporters in the process.[121]

Considering all these factors, what did the "politics of nostalgia" truly mean? The phrase had come a long way since Schlesinger coined it in the mid-1950s. Initially it referred merely to ideology: an attachment to what liberal critics saw as an outdated political tradition and what conservatives saw as the outdated strands of a tradition they hoped to revive. With Goldwater it had already taken on a broader meaning; with Reagan it took on an even broader meaning still. Now it referred not only to ideology and his conservative convictions but also to his person and to his practical politics, whether domestic or foreign. Given that Reagan frequently used the term in public speeches and, moreover, liked to talk about the past both personal and national, it must have been tempting for his critics to describe him in such a way.

On closer examination, however, their focus on nostalgia obscured not only how Reagan used the past and the radical character of his politics but also how the two fitted together. In his speeches, nostalgia was reserved largely for personal recollections. When he talked about the national past, it was not so much as a golden age, but as a long and continuous tradition that led directly into the present and extended into the future. Notwithstanding a sentimental note, the past mainly served to instill a sense of national pride in the audience and, more practically, to legitimize Reagan's politics. Here, however, social conservatism always took second place to libertarian economic ideals and policies that were not so much a throwback to earlier periods of American history—much as Reagan as well as some of his critics liked to argue that point—as a radical new departure. They went on to profoundly change American society and the relationship between citizens and the state. By dressing his politics in the clothes of the past, Reagan disguised just how radical they were. And more than a few liberals took the bait, attacking him for his nostalgia instead of warning of the disruptive character of his politics and its potential effects.

In the end, *nostalgia* was first and foremost a polemical term, suggesting that Reagan, his ideas, and his politics were all stuck in the past, offering little to solve the problems of the present and, worse still, distracting from them, leading the country backward instead of into the future. Its undercurrents made nostalgia a convenient and effective tool for partisan rhetoric, which is exactly what disqualified it as an analytical tool: nostalgia did not so much explain Reagan's politics as obscure its true nature and effects.

Although Reagan claimed to have ended the downturn and restored American self-confidence, the narrative of decline and renewal was far too well established and useful to disappear for good. When the Republicans found themselves in the minority after Bill Clinton's victory in 1992, it quickly resurfaced. In a 1995 speech, Speaker of the House Newt Gingrich called for national renewal by suggesting an unusual model: Victorian England.[122] An American politician extolling the virtues of Britain and the Victorian age was a decidedly odd event. For most Americans, Victorian England, at best, meant the novels of Charles Dickens (or the television adaptations of them), whose references to poverty, illegitimacy, prostitution, and workhouses might have rendered its usefulness as a model suspect. In any case, it is difficult to imagine Reagan looking for a role model for America beyond its own borders and tradition.

Gingrich, who had been a professor of history for a couple of years in the 1970s, did not disguise what had inspired him: "It ain't that hard to understand. Read Himmelfarb's book," he told an audience.[123] Gertrude Himmelfarb was an American historian specializing in Victorian Britain and the wife of neoconservative Irving Kristol; the book was *The De-moralization of Society*.[124]

As the title suggests, the book—which examines the moral world of Victorian Britain to compare it, favorably, to that of modern society—was a straightforward history of decline. Noting that it was less a serious historical study than a substantiation of right-wing ideas, British historian Stefan Collini doubted experts would find "anything here that they would regard as both new and true," dispatching of it as an "attempt to enlist 'history' in the service of doctrinaire moralism."[125] Of course, accusations of nostalgia were not long in coming.[126] The previous year the *New York Times* had already reported that Gingrich "knows how to market nostalgia and oversimplified remedies with Reaganesque vigor."[127] Nostalgia was also used to describe the phenomenon that inspired Himmelfarb to write her book in the first place: Margaret Thatcher's flirtation with "Victorian values."[128]

Soft-Focus Nostalgia in Thatcherite Britain

In 1983 Thatcher had been prime minister for four years. Her first term was hardly an unequivocal success given the ongoing economic recession and steadily rising unemployment. But with the first signs of economic recovery and the Falklands War to boost morale, Thatcher's fortunes were turning—so much, indeed, that she felt safe calling a general election for the summer. In January, she was interviewed on television by Brian Walden, a former Labour member of Parliament (MP) turned journalist. After discussing various other subjects, Walden turned to the issue of values, telling Thatcher that she had "outlined an approval of what I would call Victorian values." Far from rejecting the description, Thatcher immediately embraced it: "Oh exactly. Very much so. Those were the values when our country became great, but not only did our country become great internationally, also so much advance was made in this country."[129]

Although the term "Victorian values" had been suggested by Walden and not herself, Thatcher liked it so much she repeated it again and again in the months leading up to the election. In a radio interview in April, Thatcher related how she was "brought up by a Victorian grandmother," who had instilled in her certain values: "You were taught to work jolly hard, you were taught to improve yourself, you were taught self-reliance, you were taught to live within your income, you were taught that cleanliness was next to godliness," concluding that "all of these things are Victorian values."[130] After a while, however, with journalists continuing to quiz her about it, Thatcher got increasingly fed up with the subject and began to distance herself from it: "Those values are more than Victorian, they really are eternal."[131] Finally, she testily told one journalist in 1987, "They cannot be called 'Victorian values!' It is a misnomer. They are fundamental rules."[132]

For the opposition, Thatcher's extolling of Victorian values was a welcome target during the election campaign and one it continuously tried to exploit. "In view of the Prime Minister's announcement that she subscribes to many of the Victorian values," Labour MP Frank Dobson challenged the prime minister in February 1983, "will she tell the House which she most fancies reintroducing—the absence of a National Health Service, the absence of old-age pensions, the workhouse, or a long series of colonial wars?"[133] In March, fellow Labour MP William Hamilton pointed out that the "consequences of those Victorian so-called virtues and values were the cancerous growth of widespread poverty, ignorance, disease and deprivation."[134] In April, Labour leader Neil Kinnock condemned what he called "sickly Tory sentimentality": the "smug sermons from self-righteous rich Tory ladies about Victorian values" and "the antique policies that go with them."[135]

While attacking Thatcher for her comments on "Victorian values" and trying to prove her wrong by listing the social ills of the Victorian age, none of the Labour MPs accused her explicitly of nostalgia. This was left to the left-leaning *New Statesman,* whose May edition featured a special supplement on "Victorian values." Its cover was graced by "Maggie Regina," a photomontage by the artist Peter Kennard of Queen Victoria in full regalia with Thatcher's face (see Figure 2.4).[136] In an editorial entitled "Soft Focus Nostalgia," Raphael Samuel dissected and denounced Thatcher's Victorian values.[137] Following it were articles by experts on the Victorian era trying to set the record straight. From today's point of view, it is interesting to note that there was no article on imperialism and colonialism, an issue that will come up later in this section.

Thatcher's pontificating on a subject these historians, none of them conservatives, had researched for years to sell her conservative politics was clearly doubly galling. How keenly Thatcher's distortion of the past incensed historians is best illustrated by the fact that books on Victorian values kept appearing long after Thatcher herself had tired of the subject and even after she had been ousted as prime minister.[138] If anything, the critique coming from the opposition and the historians convinced Thatcher that she was right.

Figure 2.4   "Maggie Regina," photocollage by Peter Kennard of Queen Victoria with the head of Margaret Thatcher from 1983. Peter Kennard

She accused historians of misunderstanding and denigrating the national past to the point where she even held them responsible—at least partly—for Britain's decline.[139] Unsurprisingly, such accusations embittered historians even more. "She interfered shamelessly with our subject," Bernard Porter later summarized, "telling us what we should think about a whole range of historical issues, and then how we should teach it in schools."[140] In the context of this study, however, the question is not so much whether Thatcher's ideas about the Victorian age were accurate—most historians agree that they were not—but rather why she spoke about Victorian values at all and, of course, the ensuing charge of nostalgia.

Thatcher's image was certainly not one of nostalgia. A grocer's daughter from small-town Grantham, she did not belong to the establishment. Educated at a grammar school, she won a scholarship to attend a women's college at Oxford (studying chemistry, not politics or economics like so many other future MPs). As a woman she was seen as an intruder in the male-dominated corridors of power. In fact, her career was forged against her party's establishment. In contrast to Reagan, she also was not given to waxing wistfully about the past, despite the occasional reference to her father and her "Victorian grandmother." She used the term *nostalgia* rarely and almost always with a negative connotation. In 1979, for instance, she chided Edward Heath, under whom she had been secretary of state for education and science, that he "must not allow his nostalgia for the past to overcome the facts of the present."[141] Similarly, she warned on another occasion that we should not let "nostalgia for a distant past . . . cloud our judgement of today's realities."[142] Shortly before the 1983 general election, Thatcher demanded that Britain "become a world leader once again. And we must do this not out of some romantic nostalgia for past glories, but because our very survival in the modern world depends upon it."[143] In short, she could not have rejected nostalgia more forcefully.

This rhetoric corresponds with her image as an unsentimental modernizer. Samuel later reversed his view of Thatcher's nostalgia: emphasizing her "radical contempt for the antiquated and the out-of-date," he now characterized her attitude to the past as "the reverse of nostalgic."[144] Despite his retraction, however, the debate about Victorian values has often been, and still often is, read through the lens of nostalgia.[145] Samuel saw the rhetoric about Victorian values as a way of tapping into a popular nostalgic mood that had spawned phenomena such as the "conservationist outrage," "national heritage," and the "antique boom."[146] Later he believed that "the call for Victorian values" had struck a chord at the time "because it corresponded to widespread disenchantment with the modernizations of the 1960s."[147] How to reconcile these two positions? The answer may lie in Stuart Hall's formula of "regressive modernization": "the attempt to 'educate' and discipline the society into a particularly regressive version of modernity by, paradoxically, dragging it backwards through an equally regressive version of the past."[148] In Hall's eyes, Thatcher's modernization of Britain amounted to taking it back to the nineteenth century, combining the worst of old and new. Thatcher and her supporters would, of course, have disagreed, believing they were making the country fit for the future by bringing back the privateering entrepreneurial spirit Britain had lost along the way—rejecting nostalgia, they still believed in decline.

Decline was an even bigger issue in Britain than it was in the United States. First discussed in the late nineteenth century, it became something of an obsession in the 1970s as political and economic problems mounted. While historians have concentrated on economic decline, commentators at the time worried just as much about Britain's declining influence on the world stage, and an alleged decline of morals accompanying or even causing it.[149] Thatcher's own rhetoric bears this out. In the mid-1970s she was primarily concerned with the "decline of our relative power" and "this country's decline in world standing"; at the end of the decade, the economy took center stage.[150]

Ironically, Thatcher's thinking about decline was influenced by historians, particularly by Correlli Barnett, Andrew Gamble, and Martin Wiener, who made the British elite and its vanishing interest in industry responsible for the economic decline of the nation.[151] For Thatcher as well, political, economic, and moral decline were intertwined, with the last one being responsible for the first two. Although she saw decline as a long-term process whose beginnings lay in the nineteenth century, the main culprit was socialism: instead of acting as independent economic subjects, people had come to rely too much on the state.

This is where the Victorian age came into play. Every declinist narrative needs an ideal state from which things have declined, and "the Victorian era was Thatcher's golden age."[152] It fulfilled the same function for Thatcher that the 1950s did for Reagan. Like Reagan, Thatcher was opposed to everything the shorthand "the 1960s" stood for, and the Victorian age was her shorthand for "the opposite of the 1960s," as the critics of Victorian values saw quite clearly. "She seemed to have in mind her version of the 'permissive' 1960s," Asa Briggs commented, "rather than of the mid-Victorian 1860s and of the welfare state rather than of the strictly limited mid-Victorian state."[153] To this James Walvin added, "Two distinct historical epochs were singled out for praise and condemnation. The one, Victorian . . . [;] the other, the 'permissive society.' . . . The latter was the polar opposite of the former."[154] According to Peter Jenkins, "Victorian values" were "the code . . . for repudiating the 'permissiveness' of the 1960s."[155] In short, Thatcher's championing of Victorian values had little to do with the Victorian age or the British past and everything to do with the search for a positive definition of conservatism beyond the mere rejection of the liberal values of 1960s. By reacting to Thatcher's rhetoric, the Left entered into a debate about values, which unwittingly ended up giving Thatcher "a certain moral brand": the fact that the Left so vehemently rejected Victorian values made it seem as if Thatcher did indeed represent them.[156]

Victorian values were, however, not the only issue that earned Thatcher the charge of nostalgia. The other was far less benign than the "soft focus nostalgia" for a better morality: the Falklands War. The Falklands (or Malvinas) are a group of small islands three hundred miles off the coast of Argentina and eight thousand miles away from Britain still under the jurisdiction and sovereignty of the United Kingdom. Between April and June 1982, they were the subject of a war between Britain and Argentina after the latter invaded the islands. Largely because they commanded far more military power, the war ended swiftly with a British victory—though not without claiming the lives of 649 Argentinian and 255 British soldiers, as well as three islanders. The success gave the beleaguered Thatcher some respite and led her to call an early election, during which she campaigned with Victorian values.[157]

While the Labour opposition never developed a clear position concerning the Falklands War, many left-wing intellectuals attacked the war as an exercise in nostalgia. In his book *Iron Britannia: Time to Take the Great out of Britain*, published right after the war, the journalist Anthony Barnett asserted that "Thatcher's rejoicing in military victory" revealed "an almost uncontrolled nostalgia," a "nostalgia for one of the last colonies and realms of Empire."[158] Writing in the *New York Times Magazine*, the British military historian Thomas Pakenham arrived at a similar assessment. "This has been a strange nostalgic experience," he wrote, "this old-fashioned Falkland Islands war which seems to have ended by bringing to the surface, as it did, all sorts of old-fashioned emotions like patriotism and pride."[159] A patriotism that, according to Hall, thrived on "the disappointed hopes of the present and the deep unrequited traces of the past."[160] In a pamphlet written "in a fit of fury through two nights and one day as a futile attempt to intervene in the media-conducted babble of the British general election," the historian E. P. Thompson reported that other nations saw the Falklands War as "a bizarre episode, a sudden flush of imperial nostalgia, as if Britain had suddenly fallen through a time-warp into the 18th or 19th century."[161]

In all these accounts, the term *nostalgia* was used to expose the Falklands War as anachronistic. To all these observers, the war did not seem to belong in the present of the 1980s, but instead it was a regression—a fall through a time warp, as Thompson had it—to the colonial and imperial wars of the nineteenth century. In the second edition of his book, Barnett reemphasized his point, calling the war "an atavistic exercise in armed nostalgia."[162] The term *nostalgia* signified a longing to return to the days of Britain's former imperial grandeur and simultaneously portrayed it as wrongheaded: a return was as impossible as it was unwanted.

It was more than just left-wing intellectuals who believed they were observing a wave of nostalgia passing through the British public. While the war raged, two travel writers, the Briton Jonathan Raban and the American Paul Theroux, were circumnavigating Britain—Raban in a restored sailboat, Theroux by train. Their itineraries intersected at the Brighton Marina, where they met up. In the written accounts of their journeys, both writers repeatedly record their encounters with imperial nostalgia. For Raban, hearing the Falklanders speak on television evoked associations of class, patriotism, and empire: "They all talked in the voice which . . . puts you instantly and depressingly in mind of gin and tonic, cavalry twill, the next monthly mortgage repayment, Brussels sprouts, tea-cosies, *Journey's End* at the dramatic society, the Magimix in the kitchen and the Queen's head on the stamp."[163] Arriving in Blackpool in June under "mountainous storm clouds," Theroux noticed how "the Falklands news made the English nostalgic about rationing and the Blitz."[164] In keeping with his general account of Britain as a country gripped by decay, Theroux noted nostalgia not only for the time of imperial heroism but also for the time of heroic victimhood.

Although it was not so much Thatcher as the British public that was charged with nostalgia, the academic and Thatcherite Shirley Letwin felt it necessary to defend Thatcher. "For the fifty years before Thatcherism,"

Letwin wrote, "the Conservative Party struggled with Britain's imperial heritage, never quite shaking it off, a belief in or at least nostalgia for empire. Thatcherism, in its post-imperial modernity, has suffered no such hang-ups. It has concentrated instead on the revival of Britain as an independent island power."[165] On closer look, this assessment is not entirely convincing. For one, it ignores the fact that Enoch Powell had taken this position long before Thatcher.[166] More importantly, it fails to address the apparent contradiction between this policy and entering the war, nor does it explain why Thatcher chose a military confrontation over negotiating with the Argentinians and why she employed such a bellicose rhetoric, liberally seasoned with references to Winston Churchill and the Second World War.[167]

Finally, Thatcher's own words belie Letwin's claim about her indifference to the British Empire. In an interview in 1987, she reminisced about how, as a young woman, she had been "quite fascinated with India which at that time, as you know, was not independent, and as you know, part of the history of the British Empire . . . and so I thought that I would really like very much, after I had qualified, after I had got a degree, to apply to join the Indian Civil Service."[168] Though Indian independence burst Thatcher's imperialist bubble, she remained convinced that the British Empire was a good thing—not least for the colonized because it "took both freedom and the rule of law to countries that would never have known it otherwise."[169] In a remark probably aimed against the left-wing historians she so despised, Thatcher expressed her opinion that "the value of the British Empire to the world was misjudged."[170] Whether Thatcher actually believed her imperialist rhetoric—it certainly seems so—or simply addressed it at the British public, with the Falklands War it suddenly became very real.

In turn, a war produced by rhetoric produced even more rhetoric. In a speech at a Conservative rally at Cheltenham racecourse immediately after the British victory, Thatcher—evidently savoring every bite of the sweet fruit of her triumph—lambasted "the waverers and the fainthearts . . . who thought that Britain could no longer seize the initiative for herself," those "who believed that our decline was irreversible—that we could never again be what we were . . . that Britain was no longer the nation that had built an Empire and ruled a quarter of the world" and who had now been so forcefully shown to be wrong: "The lesson of the Falklands is that Britain has not changed and that this nation still has those sterling qualities which shine through our history." Britain, Thatcher concluded, had "found herself again in the South Atlantic," and now that she had found herself, she had to continue showing "those sterling qualities," she said, addressing the railway workers and National Health Service nurses who, at that time, demanded more money and now were supposed to be content with a costly military success on a faraway archipelago most Britons had not heard of until Thatcher's war.[171]

Thatcher did not hesitate to take advantage of the outcome of the war, presenting it as manifest proof that Britain's power had not declined—an idea she herself had promoted earlier—as an opportunity to get even with her detractors and, finally, using the sudden patriotic outburst to call an early election, which she won in a landslide. Of course, Thatcher could not have counted on this from the beginning. Yet, and this talent is what made her such a successful politician, once the opportunity presented itself to her, she did not hesitate to exploit it ruthlessly. Even her opponents were impressed. The historian Eric Hobsbawm called the Falklands campaign "a very brilliant operation by Mrs Thatcher and the Thatcherites," because they had succeeded in "catching a certain popular mood, and turning it in a right wing" direction. For Hobsbawm, as for many others on the left, the success of the Falklands War was not practical but symbolic: it acted as "compensation for the feelings of decline, demoralisation and inferiority."[172] It could be portrayed as an expression and a refutation of nostalgia.

As the debates about Victorian values and the Falklands War demonstrate, nostalgia had become as much part of the political language in 1980s Britain as it had in America by the same time. In both countries, debates about nostalgia in politics centered on a conservative politician in office. In contrast to Reagan, however, Thatcher was, by and large, portrayed not as a figure of nostalgia but as an unsentimental modernizer. Unlike Reagan, she rarely employed nostalgia as a rhetorical tool. Rather, her critics brought up nostalgia to characterize her use of the past. Ultimately, the British discussion revolved much more around the public mood—and unwillingness or inability to come to terms with the country's imperial past and present status—than personality.

All in all, nostalgia in the British debate fulfilled a similar function as it did in the United States. Like Reagan, Thatcher was less a traditional conservative than an economic libertarian, cladding her radicalism in the comforting language of tradition and the past. Her projects to disempower the unions, dismantle the welfare state, privatize state-owned companies, and deregulate the market smacked of radicalism and novelty. The talk about Victorian values made these policies more palatable to the voters, as the journalist Bryan

Appleyard noted: "Victorian stood for everything reassuringly old and admirable as opposed to the new and the frightening."[173] "The historical fancy-dress hides the hard edges," as Collini summed it up.[174] Drawing the same comparison, Samuel called it "modernisation in mufti."[175] In the end, all of these expressions implied the same thing: that Thatcher sold her radical politics as a return to the past, whereas, in reality, they neither marked a return nor had much to do with the past.

Nostalgia Is Not a Solution in Helmut Kohl's Germany

The Falklands War was also discussed beyond Britain's shores. In West Germany, the British management of the crisis was met almost uniformly with incomprehension and criticism. Karl Heinz Bohrer, culture correspondent in London for the newspaper *Frankfurter Allgemeine Zeitung,* felt prompted by this response to weigh in on the British side. Sometimes described as conservative or neoconservative, sometimes as liberal or radical, Bohrer was, first and foremost, a committed contrarian. The Falklands crisis made for an unmissable opportunity to cast himself as the intellectually superior dissenter, his favorite role.[176]

Initially, Bohrer had been quite disparaging of Thatcher, whom he dubbed the "white giant." In a mixture of misogyny and intellectual and class snobbery, he compared her to a "feisty housewife" and bemoaned her lower-middle-class background and the "simplicity of her thinking."[177] He only took her side when the German media came down against her in the Falklands crisis, defending her reaction and what the German media called British jingoism and accusing it in turn of "a mixture of journalistic malice and vulgar thick-wittedness."[178] Bohrer did not doubt that Britain was motivated by "national romanticism and imperial nostalgia," but for him these were superficial notions obscuring a traditional English zeal for freedom.[179]

Ignoring the criticism of Thatcher's politics at home, Bohrer equated the prime minister with her nation and praised the British for their swagger and risk-taking. By contrast—inverting the "ideas of 1914"—he characterized the West Germans as merchants who, only interested in living peaceful, affluent, comfortable, cowardly lives, preferred bribing potential enemies over saber-rattling, let alone military action. Bohrer intended to cause an uproar and he succeeded. Many readers wrote letters to the editors of the *Frankfurter*

Allgemeine Zeitung complaining about his bellicose rhetoric, as well as his lack of knowledge and compassion for the soldiers who had lost their lives.[180]

The Falklands War gave Bohrer a chance to write about one of his pet topics: the British sense of historical continuity and the West German lack thereof. Stressing that "no national disaster has ever forced" the British "to suppress their past," he implied that that was the case for the Germans.[181] England, Bohrer emphasized, "is not made up of actuality and structures but of memories and history."[182] Bohrer had been struck by this on his first visit to London as a student in the 1950s, when he had made an instant connection with British culture.[183]

When Bohrer returned as a correspondent in 1975, he found Britain much changed: London "was not swinging anymore."[184] Everywhere he looked, he saw symptoms of a "seasonal sickness" that "somewhat pretentiously was called nostalgia."[185] Whether in terms of high or pop culture, nostalgia seemed to have become a defining feature of Britain in the late 1970s and early 1980s.[186] For him, this was not necessarily a bad thing. He preferred British decadence over what he saw as West Germany's commercialism, provincialism, and philistinism.[187] Nostalgia for him was a manifestation of "how deep the sense of history is there [in Britain], how strongly the present is shaped by the past." In contrast, "people in the Federal Republic—including their intellectuals—cannot think back before the year 1945."[188] Bohrer believed that nostalgia could not exist in West Germany because it was cut off from its past by the era of National Socialism. There was simply no object, no past to feel nostalgic for, and West Germans were all the poorer for it. It obviously never occurred to him that anyone could be nostalgic for the Nazi period or that West Germany, thirty years after the end of the war, had accumulated enough past in the meantime to allow feelings of nostalgia to arise for more recent periods.

And yet not only was the "nostalgia wave," together with its alleged symptoms and manifestations, discussed almost as heatedly in West Germany as in the United States and Britain, it appeared exactly as a longing for the 1950s, as well as, more surprisingly, the Nazi period. This section first looks at how the relationship between nostalgia and conservatism was discussed in West Germany, before turning to the panic about a wave of "Nazi nostalgia," which many, particularly left-wing, commentators believed to be haunting the Federal Republic in the 1970s. Conservatives rejected this idea, and no one more forcefully than Helmut Kohl, the leader of the Christian conservative opposition at the time. Like Reagan and Thatcher, Kohl himself was repeatedly

criticized—or rather mocked—for a supposed nostalgia for the 1950s, especially when he became the front-runner of the Christian Democratic Union
(CDU), and in his first years as chancellor.

In West Germany, nostalgia first appeared in a political context in the 1970s,
soon after it had acquired its new meaning. Before that time, the term *conservative* was also rarely used, and certainly not by the CDU and the Christian
Social Union (CSU).[189] Associated with the role conservative parties played in
the demise of the Weimar Republic and the rise of Hitler and equated by the
Left with fascism in general, the term was too tainted. This changed in late
1968 when, in reaction to the student movement and the rise of the New
Left, the CDU and CSU first discussed adopting the term and then did.[190]

As the renaissance of conservatism—or at least of the term—occurred simultaneously with the nostalgia wave, it is unsurprising that some observers
saw the two as linked. Though Baacke concluded that the nostalgia wave was
largely apolitical, he nevertheless reflected at length about its relationship to
conservatism and specifically the so-called *Tendenzwende* (literally: trend re-
versal).[191] *Tendenzwende* was one of the key political terms of the 1970s in West
Germany, epitomizing what was seen as the flagging enthusiasm for reforms
and an increasing sense of conservatism.[192]

Even left-wing critics had to admit that conservatives' fortunes were
changing, that, as one article phrased it, "conservatism is in again," as part
of the more general "mood swing."[193] While some described the renaissance
of conservatism in similar terms to the nostalgia wave, others connected them
directly. A Swiss author, for instance, wrote about a "champagne conservatism" flourishing in the "updraft of a nostalgia wave."[194] Another author
warned conservatives who wanted to interpret the nostalgia wave as indicative of a change in their fortunes not to get overexcited, as nostalgia was ultimately a manifestation of "irrationality," of "idealistic hysteria."[195] The
playwright George Tabori called the "nostalgic revivals" "substitute food"
for neoconservatives.[196] As this characterization shows, parts of the West
German Left—like the Left in Britain or liberals in the United States—drew
on nostalgia to attack conservatism, implying that the resurgence of conservatism, like the nostalgia wave, was a fashionable and superficial trend and
not meant to last.

Most conservative intellectuals, however, were not sure what to make of
nostalgia. In general, they tended to dismiss it. In 1973, for instance, the
right-wing author Gerd-Klaus Kaltenbrunner distinguished between two

forms of conservatism: the first celebrated traditions, which "today are only outdated political romanticism, unfruitful nostalgia, and reactionary sentiment"; the other was synonymous with "critique, resistance, corrective."[197] It was not hard to guess with which side Kaltenbrunner identified.

Armin Mohler, former private secretary of the writer Ernst Jünger and pioneer of New Right thinking in Germany who had long labored to revive conservatism, held a similar view. There were, he admitted, nostalgic conservatives and conservatives without nostalgia, as well as nonconservatives with "intense nostalgias." But ultimately, he decided, nostalgia was not constitutive of conservatism: "Whether someone is a conservative or not cannot be deduced from whether they are nostalgic or not."[198] The conservative philosopher Nikolaus Lobkowicz—famous for calling in the police to evict protesting students from the University of Munich—wrote that conservatism precisely did *not* promise "nostalgia and artificial preservation of what has evolved historically."[199]

In summary, German conservatives in the 1970s and 1980s tended to reject nostalgia as much as their American counterparts had done since the 1950s. While they did not have a Russell Kirk from whom to dissociate themselves, they obviously still felt the need to dissociate themselves from nostalgia. For most of them, with the notable exception of Lübbe, nostalgia had nothing to do with either traditions or conservatism. On the contrary, for conservatism to succeed, it had to rid itself of any association with sentimentalism. All in all, however, the term was not as central to definitions of and debates about conservatism as it had been in the American debates in the 1950s and 1960s, which also had little to no influence on the German ones.

As in the United States, nostalgia soon filtered down from the heights of lofty intellectual debate to the realm of campaign rhetoric. In 1974 the artist Klaus Staeck designed a postcard showing current and former high-ranking CDU politicians as old men with walking sticks under the slogan, "Nostalgia is no reason to vote for the CDU" (see Figure 2.5). A member of the Social Democratic Party (SPD), Staeck never officially worked on any of its campaigns, but his artistic interventions against the Christian conservatives were gratefully received by the SPD and very popular far beyond its ranks as well. His postcard resurfaced two years later during the particularly vicious election campaign of 1976. The Christian conservative parties, trying to cast the SPD as an extremist party, ran under the rallying cries of "Freedom or socialism" and "Freedom instead of socialism."[200] In this polarized climate, the postcard's title became something of an unofficial slogan: if the conservatives

Figure 2.5 "Nostalgia is no reason to vote for the CDU," postcard by Klaus Staeck from 1974.

Klaus Staeck, VG Bild-Kunst

accused the Social Democrats of socialism, they accused the conservatives of nostalgia in return.

What nostalgia meant in this context is borne out by a second postcard Staeck created specifically for the 1976 campaign. It shows Helmut Kohl looking out of the back window of a vintage Mercedes limousine, in front of which stands Franz Josef Strauß, the ultraconservative chairman of the Christian Social Union, dressed as a chauffeur. Both are grinning happily, despite the fact their car is missing its tires (see Figure 2.6). Even without the caption "Safely into the 50s," the meaning of the picture was clear: Kohl might be the front-runner, but in reality Strauß was in the driver's seat and together the two would navigate the country nowhere but backward in time to the 1950s, the period they were reminiscent of and which they liked to invoke.

Although—or perhaps because—Staeck's satirical collages were not official party material, they show how many on the left saw the Christian conservatives: as anachronistic and nostalgic, hailing from and harking back to a bygone age. An article in a journal close to the SPD criticized the CDU manifesto as "out of touch with the times" and as a "nostalgic inventory."[201] In 1976 the SPD and the liberal Free Democratic Party, its coalition partner, won

Figure 2.6 "Safely into the 50s," postcard by Klaus Staeck from 1976. Klaus Staeck, VG Bild-Kunst

the election despite losing votes to the CDU, which only just stopped short of winning an absolute majority. It looked like the *Tendenzwende,* the mood swing toward conservatism, would sooner or later turn into an election win, not least because rising fuel prices, a struggling economy, and left-wing terrorism meant that the government was stuck in perpetual crisis mode.

In this politically polarized climate erupted a heated debate about an alleged wave of nostalgia for Hitler and the Nazi era. In the spring of 1973, domestic as well as international newspapers noticed, as *Der Spiegel* phrased it, a "suddenly awakened interest in Nazi topics."[202] Hitler, the *Frankfurter Allgemeine Zeitung* agreed, had "resurfaced."[203] "From Middle Europe to Middle America," *Newsweek* reported, "there seemed to be a sharp resurgence of interest in the man who prompted the holocaust that was World War II."[204] Throughout the 1970s many observers, particularly on the left, noticed a "Hitler nostalgia wave," "Nazi nostalgia," or a "homesickness for fascism."[205]

What were they referring to? The year 1973 was not only that of the first oil crisis and the first German analyses of nostalgia, it also marked forty years since Hitler had been appointed chancellor. This occasion would probably have passed more or less in quiet embarrassment—it certainly was not the sort of anniversary that called for celebration—had it not been for the release of a number of books, films, and other artifacts about the Nazi period, such as journalist Joachim C. Fest's voluminous Hitler biography, whose arrival was announced by a fanfare of prepublications, reviews, and a lavish advertising campaign.[206] Hailing from similar stock as Bohrer, Fest came from a staunchly bourgeois, Prussian, Catholic, and anti-Nazi family: his father, a teacher, had been banned from working by the Nazis, while Fest himself had to leave school early because, he relates in his memoir, he had carved a Hitler cartoon into a bench.[207] Like Bohrer's, this background allowed Fest to be unapologetically conservative, albeit with a liberal tinge.

His Hitler biography, displaying a mixture of revulsion toward and fascination with its subject, spent many pages on the military resistance against Hitler—who emerged once again as a demonic and irresistibly seductive villain—and almost none on the Holocaust, of which, Fest claimed, most Germans had known nothing at all.[208] West German readers were certainly grateful: the book became an instant best seller. When, four years on, Fest turned it into a documentary, reactions were much more critical. "This film is dangerous," declared the weekly *Die Zeit,* calling it a "manifestation of a questionable nostalgia."[209] A group of young, left-leaning historians published a book that discussed both the film and its reception in the context of a wide-spread "Hitler nostalgia."[210]

Fest's Hitler biography and film, which roughly marked the beginning and the end of what critics liked to call the "Hitler" or "Nazi nostalgia wave," were part of an outpouring of books about Hitler and the Nazi period ranging from serious academic tomes to dubious memoirs, picture books, and illustrated journals.[211] In addition to Fest's documentary and Hans-Jürgen Syberberg's controversial *Hitler: A Film from Germany,* there were many international productions about or set in the era of fascism such as *The Damned* (1969), *The Death of Adolf Hitler* and *Hitler: The Last Ten Days* (1973), *The Night Porter* (1974), *Lacombe, Lucien* (1974), and *Salò, or the 120 Days of Sodom* (1975), to mention just some of the best-known and most widely discussed examples. And there were other, much more dubious goings-on that had been going on for some time but only now garnered the media's attention, including the clandestine trade in Nazi memorabilia and the equally clandestine trade in records of propaganda songs and speeches.[212] Taken together, all these phenomena contributed to the impression that many West Germans longed for the Nazi period or at least looked back on it as the good old days.

In 1977, a few months after the premiere of Fest's film, the two strands, the debates about Nazi and conservative nostalgia, intersected when Horst Ehmke, a high-ranking politician of the SPD and minister for research and education at this time, warned his fellow MPs not to underestimate how the Hitler nostalgia wave was perceived abroad.[213] Helmut Kohl, the leader of the Christian democratic opposition, immediately heckled Ehmke. The topic was so contentious that the parliament returned to it the next day. Kohl took up the matter again, having looked up *nostalgia* in his *Brockhaus* encyclopedia, as he told the parliament. *Nostalgia,* he had read there, meant "yearning for the past." Did Ehmke really want to claim that there was a nostalgia for Hitler in West Germany? How could he talk such "nonsense"? Ehmke responded by asking Kohl why he was getting so upset: "There is a nostalgia wave in Germany, which concentrates on what was in the past instead of what is supposed to be in the future. There are articles and essays written about this topic!" "But not for Hitler!" Kohl interjected vehemently. "Currently, the nostalgia wave has reached the period of National Socialism," Ehmke calmly stood his ground.[214]

The exchange between Ehmke and Kohl is all the more interesting because of when it took place: on October 5 and 6, 1977, and, therefore, at the height of the so-called German Autumn, the peak of left-wing terrorism, only a month after the kidnapping of employer representative Hanns Martin Schleyer and less than two weeks before the leaders of the Red Army Faction committed suicide in prison. Given these circumstances, it may seem surprising that the German parliament had time to discuss anything else, let alone nostalgia for the Third Reich. On second glance, however, the debate had everything to do with current politics.

With his intervention, Ehmke responded to a speech by Franz Josef Strauß, who sought to blame the SPD for left-wing terrorism.[215] Ehmke defended his party at first by denying that the Red Army Faction had anything to do with the Left, or politics at all for that matter. By bringing up "Nazi nostalgia," he then returned the charge, suggesting that political extremism was not limited to the Left. Although Ehmke did not mention it explicitly, his comment could be understood as alluding to conservatism's involvement in the rise of fascism, a topic that was all the less welcome at a time when the Christian parties were rediscovering conservatism. Kohl's immediate and vehement response showed that Ehmke had hit a raw nerve.

Ehmke did not bring up an additional element that could have made his charge even more damning. There was radicalization not only on the Far Left but also on the Far Right, with neo-Nazi groups sprouting up across West Germany. Just how dangerous these groups were became clear in 1980, when Rabbi Shlomo Lewin and his partner were killed and when the bombing of the Munich Oktoberfest left 13 people dead and 219 wounded. Neither incident was ever entirely cleared up, not least because terrorism from the Right was seen as far less serious and, therefore, taken far less seriously than that from the Left.[216] For some commentators, what they defined as Nazi nostalgia and the rise of neo-Nazism were connected phenomena.

For conservatives, however, the "Hitler wave" was the opposite of nostalgia; it was a sign that, thirty years after the end of the war, West Germans were finally able to discuss the Nazi past openly. "It is entirely natural that today," Kohl told the Bundestag in his trademark roundabout manner, "where a new generation has grown up, after all democratic groups . . . put off coming to terms with the NS [National Socialist] past for long enough, that they should ask the question: Did my grandfather or even my father support Hitler?"[217] "If there ever was a Hitler nostalgia," Fest wrote, "it existed in the early 1950s, when those who had served Hitler's régime in one way or another looked back at the past." In contrast, the "new interest in Hitler" was "a first stirring of interest in our own history," something that Fest, like Bohrer, had been missing in the years before.[218]

They may even have had a point: not everything that was subsumed under the "Hitler wave" label was historically and ethically questionable, and even when it was, it may have testified to a growing curiosity, especially on the part of the younger generation, to know more about National Socialism, a subject they still learned little or nothing about in school at the time and that was seldom openly discussed at home or in public. For all its inherent problems, the Hitler wave may have helped to make such a discussion possible. If so, conservatives had done little to bring it about. Where they addressed the Nazi past, like Fest did in his Hitler biography, they often displayed exactly the apologetic tendencies for which critics decried the Hitler wave.

These were already apparent from the almost exclusive focus on Hitler—it was not for nothing that it was called the Hitler wave—a strategy employed since the 1950s to avoid addressing broader issues of responsibility and guilt. Most notably, it completely ignored the Holocaust despite the considerable knowledge available by this time. With the public television broadcast of the American TV series *Holocaust* in 1979, this was no longer possible: it made *Holocaust* a household term in West Germany and triggered a long-delayed debate about complicity in National Socialism and its crimes among large parts of German society, effectively ending the Hitler wave.[219]

Yet why did nostalgia become such a central issue in the debate about the Hitler wave in the first place? For one, the term was very prominent in West Germany at the time—as it was in the United States and Britain—especially when it came to pop cultural representations of the past, whether the 1920s or the 1950s or, in this case, the era in between. For left-wing critics, the term was particularly useful: linked to conservatism, it was the ideal stick with which to beat the conservatives. This is not to say that they did not truly worry about the phenomena subsumed under labels like "Hitler wave" and "Nazi nostalgia," but that did not keep them from instrumentalizing such terms. The strong reactions and vehement opposition to the term *nostalgia* from conservatives like Kohl show that they saw through this strategy and tried to counter it. Overshadowed by the polarized politics of the day, the debate did not evolve into an honest reckoning with the Nazi past. But it certainly shows how nostalgia was used to attack conservatism in a West German context.

Kohl himself, like Thatcher, rarely used the term *nostalgia,* and when he did it was almost always in a negative way, as in his debate with Ehmke. When, for instance, he gave a speech earlier in 1977 to commemorate an event in his party's history, he began by stating that the celebration had "nothing whatsoever to do with nostalgia but with our understanding of the continuity of history."[220] Similarly, in a speech from 1981, he said that "nostalgically harking back to earlier and allegedly better times does not offer solutions for today."[221] As vocally as Kohl rejected nostalgia, he just as fervently tried to align himself with the future. In his acceptance speech as leader of the CDU in 1973, titled "Departure into the Future," he distanced himself as much from backward-lookingness as from the "ideological utopias" of the Left, opting instead for the pragmatic middle ground of an "improvement of real living conditions."[222]

However, Kohl had not studied history for nothing. He loved peppering his speeches with references to the past and placing himself and his politics in a historical continuity almost as much as Reagan did. In line with this habit—and despite its title—he began his 1973 acceptance speech by invoking the memory of Konrad Adenauer, the first chancellor of West Germany, and of Ludwig Erhard, its portly, cigar-smoking first minister of economic affairs and Adenauer's successor.[223] If Adenauer was Kohl's revered role model, Erhard stood for a responsible and reliable economic policy. Invoking their memory over time took on an almost mythical quality in Kohl's speeches.[224] In his first government statement, he repeatedly referred to Adenauer, even going so far as to quote a whole passage from Adenauer's own first government statement in 1949.[225] Nothing could have underscored more how much he saw himself in the tradition of his predecessor.

Like Thatcher's embrace of "Victorian values," Kohl's perpetual references to Adenauer would come to haunt him. Picking up on them, the SPD politician Heide Simonis complained that, instead of providing solutions for real and pressing problems, he displayed a "nostalgic yearning" for the 1950s. Such a nostalgia may be a likeable personal weakness, but in politics, she continued, it blinded people to reality.[226] *Der Spiegel* criticized Kohl in 1983 for his "oft-cited Adenauer nostalgia" and for ignoring how much economic circumstances and policies had changed since that time.[227] Staeck's postcards, too, were puns on Kohl's history lessons.

Submitting Kohl's rhetoric to a detailed dissection, the journalist Hans-Peter Riese argued that neither his language nor his policies were borrowed directly from Adenauer. Rather, Kohl offered "nostalgically romanticized memories" and a "cheap copy of the conservatism of the 1950s"; instead of confronting voters with reality, he sold them the illusion of an "idyllic small world." The same applied to Kohl's use of the past generally, which ignored anything that could trigger "fear or feelings of guilt," enlisting it—or carefully selected parts of it—to establish a sense of community.[228] In short, Kohl used the past much like Reagan and Thatcher did: as a way to legitimize and to sell his politics by placing them in a longer historical continuity, thereby trying to invoke an impression of stability and trustworthiness. Likewise, Kohl's critics used the term *nostalgia* much like Reagan's and Thatcher's critics had: to insinuate that he was staring transfixed into the past instead of meeting the challenges of the present with new ideas and policies.

It is perhaps only fitting that a politician who liked to invoke history as much as Kohl did was, in a way, saved by history itself. By 1989, Kohl and his party seemed so hapless that some of its leading politicians planned a coup to oust him, worrying that they might otherwise lose the 1990 elections. Kohl's chancellorship could have ended then and there, much like Thatcher's premiership did the following year. And yet, as the protests in and the mass exodus from the German Democratic Republic (GDR) came to a head, the plan quietly collapsed. In October 1989, the Berlin Wall came down. A year later Germany was reunified, and Kohl went on to win the election. He remained chancellor for another eight years.

The 1990s saw Germany's most sustained and bitter debate about nostalgia yet, but it had little to do with Kohl or with conservatism—at least not in its conventional sense. Germany had hardly been reunified when observers began to note a "frightening GDR nostalgia," as SPD politician Wolfgang Thierse labeled it in a speech in the German parliament.[229] It is interesting that it was Thierse who commented on it as one of the first, as he came from East Germany himself. Most people worrying about a nostalgia for the GDR hailed from the West. By the mid-1990s the subject had become such an obsession that a new term emerged for it: *Ostalgie,* a composite of the German words *Ost* (East) and *Nostalgie* (nostalgia). Journalists flocked to the "new federal states" to report on the strange habits of their new countrymen: if East Germany had been "Kohl-onized," as some East Germans claimed, then these journalists displayed an unabashed colonial gaze.[230]

Ostalgie was—and still often is—seen first and foremost as a cultural phenomenon: the memorialization of the GDR through museums, novels, films, and so on. However, it would hardly have attracted as much attention as it did at the time, nor would it have been deemed "frightening," if it had not also been seen as politically charged. When, for instance, the German parliament initiated a comprehensive inquiry into all aspects of reunification, it took the matter seriously enough to commission two reports on Ostalgie, one by an East German political scientist and one by two West German sociologists. While the latter concluded that Ostalgie could indeed pose a danger to democracy should it develop into a sustained ideology, the former argued that even the most disgruntled East Germans wanted the return of neither socialism nor a planned economy. He also criticized existing analyses of Ostalgie for casting differences between the East and West Germans as an "East German deviation from a West German normality."[231]

Nothing better illustrates this point than the fact that West German commentators seemed to have forgotten completely that nostalgia had been discussed for almost twenty years before reunification. In the same way, very few observers noted that phenomena and practices similar to the ones portrayed as examples of Ostalgie could also be found in West Germany, that there was, thus, a complementary *Westalgie*—a term that, in a revealing turn of events, never caught on.[232] In short, the same phenomenon that was held to be normal and unremarkable in the West German case was held to be remarkable and dangerous in the East German one.

Although it was broad enough to encompass many more aspects, the debate over Ostalgie is useful for understanding how the concept of nostalgia is employed in a political context in general. West German conservatives before reunification may have had little in common with East Germans after it, but the ways in which both groups were singled out as nostalgic were not dissimilar. Ostalgie portrayed East Germans, as anthropologist Dominic Boyer has argued, "as creatures of the past, as people trapped in old habits, and as individuals frightened by change and the future."[233] And that is exactly how nostalgia was generally employed in a political context.

Whether East Germans or conservatives, nostalgia was an accusation—and one the accused usually renounced—implying that they were not merely longing for the past (that would hardly have been so contentious) but were unable or, worse still, unwilling to adapt to changing conditions, to *modernize* themselves. Implicit in this use of nostalgia was, once again, the modern understanding of time, according to which the past not only was over but had to be overcome, so that looking back to it was futile and even distracting.

Nostalgia was a convenient way of accusing someone of doing just that, while implicitly congratulating oneself for being on top of the times. This narrative and the phrase "politics of nostalgia" would return with a vengeance in the 2010s.

The Age of Nostalgia in the Era of Brexit and Trump

"Nostalgic Elderly Brexiters Have Stolen My Future," ran a headline in the *Guardian* the weekend after the UK European Union membership referendum on June 23, 2016.[234] A narrow majority of 51.9 percent of Britons had voted to leave the EU, leaving those who had voted to remain bewildered, angry, and coping with an uncertain future. Even in the headquarters of the Leave campaign, few people had expected such an outcome. Everyone was grasping for an explanation. One explanation many commentators in Britain and elsewhere landed on was nostalgia.[235]

What exactly Britons were nostalgic for was less clear. Even before the referendum, the journalist Pankaj Mishra saw the Brexiters as "pining for empire."[236] Similarly, the sociologist Kehinde Andrews observed a full-on return of "colonial nostalgia," characteristic of, though not limited to, Brexit supporters.[237] A number of further commentators made the same argument, highlighting an "imperial nostalgia" in particular.[238]

When, a couple of months later, in November 2016, Donald Trump was elected the forty-fifth president of the United States of America, many commentators again drew on nostalgia as an explanation, describing Trump's voters as driven by a "nostalgia for a white Christian America," America's industrial past, or nostalgia more generally.[239] Connecting the two events, the EU referendum and the election of Trump, a third set of articles decried the "politics of nostalgia and identity" as a broader phenomenon of the times and, particularly, of right-wing populism.[240] In an opinion piece for *Newsweek,* the political scientist Cas Mudde named "the politics of nostalgia" as one of "the main challengers of western democracies today."[241]

Many of these articles grew into book publications over time. Released in 2016, *The Shipwrecked Mind,* by the liberal political scientist Mark Lilla, took up the widespread idea of nostalgia as a reaction to accelerated political, social, and cultural change: "Every major social transformation leaves behind a fresh Eden that can serve as the object of somebody's nostalgia."[242] This is precisely what was occurring at the time, he argued. *Retrotopia,* sociologist Zygmunt Bauman's last book before his death, advanced a similar argument, detecting reaction and regression across all fields of society and all regions of the earth in what he termed "The Age of Nostalgia."[243]

In 2018 two think-tank studies, by Demos in Britain and the Bertelsmann Foundation in Germany, claimed that "a majority of the European public can be classified as nostalgic" and that nostalgia had become "endemic," a "threat" requiring "urgent attention."[244] Such apocalyptic warnings about the dangers of nostalgia were not met by sufficient evidence or by exacting standards of research. Neither of the studies defined what they meant by nostalgia, and many of the interviews they quoted even contradicted their claims, with people reporting less concern with the past than with what they perceived as problems of the present, mainly immigration, crime, and national decline.[245] For the second study, anyone answering the statement, "The world used to be a much better place," in the affirmative was classified as nostalgic, which did not leave its respondents a lot of choice and makes it seem almost surprising that it found only some 67 percent of Europeans to be thus afflicted.[246] Neither of the two studies took into account other factors or the socioeconomic situation of their respondents.

Whereas these two studies focused on Europe, others compared developments in the United States and Britain, often seeing them as indicative of larger global trends. According to the political scientists Pippa Norris and Ronald F. Inglehart, Trump had appealed to "a 'golden past' when American society was more homogeneous, US leadership of the Western alliance was unrivalled, threats of terrorism pre-9/11 existed only in distant lands, and gender roles for women and men reflected traditional power relationships," while the Leave campaign had harked back "nostalgically to a time before Britain joined the EU, when Westminster was sovereign, society was predominately white Anglo-Saxon, manufacturing and extracting industries . . . still provided well-paid and secure jobs for unionized workers, and, despite the end of empire, Britain remained a major economic and military world power."[247]

Using Brexit as a case study to investigate "the role of nostalgia in driving global politics," Edoardo Campanella and Marta Dassù diagnosed an "epidemic of nostalgia"—note the widespread use of medical, pathologizing metaphors—as well as an "age of nostalgia" and a "time of regression and pessimism."[248] The political scientist Colin Crouch saw what he called "politicized pessimistic nostalgia" as a hotbed of right-wing populism.[249] The journalist and historian Anne Applebaum also included a chapter titled "The Future of Nostalgia" in her book *The Twilight of Democracy*—a reference to Boym, whose works many of the other books mentioned here also quoted.[250] Finally, there were a number of commentators advancing the idea of an "imperial" or "colonial nostalgia" in Britain that they saw as at least partly responsible for the Brexit vote.[251]

Given the existence of these analyses, one would expect the Leave campaigners to constantly have talked about the past. However, the aforementioned studies offer few concrete examples. In addition to obsessing about the Leave slogan "Take back control," they frequently draw on the same examples to drive home their point. Boris Johnson's oft-quoted remark in the *Daily Telegraph,* dating from May 2016, that "Napoleon, Hitler, various people tried this out, and it ends tragically. The EU is an attempt to do this by different methods," undoubtedly referred to the past; it is less obvious what, if anything, made it nostalgic.[252] Another favorite was Jacob Rees-Mogg's postreferendum Greatest Hits album of British history: "This is the Magna Carta," he proclaimed at the Conservative Party conference in October 2017, "it's the Burgesses coming to Parliament, it's the Great Reform Bill, it's the Bill of Rights, it's Waterloo, it's Agincourt, it's Crecy. We win all of these things."[253] Showing how Rees-Mogg misrepresented the past, the historian Richard J. Evans accused him of putting forth a nostalgic reading of the nation's past.[254]

What Evans means here, however, seems to be that he distorted the past, because Rees-Mogg, like Johnson and other Leavers, evoked the national past in a heroic, patriotic mode, invoking feelings of pride, not mourning or yearning. A comment by Applebaum is revealing in this context. "Or maybe the expression 'nostalgia' is incorrect," she suddenly stops to reflect, "because my friends in and around the *Spectator* did not think that they were looking backward."[255] This holds true for Leavers more generally. As in the examples discussed before, nostalgia was something ascribed from the outside by the Remainers—or journalists and academics sympathetic to Remain—to the Leavers, who naturally rejected the label. "Brexit Isn't about Nostalgia. It's about Ambition," declared the journalist and historian Tim Stanley.[256]

What is more, they employed the nostalgia argument themselves against the other camp and particularly against the EU. "The EU is an institution rooted in the past and is proving incapable of reforming," said Michael Gove in the run-up to the referendum.[257] "In 1975," David Davis agreed, "the EU was the bright future, a vision of a better world. Now it is a crumbling relic from a gloomy past."[258] Obviously, two could play at the same game. While the charge of nostalgia was more often leveled against the Leave side, Brexiters' use of it further underscores its polemical nature.

Portraying the opposite side as nostalgic did not contradict but rather complemented the overall rhetoric of the Leave side. Of the more than fifty speeches, interviews, and op-eds published on the website of Vote Leave, only a few refer to the past at all.[259] If something stands out in them, it is their insistence on a bright future after Brexit, ranging from general remarks, such as Andrea Leadsom's claim that "the UK has a superb future waiting for us outside the EU," to specific promises such as the famous bus announcing 350 million pounds more for the National Health Service.[260] Their whole rhetoric is encapsulated in Gove's call to "leave an EU mired in the past and embrace a better future."[261] These quotes reinforce Applebaum's point: if anyone was looking to the past in the eyes of the Leavers, it was the Remain camp: leaving the EU was all about the future. Their critics might have thought them optimistic to the point of delusion, but nostalgia—however defined—is harder to make out.

Dubious as such claims may have been, they gave the Leave campaign a clear advantage in mobilizing the electorate, even more so because the Remain side, after years in which politicians from all parties had scapegoated the EU, never managed—or even tried—to come up with their own positive vision of the future. Instead, Remain spokespeople resorted to warning against a future outside the EU. In a speech at the British Museum in May 2016, for instance, David Cameron criticized the Leavers for "asking us to take a massive risk with the future of our economy and the future of our country" and culminated his speech with the warning that the "future of your entire country is at stake."[262] Of the future within the EU, he had nothing to say. The Leavers seized on this rhetoric and, brandishing it as "Project Fear," turned it against the Remainers.

The Brexiters were also not alone in trying to bolster their case by citing the past; the Remain camp did much the same. Cameron quoted almost the identical examples Rees-Mogg would dwell on more than a year later—"Blenheim. Trafalgar. Waterloo. Our country's heroism in the Great War"—to make the opposite point.[263] For him, Britain's historic entanglement with the rest of Europe was an argument for remaining in the EU. Unsurprisingly, Cameron's excursion into the British national past was also met with criticism, this time from historians sympathetic to the Leave cause. "He employed cod history, absurd conjecture, total non sequiturs and one straightforward untruth," fumed the journalist and historian Andrew Roberts in the *Daily Mail*.[264]

Frequently invoking the same historical episodes, the two camps' views of the past could not have been more different. This difference became undeniably clear when they touched on the Second World War. The journalist Fintan O'Toole noted "a very deep underlying division about the meaning of the second world war" behind Brexit.[265] For the Brexiters, the Second World War meant British victory, and they conveniently forgot that Britain owed its survival to its allies; for the Remainers, it stood for the clash of extreme nationalisms and the self-destruction of Europe, which, in their eyes, included Britain. In this regard at least, the 2016 referendum looked like a replay of its predecessor of 1975, when the Second World War—at that point far more present in many people's minds as a lived reality—also served as an argument for both staying in the European Economic Community and leaving it.[266]

Despite the Leavers' branding the Remain campaign "Project Fear," they capitalized on fears themselves. Of the fifty-odd items listed on the Vote Leave website, almost a tenth refer to "migration" or "immigration" in their titles, with many more addressing these issues. Both stoking and exploiting fears about migration to Britain, Leave campaigners—falsely—claimed before the referendum that Turkey was about to join the EU.[267] The Remain campaign had little positive to say on immigration as it had little positive to say about the EU altogether. Given how important immigration and antimigration sentiments were in the campaign, it is surprising how many studies focus on nostalgia and the use of the past in the Brexit debate, rather than on the more obvious issues.

In the case of Trump, many observers based their claims of nostalgia on his campaign slogan "Make America great again," which, like some of his rhetoric, was borrowed directly from Reagan. Like that of the Leavers, however, Trump's rhetoric was more ambiguous than the nostalgia charge suggests. Unlike Reagan, Trump neither employed nostalgic tropes nor referred to any specific events or periods in the past; rather he gestured toward a temporal narrative that could be said to imply a nostalgic view of the past, creating a void his audiences could fill with their own meanings, memories, and feelings.[268]

Trump's inaugural address can be seen as representative of this rhetoric. Starting with "for many decades," Trump enumerated how the United States had been cheated and exploited by other countries, while its own economy suffered. Unlike other presidents (or the Leavers), Trump did not conjure up past moments of national greatness. Instead, he vilified the recent past. Like Reagan in his inaugural, Trump presented a negative foil against which he then set his vision for the future. His speech—much bleaker than Reagan's—continued in this vein, juxtaposing the period of decline to the prospect of a brighter future under his leadership, closing with the chant-like pledge, "Together, we will make America strong again. We will make America wealthy again. We will make America proud again. We will make America safe again. And, yes, together, we will make America great again."[269] This was Trump's campaign rhetoric in a nutshell: the image of a nation in crisis—weak, poor, humbled, unsafe, and certainly not great—and, contained in "we will . . . again," a rhetorical device that could be said to simultaneously invoke the future and the past, culminating in the promise to return the country to an undefined golden age.

On closer examination, the rhetoric employed by politicians and their uses of the past appear to be more complicated and nuanced than the nostalgia argument allows for. More importantly, even when they were still cast in a central role, that role had changed since the 1980s when Reagan, Thatcher, and Kohl were accused of nostalgia. Now, politicians were no longer portrayed as nostalgic themselves but as manipulators who triggered, fed into, and, most of all, exploited nostalgia for their political gain: nostalgia was "activated and harnessed by politicians and political movements"; it was "skillfully employed by populist political entrepreneurs"; "nationalist leaders" were "keen to resort to nostalgic arguments to mobilize their citizens."[270] In short, it was not the politicians who were nostalgic but the people voting for them. These were often equated with the "white working class," the former constituency of the left. In *The New Minority,* for instance, the sociologist Justin Gest characterized the "white working class" as "consumed by nostalgia," based on case studies of two communities in the United States and Britain.[271] Despite the book's being conceived before 2016, its publisher advertised it as explaining "the rise of Donald Trump, UKIP, and the European Far Right."[272] Now other commentators picked up on this interpretation.

Given the focus on voters, one would have expected such studies to pay them more attention. Yet even when they did, as in the two think-tank reports, their results and the ways they reached them were so flawed and superficial as to render them virtually useless. In fact, it often seems that they used nostalgia as a universal explanation in order to avoid looking any closer at other factors. They never even considered that, for people saying that "things were better in the past," some things—salaries, job security, social security, living standards, rents, health care, and so on—were indeed better in the past and had declined as a result of changes in the economy and welfare systems since the 1980s, and that, therefore, the respondents may have held justified grievances. Instead, these studies, infused by neoliberal ideology, blamed whatever grievances their respondents expressed on a wrong attitude to the world, a mental health problem—nostalgia. Given its origins in medical language, the term was ideally suited to pathologize, and that was exactly what it was used for.

By distinguishing between those who are not nostalgic, who mastered the challenges of modernity (not least because they were well educated and middle class), and those, the "white working class," who did not, these studies turned nostalgia into a marker of identity. Only the idea of a "white working class" does not survive closer scrutiny intact. Pretending to bring class back into the equation, analyses capitalizing on this term, effectively turn a social category into an ethnic one. But not only are working-class communities often "more likely to be ethnically diverse than their middle-class counterparts," several studies have shown that the Leave camp and Trump attracted a broad and diverse coalition of voters, so that neither can be understood in terms of "working class revolts."[273] The idea of the nostalgic "white working class" was a means of scapegoating.

When it comes down to it, the critique of nostalgia was not unlike David Goodhart's embrace of it in *The Road to Somewhere*. The book showed the world—or Britain at least—as inhabited by two tribes with opposing worldviews: the cosmopolitan "Anywheres," a.k.a. "citizens of the world," who "broadly welcome change and are not nostalgic for a lost Britain," and the rooted "Somewheres," who are.[274] Not class, race, gender, education, or religion, but nostalgia—short for an emotional attachment to the nation-state and its past—here becomes the central category for defining and dividing people, with the implicit assumption that those who are not nostalgic for "somewhere" cannot be trusted. Where Goodheart, an Eton- and university-educated journalist living in London and, thus, a fully paid-up member of the "metropolitan elite" against which he polemicizes, obtained his insights into the hearts and minds of "ordinary Britons" remains opaque. Sympathetic to the "Somewheres," he was frequently criticized for defending xenophobic and racist attitudes.[275] One of the very few contributions to take a positive view of nostalgia,

The Road to Somewhere underscores how the whole debate used nostalgia in a partisan way to define opposing identities.

The claim that an obsessive concern for the national past drove Britons to vote Leave is also contradicted by the responses to the 2016 Spring Directive on the EU referendum by the Mass Observation Project at the University of Sussex.[276] While the past hardly crops up at all in them, one topic outweighs all others. A fifty-five-year-old woman from Chester, a seventy-five-year-old retired schoolteacher from Leicester, a fifty-seven-year-old unemployed retail worker, an eighty-six-year-old retired local government officer from West Sussex, a sixty-five-year-old woman working as a researcher and writer, a seventy-five-year-old retired library assistant—to mention but a select few—all cite immigration as their primary reason for voting Leave; an online retailer from Salisbury confesses to being "terrified by the flood of all those young men" about to come to the country in the wake of Angela Merkel's decision to "open the doors."[277] There were other reasons as well: a female ex–factory worker "was fed up with a foreign country telling us what to do"; a seventy-three-year-old housewife and former bookkeeper did not "like the Human Rights Act"; and a ninety-three-year-old retired decorator feared "the loss of our identity as an independent, English speaking, Christian country with a proud historical background"—one reference anyway, if oblique, to the national past.[278] Naturally, neither the Mass Observation Project nor the selection presented here is representative. Still, it suggests that "ordinary" voters made up their minds primarily based on present concerns and topical news items.

Like the rhetoric by Leave campaigners, the responses to the Mass Observation Project directive—as well as the findings of the think-tank studies, if they are read against the grain—suggest another meaning for nostalgia in the debates at the time: as code for racism. Nothing demonstrates this better than a speech by Vince Cable, the leader of the Liberal Democrats, given at their annual party conference in 2018. Coming to the issue of Brexit, Cable told his audience that "75 per cent of under 25s voted to Remain. But 70 per cent of over 65s voted for Brexit. Too many were driven by a nostalgia for a world where passports were blue, faces were white, and the map was coloured imperial pink."[279] Although Cable said nothing that liberal and left-wing commentators had not already said countless times since the referendum, his remarks—perhaps because they came from a politician—immediately caught the public's attention, causing outrage in the pro-Brexit faction and approval in the Remain camp. Cable was universally seen to have called Leave voters racist, a charge he strongly denied.[280] And yet accusing Brexit voters of nostalgia was nothing if not a roundabout way of suggesting that they held racist and xenophobic attitudes—as Cable's critics clearly and correctly understood—as well as that these attitudes and the people holding them belonged in the past. The fact that Cable ultimately said much the same as many of the studies quoted earlier says a lot about them: mainly that *nostalgia* functioned as a partisan term, which makes it unsuitable for analytical purposes.

Conclusion

Nostalgia had come a long way from Schlesinger's phrase "the politics of nostalgia" to the diagnosis of an "age of nostalgia" after the EU membership referendum and the election of Donald Trump. First meant as a critique of certain conservative ideas and the rediscovery of conservative thought in postwar America more generally, by the 1960s it had already attached itself to politicians who championed such ideas. When these politicians gained power, from the late 1970s onward, nostalgia also resurfaced in political language. Its meanings broadened yet again when it was applied to larger groups: first, in the 1980s, to describe the national mood surrounding the Falklands War in Britain, and then, in the 1990s, to criticize East Germans seen as mourning the demise of the GDR and resisting integration into the new, reunified Federal Republic and capitalist, democratic Western modernity. Following the EU membership referendum and the election of Trump, the three strands coalesced: nostalgia now appeared connected to ideas and attitudes like nationalism, racism, and xenophobia; it described politicians like the Leavers and Trump, as well as the vast sections of the population that had voted for them.

Although nostalgia sometimes surfaced in confrontations between conservatives or within the left—for instance, in the debates between various factions of the British Labour Party—it was, throughout this period, mainly used to attack conservative ideas, politicians, and projects.[281] If this was one common denominator, the word *attack* already suggests another one: in politics nostalgia appeared rarely as anything other than an insult. No one ever defended nostalgia, claimed it for themselves, or admitted to relying on it. Reagan is no exception here: insofar as he used the term and insofar as he could be argued to employ nostalgic sentiments in his rhetoric, he only ever did so in a personal, never a political, sense. When it came to politics, he rejected nostalgia in the same way everyone else did. More than in any other field, in politics *nostalgia* carried overwhelmingly pejorative connotations. What constituted these connotations? And what made *nostalgia* so useful as a term that it kept reappearing over such an extended period?

The first answer pertains to nostalgia's emotional quality: labeling someone nostalgic implies that they are acting emotionally, and hence not rationally. This criticism has a long history because emotions or emotionality has historically often been used to call someone's right to political participation into question—for instance, in denying women the vote. It also has the added benefit of portraying the person making the charge as a rational actor. The second answer is even more important, and it also explains why the accusation of nostalgia is mostly aimed at conservative politicians and causes: it ideally fits in with the larger temporal understanding of politics. Politics is often conceived of in spatial terms—namely, in terms of the nation-state and who is, and who is not, part of it. However, at least since the French Revolution, temporal categories have been equally important in the way people think about politics. Indeed, time and politics are so intertwined that there has been little reflection on the temporality of politics until just recently.[282]

Also since the French Revolution, the temporal understanding of politics has appeared most obviously in the broad distinction between progressive and conservative creeds and camps. While progressives aim to change, conservatives want to maintain the status quo or, in Hartmut Rosa's definition, "progressive politics strives toward an *acceleration* of the expected development of history, conservative politics toward its *deceleration* or temporary suspension."[283] As conservatism implies "an attachment to the past rather than to the future, and a condemnation of utopian designs," it is only natural that the nostalgia accusation was more readily applied to conservative than to progressive politics.[284] Both concepts, however, rely on the modern understanding of time as linear and dynamic.

If the distinction between progressive and conservative ever made sense, it became less and less coherent as the modern understanding of time was increasingly called into question. Simultaneously, and likely as an effect, the distinction between progressive and conservative has begun to blur since the 1970s as well, as historians Emily Robinson and Martina Steber have argued: both camps began to talk about the past *and* the future, wanted to both move forward *and* conserve.[285] Conservatives found themselves increasingly under pressure to adopt the language of change and progress in order to hold their ground in an age of progressive politics after the Second World War. In the 1970s and 1980s, politicians such as Thatcher and Reagan still dressed their rhetoric in the language of conservatism, but many of their policies, especially their economic policies, were liberal or even radical, earning both of them criticism from conservatives in their own parties. At the same time, progress came under increased scrutiny from both the right and the left as its high costs, particularly to the environment, became more obvious. As a result, progressives took on board some ideas that could be characterized as conservative—for instance, when it came to the environmental movement. Despite this blurring of differences, the old labels and the established temporalization of politics did not vanish, as the debate over the "politics of nostalgia" also bears out.

Nostalgia works so well in a political context because it not only fits the established temporal understanding of politics, it also reproduces it. In a political context nostalgia has, as we have seen, little to do with yearning, longing, or sentimentalism. Rather, it signifies the fact that something (an idea, a person, or a group of people) is oriented toward the past (backward-looking), of the past (anachronistic), or stuck in the past (unable to adapt to changing circumstances). Like accusing people of being emotional, denying them coevalness has a long tradition in Western thinking as a strategy of "othering." The most obvious example is the distinction between "backward" and "civilized" or "modern" people or societies, which was bolstered by ethnography and drawn on to justify colonial projects.[286] However, the same technique has also been applied to people or groups within a society.

A famous example is the idea of the "contemporaneity of the non-contemporaneous," sometimes also translated as the "simultaneity of the non-simultaneous" (in German: *Gleichzeitigkeit des Ungleichzeitigen*). First coined by the German art historian Wilhelm Pinder in 1926, it was taken up by the philosopher Ernst Bloch—in his 1935 book *Heritage of Our Times*—and later popularized by Reinhart Koselleck.[287] Because Koselleck developed it into a much broader theoretical concept, it is sometimes forgotten that Bloch used it in a specific political context. Bloch finished his book in Switzerland, where he had fled to escape Nazi persecution. Unsurprisingly, his thinking at the time was driven by the urge to make sense of fascism, which, in Bloch's Marxist understanding of history, did not make any sense at all. As a Marxist,

Bloch had expected that the world revolution—and the classless society supposed to follow it—would be imminent. Instead, he was confronted with National Socialism. As a philosopher, Bloch solved the problem in an ingenious philosophical way: he declared that the Nazis—or, to be exact, those who voted for them: the young, the peasants, and the middle class—present as they undeniably were, were not *of* the present. "Not all people exist in the same Now," he wrote in *Heritage of Our Times*. "They do so only externally, through the fact that they can be seen today. But they are thereby not yet living at the same time with the others."[288] Fascism, it turned out, did not disprove Marx's historical materialism; the Nazis did not contradict it. They were a residue, a last gasp of the old era, mere zombies. Although they were very much part of his present, and, indeed, a threat to his life, Bloch got rid of them—philosophically at least—by relegating them to a past to which they would inevitably return.

As a temporal figure, nostalgia is closely related to Bloch's formula of the "contemporaneity of the non-contemporaneous." Whether it was applied to conservatism—new, neo-, or in general—to Reagan's anti-Soviet rhetoric, Thatcher's "Victorian values" and Falklands War, Kohl's enthusiasm for Adenauer, or Brexit and Trump (and their voters), nostalgia served as a way to declare them "non-contemporaneous": while they were, obviously, present—the EU membership referendum had been lost; Trump had won; xenophobia, racism, misogyny, and so on continued to exist—ultimately, they were not; they were things of the past, they just did not know it. To declare something or someone else "non-contemporaneous" is a shrewd rhetorical strategy: it denies them legitimacy—better still, it denies them a place in the here and now—and allows the speaker to claim the moral high ground for themselves. It must be especially soothing in a moment when a political fight has been lost.

In the long run, however, this strategy is not only self-deceiving but also dangerous. It implies that it is both unnecessary to engage with a political other and impossible—the other is, after all, not part of one's own present. By declaring conservatism a matter of nostalgia, liberals like Schlesinger persistently underestimated its power—until they found themselves faced with a conservative majority. Likewise, banishing racist and other hateful attitudes to the past is wishful thinking: it neither makes them less present nor successfully eradicates them.

The strategy becomes even more problematic when whole groups of people are written off as nostalgic. In the debate over Ostalgie, some East Germans, justifiably feeling that they were neither taken seriously nor accepted as equals, defiantly reclaimed it, fashioning exactly the kind of East German identity the critics had warned of in the first place. Similarly, nostalgia has been used to pathologize and to other Leave and Trump voters. Rather than explaining how they voted as they did, this strategy prevents a deeper examination of structural causes. Instead of explaining how societies work, it further divides them. Because all people that "can be seen today" do, after all, live "at the same time with the others," they somehow need to find ways to cope and engage with one another.

From this perspective, it would be best if the term *nostalgia* could be struck from the political vocabulary altogether. And yet, as long as politics is conceived of in temporal terms, of progressive and conservative, of backward- and forward-looking—and it still very much is—that seems unlikely. Under such conditions, nostalgia is far too useful an accusation to simply fade away. For the time being, it would be good if we could at least strike the term from the vocabulary of political analysis. If it is acceptable for use in partisan rhetoric, then it is definitely unsuitable for political analysis. At the very least, we need to acknowledge its long and checkered career in politics, its ideological underpinnings, and its pejorative and polemical connotations and the dangers that reside not so much in alleged "politics of nostalgia" as in an imprecise language.

Three

Reviving

The Past in Popular Culture

Since the term *nostalgia* first became common currency, no area of life has been associated with it more than popular culture. From Alvin Toffler onward, intellectuals frequently drew on revivals of past styles in music and fashion or used films and television series set in the past as examples to substantiate their claims that nostalgia had become omnipresent. At the same time, film, music, and fashion critics drew on nostalgia to explain the existence and appeal of pop cultural revivals. The two lines converged in the discussion of the "nostalgia wave" in the 1970s, which, to a large extent, was inspired by a revival of 1950s rock and roll at the time. The 1970s also generated a new term for revivalism with *retro*. Originating in France in the debate about *la mode rétro,* discussed later in this chapter, the word soon entered many other languages. Quickly the two terms, *nostalgia* and *retro,* became conflated to the point where they were used almost interchangeably. What

Fredric Jameson called the "nostalgia film" drew on examples also discussed as retro, a term he used as well, and the same holds true for Jean Baudrillard. Simon Reynolds starts out by distinguishing between retro and nostalgia only to end up equating them: for him nostalgia is complicit in—if not responsible for—pop culture's full-on plunge into "retromania."[1] By contrast, art historian Elizabeth Guffey, in her overview of the history of retro, calls for differentiating between the two terms because "retro is not nostalgia."[2]

While both concepts can appear in a positive or neutral way—there is no dearth of radio stations, TV shows, and shops sporting either the word *nostalgia* or *retro* in their titles—in intellectual discourse they, and *nostalgia* most of all, usually carry a negative, pejorative connotation. Similar to the critics of nostalgia discussed in Chapter 1 and the critics of conservatism discussed in Chapter 2, critics of pop culture use the term *nostalgia* mainly as an indictment. More specifically they use it, as we will see, first in an emotional sense, implying that people returned to the pop cultural past because of a personal, sentimental attachment; second in an aesthetic sense, synonymous with *kitsch;* and finally in a temporal sense, to denote an orientation toward the past and an inability or unwillingness to go with the times, forsaking innovation and originality for imitation and repetition.

The last aspect, which the pop cultural critique shares with the other critiques, is the most important one, and as in the other instances, it was based on an implicit modernist understanding of time. Pop culture critics tend to conceive of time as homogeneous and linear, as a straightforward timeline. By contrast, the word *retro* implies a cyclical temporality: every style (or aspects thereof) returns after a certain number of years. One of the first to observe this process, or, at any rate, to put it into writing, was the British curator and historian James Laver in his 1937 book *Taste and Fashion*. "Laver's Law," as his scheme was later dubbed, stipulated that a garment was subject to a distinctive cycle: ten years before its time it was perceived as indecent, then as shameless, until it finally became smart, only to quickly fall out of fashion: perceived as hideous after a mere 10 years, it took a good 150 years for it to become beautiful—or back in fashion—again:[3]

Indecent   10 years before its time

Shameless   5 years before its time

Outré (daring)   1 year before its time

Smart	———
Dowdy	1 year after its time
Hideous	10 years after its time
Ridiculous	20 years after its time
Amusing	30 years after its time
Quaint	50 years after its time
Charming	70 years after its time
Romantic	100 years after its time
Beautiful	150 years after its time

The cyclical nature of retro does not fit in with—contradicts even—the modern understanding of time: if there is no progress, there must be decline for the pop culture critics. Reynolds even dates the exact point from which pop culture declined, when he notes an "absence of revivalism and nostalgia during the sixties" followed by a period in which "nostalgia became steadily more and more bound up with popular culture." Gradually increasing—or rather worsening—this development reached its peak with the new millennium: "Instead of being the threshold to the future, the first ten years of the twenty-first century turned out to be the 'Re' Decade."[4]

Reynolds's chronology, however, is dubious on two counts at least. For one, it can be accused of nostalgia itself, as the 1960s emerge as a dynamic, nostalgia-free golden age from which pop culture began its decline in the 1970s and reached its nadir in the 2000s, at the time of writing. Worse still, it is false: as Raphael Samuel notes, revivalism has been a "leitmotiv of European culture ever since the quattrocento's discovery (or rediscovery) of classical antiquity."[5] Laver's law bears this out for the area of fashion. "Pastiche and nostalgia have been pervasive in popular culture throughout the twentieth century," historian Elizabeth Wilson, too, argues.[6]

This chapter takes up these objections. Starting with the 1970s debates about the nostalgia wave and *la mode rétro,* it then jumps back to the 1950s and the 1960s to show that many of the issues at stake in these debates were—contrary to Reynolds's claim—already present in the preceding decades. Indeed, this chapter shows that if any decade could be said

to have invented retro, it was not the allegedly nostalgic 1970s but the supposedly future-looking 1960s. The chapter then continues with the 1980s, tracing
the development of the debate up to the present. Jumping between decades
and tracing elective affinities between them, the chapter hopes to break up
and complicate the established chronology. Positioning itself against the cliché
of retro as imitative and derivative, a mere replica of past styles, it argues that
looking back is a source of inspiration rather than a sign of stagnation. In following these various strands of revivalism and the critique of them, it examines
the role of the concept of nostalgia in how they are perceived, explained, and
criticized and thereby how nostalgia's meanings changed and shifted.

The 1950s Revival of the 1970s

For many observers, one of the most surprising things about the beginning of
the 1970s was the degree to which they seemed enthralled by the past. The
past, and the 1950s specifically, was felt to be "charging back at us," bringing
the present up to the "edge of nostalgia shock," warned the *Saturday Review*
in 1971.[7] In a 1972 cover story titled "The Nifty Fifties," *Life* reported, "It's
been barely a dozen years since the '50s ended, and yet here we are again,
awash in the trappings of that sunnier time, paying new attention to the old
artifacts and demigods."[8] "In the grand sweep of American history," *Newsweek*
declared a few months later, "the 1950s were one of the blandest decades ever.
But now a revival of those very same quiet years is swirling across the nation
like a runaway Hula-Hoop."[9] Obviously, *Newsweek* had its doubts about the
revival, evoking such "grim memories as Korea, Suez, Hungary, Sputnik and
economic recession" to counter it, but to little avail.[10] "Must we be nostalgic
about the fifties?" writer Thomas Meehan also wondered—obviously, many
Americans were because, in his words, "an enormous number" of them were
"looking back on the decade as a shimmeringly serene and happy time."[11]

The return of the 1950s was not limited to the United States. In Britain,
too, the "'fifties and all the cult heroes associated with that period, again became high fashion," as the *Evening Standard* put it in 1972, confirming a
year later: "The 'fifties revival has definitely come to stay."[12] Drawing on some
of the same examples as American and British writers, the German cultural
historian Wolfgang Schivelbusch in 1973 observed a "nostalgic wave" resurrecting the 1940s and 1950s—although the 1950s revival would not really

take off in West Germany until the end of the decade.[13] In 1978, the weekly *Der Spiegel* led with "The Myth of the 50s: The Yearning for the Miracle Years," reminiscent of *Life*'s earlier issue on the "nifty fifties."[14]

Initially, the 1950s revival was mainly a revival of 1950s rock and roll. Suddenly, rock veterans like Chuck Berry, Bill Haley, Jerry Lee Lewis, and Little Richard, some of whom had fallen on hard times or slipped into obscurity by then, found themselves in demand again. In histories of rock, this development usually begins with the Rock Revival at the Felt Forum in New York in 1969, allegedly the first ever revival concert.[15] However, developments in Europe predated those in the United States. At the low point of his career, returning from touring US Army bases all over Germany, Haley played a triumphant concert in Paris in 1966, where audiences welcomed him with banners and cheers, and this enthusiasm repeated itself shortly thereafter in Amsterdam.[16] Two years later, he experienced an equally raucous welcome when he toured the United Kingdom, with his signature song "Rock around the Clock" even returning to the charts.[17] "A good many of our bookings come from many parts of the world where people want to be nostalgic about rock & roll," Haley explained. "We have always been defenders of rock and now we find ourselves showing how it is played, describing it to people and generally keeping it alive."[18] Entering middle age, Haley had transformed from a menace of middle-class society into a gatekeeper of rock and roll lore, passing it on to the next generation. Happy about his unexpected comeback, Haley seems to have been at ease with his new role as elder statesman of rock. Other performers were more critical: they did not want to be antiquarians, playing their old songs over and over again, but taken seriously as contemporaries with new material to offer. Audiences, however, saw the performers of the 1950s as just that, expecting them to play the songs they were best known for.[19]

To some extent the rock and roll revival was the brainchild of Richard Nader. Born in 1940, he had grown up listening to rock and roll, turning his hobby into a job by becoming a disc jockey. During the "British Invasion" in the 1960s, he resolved to bring back the acts he had grown up with during the 1950s. The task was more difficult than he had assumed. It took him over four years to get the show off the ground because tracking down and convincing the performers of that era to participate was not as easy as he thought. In 1969 he rented the Felt Forum in New York, quickly selling out its 4,500 seats. One year later, the revival had gathered enough momentum for Nader to move his show to the 20,000-seat auditorium of Madison Square Garden.

He continued to organize revival concerts throughout the 1970s, in both the United States and Europe.[20] At the outset, these concerts were aimed at people like Nader himself, people who felt, as he said, the "world isn't the one they were brought up in, and they're not quite comfortable with the new thing. But the Revival gives them that womb again, it gives them that security, that escape."[21] Though he did not use the term *nostalgia,* what he said fed into how critics perceived the revival.

Quickly, however, the shows attracted a new constituency: the adolescent rock fans of the present. They flocked not only to Nader's revival concerts but also to their British equivalent, the London Rock and Roll Show of 1972, which was released as a concert film the following year.[22] Organized by brothers Ray and Ronald Foulk, who had previously staged festivals on the Isle of Wight as a kind of British Woodstock, it took place at Wembley Stadium.[23] The London Rock and Roll Show featured much the same acts as its American predecessors: Haley, Bo Diddley, Chuck Berry, Little Richard, and Jerry Lee Lewis, among others. Despite its all-star lineup and the crowds of people descending on Wembley, the show received some criticism. "It's a fossil scene," said Mick Jagger after the concert.[24] The *Guardian* called it an "extraordinary historical peep show" and "a treat for teddy boys, fifties nostalgics, and musical archaeologists"; the *Financial Times* expressed "relief that this was (hopefully) a once a decade overdose of nostalgia."[25] Such hopes soon proved to be wrong: revival concerts quickly became a regular part of the pop music circuit.

Although the show attracted older people, who had been reared on rock and roll and saw the concert as a chance to revisit their youth, the audience mainly consisted of younger fans, as both the film and pictures of the audience bear out. They mainly show people in their twenties, clad in the long-draped coats with velvet collars and other garments worn by the Teddy Boys in the 1950s (see Figure 3.1). Indeed, it was not the former Teddy Boys, as the *Guardian* thought, but younger people who adopted their style and updated it who were the main constituency of the rock and roll revival.

But where did the Teddy Boys and Girls of the 1970s get their authentic-looking gear? Flea markets and secondhand shops were essential. As was the boutique Let It Rock in the King's Road, run by a flame-haired art school graduate called Malcolm McLaren, who was still relatively unknown at that point, and his equally unconventional girlfriend Vivienne Westwood. Repelled by the hippies frequenting the surrounding boutiques and attracted to the tough-looking and tough-acting Teddy Boys, McLaren and Westwood

Figure 3.1   The 1950s revived: Rock fans at the 1972 London Rock and Roll Show dressed as 1950s Teddy Boys. Trinity Mirror / Mirrorpix / Alamy

copied their look. When they took over the shop in the King's Road, they turned it into a time machine. McLaren designed the interior to look like an "imitation of a kitsch fifties front room," decorating it "with authentic Festival of Britain-era wallpaper" and the paraphernalia of the decade, such as "a period fridge painted bubblegum pink and black, teak sideboards and formica display cabinets. Rock 'n' roll blasted from a jukebox."[26]

McLaren and Westwood sold whatever apprentice Teds needed to feel authentic: "Brylcreem, novelty socks decorated with musical notes, plastic earrings and black leather ties with see-through plastic pockets," as well as "handbills for fifties films and secondhand records from that time."[27] Mainly, however, they sold period clothes. As these were often not in the best of shape, Westwood started to repair them. Soon she made entire outfits herself. A schoolteacher with no formal training in tailoring, it was here that Westwood's career as a fashion designer began. In the film about the London Rock and Roll Show, McLaren is seen hawking her T-shirts; Westwood remembers, "We sold quite a lot of stuff that day and made over a thousand pounds."[28]

Westwood and McLaren may have been pioneers, but they were not alone. "Fashion has been flirting with the 'fifties for months now," reported the *Evening Standard*.[29] "Many fashion houses, boutiques and department stores are stocking up not only on the actual clothes that were popular then," *Newsweek* told its readers in 1972, "but also on a new line of '70s clothing featuring '50s accents."[30] Starting out in one area of popular culture, the revival quickly branched out into others. As it did, Westwood and McLaren got bored with the Teds. Says Westwood, "They weren't such rebels after all."[31] Roughly the same age as Nader, they took an interest in the 1950s because identifying as Teds was a way to rebel against the hippie counterculture that dominated the scene in the 1960s. In 1974, they renamed their shop SEX and made it a hotbed for the burgeoning British punk scene—the Sex Pistols, named after it, were conceived largely as advertising. Backward-looking as the 1950s revival may have been, it fed directly into one of the major cultural innovations of the 1970s: "There is a paradox right at the heart of punk," Simon Reynolds observes: "this most revolutionary movement in rock history was actually born from reactionary impulses."[32] After all, punk was, as Nancy Spungen, girlfriend of Sex Pistols bassist Sid Vicious, declared, "just real good basic rock & roll . . . real basic fifties and early sixties rock."[33] She may have been overstating things, but the rock and roll revival of the early 1970s doubtless inspired and instigated the emergence of punk as one of the major new styles of the era.

It also introduced a completely "new breed of entertainer": "contemporary groups that dress, perform and sometimes live like their '50s predecessors."[34] The most famous of them was Sha Na Na, a group of undergraduates and PhD students from Columbia University (see Figure 3.2). Initially performing rock songs from the 1950s on campus during the student protests of the 1960s, they soon attracted larger audiences. Thanks to Jimi Hendrix, a fan, they appeared right before him as the second-to-last act at Woodstock in 1969. The documentary film shows how audience members watched in disbelief as the golden-suited dancers went through the motions of "At the Hop."[35] Greeted with skepticism at first, Sha Na Na left the stage to loud clapping and cheers. Later that year they performed at Nader's Rock Revival concert, where they "excited the crowd the most" of all performers.[36]

Sha Na Na specialized in rock and roll and doo-wop songs from the 1950s but rearranged them and performed them at a faster speed (their version of "Rock around the Clock" was thirty seconds shorter than Haley's). With Sha Na Na, the outfits and show were as important as the music—if not more.

Figure 3.2   A "brilliantly crystallized dream from the past"? The pop group Sha Na Na showcasing a mixture of 1950s-influenced styles in 1972. Archive PL/Alamy

Their success "always hinged more on their style than their sound."[37] While their "greaser look"—slicked-back hair, ducktails, and black leather jackets—was reminiscent of the rebels Marlon Brando and James Dean had played in 1950s films, the same could not be said of their golden jackets and pants—and even the greaser look they exaggerated for comic effect. Furthermore, the style did not at all fit the music they were performing because doo-wop groups of the 1950s usually wore evening suits.[38] Still, the group often served as proof of 1950s nostalgia: the *Life* issue on the 1950s revival devoted an entire page to them, and Jan Hodenfield from *Rolling Stone* called them a "brilliantly crystallized dream from the past."[39]

The band itself, however, rejected the association with nostalgia. "They're role-playing," their manager told Hodenfield. "They don't like being regarded as quaint curios of the past or being limited by nostalgic bullshit. . . . Generally, the Fifties themselves are irrelevant to them."[40] Alan Cooper, one of the lead singers, stressed their creative approach to the repertoire they performed: "We're cleaning it up, making it tighter, the sound is clearer. . . . We're giving the old songs a contemporary impetus. . . . We are not regressing," he insisted.[41] "I really don't think it's escaping into the past," concurred bandmate Richard Joffe. For him the revival was not motivated by nostalgia, as "most of the kids who are involved in it have no memory of the 'fifties as they were children or unborn at the time."[42]

As these quotes demonstrate, Sha Na Na rejected the term *nostalgia:* neither they nor their audiences longed for the 1950s or wanted to escape the present. As a band they combined different cultural influences and styles of music and performance without direct historical referents. Their act was a collage of elements, taking selected associations with 1950s pop culture and often exaggerating and updating them for contemporary tastes. As a result, they produced something that would have been unthinkable in the 1950s and that was entirely of the 1970s. Sha Na Na also disproved those critics who saw the "nostalgia wave" of the 1970s as a backlash to the revolutionary 1960s: not only did Woodstock and the Rock Revival happen in the same year, in Sha Na Na they shared at least one act—retro was not the antithesis to the sub- and countercultural experiments of the 1960s, it grew directly out of them.

If there was a backlash, it was to be found more in the music itself. For Joffe, rock music had gotten "very introverted and very cerebral and very instrumental."[43] "Acid rock, blues rock," one of his bandmates agreed, "is not happy music. It's introverted music. . . . We're playing happy music and we get happy audiences."[44] There had been a widespread impression since the late 1960s that rock had gotten too far away from its roots, that it had become too serious, too complicated, too artsy. At the same time, it was, twenty years after its first appearance on the radio, possible to look back on its history, as the many rock histories coming out at this time demonstrate.[45] With the Beach Boys in decline, the Beatles disbanded, Bob Dylan withdrawing from the public, and the deaths of Jimi Hendrix and Janis Joplin, 1970 felt like a caesura in the history of rock, even something of an endpoint. It even had an obituary: "American Pie," Don McLean's song released in 1971.

But that was hardly the first time that rock seemed to have lost its momentum. Interviewed by *Newsweek* in 1972, a disc jockey compared the present situation to the early 1960s: "That was when there was the first oldies craze, because there was a big lull in music and the population was waiting for something to happen. Finally the Beatles came along in '64. We are in the same lull now, and the '50s are filling in."[46] While there is something to the theory that revivals bridge the gap between more creative periods, it overlooks the fact that revivals can be a creative force themselves, informing new artistic developments such as punk.

From music and fashion, the rock and roll revival spread into the theater and film. In 1971 the musical *Grease,* set among high schoolers in the 1950s, premiered and, running for over three thousand performances, surpassed all preceding Broadway musicals in staying power. Although it too was often seen as evidence for a 1950s nostalgia, it viewed the era, as one critic noted, "with a condescending smile and a touch too much of camp parody."[47] Like Sha Na Na, it exaggerated for comic effect, playing the 1950s for laughs rather than sentimentality. It was only fitting, then, that Sha Na Na made a cameo appearance when *Grease* became a film in 1978.

The best-known and most discussed example of the 1950s nostalgia wave was, however, George Lucas's film *American Graffiti*—and that was despite its setting of 1962. Opening to the sounds of "Rock around the Clock," the film was infused with rock and roll: every scene in the film was accompanied by a song from the period. The resulting copyright costs of about $80,000 were considerable for what was otherwise a comparatively cheap film. In the end, there was no money left for a traditional score, a problem Lucas turned into an advantage: *American Graffiti* became the first American film entirely to rely on preexisting songs, which added much to its style, period feel, and success.[48]

For Jameson, *American Graffiti* was the "inaugural film" of the "new aesthetic discourse" he called "nostalgia film." In his eyes, *American Graffiti* strove to "recapture . . . the henceforth mesmerizing lost reality of the Eisenhower era," turning the 1950s into "the privileged lost object of desire."[49] Enormously influential, his reading shapes how the film is generally understood today. Peeling back the layers of interpretation that have accumulated over time, media scholar Michael D. Dwyer has put forth a different one. In particular, he draws attention to the film's ending, when Curt, the main character, decides to leave his hometown to go to college on the East Coast (where the student movement is already brewing), while John, whose drag racing and white T-shirt mark him as the quintessential 1950s character, ends up killed in a car accident. "*Graffiti* reminds its viewers that there is simply no way back to the Fifties," Dwyer concludes.[50] In his reading, *American Graffiti* emerges less as a nostalgic film than a film about the dangers of nostalgia and the need to move on.

While Dwyer's interpretation relies on the film itself, it is backed up by its director. "Originally I didn't think about it as nostalgia, even though it took place in 1962," Lucas said in an interview in 1972. "The film is about teenagers; about teenagers moving forward and making decisions about what they want to do in life. But it's about the fact that you can't live in the past, which is part of that same idea. You have to move forward, things can't stay the same; essentially that's the point of the film. No matter how much you want things to be the same, they won't and can't; everything is always changing, and you have to accept change."[51] Not unlike the members of Sha Na Na, Lucas rejected nostalgia as a main motivation for his film: if there was an element of it, it was there mainly to show that it was impossible to "live in the past" because it was important to "move forward" and to "accept change." If anything, this message would make *American Graffiti* an antinostalgia film.

Many critics at the time understood the film in this way. "When I went to see George Lucas's 'American Graffiti,'" Roger Ebert opened his review, "that whole world—a world that now seems incomparably distant and innocent—was brought back with a rush of feeling that wasn't so much nostalgia as culture shock." Releasing a flood of half-forgotten memories, the film did not make Ebert yearn for the past; instead it drove home to him how "incomparably distant" the passing of time had rendered it, "how far (and in many cases how tragically) we have come." To Ebert it seemed as if "whole cultures and societies have passed since 1962," so remote did the era seem to him only eleven years later.[52] The term *culture shock* inevitably brings to mind Toffler, who used the same term to describe the accelerated pace of change. By reenacting the past, pop cultural artifacts like *American Graffiti* or Sha Na Na made people confront the distance between past and present, instigating a range of different reactions from remembering to mourning to shock.

American Graffiti was very popular in the United States and quickly became a classic, inspiring a number of similar films and television series, such as the long-running 1950s-set sitcom *Happy Days* (1974–1981). At the same time, filmmakers in other countries also turned to the 1950s. Despite arriving in theaters a couple of months earlier, the British film *That'll Be the Day* has been called a "British Graffiti." Also dealing with growing up in the 1950s—and the role of rock and roll in adolescence—it has been interpreted as a nostalgia film as well.[53] *That'll Be the Day* centers on Jim MacLaine, played by the singer David Essex, who drops out of school after being seduced by the sweet song of American rock and roll and Hollywood films only to end up working lowly jobs as a deckchair attendant and as a barman in a holiday camp, where he is taken under the wing of an older drifter, played by Ringo Starr. At the end of the film, Jim returns to middle-class respectability, marrying and taking over his father's shop, until the lure of the rock and roll lifestyle calls him away yet again.

Like *American Graffiti, That'll Be the Day* was built "upon a collection of old songs from different artists that would be sold on a soundtrack," making it, in fact, the first film to go down this route.[54] Ironically, however, its makers followed almost the exact opposite approach of Lucas's. Instead of paying for copyright, David Puttnam, the film's producer, put in the songs later on to secure additional funding for his film: still lacking 100,000 pounds, he went to the music label Ronco and guaranteed that he would feature a minimum number of rock classics on the soundtrack, which they then could release as a double album.[55] Ronco not only agreed but spent additional money on cross-promotion. Puttnam and his scriptwriter then returned to the script, "marking it every so often where they could put a record player or radio in the scene. Characters took to wandering along beaches and through fairgrounds, *anything* to squeeze in the necessary tracks."[56] *That'll Be the Day* may have been set in the past, but the casting of well-known rock stars like Essex and Starr and the close cooperation with the record industry made it a pioneering film.[57]

On the surface, however, the modern production methods were less evident than the period setting. "Here is a nice bit of nostalgia," *Variety* gave the film short shrift.[58] In the *Observer* George Melly praised the film's "amazing period accuracy," for which, incidentally, none other than Vivienne Westwood was responsible (despite considering Essex and Starr "two complete fools").[59] Praising the film's period accuracy, Melly perceived it nonetheless as "a great threat for all us nostalgic scelerotics of the Fifties."[60] How so? While later publications are quick to subsume *That'll Be the Day* under the nostalgia label, its contemporary reception was, as the quote by Melly implies, less straightforward. For the film critic Julian Fox, *That'll Be the Day* marked a new development in the history of cinema insofar as it turned to the most recent past, holding up "one's own youth and the memory of it . . . as a mirror for the delight and absorption of cinemagoers even younger than oneself."[61] Fox was not at all pleased with that. "Sitting through *That'll Be the Day* is like looking through the wrong end of a telescope," he complained. "For the first time in a lifetime's avid cinema-going, I really began to feel my age! To see one's antediluvian childhood reflected on the wide screen—that is the unkindest cut of all." Melly's and Fox's reviews of *That'll Be the Day* antici-pated Ebert's reaction to *American Graffiti:* all three were taken in by how the films conjured up a past they saw as their own, but rather than the "warm bath" to which Ronald Reagan frequently compared nostalgia, they experi-enced it as a cold shower, making all too plain to them how much time had elapsed since their youth. Wondering why the film felt like a "historical doc-ument," Fox came to a similar conclusion as Ebert: "Surely it is because so *much* has happened in the world."[62]

"They'll demand a sequel," David Puttnam told his scriptwriter even be-fore *That'll Be the Day* opened in the cinemas. And so it came to pass: fol-lowing the success of the first film, the two sat down to write *Stardust*. Coming out in 1974, the sequel takes up the story of Jim MacLaine in the mid-1960s, when his dream of becoming a rock star has come true, and continues it into the present of the early 1970s. But as he is haunted by the media, driven by a relentless American manager, and becomes addicted to drugs, the dream turns out to be a nightmare, and Jim dies of an overdose. Despite such a dire ending, the film was very successful at the British box office, but it hardly made any impact abroad.[63]

Marketed with the tagline "Remember the 60's?," *Stardust* suggested that the 1950s revival was already on its way out and going to be replaced by one of the 1960s. And sure enough, after the 1950s revival, the 1960s equivalent was only a matter of time, and so the Mods followed the Teddy Boys, much as the original Mods had followed the original Teds back in the 1960s.[64] Al-ready on the way, the Mod revival was much aided by the 1979 film *Quadro-phenia*. Based on the rock opera of the same name by the Who, who had been part of the Mod subculture, it was set in 1964—exactly fifteen years earlier—and told the story of Jimmy Cooper, a sort of 1960s doppelgänger of Jim MacLaine. Estranged from his parents and bored by his job in a mail room, Jimmy joins the Mods, taking part in such typical Mod activities as partying, popping pills, riding around on his scooter, and brawling with rockers.

In a way, *Quadrophenia* did for the Mod culture of the 1960s what *American Graffiti* and *That'll Be the Day* had done for rock and roll. Yet when reviews of the film mentioned nostalgia at all, they only did it to refute the categorization. *Quadrophenia* was not "being played for nostalgia" but "very realistic," remarked one reviewer.[65] The "nostalgia industry has taken a curiously tough turn," observed another, characterizing the film as "a statement of vitriolic despair."[66] By 1979 many articles carried titles such as "The Return of the Mods" or "Mods: The Second Coming," mentioning *Quadrophenia* as one reason for their resurgence.[67] Compared with the rock and roll revival at the beginning of the decade, however, that of the Mods was much more limited, hardly reaching beyond Britain, and less centered on music than on style. It also blew over much more quickly.

The year *Quadrophenia* came out, 1979, was also the year when *The Day Elvis Came to Bremerhaven* (*Der Tag an dem Elvis nach Bremerhaven kam*) was shown on West German public television. Focusing on a group of young people in the 1950s and their love for rock and roll, which also featured on the soundtrack, the film could perhaps be seen as a kind of West German answer to *American Graffiti*—had *Der Spiegel* not insisted that it definitely was no "German Graffiti."[68] Indeed, the film was further removed from *American Graffiti* than *That'll Be the Day,* with the German teenagers being even worse off than Jim MacLaine, suffering under their parents and at their mundane jobs, their boredom communicated by the excruciatingly slow pace of the film, made even slower by the comparison with the fast-paced American production. As in *That'll Be the Day,* rock and roll figured not so much as part of everyday life but as an alternative space, a vision of a more exciting life free of repression and social constraints. The arrival of Elvis Presley in Germany to complete his military service, from which the film derives its title, is shown in documentary style in black and white, almost as a collision of two irreconcilable worlds. No one accused *The Day Elvis Came to Bremerhaven* of nostalgia. *Der Spiegel* even attested that here "looking back to the 1950s defies nostalgically soothing feelings."[69] It also defied success.

No doubt the film would have been more successful had it bought into the 1950s revival or the "homesickness for the false fifties," as *Der Spiegel* called it in 1978. Leaving out all that was inconvenient, popular images of the 1950s offered "nostalgic bliss," the paper argued, quoting a wealth of examples from exhibitions and novels to music festivals and, of course, fashion.[70] Fighting against the nostalgic reshaping of the past, Der Spiegel stressed the repressive climate of the era, and yet it immediately subverted its own undertaking by illustrating its historical interventions with pictures of dancing teenagers and films of the era.[71]

Similarly, an exhibition Der Spiegel drew on referred to the current "nostalgia for the 1950s"—particularly among young people who had no memories of the era—and was itself contributing to a "revision of the 1950s."[72] The accompanying catalog was one of many books about the 1950s—almost all of them heavily illustrated with images from the period—that came out in quick succession in West Germany in the late 1970s.[73] Like the Der Spiegel article and the exhibition, they inhabited an ambivalent position toward nostalgia. As one reviewer remarked, these books offered "not only nostalgia": "Browsing through [them] one couldn't stop being astonished at how long all this has been gone and how alien it is, how much has changed since then."[74] In other words, the reviewer experienced a feeling similar to that of the reviewers of the films set in the 1950s: not so much a sentimental yearning for a period of their past as shock at how much the world had changed in less than two decades. While these books may be the most durable result and lingering reminder of the 1950s revival in West Germany, it also manifested itself elsewhere. In 1978 Bravo, Germany's most popular youth magazine, featured the "Superstars of the 1950s"—Marilyn Monroe, Elvis Presley, and James Dean—on its cover.[75]

As this bears out, the 1950s revival was a transnational phenomenon, much as the rise of rock and roll and the global spread of Hollywood, Coca-Cola, jeans, and other icons of American consumer culture had been in the original 1950s. At the same time, what the 1950s meant differed between national contexts. In West Germany there was a much bigger insistence—at least on the part of the critics—on its darker aspects, given that the country had just emerged from National Socialism, which the new pop and consumer culture of the 1950s had glossed over.

Despite such differences, the term nostalgia appeared without fail whenever music, film, or fashion revisited the recent past in the 1970s. It was mostly used by critics, however, and those they applied it to usually rejected the term—less because of its increasingly pejorative connotations and more because they did not feel that it adequately described their motivations or the ways they used the past. Picking up on selected elements—often in highly ironic ways—they saw themselves as creating a new culture for the present. Some critics only evoked the term to dismiss it: instead of being tempted to wax wistfully about the past, they felt shock at seeing their childhood and youth reproduced and at what they, in the tradition of Toffler, perceived as accelerated change. In both instances, a defining characteristic of the 1950s revival in the 1970s was the impression that the 1950s, after a mere fifteen to twenty years, already felt like the distant past. All of these nuances cast doubt on the accuracy of the term *nostalgia* for this particular revival. In France a similar discussion—or one triggered by similar phenomena—had little recourse to nostalgia, resulting in the introduction of a new and rival term: *retro*.

The 1940s Revival: The Invention of Retro

Not unlike an English country house murder mystery, the history of retro began with a death in polite society. In January 1971 Paris's finest met in a salon in the Rue Spontini, in the western part of Paris between the Arc de Triomphe and the Bois de Boulogne, to examine the newest haute couture creations. The last collection—high point and conclusion—came from Yves Saint Laurent, one of the chief representatives and innovators of high fashion. This time, however, YSL—as he was affectionately called—had taken innovation too far, or rather he seemed to have renounced it altogether. Before the eyes of an aghast audience, the fashion of the 1960s drew its last breath and expired. French fashion journalists, normally fiercely patriotic, were appalled, as were their international colleagues. *Combat* found the collection "repulsive" and "reprehensible," the *Guardian* "a tour de force of bad taste" and an "exercise in kitsch," the *International Herald Tribune* "truly hideous."[76] Quoting with relish the damning reviews, *Time* dubbed the master "Yves St. Debacle."[77] What had happened?

Saint Laurent had violated both the laws of fashion and political correctness. Instead of moving forward, continuing with the trends of the 1960s and projecting them into the future, he had looked back to the past. In retrospect, his collection seems like a toxic toast to Roland Barthes's *Système de la mode,* which had appeared only a few years earlier in 1967. Like other fashion theorists before him, Barthes had understood fashion as belonging "to all the phenomena of neomania which probably appeared in our civilization with the birth of capitalism": it intrinsically strove for newness.[78] If fashion had a history at all, it denied it. Saint Laurent had other ideas. Asked why he had gone back in time, opting for a "retro look," he quipped, "What can we really call 'new' in fashion?"[79] A greater sacrilege was hardly imaginable.

Or was it? What scandalized people even more than the backward-looking nature of Saint Laurent's collection was the era it looked back to: "velvet turbans spiraling skyward, enormous boleros in green fox or black monkey fur, short jackets with square shoulders and narrow braided lapels, little jersey dresses whose bias cutting, drape, and gathering clung brashly to the body, high-heel wedges and ankle-strap shoes, bold makeup"—anyone who knew a thing or two about fashion felt "projected back to the 1940s."[80] The 1971 collection did not simply go back in time, it made straight for the period of the German occupation during the Second World War, the darkest chapter in recent French history. Not only did it offend tastes by dismissing such beloved icons of 1960s style as the mini skirt, it was morally repugnant, reminding people of a period they still remembered though they would have much rather forgotten about it. *Combat* speculated whether the models' heads had been shaved "by the Free French forces"; *Le Figaro*—in one of the few instances where the term appeared—asked whether Saint Laurent was "nostalgic for that era."[81]

Saint Laurent had expected a scandal, and though the scandal he caused might have exceeded his expectations, he stood firm. "What do I want to do? Shock people, make them stop and think. What I'm doing is closely related to what's going on in contemporary American art. Young people have no memories."[82] Like the Pop artists to whom he referred here, Saint Laurent looked for inspiration in everyday styles and fashions. His main defense, however, which, in the eyes of his detractors, probably added insult to injury, was that he was making fashion for young people, young people who had no recollections of the occupation and therefore did not feel offended by the collection.

A poor excuse? Not necessarily. Saint Laurent had indeed, as *Elle* reported, designed the collection with young people in mind and one young woman in particular: Paloma Picasso. The daughter of Pablo Picasso and Françoise Gilot was something of a role model for young women at the time who created their looks with secondhand clothes: "Like her, they're going to the flea market to buy the dresses and 'platform' shoes that their mothers threw out twenty-five years ago."[83] When Saint Laurent met her for the first time a year earlier, he had been impressed by her style, the effect of which soon became visible in his own designs.

Interviewed many decades later, Picasso recalled the shock people had felt on that winter day in the Rue Spontini, a shock she had a hard time comprehending. "As far as I was concerned, putting together what we call a 'look' or 'style' today was just a spontaneous, almost crazy urge. Flea markets had appealed to me for years. . . . We preferred clothes that had been lived in, used, and individualized over anything that could be bought new."[84] Retro, therefore, did not begin with haute couture and fashion designers but with young women who, rejecting both designer and mass-produced fashion, experimented with affordable secondhand clothes (see Figures 3.3 and 3.4).[85]

Like the rock and roll revival, the retro look came straight out of the counterculture. The hippies were the first to exchange department stores for flea markets and secondhand shops or self-made clothes. While Picasso and her friends were certainly not hippies, they shared in this ethos. Known as "anti-fashion," the trend soon caught on in much wider circles of young people.[86] It was also not limited to France. As *Women's Wear Daily* noted in 1971, the "40s look . . . had been around London and the East Village for some time."[87] Saint Laurent merely injected the trend into high fashion. The ensuing scandal did the rest: it put a name to the trend and popularized both.

Yet the 1971 collection is only half of the story. To fully understand the emergence of retro, we also need to consider its counterpart: anti-retro. "Anti-rétro" was the title of an interview the *Cahiers du cinema* conducted with Michel Foucault in 1974 about a number of films set in the era of fascism and the German occupation, which had been released beginning in the late 1960s, particularly Louis Malle's 1974 film *Lacombe, Lucien*.[88] *Lacombe, Lucien*—like the novels of Patrick Modiano, who wrote the script for the film—portrayed the occupation era in a new light. Instead of heroizing the resistance and condemning the collaboration in black and white, it opted for shades of gray. A tiny accident like a punctured bicycle tire could lead a person who could just as well have joined the resistance to collaborate with the Nazis, as was the case for Lucien in the film. At the time, this break with convention—set against the political background of the election of conservative Giscard d'Estaing as president of France in 1974—was just as scandalous as the 1971 collection.[89] For Foucault the "old Pétainist right, the old collaborationist, Maurrasian and reactionary right which camouflaged itself as best it could behind de Gaulle, now considers itself entitled to produce a new version of

Figure 3.3   "Putting together a look": Paloma Picasso, on the left, with friends, wearing secondhand clothes from the 1940s in 1971. © AGIP / Bridgeman Images

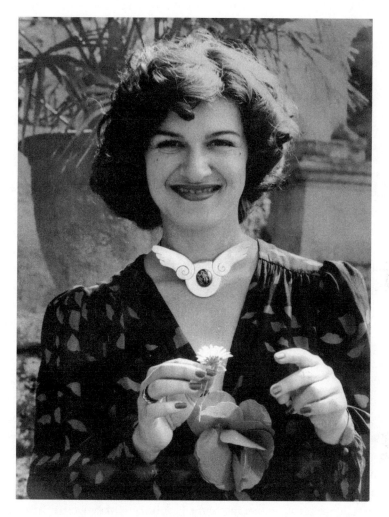

Figure 3.4   Scandalous clothes? Paloma Picasso wearing one of the dresses from Yves Saint Laurent's 1971 collection. Keystone Press/Alamy

its own history."[90] And films like *Lacombe, Lucien* contributed to the white-washing of the collaborators by downplaying their agency and therefore their responsibility. This was not at all how Malle and Modiano, whose father had been persecuted as a Jew, had intended the film to be interpreted. Rather, they wanted to puncture the idea—like the bicycle tire in the film—that all French people had been part of the resistance, an overdue correction in their view.

As it dealt with the memory of the German occupation, the controversy about *la mode rétro* was a specifically French debate and resonated little outside the country. Nevertheless, it shared a lot of common ground with the controversy about "Nazi nostalgia" raging in West Germany in those years, which also revolved around the memorialization and popular representation of National Socialism. One of the few people to connect the two was the historian Saul Friedländer. In his autobiography he remembers how, in the early 1970s, he "caught a glimpse of weird mutations in the representation of the Nazi years, both in Germany and elsewhere in Western Europe. A strange sort of countermemory was appearing: in Germany it was dubbed the Hitler Wave (*die Hitlerwelle*), in France the retro fashion (*la mode rétro*)."[91] What both terms tried to get at was a resurgence of the fascist past not as serious history but in—at least in the eyes of critics—superficial and trivializing ways in popular culture that threatened to trivialize this past itself. Soon the two terms began to overlap more and more as *retro* lost its connection to *la mode rétro* and politics.

The first example for the use of *retro* in the English language given by the *Oxford English Dictionary* is a 1972 article in the *Chicago Tribune* about Saint Laurent.[92] In 1976, the fashion writer Clara Pierre employed the term—still with a capital letter and accent—connecting it to the flea markets and catwalks of Paris. Nonetheless, she saw it as characteristic of the 1970s generally. For her, retro "was nothing so simple as not being able to face our own times, as some have suggested. It was not just that a whole generation of young women was being unnerved by future shock." Rather, she explained, it was the absence of the future or any idea thereof: "If you weren't going forward, you gotta go back."[93] Hence, Pierre not only linked retro to Toffler but also understood it in much the same way nostalgia was understood at this time: young people were turning to the past because they were unable or unwilling to face the future—or, worse still, did not believe in a future at all. By the end of the 1970s, retro still appeared as a recent development but now divorced from its original French context. "Will the 'retro' look make it?" asked the *New York Times,* for instance, in 1979.[94]

When the interview with the *Cahiers du cinéma* was translated into English, "la mode rétro," which they defined as "the snobbish fetishism of period effects (costumes and settings) with little concern for history," became "retro style."[95] Others translated it simply as "Forties revival" to account for its original meaning.[96] The term *nostalgia* rarely appeared in the French debate. In *Simulacra and Simulation,* however, Baudrillard used both in connection with each other.[97] His chapter on nostalgia, entitled "History: A Retro Scenario," begins by observing the "omnipresence of fascism and of war in retro," obviously a reference to *la mode rétro*.[98] Jameson characterized the "nostalgia film" in much the same way, adding at the end, "what the French call la mode rétro," translating the term as "retrospective styling."[99] Rather than differentiating between retro and nostalgia, he declared the two to be identical. Whereas Jameson still knew about the origins of the term, *retro* soon came to characterize the return or revival of any period of the past.

In the eyes of its critics, retro revolved not around the past but the present; it used the past in an easygoing, careless, and decontextualized and, therefore, exactly not nostalgic—in the sense of yearning for the past or sentimentalizing it—manner. Of course, *Le Figaro*'s suggestion that *la mode rétro* was nostalgic for "that era" was a calculated exaggeration. With no memories of the occupation era, Picasso and her friends appropriated artifacts of the 1940s unaware of their original context. Saint Laurent used them because he sensed that tastes were changing and because he welcomed a potential scandal and the chance to attract publicity. Likewise, the debate about *la mode rétro* was less about the past than how it was remembered in the present. Seeming to look back, retro was, in fact, looking around in the here and now. Much the same could be said about the 1950s revival in the United States, Britain, and West Germany.

While the concepts retro and nostalgia are clearly related—emerging at around the same time and dealing with similar phenomena—some writers have warned against conflating them. Raphael Samuel sees retro precisely not as nostalgic when he notes an "absence of sentimentality about the past" as one of its major characteristics. Retro, he argues, is "untroubled by the cult of authenticity," and nothing brings this home as much as fashion.[100] Similarly, Elizabeth Guffey distinguishes between ironic retro and sentimental nostalgia.[101] While *retro* in the initial French debate was at least as polemically charged as *nostalgia,* and although critics have continued to attack it, it gradually lost its overwhelmingly pejorative connotation—unlike *nostalgia*. This makes it a more neutral and, therefore, preferable term. If the debate over *la mode rétro* shows anything, then it is that pop cultural references to the past do not have to be understood in terms of nostalgia. The same conclusion can be drawn when we turn to the period preceding the discussions of the nostalgia wave and *la mode rétro,* which, according to Reynolds and other commentators, distinguished itself through an absence of nostalgia.

Postwar Revivalism

"Forty years ago, the word 'Victorian' was simply a term of abuse; it stood for all that was stuffy, heavy, and overladen with ornament. . . . No one dreamed of collecting 'Victoriana.' . . . Now, a generation later, all that is changed," wrote James Laver in 1966, providing a provocative illustration of the law named after him.[102] Indeed, the Victorian age is a good example for Laver's observation that a style is perceived as hideous as soon as it has fallen out of fashion, and while the term may have a specifically British ring to it, the stuffy, overladen style Laver depicts here was really universal to the nineteenth-century bourgeoisie.

Except for among some precocious Oxford aesthetes who had already collected Victoriana in the 1920s and 1930s to stand out from, and to spite, mainstream opinion, the Victorian age was seen as having one of the most terrible styles ever to have existed, and this opinion remained virtually unchanged until after the Second World War.[103] More rapid than Laver's law allowed, it still took a good fifty years until the art, design, and fashion of the Victorian era managed to climb from "hideous" to "charming" on Laver's ladder.

In Britain the first sign of a reevaluation of the Victorian age came in the 1950s with the Festival of Britain—at least insofar as it commemorated the Great Exhibition of 1851. In truth, the festival espoused exactly the future-oriented values commonly associated with the 1950s, with the jubilee "really no more than a pretext" for the celebration.[104] A pretext, moreover, that quickly slipped the organizers' minds, as James Gardner, one of the festival designers, remembered in 1975: "Everyone had forgotten that we must have something, or should have something, about 1851."[105] The last-minute solution: a miniature copy of the Crystal Palace of 1851 in glass and steel.[106] Completely dwarfed by another "act of homage" to the famous engineering feat of the nineteenth century, the futuristic, flying saucer–like Dome of Discovery, the mini Crystal Palace seemed to embody how the future overshadowed the past in 1950s Britain.[107]

Whereas the Festival of Britain on the South Bank forgot the past by commemorating it, three and a half miles to the west in South Kensington, its resurrection had already begun. In the year before the festival, the Victoria and Albert Museum (the V&A) had published a catalog to commemorate the Great Exhibition.[108] Small and flimsy, it nevertheless marked an important moment, as the V&A would become instrumental in rehabilitating the Victorian era as well as subsequent periods. Inspired by the events of 1951 and irritated by the absence of the decorative arts at the festival, the V&A followed up the album with an Exhibition of Victorian and Edwardian Decorative Arts in 1952.[109] Opposed to the undertaking, architectural critic Reyner Banham hoped it would spell the "death of the cult of fashionable Victoriana" by exposing "the tawdriness of the interior decorator's XIX Century fancy"— which implies that Victoriana must already have had something of a comeback at the time.[110]

Crediting the exhibition with altering the "public approach to the decorative arts of that period," curator Barbara Morris certainly did not share Banham's views.[111] No doubt it contributed to the rediscovery of the Victorian age that had been brewing for a while. It gathered more pace with the foundation of the Victorian Society in 1958, an amenity society aimed at saving the architectural heritage of the Victorian age from destruction (it will feature in greater detail in Chapter 4). Still, the V&A took until 1964 to open its first gallery devoted to the Victorian period.[112]

Naturally the reevaluation of nineteenth-century art and design was not limited to Britain. In 1960, the Brooklyn Institute of Arts and Sciences held an exhibition on Victorian art in the United States, conceived as "a first attempt to consider the many varied tendencies of the period." Stressing their pioneering role, the curators in New York also acknowledged "the renewed interest of the public in objects that have largely been ignored for almost half a century."[113] Museums may have reacted to a shift in taste; they certainly did much to advance it. By exhibiting artworks that had been slumbering in their vaults for decades, they not only brought the Victorian age back into the public domain but, by stamping it with their seal of approval, raised its cultural profile. Much more than mere archives of the past, museums acted as tastemakers and trendsetters. By the end of the 1960s, Victorian art was fully rehabilitated to the extent that a 1970 *Victoriana Collector's Handbook* spoke of a veritable "cult." If this was true, the handbook could easily be seen as something like a catechism—which did not keep it from speculating that the cult sprang "from a nostalgia for the past that is symptomatic of our times": a good example of how the nostalgia discourse infiltrated even those texts it saw as part and parcel of the phenomenon.[114]

Limited to the rediscovery of the art, architecture, and design of the Victorian period, the revival did not extend to fashion: there was no comeback of the crinoline or upturned collars—not yet at least. What did come back in postwar Britain, however, if in a limited way, was Edwardian fashion. After the Second World War, London tailors tried to curb the influence of American fashion by bringing back dandified Edwardian styles in the form of long jackets with flaps and velvet collars, as well as brocade waistcoats. Aimed at an aristocratic, upper-class clientele, the trend carried, for Laver at least, an "undoubted element of nostalgia."[115] According to critic Nik Cohn, the clothes acted as "defences against the new order" of the welfare state and the classless society.[116]

In contrast to this original intention, it was among working-class adolescents, first in London and then in other big cities, that the style really caught on. Combining the Edwardian jackets with tight drainpipe trousers or jeans and heavy shoes, they adapted it to their own tastes. Ducktail haircuts and long sideburns completed the Teddy Boy look, as it was called, in a reference to Edward VII. Working-class youths with a bit of money to spend, the Teddy Boys lived in the here and now, listening to American rock and roll and riding around on motorbikes. The first real youth subculture, the Edwardian style to them was not about the past but a way to stand out in the present, particularly from the restrained, boring, ill-fitting high-street fashion of the time. They pioneered the strategy in which adopting a past style became a method to rebel against mainstream fashion and, by extension, mainstream culture, a pattern that would repeat itself in the following decades. In this way, the Teds "provided the blueprint for all future teenage cults."[117] And nothing better illustrates this than their comeback in the 1970s, when the masculine, working-class, rough Teddy Boy style and attitude provided a counterpoint to the hippies of the 1960s, who, it turns out, themselves looked back to earlier times.

The Art Nouveau and Art Deco Revivals of the 1960s

As the 1950s gave way to the 1960s, the revival broadened. In *Future Shock* Toffler mentions the "spread of Edwardian styles" as well as the "revival of Art Nouveau" as examples of the "tremendous wave of nostalgia in society" he observed.[118] Looking back from the vantage point of the 1980s, design historian Bevis Hillier even claimed that the "nostalgia movement began with the Art Nouveau revival."[119] Back in the 1960s, however, revivalism was not as yet firmly linked to nostalgia.

Again, museums played important roles in the revival, with the Kunst-gewerbemuseum Zurich staging a first big exhibition on Art Nouveau as early as 1952—incidentally, the same year as the V&A's show on Victorian and Edwardian art, which also contained a number of Art Nouveau pieces.[120] A skeptical reviewer saw this as a sign "of a renewed interest in the style known as *art nouveau,* though mercifully not as yet of any revival of its use."[121] Perhaps not quite yet, but it was not long in coming. Further Art Nouveau shows followed in Munich in 1958, as well as New York and Paris in 1960.[122] The last was curated by the German émigré art historian Peter Selz, who cred-ited the Zurich show with rehabilitating a style that had until recently been seen as "the extravagant conclusion of a tasteless era."[123] For Selz, Art Nou-veau was not so much a style of the past as the beginning of the present: it had set "the stage for developments which followed with such extraordinary rapidity in the twentieth century."[124] Further exhibitions and book publica-tions wore down the last resistance.[125] "For a decade the revival of art nou-veau has been building in nostalgic museum shows in London, Munich and New York," now it was mainstream, *Time* noted in 1964.[126]

In Britain, the V&A staged two shows on artists closely connected to Art Nouveau, both masterminded by the art historian Brian Edmund Reade. In 1963 the museum paid tribute to Alphonse Mucha, a Czech artist, who ex-emplified Art Nouveau's ethos that art should climb down from the ivory tower to transform everyday life by creating both an elaborate cycle of his-torical paintings and advertising posters for products such as beer, biscuits, and perfume.[127] None other than Reyner Banham, condemner of the Victorian style, celebrated Mucha's modernity. Reviewing the exhibition, he stressed how Mucha had worked "with the mass media in such fields as posters, pack-aging, book-design, and prints for home decoration . . . strikingly like the way some pop artists do today," and went on to compare him to such con-temporary artists as Peter Blake.[128]

Reminded by Art Nouveau of contemporary art, critics declared it con-temporary itself. In fact, it was the other way around, and the critics merely lagged behind the Pop artists who had looked to Mucha and Aubrey Beard-sley—to whom the V&A devoted a retrospective in 1966—for inspiration.[129] If anything, Beardsley's expressionist style and the frequently obscene con-tent of his drawings were even further removed from any idea of the good old days than Mucha's work. He was celebrated as "England's chief pioneer of modern art" and "the most cool cat," whose art still—or once again—seemed fresh and modern, if not disturbing and unsettling as well: while the V&A retrospective sought to establish him as a great forgotten genius, the London police went around seizing reproductions of his work in London book-shops because they were seen as obscene.[130] Naturally, this only increased his countercultural cachet. When George Melly visited the exhibition, he found it packed with "art students, some were beats, others could have been pop musicians, most of them were very young, but almost all of them gave the impression of belonging to a secret society. . . . I had stumbled for the first time into the presence of the emerging underground."[131] Whether or not Melly was exaggerating, the Beardsley exhibition clearly was a defining mo-ment: for a London counterculture on the lookout for its own distinctive style, it provided an inspiring and exhilarating template.

Other voices bear out his account. "London in the late 1950s had been very grey, filled with bombed-out sites," Michael Rainey, the owner of the fashionable boutique Hung on You, decorated in a style reminiscent of Beard-sley, remembered. "It was a very stiff, authoritarian climate. . . . We were coming out of a dark cloud of hypocrisy and moralizing. Beardsley's languid, relaxed drawings chimed with our desire for a more laid-back society."[132] Beardsley became a posthumous celebrity. His drawings were venerated, his style copied by many artists of the day. The cover art of the Beatles' 1966 album *Revolver* by the German artist Klaus Voorman was inspired by his draw-ings, as was the 1968 Beatles film *Yellow Submarine*. Beardsley also appeared on Peter Blake's cover for *Sgt. Pepper's Lonely Hearts Club Band* (the first person on the left in the second row from the top).[133]

Another field where Art Nouveau was of great influence was fashion, both through secondhand clothes bought in secondhand stores or at flea mar-kets and through young designers seeking inspiration, blending old and new materials and styles.[134] Swinging London saw a mushrooming of bou-tiques like Hung on You, Granny Takes a Trip, and Biba along the King's Road in Chelsea and Carnaby Street in Soho, immortalized by the Kinks in their 1966 song "Dedicated Follower of Fashion."[135] While Mary Quant popular-ized the mini skirt, the most iconic garment of the 1960s, Barbara Hulanicki turned to the past for inspiration. Her designs incorporated historical influ-ences almost from the beginning. In 1966 she created a gown combining elements of several different eras: the high-necked collar of the Edwardian period and the puff sleeves of the early nineteenth century with the high waist and full skirt of the Regency era, a "1966 version of a Victorian christening

Figure 3.5 The 1960s swinging to the tunes of the past: The Art Nouveau–inspired interior of the Biba Boutique in Kensington. Pictoral Press Ltd/Alamy

robe," as the *Daily Express* described it.[136] This was the first of many designs combining elements of different historical styles. Hulanicki's chosen colors—dark brown, purple, plum—were nothing like the bright colors usually associated with 1960s fashion; they were "very Alphonse Mucha, Klimt, that period. They were Art Nouveau colors."[137] In keeping with her designs, the interior of Hulanicki's boutique Biba, like the Biba logo designed by Antony Little, an artist and illustrator heavily influenced by Beardsley, channeled Art Nouveau (see Figure 3.5).[138]

In interviews Hulanicki frequently spoke about the appeal of the past and its influence on her fashion, describing it in terms of a nostalgia that was not yet tainted by the debate of the 1970s. "At the moment it's the 30s that fascinate me," she said in 1966. "I wallow in old books and the films they've been showing on TV. It's the glamour of nostalgia I suppose."[139] "For me, Art Nouveau is never still, *always* convoluted, unlikely to be boring," she told a journalist the following year. "Indoors, the elements of the style can produce real warmth and nostalgia, which I find bewitching, and, of course, it's all a trifle decadent."[140]

For Hulanicki, nostalgia seems to have expressed not so much a sense of loss or yearning as a vague, positive feeling—"warmth," notions of stylishness, "glamour," "decadence"—and the idea that people had more taste in the past, and fashions were more elegant. Likewise, in her designs, she never simply copied a specific style; instead she mixed different influences together, ultimately creating fashion for the present. What Hulanicki called nostalgia was not the escapist, derivative dead end critics imagined, but an inexhaustible well of inspiration. Although they drew on the past, her designs were perceived as entirely of the moment, if not the future: "The whole Biba scene makes you feel like you're in tomorrow," the *Chicago Times* commented in 1968.[141]

Already in 1966 *Time* had featured London on its cover as "the Swinging City." In the accompanying article, Piri Halasz celebrated it as the capital of the global youth culture, extensively describing its fashion scene, boutiques, and nightlife.[142] To some extent, her article made London into what she had described, attracting the eyes of the world to it. The "British invasion" of the mid-1960s did the rest, popularizing British youth and pop culture around the world. Via these routes, the Edwardian- and Art Nouveau–inspired dandified British look found its way into American fashion and the fashion of the 1960s more generally.[143]

Like Hulanicki, the counterculture was not aiming to preserve or authentically reproduce Art Nouveau styles; in the end, it was not even that interested in Art Nouveau as such. The German historian Jost Hermand, somewhat unfairly but not incorrectly, accused it of using the style "purely as a legitimization of their own ideas" and of only being interested in its "snobbish, exquisite, lewd, monstrous, old-fashioned and kitschy" elements.[144] Indeed, the counterculture did not conserve the past; it treated it like a treasure trove, mining it for its own purposes, using whatever chimed with its ideas and requirements and discarding everything else—much as Hulanicki did in her fashion designs.

However, this does not explain the elective affinities between the counterculture and Art Nouveau: What attracted young people in the 1960s to the overcrowded, ornamental, turn-of-the-century style? One explanation may lie in the German term for the style: *Jugendstil*, literally "youth style." Art Nouveau was not simply a new style; it consciously broke with Victorianism. It was a rebellion against the stuffiness, complacency, and conservatism of the nineteenth century. For young people in the 1960s, the exaggerated, expressive curves of Art Nouveau were, as *Time* concluded, "a revolt against the grim, stark, formless, spiritless expression of much abstract art and modern architecture," much as short skirts and colorful clothes or the anti-fashion of the hippies were the antithesis to the nondescript dark suits and dresses of the 1950s.[145] Earlier youth movements, with their rejection of traditional values and social conventions and an emphasis on nature, sensuality, vegetarianism, and sexual liberation, anticipated many ideas of the 1960s—or, the other way around, many older ideas were taken up and adapted by the 1960s counterculture. It is no wonder, then, that the hippies reminded observers of this ancestry.[146]

Like the first youth style, its second coming quickly faded away. When "Art Nouveau-inspired swirls embellished soft drink ads" and the style was completely commercialized, the youth and counterculture lost interest.[147] Yet it did not "require a Nostradamus to predict that the Art Nouveau revival would be followed by a twenties and thirties revival," as Bevis Hillier foresaw in 1968.[148] The very term for this style, Art Deco, a retrospective invention to sum up the often quite diverse and disparate decorative and architectural trends of the interwar period, was itself a product of the revival.[149] And like preceding revivals, this one also began with a museum exhibition, the *Les Années 25: Art Déco / Bauhaus / Stijl* show at the Musée des Arts Décoratifs in Paris in 1966—the same year as the Beardsley exhibition at the V&A. The accompanying catalog observed how detested the style had been before the passing of time had bestowed on it "the nostalgic prestige of time lost and regained."[150] It was followed by many other shows across Europe and the United States, usually accompanied by sumptuous exhibition catalogs, in addition to which publishers brought out coffee-table books on Art Deco and the 1920s style.[151]

"Art Deco, more than Art Nouveau, captures us because of its heady nostalgia," Roy Strong, the director of the V&A, believed.[152] Like the rediscovery of Art Nouveau, that of Art Deco had a lot to do with contemporary sensibilities. For the architectural critic Deborah Stratton, the interwar period "was one of rapid, breath-taking change," a "hectic, frantic, tenuous world" to which people of the late 1960s could easily relate as "we are no more stable now." She also saw in it "the beginnings of what we now take for granted—of functional design, combined with beauty of form."[153] Much like Art Nouveau before it, Art Deco was rediscovered because of a felt similarity between then and now.

Hillier, in particular, drew attention to the affinities between Pop Art and Art Deco, to which Saint Laurent also referred when defending his 1971 collection.[154] A fan of Art Deco, Andy Warhol collected everything "from unabashed kitsch to the rare and exquisite."[155] Roy Lichtenstein, too, spoke about his admiration for a style resembling "a discredited area, like the comics."[156] Like the comics, Lichtenstein used Art Deco as raw material for his artworks as early as the mid-1960s. The Art Deco revival, consequently, did not wait dutifully in the wings until Art Nouveau had fallen out of favor; the two revivals occurred simultaneously, appealing to different constituencies: while the counterculture was inclined to refer to Art Nouveau, Pop Art drew on Art Deco—which does not mean that there was not a good deal of overlap.

Pop Art and Art Deco also shared a similar ethos: not only did they both elevate everyday objects, popular culture, and industrial methods of production, they also emulated them, most famously in Warhol's *Campbell's Soup Cans* prints and Lichtenstein's comic paintings. When Warhol called his studio a "factory" and Lichtenstein spoke of "industrial painting," they both sought to provoke the traditional art world by embracing the aesthetics of industrial mass production. Lichtenberg felt attracted to the 1930s not because they seemed antique but, on the contrary, because "they were much more modern than we feel we are now."[157]

By 1972, Art Nouveau had almost been "totally eclipsed by Art Deco," as a guide for collectors observed.[158] "By the early seventies," Clara Pierre noted at the end of the decade, "we were wallowing in *la nostalgie* to the brim, from flea-market fashion to Art Deco ashtrays to kitsch, until we had nearly managed to forget who we were," repeating the idea that looking back was a distraction from the here and now.[159]

Like the rediscovery of Art Nouveau, that of Art Deco reverberated in the fashion world, the designs of Hulanicki again providing a good example. In the late 1960s and early 1970s, she no longer harked back to the Victorian and Edwardian eras but instead to the 1920s, 1930s, and 1940s. Art Deco and animal prints, fake fur, skullcaps, feather boas, and platform shoes became part of the new Biba look. Expanding her business, Hulanicki found the ideal surroundings in a 1930s department store in Kingston High Street, whose original Art Deco fittings she had previously restored. Opening in 1973, Big

Biba instantly became London's new prime fashion emporium, allegedly attracting a million people a week, as well as becoming a favorite hangout for the early 1970s glam rock scene.[160]

No one less than David Bowie, with his well-known fascination with the 1930s, praised Big Biba's "up-to-the-minute appearance combined with a lovely, nostalgic feel of the Thirties."[161] Others found this nothing less than obscene. The filmmaker Dennis Potter called Big Biba a "tat palace in Kensington High Street which has timed its Thirties décor to such perfection that it only wants a pavement band of the unemployed outside."[162] Soon, however, it was the Biba staff that found itself out of work. Thanks to the volatile economy and property market, the store had to close in 1975.

The 1920s revival may have begun in 1966 when it came to art and design, but in other areas it was already well under way. As early as 1962, the German sociologists Helmuth Plessner and Theodor Adorno observed an increasing mythologization of the 1920s. Vague on details of what was revived, they were firm in their judgment. Having witnessed the demise of the Weimar Republic and the rise of the Nazis, which had driven them both into exile, they invoked their memories of the era against any attempt to idealize it—to little avail as it turned out, as the real 1920s revival was yet to come.[163]

The rediscovery of the 1920s also extended to film. While Hollywood had begun to revisit the interwar period as early as the 1950s—in *Some Like It Hot* (1959) or *Singin' in the Rain* (1952), for instance—the real 1920s craze arrived in 1967 courtesy of *Bonnie and Clyde*. Focusing on some rather unlikely—though extremely stylish—characters and inviting audiences to identify with them, it portrayed violence in a way no film had done before: blood spurted, wounds gaped, brains sputtered. When it came out, it was panned by many critics and by none more than Bosley Crowther, longtime film critic for the *New York Times,* who thought it "strangely antique, sentimental claptrap."[164] It was nothing of the sort for the young, as yet unknown critic Pauline Kael, who rode to the film's defense with all critical guns blazing—a conflict of opinions pointing to a larger generational conflict. As the queues of people, especially young people, in front of cinemas became longer and longer, many critics changed their opinion. Out of tune with the tastes of the times, Crowther was demoted, while Kael's star rose.[165]

Bonnie and Clyde warrants closer attention not only because of its popular success and long-term influence but also because it was—though absent from Jameson's list—criticized as one of the first "nostalgia films." Indeed, apart from its graphic violence, nostalgia was one of the chief sins the film was reproached for—it "slithers easily into nostalgia," the *Village Voice* was not alone in observing.[166] Even for Kael, the film appealed to audiences partly because of "our nostalgia for the thirties."[167] For the film scholar Paul Monaco, *Bonnie and Clyde*'s "mixture of vagueness and precision" was one of the key characteristics of nostalgia in a film, and he also charged it with stylizing, simplifying, and sentimentalizing the past. The fact that its main audience was too young to have witnessed the Great Depression did not give him pause: they were "prepared by the media and their parents to respond to this movie nostalgically."[168]

This was definitely not how its authors, David Newman and Robert Benton, had intended the film. In their thirties when they wrote the script, they were heavily into the French New Wave and, if not part of it, certainly sympathetic to the counterculture. For them, Bonnie and Clyde were interesting because they felt "out of their time in the 30s." "If Bonnie and Clyde were here today, they would be hip," the writers thought. "Their values have been assimilated in much of our culture—not robbing banks and killing people, of course, but their style, their sexuality, their bravado, their delicacy, their cultivated arrogance, their narcissistic insecurity, their curious ambition have relevance to the way we live now."[169] For the creators of the fictionalized Bonnie and Clyde, the two were interesting not as historical but as contemporary characters, and they were hardly alone in this. With the tagline "They're young . . . they're in love . . . and they kill people," the film was geared toward the young, and for them it carried a clear message: "It says 'fuck you' . . . to a generation"—the generation of their parents.[170] The resentment of older viewers like Crowther only heightened the film's attraction for the young. Far from invoking wistful memories, it was perceived as a call to arms. The real Bonnie and Clyde may have been small-time crooks, but in the climate of the 1960s, they became revolutionaries—as well as revolutionary style icons.

Bonnie and Clyde was also the starting pistol for what came to be known as "New Hollywood": the arrival of a new generation of filmmakers who, inspired by the French New Wave and aided by the weakness of the major Hollywood studios at the time, gained more artistic autonomy and, inadvertently, ended up saving Hollywood. When looking for subjects, many of these young directors, doubtless inspired by *Bonnie and Clyde,* turned to the past and particularly to the interwar period. In *Thoroughly Modern Millie* (1967) a young flapper tries to make her fortune in 1922 New York by marrying a successful businessman; in *They Shoot Horses, Don't They?* (1969) the prize is $1,500 for the winner of a dance marathon, but the competition is vicious, and there is blood on the dance floor by the end of the film; in *Boxcar Bertha* (1972) a gangster couple tries to rob a train; in *Paper Moon* (1973) the gangsters are a nine-year-old girl and her father; in *The Sting* (1973) they are two handsome grifters in 1930s Chicago; *Dillinger* (1973) shows "the gangster's gangster"; *The Way We Were* (1973) tells a love story backward from the 1950s to the 1930s; similarly, *The Godfather II* (1974) crosscuts between the 1950s and the early twentieth century; *Chinatown* (1974) is an homage to the film noir of the 1930s while simultaneously subverting it; *The Great Gatsby* (1974) is an adaptation of the F. Scott Fitzgerald novel that contributed so much to the myth of the Roaring Twenties; and *Thieves Like Us* (1974) is another gangster film. *The Day of the Locust* (1975) and *The Last Tycoon* (1976) are as good as any to conclude this list, as they allowed contemporary Hollywood to hold up a mirror to itself by looking to its own past.[171] The 1920s and 1930s were, indeed, very present in the cinema of the 1970s.

However, most of the films were set in the era of the Great Depression and thereby exactly not in the "good old times." The rediscovery of this era may have had less to do with Laver's law than with the depression—political, economic, and mental—the United States found itself in following the murders of the Kennedys and the leaders of the civil rights movement, the drawn-out debacle of Vietnam, and the equally bloody end of the counterculture with the Manson murders, to which the 1970s added Watergate and the oil crisis. Against this backdrop, it was perhaps only natural that Americans remembered "the last great domestic crisis in the United States prior to the protests of the late sixties."[172]

The charge that 1970s pop culture simply glossed "over such crises as the 1926 General Strike and the Great Depression" does not ring true for most of these films.[173] It is difficult, for instance, to find a less glamorizing film than *They Do Shoot Horses, Don't They?*, with its vivid depiction of despair, culminating in the killing of Jane Fonda's character like the wounded horse of the title. *Chinatown* also exhibited "very little nostalgia for the time period portrayed in the film. . . . Instead of creating yearning for a bygone time, the film works to expose inequalities present in the 1970s."[174] Others see it as "mourning the death of the 1960s dream."[175] Despite their often meticulously re-created period settings, these were intensely contemporary films, using history to address problems of the present like social inequality, poverty, and corruption, a common denominator that is probably more obvious in hindsight than it was when they came out.

The films also amplified the ongoing rediscovery of the fashion of the period. Bevis Hillier even went so far as to make *Bonnie and Clyde* responsible for the replacement of Art Nouveau with Art Deco.[176] Its costumes—Clyde's wide-lapelled pinstriped suits, spectator shoes, and fedora hats reminiscent of the gangster movies of the 1930s but "channelled through the cool sophistication of the French New Wave," and Bonnie's maxi skirts, silk neckties, and berets "period clothes made unrepentantly modern"—influenced the fashion of the era within and beyond the counterculture.[177] Though modernized, such clothes were far removed from the mainstream fashion of the 1960s (as well as the 1920s and the 1930s). All the more reason why they struck a chord with the fashionable young, who—regardless of gender—could suddenly be seen walking around in gangster suits, like the one Faye Dunaway wore in a 1968 fashion shoot for *Life*.[178] While not every woman may have gone for this style, the long dresses Dunaway wore as Bonnie contributed to the demise of the mini skirt.[179] A particular favorite was Bonnie's beret, which became an international icon of the counterculture. In a piece on the style of the 1960s, the British writer Angela Carter imagined a girl completing her outfit with "her old school beret dug out of the loft because she saw Faye Dunaway in *Bonnie and Clyde*."[180] The girl in question could have been a young German feminist like Alice Schwarzer, who remembered how she went to demonstrations "wearing . . . the full Bonnie look, beret included."[181]

Similarly influential was *The Great Gatsby*. Its producers wanted none other than Barbara Hulanicki to design the costumes—a token of how successful she had become as an international fashion designer and how much her designs were associated with bringing back the styles of the interwar years.[182] In the end, however, Robert Redford's clothes were designed by Ralph Lauren, for whom Fitzgerald's book was the "strongest, lifelong influence."[183] Lauren used his involvement in the film to bring out his own 1920s-inspired line of menswear, including white collars on candy-striped shirts as well as white and pink suits. He combined designs from the era with the comfort of contemporary fashion, effectively creating an entirely new style. "What the consumer *thinks* is period isn't really what he wants to wear today," Lauren explained, "so I've translated it. The look is contemporary and updated, and it still looks like what Gatsby was all about."[184] By collaborating with one another, filmmakers and designers both fed off each other and promoted each other's products as well as contributing to a sense of revivalism encompassing the whole of pop culture.

Except perhaps for music, where the tendency to seek inspiration in the past was not as obvious as it would become later on, given that the 1960s were one of the most inventive, experimental, and avant-garde periods for rock music. Yet precisely because rock was becoming ever more elaborate, some artists already had begun to return to the roots of rock and roll, as Bob Dylan started to do with his blues- and country-infused—as well as electrified—albums of the mid-1960s.[185] Notably, none of these artists were accused of nostalgia and neither was folk music, the genre Dylan started out in and which had provided so much of the soundtrack of the counterculture, despite the fact that it harked back not only to the folk revival of the 1930s and 1940s but also to preindustrial times and the rural, subjects usually perceived as inherently nostalgic.[186] Whether a revival was nostalgic or not lay in the eye of the beholder.

Perhaps the most conspicuously backward-looking album of the 1960s came from Britain: the Kinks' *The Kinks Are the Village Green Preservation Society*. Unable to keep pace with the boundlessly innovative Beatles (who, nevertheless, "could well be labelled retro themselves" for adopting older styles), falling in popularity, and barred from touring the United States, the Kinks took an extreme step in the opposite direction, rejecting internationalism and experimentalism in favor of the simple, quaint, and parochial—their new album was "appallingly out of sync with the time" and quite deliberately so.[187] The theme song's indictment of office blocks and skyscrapers was not meant as a joke. "When you look around now at the terrible architecture in England," lead guitarist Dave Davies later wrote in his autobiography, "it serves as a constant reminder of how thoughtless and naive post-war Britain was. They tore down lovely Victorian terraced houses all over London and replaced them with cold, ugly office blocks; they carved up beautiful countryside to build more roads."[188] In the face of modernist destruction, the album celebrated village greens and variety theater, draft beer and custard pie, Tudor houses and antiques. In an interview with the *Melody Maker*, Ray Davies declared that "we are all for that looking back thing."[189] What may have appeared eccentric in the moment was really ahead of its time: had it come out a few years later, the album would have been cited as evidence for the nostalgia wave. The fact that it did come out in 1968 shows, once again, that many of the phenomena and practices subsumed under the nostalgia label were already in evidence in the 1960s.

Indeed, surveying the cultural landscape of the 1960s does not provide much evidence for Reynolds's claim—and the common stereotype—that revivalism was absent before the 1970s. If anything, the era initiated revivalism as it came to be known and understood in the following decades by bringing back elements of both the 1900s and the interwar period. Far from plucking them out of thin air, the 1960s produced new styles, sounds, and subjects by drawing extensively on the past. *Nostalgia* as a term already appeared frequently in this context, yet it was used in a more ambivalent and open way than it would be from the 1970s on. Overall, however, it was used by critics and usually with the pejorative connotation that would come to dominate in the 1970s.

So why were phenomena, practices, and attitudes that were, by and large, not perceived as nostalgic in the 1960s evaluated differently in the 1970s? Of course, there were some slight differences. Dylan's appropriation of 1950s rock and roll was arguably more subtle and also more creative than Sha Na Na's, but that holds true for many musicians of the 1970s appropriating earlier styles as well. And it's harder to see why the 1950s revival should be more nostalgic than the preceding revivals. Whether something was categorized as nostalgic or not, therefore, was ultimately a matter of taste, which goes to show that nostalgia was also an aesthetic category and clearly a negative one, applied to those uses of the past that critics rejected but not to others. Then again, the nostalgia critique of the 1970s may have had less to do with the actual examples at which it was aimed than with the overall changing cultural, political, and social landscape. The failure of the counterculture and the rise of conservatism, the growing pessimism about and the rejection of the idea of progress and, as its flipside, the critique of nostalgia, may have led critics to perceive artifacts dealing with the past more critically than they had in the climate of the 1960s, when they were associated with the counterculture. What was new in the 1970s, then, was not the fact that fashion and pop culture drew on the past, but how this was seen and assessed by the critics. The obvious next question is, what happened after the 1970s?

The "Re Decade": The 1980s

"The fabric of the universe was sort of a botch-up job, to be quite frank. We made it in only seven days. You see Kevin, there are holes in it," explains a character in the 1981 film *Time Bandits,* which can be seen as symbolic of a more complex postmodern understanding of time: due to the porous nature of the universe, the protagonists are not only able to travel through time, they do so in a nonlinear way, jumping arbitrarily between various periods.[190] And what they encounter there is as botched up as the universe itself. *Time Bandits* certainly leaves little of the "great man theory of history," portraying, in the words of David Lowenthal, "Napoleon as obsessively touchy about his shortness and Robin Hood as a Mafia-type lout."[191] In general, the past emerges as "messy, disorganized, and decidedly hostile," as a contemporary reviewer noted.[192] *Time Bandits* contradicts the claim, made by film scholar Andrew Gordon in the late 1980s, that the "recent explosion of time-travel films represents a pervasive uneasiness about our present and uncertainty about our future, along with a concurrent nostalgia about our past."[193] The past often did not come off much better.

With its jumbled-up timelines, *Time Bandits*—as well as many other time-travel films of the era—can also be seen as symbolic of the changing nature of retro. In the 1960s and 1970s, it may just have been possible to think of retro as having distinctive and coherent cycles, the return of a style after a certain number of years, the 1920s in the 1960s, the 1950s in the 1970s, and so on. From the 1980s onward, however, different periods of the past came to blend into one another more and more.

After the preceding revivals, it was only logical to expect a 1960s revival—already foreshadowed by the Mod revival of the 1970s—and it was not long in coming. "Now the 60s are back," music critic Robert Palmer noted in the *New York Times* in 1985. Unlike most other commentators, Palmer saw revivals as neither negative nor nostalgic; to him it was even possible that "the rock of the 60s revival could become more interesting than much of the music that originally inspired it."[194] "Yes, it was 1985," confirmed British journalist Julie Burchill a year later, "that was the year, that was, when the sixties revival which had threatened since the start of the eighties laid down the first solid foundations for the big sweep."[195] "Oh, God! The Sixties are coming back," exclaimed the satirist and self-confessed "retired hippie and former pinko beatnik" P. J. O'Rourke in *Rolling Stone* in 1987. "What if my friends and I had tried to revive the Forties?" he asked, addressing the youths he held responsible for the revival and conveniently forgetting that his own generation had borrowed heavily from the past.[196] That same year, the sociologist and former president of the Students for a Democratic Society Todd Gitlin noted a "curious sort of sixties revival—an amalgam of mystique, travesty, and serious occasion."[197] "As the Eighties recede, we find ourselves caught in the riptide of a Sixties revival. There are films, histories, and memoirs of what has been made to seem a sort of golden age," wrote Peter Collier and David Horowitz, two former members of the counterculture turned conservatives.[198]

The 1960s revival manifested itself in much the same way as previous revivals had. "We are awash in sixties nostalgia," declared British journalist James Collins with an eye to fashion in a 1991 issue of *Spy* magazine with the title "What Year Is It, Anyway?," whose cover featured a photomontage of Princess Diana as a hippie. "Since around 1987," Collins contended, "all couture has looked as if it had been designed one spring day in the 1960s."[199] "The sixties are back with a vengeance," concurred *New Yorker* fashion critic Holly Brubach, dedicating an entire column to the phenomenon. For her, "nostalgia has come full circle, and we've ended up back at the start of the seventies," where it had all begun.[200] Again the fault did not lay with her own generation but with the present youth. "The people most enthusiastic about the revival of the sixties," she noted, "seem to be those too young to have participated in the real thing."[201] As with earlier revivals, that of the 1960s was driven less by people looking back to their past than by the following generation.

O'Rourke and Gitlin reacted in just as alienated a way to seeing their salad days reenacted, revived, and remembered as Ebert and Fox had done a decade before—which did not stop O'Rourke from lamenting "that it's been straight downhill ever since."[202] For others, the 1960s represented precisely the moment when things had gone downhill. Entitled *Destructive Generation*, Collier and Horowitz's book about the 1960s was meant as an indictment of the period and as an antidote to its nostalgic re-creation in the present. As Burchill noted, 1985 was not just "the year of the sixties revival—it was the year of the sixties reviled."[203] Over time the conflicts of the 1960s had turned into a conflict over their meaning and memory: "While the 1970s disappeared before they even ended and the 1950s succumbed to a nostalgic fog, the 1960s stay hot," a historical survey published in 1994 noted.[204] Yet both the

1950s and 1960s—or rather the retrospective images of them—were mobilized in political and cultural clashes, as we saw with Reagan's rhetoric in Chapter 2.

The 1950s may not, may never, have been as hot—in the sense of contentious—as the 1960s, but they nevertheless continued to exert a powerful influence on the popular imagination far beyond the 1970s. "It is the eighties, but the fifties live again," a 1985 guide titled *Fifties Style* asserted. "Postwar furniture, the latest and hottest entry into the antiques market, is quickly snapped up by private collectors and museums on both sides of the Atlantic. Movies and plays set in the 1950s continue to attract crowds. Many of today's magazines, record albums, and advertisements offer stylish updates of fifties graphics."[205] Fashion could also be added to this list. "There's a fifties revival in full swing," declared the *Guardian* in 1983.[206] Compared with the previous decades, the 1980s saw a return to more conservative styles—matching the more conservative politics of the era—in which designers borrowed from the postwar era.[207]

In the cinema as well, the 1950s remained the preferred period to go back to, as *New York Times* film critic Michiko Kakutani noted in 1984.[208] Not only was there no *American Graffiti* for the 1960s, it was hard to imagine one, given the decade's historical background: most films about the 1960s coming out since the late 1970s, such as *Apocalypse Now* (1979), *Platoon* (1986), *Full Metal Jacket* (1987), *Good Morning, Vietnam* (1987), *1969* (1988), *Born on the Fourth of July* (1989), *In Country* (1989), and *Casualties of War* (1989), dealt with the Vietnam War, suggesting that this event dominated the public's memory of the decade.

There were more lighthearted entries too, mainly in the form of two popular TV sitcoms, *Family Ties* (set in the 1980s, broadcast 1982–1989) and *The Wonder Years* (set in the 1960s, broadcast 1988–1993), both of which dramatized generational tensions—between hippie parents and their conservative children in the former and between conservative parents and hippie children in the latter—and played them for comic effect.[209] In both political rhetoric and pop culture, the conflicts of the 1960s still seemed to resonate in the contemporary world. Even if pop culture displayed a degree of sympathy for the values of the counterculture, it ultimately portrayed them as something people had to grow out of, rejecting them for the individualism and neoliberal free-market ideology of the Reaganite present.[210] So it was much safer to stick with the mythical 1950s, as films continued to do throughout the 1980s with, for instance, *Rumble Fish* (1983), *Peggy Sue Got Married* (1986), *Blue Velvet* (1986), and *Stand by Me* (1987).

In 1985, the same year journalists started to note a resurgence of the 1960s, the 1950s hit it big again at the box office with *Back to the Future,* in which the teenager Marty McFly accidentally travels from 1985 to 1955 and meets his teenage parents. Though it was ignored by Jameson—perhaps because it was not highbrow enough—many other critics understood *Back to the Future,* with its meticulous reconstruction of the 1950s and its emulation of the pop culture of the era, as the prime example of a "nostalgia film."[211] However, as in others cases, the film does not easily comply with this reading. As a contemporary review noted, it put "nostalgia gently in perspective," with both the director and the protagonist taking "a bemused but unsentimental view of times gone by."[212]

Indeed, when Marty arrives in the 1950s, he does not find the "good old days" his mother likes to rhapsodize about. In fact, as it turns out, everything that has gone wrong for his family is rooted in his parents' experiences in the era. Breaking the oft-defied first rule of time travel—do not alter the past, because doing so may change the present—Marty does just that. When he returns to 1985, he finds his parents transformed from a bullied employee and frustrated alcoholic housewife to an affluent and successful couple. Paralleling the film with Reagan's rhetoric, Michael D. Dwyer views them as closely related: "Marty embodies the Reagan-Era disaffection with an America that was not living up to its postwar promise."[213] By repairing the past—much as Reagan sought to repair what had gone wrong in American history—Marty fixes the present. While it revisits the 1950s, the film ultimately revolves around the present of the 1980s and is enthralled with the future, for which Marty sets off at its end. Taking her cue from Jameson, critic Vivian Sobchack understands *Back to the Future* as "a generic symptom of our collapsed sense of time and history," and the same could also be said for *Time Bandits* and other time-travel films of the period.[214] *Back to the Future* also crops up in Tom Shales's article about the "Re Decade" as "a phrase that almost sums the Eighties up."[215]

If "for Americans at least the 1950s remain the privileged lost object of desire," as Jameson notes in his discussion of the "nostalgia film," a similar claim could be made for the period preceding and following the First World War when it comes to Europeans—or at least to European films of the 1980s.[216] Starting in 1981 with the television series *Brideshead Revisited,* about the

decline of an aristocratic family, and the film *Chariots of Fire,* about the unexpected success of two British athletes at the 1924 Olympics, the British
film industry churned out a succession of films and television series set between the mid- to late nineteenth century and the Second World War, usually in the countryside or colonial India and often based on novels, such as
Quartet (1981), *Heat and Dust* (1982), *Gandhi* (1982), *Another Time Another
Place* (1983), *A Passage to India* (1984), *The Jewel in the Crown* (1984), *Another
Country* (1984), *A Private Function* (1984), *A Room with a View* (1985), *Hope
and Glory* (1987), *Maurice* (1987), *Personal Services* (1987), and *Howards End*
(1992). By the early 1990s, they came to form a distinctive genre—the "heritage film"—the unifying characteristic of which, in the eyes of its critics, was
that all these films were "nostalgic in that their pasts were represented as entirely better places."[217]

Although Andrew Higson, who coined the term, referred to the "heritage
debate" only indirectly, it clearly exerted a big influence: both debates—
the one about heritage proper and the one about heritage film—drew on
nostalgia to explain the public interest in the past.[218] While the heritage
critics, more concerned with the conservation movement and museums, had
little time for film, or pop culture more generally, most of them could not
avoid mentioning *Brideshead,* so popular was it at the time.[219] In the United
States, *Brideshead* was hugely successful as well, continuing "Britain's cultural
colonization of America," as the critic of the *Times* claimed patriotically if
exaggeratedly.[220]

It was not just the elegiac tone of Evelyn Waugh's novel, on which the
series was based, that suggested nostalgia. "In the depth of an English recession, when the country is depressed and gray," producer Derek Granger
openly acknowledged, "we come out with a nostalgic production of a nostalgic novel which looks back romantically at the upper classes—the exotic
life of great elegance and wealth."[221] In the United States, it had, surprisingly,
no bigger fan than Shales, who, try as he might, could not come up with
a better term to characterize it. "The word 'nostalgia' has taken on such a
cloying, superficial meaning through overuse that you wouldn't want to apply
it to *Brideshead,*" he noted, "except that the program does evoke, sensually
and spiritually, the particular mood of the world between wars, and also of a
time when—or so it now seems—people still controlled technology, rather
than the other way around."[222] Implying that this was exactly what had
come to pass, Shales's defense of *Brideshead*'s nostalgia throws an interesting

light on his attack on the 1980s as the "Re Decade" four years later. It highlights both his skeptical attitude toward technology, also palpable in the later text, and his view of the past as slower, more ordered, and more controlled, a view that itself could be called nostalgic.

Even more than *Brideshead*, *Chariots of Fire* profited from its success in the United States. Opening to poor box office results at home, it became a hit only when it was rereleased after winning four Academy Awards, among them Best Picture. When the Falklands War ended soon afterward, the two events became closely linked as signs of Britain's resurgence and the neoliberal zeitgeist. The film had a prominent fan in Reagan, who repeatedly quoted it to illustrate his message of individualism, self-reliance, the will to succeed, and freedom.[223] The conservative attempts to co-opt *Chariots* have determined how it has been viewed ever since, much to the chagrin of its director, producer—none other than David Puttnam—and screenwriter, who all stood firmly on the left and thought of their film as antinationalist and antiestablishment.[224]

Like *Chariots, Brideshead* quickly became equated with Thatcherism—one critic called it a "truly Thatcherite text"—and so did the heritage film as a genre: it was "symptomatic of the crisis of identity through which Britain passed during the Thatcher years," "symptomatic of cultural developments in Thatcherite Britain."[225] As in the critique of heritage more generally, in this particular instance, the accusation of nostalgia was also directly linked to Thatcherism and an alleged Thatcherite yearning for past national greatness.

The critique of the heritage film, however, met with more resistance than the heritage critique. In an early response, Alison Light argued that the films should be understood in the context not of Thatcherism but of liberalism.[226] Expanding on her objections, others stressed that many of the films revolved around characters from marginalized groups—mostly women, but also homosexual men, Jews, and social outsiders—and that they therefore could be seen as questioning rather than affirming traditional conservative ideas of gender, sexuality, and class.[227]

Apart from coming out in quick succession and being set in the past, the heritage films were distinct from one another in almost every other respect, so it is reasonable to ask whether they constitute a genre at all—especially as their critics never elucidated how they differed from earlier historical films and period dramas. It is also worth pointing out that roughly a third of the films listed earlier were not even made by British filmmakers or companies at all but by Merchant Ivory Productions, which consisted of American director James Ivory, Indian producer Ismail Merchant, and screenwriter Ruth Prawer Jhabvala, who was of German Jewish descent.[228] Given their multicultural backgrounds, they were unlikely proponents of a glorification of the British nation let alone the empire. Likewise, the audiences attracted to these films were very diverse and, accordingly, understood them in different ways.[229] Just like the films' creators, they were also not primarily British: following in the tradition of *Brideshead* and *Chariots,* many of the later heritage films appealed to the international market, which may explain why there were so many of them: in a disastrous state in the early 1980s, the British film industry tried to capitalize and replicate the success of *Brideshead* and *Chariots*. In a way, then, the critics espoused a much narrower, national view than the films they criticized.

This argument is further substantiated by the fact that the similarly stricken film industries in other European countries behaved in much the same way. Quickly, the term *heritage film* no longer only applied to British films but also to French ones such as *Le retour de Martin Guerre* (1982), *Danton* (1983), *Un amour de Swann* (1984), *Un dimanche à la campagne* (1984), *Jean de Florette* and *Manon des Sources* (1986), *Camille Claudel* (1988), *La gloire de mon père* (1990), and *Tous les matins du monde* (1991).[230] Set in the past and often in the countryside, these films were also seen as nostalgic and as aesthetically and politically conservative, despite coming out under the government of Socialist president François Mitterrand, which subsidized and promoted them.[231] The German film industry, too, adopted the heritage film formula, if somewhat later in the mid-1990s.[232] By then, the heritage film had become a mainstay of European cinema on both national and transnational levels in the form of coproductions.[233] Consequently, their exploitation of history and high culture was less indicative of an infatuation with the past than a strategy to utilize them as unique resources to compete with Hollywood in the present.

The debate about heritage films again expanded the meanings of nostalgia: initially associated with the recent past just within living memory, the term soon came to apply to more remote periods. Moreover, functioning as an aesthetic category, it implied that heritage films were affirmative and conservative in terms of both content and form: a preference for spectacle over narrative, style over substance, popular over highbrow tastes.[234] In fact, the whole debate is reminiscent of Dwight Macdonald's critique of what he called "midcult": midcult, he wrote, "pretends to respect the standards of High Culture while in fact it waters them down and vulgarizes them."[235] Similarly, the heritage film was accused of drawing on highbrow literature and cinematic conventions to please its audience instead of challenging it; in other words, it was seen as peddling kitsch.

Perhaps surprisingly, the popularity of heritage films was also reflected in fashion, where nineteenth-century styles fit in with the overall trend toward more conservative and traditional attire. The fashion magazine *Harpers & Queen,* for instance, promoted the "Brideshead look."[236] Borrowing from the 1950s and 1960s, fashion simultaneously began to cast its net much wider in the 1980s, trawling hitherto unplumbed historical depths, especially when it came to haute couture and subcultures.

"I felt it was time I did something new," Vivienne Westwood told journalists in 1981 on the occasion of her first fashion show.[237] What's more, the whole 1980s "reflected a constant search for novelty."[238] Yet as in preceding decades, the search for novelty often led people back to the past. That is certainly how it was for Westwood, who even went so far as to research historical styles in the V&A's library, proudly claiming to be "the first modern-day designer to exactly copy the cut and construction of historical dress."[239] Having started out in the early 1970s by replicating 1950s clothes, a decade later she burrowed all the way back into the eighteenth century. For Westwood, this was a conscious decision that had little to do with the past and everything to do with the present: "We just spent 10 years re-assimilating the '30s through the '70s," she said. "The '80s will be a technological age for which we need to equip ourselves with a feeling of human warmth from past ages—of culture taken from the time of pirates and Louis XIV."[240] To this era Westwood now turned, bringing back even such unlikely candidates for revival as the corset and the crinoline.[241]

Initially conceived to promote Malcolm McLaren's newest pet project, the band Bow Wow Wow, the "pirate look" soon became a much wider phenomenon. As had become their habit by that point, Westwood and McLaren refurbished and renamed their Chelsea shop to go along with the stylistic shift: made to look like a pirate ship, the World's End—as it was now called—sported a giant clock or rather anticlock: showing thirteen hours, its arms ran counterclockwise. Nothing could have better symbolized postmodern temporality: time was not simply moving backward, it was completely out of joint.

Westwood's newest creative phase came full circle when the V&A commissioned her to make a custom outfit for its permanent collection, thus elevating her historically inspired design into a museum piece.[242]

The pirate look was reminiscent of a wider British subculture called New Romanticism. While it also referred to pop acts such as Bow Wow Wow, Adam and the Ants, and Spandau Ballet, it was mainly a fashion movement that, in response to the coldness of punk, emphasized warmth, sentimentality, and emotion, taking its cue, obviously, from Romanticism.[243] "The New Romantic look . . . is jolly, extravagant, and must be lighthearted relief for the jeans-and-sweatshirt generation who have had precious little chance to dress up," *Times* fashion columnist Suzy Menkes explained.[244] Compared with punk's tendency toward uniformity, it was also highly individualistic and elitist.

New Romanticism signaled a new departure in retro. Not so much in that it jumped as far back as the eighteenth century—that had already happened in a more limited way in the 1960s—but in the carefree way it jumbled up the periods. "You spent your day at St. Martin's," remembers design professor Iain R. Webb of his student days at London's premier fashion college, "making an outfit to wear that evening, and if you decided to be a historical character, then that's what you were. And then another time it might be that you dress up as some kind of diagonally-cut, future robotic person; and it was fabulous from that point of view."[245] In the eye of such diversity, it was near impossible to characterize the New Romantics. "Some look like science fiction. Some like extras from a Restoration comedy. Gangster suits. Robin Hood outfits. Big hair. Whitened faces. Many wear perverse combinations that defy journalistic shorthand."[246] Unable to come up with common denominators, journalists settled for lists.

What was true for the New Romantics was true for fashion in the 1980s more generally. A decade where "just about every style since the crinoline" resurfaced eluded easy generalizations.[247] In their stead, more lists appeared: the 1980s saw the revival of "Art Deco from the 1930s, Abstract Expressionism and film noir from the 1940s, commercial kitsch from the 1950s, rock music and countercultural experimentalism from the 1960s," or, in short, revivals of all the styles revived before.[248] But revivalism did not stop there: "Pirates, Buffalo Gals, New Romantics, rockabilly, new psychedelia, Hassidic ringlets, white dreadlocks, bobtails, Victorian fetish wear, zoot suits and Dickensian urchins erupted on to the streets. The 1930s, 1940s, 1950s and even the 1960s were cannibalized, recycled, refracted and sprinkled with Third World and

ethnic references."[249] In short, 1980s revivalism involved many different influences from many different eras coexisting and amalgamating, and that
quicker and quicker, it seemed. The decade was not yet over when historian
Angela McRobbie noted an "accelerating tendency in the 1980s to ransack
history for key items of dress," as well as fashion's penchant for borrowing
and referencing in an "eclectic and haphazard manner."[250]

For McRobbie this trend was neither necessarily negative nor nostalgic.
For her, nostalgia indicated "a desire to recreate the past truthfully," while
the appropriation of past styles in secondhand fashion evinced a "willful an-
archy and an irrepressible optimism."[251] Following McRobbie's differentia-
tion, Westwood's designs might be called nostalgic, insofar as she immersed
herself in the study of past fashions. Yet as Westwood said herself, she was
unconcerned with historical authenticity, making fashion for the present oriented toward present-day sensibilities, and the same could be said of New
Romanticism and other 1980s youth cultures that mixed elements of past
styles without any regard for their origin or context.

Nevertheless, nostalgia became an even more important ingredient of the
pop culture critique in the 1980s. "We are inundated by images from the
past, swamped by the nostalgia that is splattered all over Thatcherite
Britain," exclaimed music critic Jon Savage in a 1983 article titled "The Age
of Plunder." Over the course of his article, his argument shifted, concluding,
"It is a characteristic of our age that there is little . . . of any *real* sense of
history, as THE PRESENT is all that matters."[252] How was it possible for the
present to be swamped by the past and, at the same time, interested only in
itself? Because it drew on the past in a decontextualized and dehistoricized
manner, using only those elements resonating with itself.

Savage was far from the only one to think along these lines. As we have
seen, the critics of postmodernity and heritage came to much the same conclusion. "In the fantasy culture of the 1980s there is no real history, no real
past," Elizabeth Wilson argued in the early 2000s, sounding almost like
Jameson here; "it is replaced by an instant, magical nostalgia, a strangely un-
motivated appropriation of the past."[253] Critics lamented the loss of a "real
past," without ever specifying what this was supposed to mean: How could
the past, which, by virtue of being past, had no ontological existence, be
"real," and how could anyone access this supposedly "real past"? In any case,
nostalgia was antithetical to it, denoting both the past as "fantasy"—that is,
distortion—and a decline of the sense of history. In the pop culture critique

of the 1980s—as in postmodern criticism generally—it came to mean the opposite of what it once had meant: it no longer described a yearning for the past but, on the contrary, the inability to perceive the past as different from the present, a present that, much as fashion and film had, increasingly took in all periods of the past.

From Revivalism to Presentism

"What's new in fashion?" asked Suzy Menkes in 1993, advising her readers, "You should be asking, What's old? . . . After a decade that celebrated all that was new, shiny and sleek," she continued, contradicting the self-characterization of the 1980s as a decade of revivals, "old is beautiful."[254] After the 1950s revival in the 1970s and the more limited 1960s revival in the 1980s, pop culture critics did not have to be clairvoyant to expect one of the 1970s in the 1990s. "It's 1988—and the 1970s are back!" satirist Tony Hendra duly obliged the expectation as early as 1988.[255] "The 70's (Stayin' Alive) Won't Die (Stayin' Alive)," the *New York Times* declared in 1991, noticing how those "who actually took part in the decade that taste forgot" rather hoped to forget the decade, whereas "many of today's 70's revivalists were pre-teen-age, if not toddlers."[256] Like preceding revivals, that of the 1970s was mainly driven by young people, proving wrong those who had prophesied that the 1970s were too marked by revivalism to ever be revived themselves.

The influence of the 1970s was especially apparent in fashion, both in haute couture and, perhaps even more so, in streetwear, where it became more conspicuous as the decade went on, especially with the return of such iconic—and subsequently widely ridiculed and reviled—1970s styles as bell-bottom trousers and platform shoes.[257] There was also no dearth of films and television series set in the period, such as *Dazed and Confused* (1993), *Jackie Brown* (1997), *Boogie Nights* (1997), *Velvet Goldmine* (1998), and *That '70s Show* (1998–2006). "Behold! The 1970s! Which happened again in the 1990s," observed Michael Bracewell, looking back on the decade as it ended.[258] For the critic Chuck Klosterman, nostalgia for "the unexperienced seventies" was "central to everything" about the 1990s. But the longing was of a different sort, not like "people of the seventies had longed for the fifties. It was not nostalgia for a time that was more wholesome. It was nostalgia for a time when you could relax and care less."[259] And yet, the prominence of acceleration in the thinking about nostalgia in the 1970s suggests that it was already understood as a yearning for a past retrospectively construed as slower than the present.

In general, both the revival and how it was described followed a well-established formula—with the important difference that the 1980s trend of coexisting and overlapping revivals became even more salient: there was never just one style coming back at any one time. In addition to revivals of more recent styles, the 1950s and 1960s lingered on long after the initial revival had ended or were revived again.[260] The "sixties are swinging once again," observed the *Guardian* in 1995.[261] "London swings! Again!" concurred *Vanity Fair* in 1997, referring explicitly to the by now legendary 1966 *Time* article about "Swinging London." "There's more than a little self-conscious similarity between London's 60s and 90s," it proceeded, "because Britons in their 20s and 30s—the current tastemaking generation—have studied their forebears well."[262] For *Vanity Fair* this was a good thing: the success of bands like Suede, Blur, Oasis, and the Spice Girls—Britpop, in short—fashion designers like Alexander McQueen, and artists like Damien Hirst signaled a return to form and the global importance of British culture not seen since, and for this reason reminiscent of, the "British invasion" of the 1960s. Other commentators, Simon Reynolds for one, saw Britpop and its references to the 1960s as unimaginative and derivative, a backlash against the "multiracial, technology-mediated nature of UK pop culture in the '90s."[263] Positioning himself against this characterization, musicologist Derek Scott argues that "Britpop drew upon a rich diversity of former styles, and not just those from a single decade."[264] Indeed, for most people at the time, Britpop, far from being nostalgic, was full of optimism, a celebration of the here and now and a part of "Cool Britannia."[265]

The 1960s—and the British 1960s in particular—now also exerted a stronger grip on the cinema with remakes of classics of the era such as *The Avengers* (1998), *The Fugitive* (1993), *Mission Impossible* (1996), *The Mod Squad* (1999), and *The Saint* (1997), as well as films poking fun at the pop culture of the era like *Austin Powers: International Man of Mystery* (1997).[266] In addition to the 1970s appearing again in the 1990s, the decade also brought a "triumph for Sixties revivalism," as Bracewell remarks.[267] But that was not all.

"Prepare for a shock," the *Observer* warned its readers in 1995. "Halfway through the Nineties, the Eighties are making a comeback. The fashion and music industries are gearing up for the revival to end all revivals." As fashion journalist Sarah Mower told the paper, "Fashion used to do one decade at a time, but now they're all playing simultaneously."[268] In the same year as the *Vanity Fair* feature on the return of the 1960s, more and more articles started announcing a revival of the 1980s.[269] "Nostalgia for the 80's? . . . Isn't this taking our mania for cultural recycling too far, too fast?" Michiko Kakutani wondered in 2001, reciting a host of examples from fashion and film as proof that, indeed, the 1980s were back.[270] "The 70's are so 90's. The 80's are the thing now," Reynolds noticed the following year. Yet as the 1980s themselves had been so marked by revivalism, retro now reached the level of "second-order recycling."[271]

The vice president of the music channel VH1, which specialized in retro shows about past decades, complained to a *New York Times* reporter how much harder it was to turn members of Generation X nostalgic, because they were more critically minded and knew that "things weren't that great" in the past. In any case, time was running out: as the 1980s revival had lasted for as long as the original decade, something new was called for in the "ever-quickening cycles of cultural nostalgia."[272]

Lisa Armstrong, fashion editor at the *Times,* noticed it too. Misquoting Laver, she reminisced in 2006 about how, in the past, it had taken a "decent 20-year interlude" before an old style could be revived. That was not true anymore, because "here we are, attempting to spin nostalgia from something so recent it's practically still the present tense." She meant the 1990s. "Or maybe it's not nostalgia," she added pensively. If *retro* was becoming an "almost meaningless term," she mused, maybe *nostalgia* was as well.[273] Even more confusingly, only two months later she announced that the "Eighties revival is finally upon us."[274] Alternatingly proclaiming revivals of the 1980s and the 1990s, taken together these articles resemble nothing as much as an increasingly frantic game of table tennis.

The match did not slow down in the next decade. "The 90s are back," announced the *Guardian* in 2016.[275] Which did not keep the *New York Times* from noting the same year how the "formerly irredeemable 1980s . . . are creeping back to the fore," followed shortly by "the return of the '90s."[276] "Why do we keep going back to the 80s?" the *Guardian* asked in 2017.[277] "Help! The '80s are back," exclaimed the *New York Times* in 2018.[278] "Why is pop music suddenly obsessed with the late 90s?" *Vanity Fair* asked the same year.[279] "The whole concept of the Nineties continues to haunt the pop imagination, epitomizing everything our sorry excuse for a decade fails to be,"

Rolling Stone agreed, managing both to criticize the 1990s revival as proof of the present's lack of originality and to celebrate the 1990s as superior to the present in the same sentence.[280] Also in 2018, the *New York Times,* noting how fashion items of the 2000s had found their way back into circulation, wondered whether a "fatal shortening of the cycle" was occurring.[281] Vanessa Friedman, its fashion critic, commented in 2021 on how the 1990s were back, adding, "But then, so are the 1980s, the 1970s and the 1960s." Like Laver eighty years earlier, journalists were looking for rules and patterns in revivalism. "But the truth is," Friedman acknowledged, "the days of a single, overriding trend are long gone."[282]

While journalists, critics, and pundits still talked about "revivals," "retro," and "nostalgia" as a matter of course whenever fashion or pop culture turned to the past, the increasing frenzy with which they proclaimed the arrival of ever-new revivals, alternating from year to year, sometimes even from month to month, between the 1980s and 1990s, and occasionally earlier and later decades, shows how these concepts made less and less sense, let alone explained anything. What began in the 1980s had become inescapable by the 2010s: distinctive trends, and with them distinctive revivals—neatly corresponding to a decade and arriving after a certain number of years—no longer existed, giving way to a multiplicity of coinciding, overlapping, and converging styles and, with them, times. More than ever it became clear that revivalism was a form of—if not identical to—presentism: the past was no longer past; instead it was part of the ever-expanding reservoir of references only someone schooled in the history of fashion and pop culture could pinpoint to any one period—or perhaps not even they anymore, given how elements from various periods mixed with one another.

Conclusion

From the 1960s to the present, nostalgia has been integral to understanding pop culture's penchant for revisiting its own past, both as a way to explain its appeal and to criticize it. Its negative undertones have become stronger over the years. In the 1950s and 1960s, the term still frequently appeared in a neutral or even positive manner, but from the 1970s onward it acquired an overwhelmingly pejorative and polemical connotation to the point where it— as in the notion of the nostalgia wave—came to characterize an entire decade as obsessed with the past. At this time nostalgia appeared mostly as an emotional category: it explained pop culture's backward-looking aspects as a yearning for a past seen as superior to a present experienced as deficient.

Not everyone was convinced. In contrast to the widespread view that nostalgia becomes more pronounced with age, older people for the most part were not the driving force of revivalism. Some even took a decided stand against it, invoking their memories of the period revived to counter what they saw as sentimental glamorization. Others reacted with shock or irritation when they saw the culture of their youth re-created because it revealed how much time had elapsed since then, how much the world had changed, and how much older they had become. While this experience could be called nostalgic in an Ankersmitian sense—as an experience of the distance and difference between past and present—that meaning was not what the critics who used the term had in mind.

Rather, throughout the period, young people were the motor of revivalism, despite, or perhaps because of, the fact that they had no personal recollections of the periods revived. They appropriated the past in ironic, selective, and decontextualized ways, adopting whatever struck a chord with the present, or fulfilled a function in it, and discarding everything else. Which also explains why the critique from people who had lived through the era had so little effect: revivals never were about a period in its entirety but about certain, mostly pop cultural, artifacts.

Finally, those participating in the revivals usually rejected nostalgia as a characterization—not so much because of its negative connotation, but because they saw themselves not as longing for the past but as using it in creative ways. All of which makes the application of the nostalgia label—at least in the sense of yearning—to retro questionable and supports the position of those critics, like Samuel and Guffey, who call for differentiating between retro and nostalgia.

But nostalgia also appeared as an aesthetic as well as an emotional category. This became especially apparent in the discussion of the "nostalgia film" and the "heritage film" in the 1980s. Already in 1964, many phenomena discussed as evidence of nostalgia in the 1960s not coincidentally also appeared in Susan Sontag's essay "Notes on 'Camp,'" such as "Aubrey Beardsley drawings," "women's clothes of the twenties," and Art Nouveau, which she acknowledged as "the most typical and fully developed Camp style."[283] To a large degree the terms *nostalgia, camp,* and *kitsch* were all more or less synonymous, referring to styles—usually of a former era—perceived as imitative, exaggerated, and certainly at the opposite end from high art and avant-gardism. If Adorno defined *kitsch* as "devalued forms and empty ornaments from a formal world that has become remote from its immediate context," he could have been speaking about nostalgia.[284] "Critics mock nostalgia's kitschy absurdities," Lowenthal noted.[285] "Nostalgia is to longing as kitsch is to art," wrote Charles Maier, equating the two concepts.[286] Here nostalgia stood for both a debased aesthetic and a debased form of longing. Often enough the two were treated virtually as one.

Mostly, however, nostalgia appeared as a temporal category, a way to dismiss retro because of its wrong—that is, backward-looking—nature, which violated the modern idea of time. Since the early 1970s, revivalism has been understood in terms of cycles: a certain style—or aspects thereof—returning after a certain number of years, usually between 15 and 20. "Fifteen years on begins the aging process for fine nostalgia," as the *Saturday Review* had it in 1971.[287] That was, of course, a very short time span compared with the 100 to 150 years supposed to elapse between an original style and its revival according to Laver. Many critics, therefore, commented on the "enormous acceleration in the apparatus of revivalism," as Roy Strong wrote in 1974.[288] Fashion critics continued to stress how Laver's law had "radically accelerated . . . from intervals of a century or so to periods of 50 years, and then to ten or fifteen years, and then to five or six," as Jamie Wolf noted in 1980.[289] Nevertheless a fashion historian interviewed by the *New York Times* in 2018, almost twenty years later, made exactly the same point: "Before, the cycle was 20 years, but now it can be five."[290] By contrast, other critics like Reynolds and Armstrong remained convinced that revivals appeared "punctually after roughly 20 years."[291]

Both versions have a point: while there may have been a degree of acceleration, it still takes a good fifteen to twenty years for a full-blown revival to emerge. Overall, however, the disparity shows how questionable all such attempts at generalization are: revivalism is too erratic and too eclectic to be reduced to a set of overall patterns or generic rules. Also, none of these authors discuss when and how a revival ends, usually taking for granted that one recedes as the next arrives. From the beginning, however, revivals of different periods were feeding into one another. In the fashion of the 1970s, references to the 1920s, 1940s, 1950s, and 1960s already coincided with one another. And every new revival contained traces of earlier ones: reviving the 1970s meant also reviving all these earlier styles revived during the 1970s, so that different versions of different periods were present at the same time, one layer on top of or next to the other. Consequently, it is more and more difficult to differentiate between distinctive revivals at all.

Whatever else they may be, the retro cycles contradict the idea of a steady, straightforward, linear pop history. What emerges is a combination of linear, cyclical, and overlapping times: fashion and pop culture move forward by constantly drawing on their pasts. Critics, however, arguing that pop culture recycles its past because it is unable to produce anything new, tend to perceive this as decline. Indeed, there has been no decade since the 1970s that some cultural critic has not declared inferior because of its backward-lookingness. "There won't be anything of the seventies to revive" because they had themselves amounted to nothing but revivalism, declared Kennedy Fraser in 1981.[292] "People think the Eighties have no texture, no style, no tone of their own. They don't. They have the texture and style and tone of all the other decades," Tom Shales wrote similarly in the 1980s, doubting whether they would amount to a decade at all.[293] "What is the signature design style of the 1980s and early '90s?" James Collins asked, answering the question himself with: "Retro."[294] "It could be said that we haven't had any new popular culture in the 1990s," Michael Bracewell suggested in 2003, "we've simply had the recent past again."[295] Enter Reynolds: "Instead of being about itself, the 2000s has been about every other previous decade happening again all at once."[296]

Taken together, these voices suggest that fashion and pop culture have been in continuous decline since the 1970s, with every new decade worse—in the sense of more backward-looking—than the preceding one. If not all critics might go as far as that, Reynolds certainly does. To him, the 1960s mark the unmatched high point in the history of popular culture—not only due to their innovatory impact but also because of the "absence of revivalism and nostalgia." In his history of retro, the 1960s are the peak from which things went down continuously and inexorably. Yet not only does this narrative misrepresent later decades, it also misrepresents the 1960s, which, as we have seen, instead of being devoid of revivalism, could be said to have pioneered it. By turning the 1960s into a golden age, Reynolds replicates exactly the sort of nostalgic narrative he criticizes, even recycling earlier tropes, such as Shales's "Re Decade," which could be said to render his critique almost as derivative as what he is accusing retro of.[297]

Arguing from the perspective of the modern understanding of time as homogeneous and linear, pop critics like Reynolds, Mark Fisher, and Owen

Hatherley are unable to account for the return of the past and reject what they see as the "simultaneity of pop time," in which past and present blur to the extent that they become indistinguishable.[298] Based on their observation of pop culture, they arrive more or less at the same conclusion as the critics of heritage, postmodernity, and presentism, which, of course, were also at least partly informed by examples from pop culture. In fact, *presentism* might have been a better term, as *nostalgia* here largely lost its association of yearning and came to signify the presence of the past—or rather of various pasts—in the present and the concomitant inability to view the past as distinct from it. A more accurate term might again be *pluritemporality* because it captures the multiplicity of different times available and intersecting in any given present.

The unanimous rejection of retro raises the question whether it is at all possible to understand it as something other than nostalgia and decline: Is no one standing up for it? In fact, most people could be said to do so simply by engaging in retro phenomena and practices as both producers and consumers of the kind of fashion, films, and music that critics characterize as nostalgic. Outspoken advocates of retro, however, are harder to find. In the 1980s and early 1990s, Angela McRobbie defended the "second-hand, do-it-yourself plundering of culture" against the condescending postmodernist critique as potentially subversive.[299] In his article "The Ecstasy of Influence" from 2007, the American writer Jonathan Lethem does not mention retro explicitly but applauds "appropriation, mimicry, quotation, allusion, and sublimated collaboration" as the "sine qua non of the creative act, cutting across all forms and genres in the realm of cultural production."[300] Lethem does not distinguish between high art and pop culture, taking it as a given that both thrive on conscious and unconscious, explicit and implicit borrowings. In doing so, he reveals the hidden bias of the retro critique, which blames pop culture for the same thing usually venerated in high culture: whereas the one, in borrowing from the past, is revered for its intertextuality, the other is chided for its nostalgia. Lethem's punch line: his entire text is a self-conscious collage consisting of quotations from many other texts.

And yet it manages to say something original, whereas the retro critique, perpetually presenting nostalgia as a new phenomenon, is going around in circles. "My target," Lethem clarifies in an afterword he added later, "was the reactionary backlash at what Internet and sampling culture happened to make (even more) obvious: the eternal intertextuality of cultural participation—of reading, writing, making things from other things."[301] In this reading, retro and revivalism are nothing new but merely new manifestations of much older—eternal, as he says—cultural practices that, instead of undermining creativity, enable it. Culture never starts completely from scratch; every new generation continues to weave a cloth started in time immemorial.

Where does this leave the history of pop? Is there a way to write it as a history that accounts for its pluritemporality? A straightforward, linear, chronological history clearly cannot. Instead, it might be helpful to think of other visual metaphors than the arrow or the timeline. In the 1970s, artists like Pete Frame in Britain and Bruce Burton in the United States, for instance, started to visualize the developments of bands and genres in rock music through family trees. Unlike the timeline, the tree allows for the coexistence and simultaneity of many different developments.

The image of the tree evokes rhizomes, subterranean plant stems that emanate in all directions without a clearly definable beginning, middle, or end. At about the same time Frame and Burton began to draw their trees, postmodern thinkers Gilles Deleuze and Félix Guattari used the rhizome as a metaphor for a postmodern, nonhierarchical organization of knowledge.[302] While they thought of the rhizome in spatial rather than temporal terms, it might be useful to adopt their metaphor for temporal processes.[303] This might allow us to fashion narratives that account for both linearity *and* simultaneity, that show the artificiality of chronology by disrupting it and by drawing attention to coinciding, competing, and intersecting developments, as this chapter has, in a limited way, tried to do. Such a history would be able to explain retro and revivalism not as aberrations, as a symptom or result of nostalgia and a sign of cultural decline, but as essential to popular culture.

Four

Reliving

The History Boom

The writing seemed to be on the wall for history in the 1960s. While J. H. Plumb had already declared the past dead in 1966, the American historian C. Vann Woodward went a step further. In an overt reply to Plumb, he titled his presidential address at the annual meeting of the American Historical Association in 1969, "The Future of the Past." Did it have one? Judging by its present, Woodward was not very optimistic. Whether in the estimation of students, the public, or other disciplines, history was in steep decline. "It is not inconceivable that our civilization may, one day," he quoted the French historian Marc Bloch, "turn away from history, and historians would do well to reflect upon this possibility."[1] This day, Woodward believed, might be imminent. One year later, Reinhart Koselleck, addressing the American Historical Association's German equivalent, the German Historikertag, was

equally pessimistic, perceiving "our discipline as such to be called into question," a sentiment many leading West German historians shared at the time.[2]

From today's perspective, such prophecies of doom can seem almost
comical—we know how the story continued. And yet, if the critics of presentism are right and we have indeed entered a presentist age, we might be
closer to the moment Bloch foresaw than ever before—certainly closer than
the 1960s. Because as such gloomy assessments continued to come out, things
began to change: history was about to become more popular than it had ever
been—or at least this was how many contemporary observers saw it in the
context of the "nostalgia wave." In the late 1970s Hermann Lübbe mocked
those historians who, despite all evidence to the contrary, still lamented the
lack of popular appreciation for their discipline—only to note a few years later
that these laments had finally ceased.[3]

If Lübbe expected historians to be pleased with this broader reception,
he would soon be disappointed. As the public's interest in history grew, they
now began to worry about the exact opposite: that there was too much past,
that it was swallowing up the present, diverting attention from the future,
while itself being transformed into the "good old days," an object of nostalgia.
As we saw in Chapter 1, this was, in a nutshell, how many historians—and the
heritage critics first and foremost—understood and explained popular engagement with the past or what they called "heritage."

Where was their evidence? Where was it not! "The past is everywhere,"
David Lowenthal's book began, and though he and his fellow heritage critics—
as well as their most formidable opponent, Raphael Samuel—did indeed look
nearly everywhere, there were four practices that all of them zeroed in on.[4]
First, there was historic preservation, which had transformed from a niche,
elitist pursuit into a popular cause. Second, there was the enormous growth
in the number of museums, which prompted Robert Hewison to investigate
what he termed, polemically, the "heritage industry." Slightly less prominent
but still of concern were the third and fourth, the "vogue for historical
re-enactments" and the "ancestor-hunters," Lowenthal's label for people conducting family history research.[5] All four practices also cropped up in Michael
Kammen's book about heritage—and nostalgia—in the United States.[6]

The critique established in the 1980s had a long-reaching effect: the association of these practices with nostalgia has never really gone entirely away.
Quoting Lowenthal, Daniel T. Rodgers argues in *Age of Fracture* that nostalgia

was indeed "everywhere" in the last quarter of the twentieth century. "One saw it across the fractured terrains of civil society in the growing interest in local history museums and heritage sites," he writes. "One saw it in the new platoons of adult men, garbed in quaint clothing and bearing period arms, devoting their off-work hours to reenactments of the Revolutionary and Civil War battles. One saw it in the rage for family histories and growing lines at the genealogical libraries."[7] Again, these practices serve as evidence of a growing sense of nostalgia, while conversely nostalgia explains the popularity of these practices. The persistence of this explanation makes it even more important to scrutinize it: What did—and, indeed, does—nostalgia mean for the heritage critics and historians more generally? And can it really explain the rise of what is more neutrally labeled—in a term that also emerged in the 1970s—public history or the "history boom"?[8]

These questions are at the heart of this chapter. While Chapter 1 discussed the heritage critique and its understanding of nostalgia on a more abstract and general level, this chapter will take a closer look at the examples on which it relied. Using the four practices singled out both at the time and by later historians—historic preservation, the museum boom, historical reenactments, and family history—as case studies, it examines how the concept figured in these debates. As in the case of politics and pop culture, *nostalgia* here took on different, though often overlapping, connotations. Each case study will concentrate on one predominant meaning.

In the critique of historic preservation, for instance, nostalgia suggested that conservationists viewed the past as superior to the present. The new types of museums came under criticism for allegedly turning the past into a form of entertainment by drawing on performative elements that allowed for more immersive, interactive, and experiential engagements. Because these elements appealed to emotions and because *nostalgia* had an emotional connotation, the term also acted as code for emotions in general. This applies equally to historical reenactments, which had pioneered the "reenactive engagement" that museums began to adopt in the 1970s.[9] But discussions of nostalgia in reenactments revolved also around the experience of time, or what critics—but also many participants, as we will see—saw as an element of escapism. All these elements were reason for criticism, as was the involvement of amateurs—most apparent in the rejection of popular genealogy. Here *nostalgia* usually implied escaping the present as well as distorting the past.

As in the preceding chapters, *nostalgia,* therefore, carried mostly pejorative connotations when it came to popular history. To reach beyond the perspective of the critics and paint a fuller picture, the chapter also considers the view of the practitioners by asking whether and how they used the term *nostalgia,* as well as what other motivations they cited for engaging with the past. For practical reasons, it relies mainly on examples from Britain, though it compares them with developments in other European countries and the United States to highlight their transnational character.

The Heroic Period of Conservation

Ever since 2007, travelers arriving on a Eurostar train at St. Pancras International Station in London may have wondered about the slightly curious statue located on the concourse: a portly, elderly man in a three-piece suit and a mac, clutching a bag in his left hand, his right securing his hat on his tilted-back head, as he gazes up into the wrought-iron and glass roof of the station (see Figure 4.1). The statue is of the English poet laureate John Betjeman, but the reason it stands there is not his poetry—or at least, not primarily. Instead, it has been given this place of honor because, without Betjeman and his fellow conservationists, St. Pancras Station and Hotel might no longer be standing there themselves, at least not in their original form. After Euston Station, a ten minutes' walk up the road, had been demolished in 1962, St. Pancras was next on the list.[10] This was a common enough story at the time. A year after Euston Station, Pennsylvania Station in New York was demolished.[11] By that time, Berlin had already razed Anhalter Bahnhof, the grandest of its old station buildings, while in Paris the Gare d'Orsay, also earmarked for destruction, was saved just in the nick of time by its transformation into the Musée d'Orsay.

The postwar era was not a good time for old buildings—particularly when they had originated in the nineteenth century. As some outstanding buildings as well as many lesser-known ones were reduced to rubble and new ones rose in their stead, people increasingly began to have second thoughts. Gradually, the conservation movement, transforming from a small, elitist cause into a popular movement, became more and more successful in saving endangered buildings. Retrospectively, the years between the mid-1960s and

Figure 4.1   Conservator conserved: Statue of poet and preservationist John Betjeman
at St. Pancras Station in London. Backyard Productions / Alamy

the mid- to late 1970s came to be called the "heroic period of conservation" or "the preservation decade."[12]

Not everyone welcomed this development. "Nostalgia when organised can be positively harmful, and the most obvious example of this is the conservation movement," complained the historian Douglas Johnson in 1978.[13] At the same time that critics of conservation liked to accuse it of a nostalgic attitude toward the past, intellectuals writing about the nostalgia wave often drew on it as an example: to them its success was one of the most conspicuous signs of a new obsession with the past. This makes historic preservation a useful case study for examining both the new engagement with the past and the critique of it as nostalgic. To understand why it was perceived as nostalgic and what nostalgia meant in this regard, this section will initially examine the postwar situation more closely, as well as the shift from urban renewal to conservation, before analyzing the rhetoric and motivations of the conservationists and their critics.

The postwar era was a boom time for modern architects and urban planners. The destruction caused by the wartime bombings allowed for hitherto unimaginable interventions into the urban fabric. The "blitz has been a planners' windfall" as the British scientist and first director of UNESCO, Julian Huxley, observed.[14] Even without this tailwind, a growing urban population and the increasing car traffic called for new approaches to urban planning. American cities, free of wartime destruction, launched massive building programs, tearing down whole districts to make way for new highways, bridges, and housing to the extent that, despite all their differences, the urban renewal programs on both sides of the Atlantic looked "remarkably similar."[15]

Alongside the imperative to accommodate the new came a distinct dislike of the old. Turning against tradition, and the Victorians in particular, modern architects had set out since the interwar period to create, in the words of the German-born British architectural historian Nikolaus Pevsner, "a new style of architecture entirely independent of the past."[16] Bauhaus founder Walter Gropius even went so far as to strike architectural history from the curriculum altogether when he became a professor at Harvard.[17] After the war, architects started to strike down the built architectural history too. This would not have been possible without the consent of large parts of the public, as well as politicians such as Prime Minister Harold Wilson, who, in 1967, celebrated Britain's urban renewal program: "All over the country the grime, muddle and decay of our Victorian heritage is being replaced and the quality of urban life uplifted."[18]

If one type of building was considered especially grimy and decaying and, therefore, under heightened threat of demolition, it was the railway station. As commuters increasingly took to the roads and long-distance travelers to the air, railway companies recorded mounting losses. Britain, the nation that had pioneered the railways, was a case in point. When the engineer Richard Beeching became chairman of British Rail in 1961, he pulled the emergency brake. In a plan later to become infamous as the "Beeching Axe," he recommended closing five thousand miles of track, shuttering 2,359 local stations, and getting rid of 160,000 jobs; only some profitable routes were to be modernized.[19]

To signal the dawn of this new railway age, London's Euston Station, together with the bombastic Doric arch serving as its entrance (see Figure 4.2), was to be replaced with a modern building. No one less than Betjeman himself had advocated tearing down the station in the 1930s, adding, "and if the arch must be demolished, then that is that too."[20] Thirty years on and with a newfound appreciation of Victorian architecture, his attitude had changed. Now he defended the Euston Arch as an expression of the "courage and swagger of a time which was convinced of a glorious future."[21] In the future of the 1960s, however, steam no longer symbolized progress but rather, if anything, its opposite: the old times of industrial grime and squalor, which people like Wilson wanted to leave behind. In contrast, Betjeman, the "poet of nostalgia," with his "nostalgia . . . for the Victorian past" and his "nostalgia for steam engines," appeared eccentric, anachronistic, or, in short, nostalgic.[22]

Bound together by an interest in preservation—as well as a heartfelt mutual loathing—Betjeman and Pevsner had both been founding members of the Victorian Society in 1958, the latest of Britain's conservation societies. Together they campaigned on behalf of the Euston Arch by writing newspaper articles and lobbying politicians.[23] When this showed little impact, a group of seventy-five young architects and students staged a protest at the station.[24] A few days later, Prime Minister Harold Macmillan met with a delegation of conservationists, including Betjeman and Pevsner, but ultimately decided not to intervene because of both the costs and the inevitable delay of the building project.[25] In November 1961 the demolition crew set to work.

The conservation movement had lost an important battle, but the war over the future of Victorian architecture had only just begun. The new station at Euston had hardly been finished when British Rail announced that St. Pancras

Figure 4.2 Arch enemies: Like the Euston Arch, seen here before its demolition in 1962, many nineteenth-century buildings were despised by the modernist zeitgeist. Arcaid Images/Alamy

Station was also under review. To its dismay, it found that conservationists had not dragged their feet in the meantime: following their defeat, they tried to get as many stations listed—that is, given protected status—as possible, with St. Pancras on top of the list. Their endeavors bore fruit in 1967 when it was declared a Grade I building, the highest category.[26] This made its demolition not impossible, but much harder. Tired of fighting, British Rail decided to simply let the building rot away. It was not until 2007 that the station reopened as a Eurostar terminal—with the bronzed Betjeman proudly standing on its concourse.[27]

Figure 4.3   The best-dressed picket line: AGBANY protest against the demolition of Pennsylvania
Station in 1962. Courtesy of David L. Hirsch

In July 1961, the very same month the British government announced that
not only Euston Station but also its arch were to be demolished, Pennsylvania
Railroad revealed that New York's Pennsylvania Station would be razed to
street level to make way for a new Madison Square Garden.[28] As in London,
resistance came mainly from civic societies such as the Municipal Art Society
of New York and the National Trust for Historic Preservation, and soon from
young architects as well.[29] Founding the Action Group for Better Architecture in New York (AGBANY), they staged protests in front of Penn Station in
1962, wielding placards reading, "Save Face—Keep Penn in Place," "Don't
Amputate—Renovate," and "Don't Demolish It! Polish It!" (see Figure 4.3)[30]
Local papers called it "the best-dressed picket line in New York history."[31]
Ultimately, however, the protestors had to concede defeat. "Pennsylvania Station succumbed to progress at the age of fifty-six," architectural critic and
conservation advocate Ada Louise Huxtable wrote in her obituary of Penn
Station in the *New York Times*.[32]

When Grand Central Terminal was put under review a few years later, however, the ground was well prepared. Thanks to the lobbying of conservationists, New York had passed the Landmarks Preservation Law in 1965 to
safeguard other buildings.[33] The railway company fought the decision through

the courts until, in 1978, the US Supreme Court decided to uphold it.[34] The ruling itself became something of a landmark, not only for New York but for the United States in general: "Since then, the preservation ethic has dominated in American cities."[35]

The destruction of the Euston Arch and Penn Station, and the survival of St. Pancras and Grand Central, took on near-mythical proportions retrospectively as turning—if not starting—points of the modern conservation movement.[36] Something of an exaggeration, this view is not entirely incorrect. By the end of the 1960s, conservation was in a much better position than at the beginning of the decade. In 1966 President Lyndon B. Johnson signed into law the National Historic Preservation Act, creating the National Register of Historic Places, the list of National Historic Landmarks, and the State Historic Preservation Offices.[37] In Britain, the Civic Amenities Act of 1967 and the Town and Country Planning Act of 1968 extended both the meaning and the powers of conservation.[38]

These developments were not unrelated. Organizations in the United States, believing that historic preservation in their country was "less orderly and less neatly defined than in Europe," looked abroad for models and advice.[39] The American National Trust was modeled on the British one, and in 1966 the New York conservationist Margot Gayle, after meeting Pevsner in London, founded an American Victorian Society.[40] The same year, the Special Committee on Historic Preservation of the United States Conference of Mayors visited eight European countries to study their preservation efforts, concluding in its report that "we have much to learn from European experience."[41] Perhaps the destruction of nineteenth-century buildings escaped their attention because, from today's point of view, the parallels seem far more striking than the differences.

Having saved St. Pancras and Grand Central and raised public awareness, with new conservation societies being founded and new laws coming into force, the conservation movement was able to face the 1970s with confidence. If the 1960s saw the transition from campaigns by eminent individuals and learned societies to direct action, the 1970s brought full-blown protests with demonstrators who were neither experts nor architects but concerned citizens. Not just in big cities, across the country people got together, forming protest groups and conservation societies to save buildings threatened with demolition. The Civic Trust, founded in 1957 as an umbrella organization for local conservation societies in Britain, reported in 1977 that its membership had surpassed 300,000.[42] And this was nothing in comparison to the National Trust for Places of Historic Interest or Natural Beauty, founded in 1895, whose membership grew by leaps and bounds from just 7,850 in 1945 to 157,000 in 1965, a quarter of a million in 1970, half a million in 1975, and 2 million in 1981.[43] Taken together, these examples bear out conservation's development into a "populist movement."[44]

This development was not limited to Britain. In Germany, too, conservation was frequently referred to as a "popular movement" in the late 1970s.[45] In the United States, *Progressive Architecture* proclaimed a "nationwide passion for preservation," which was "no longer seen, as it once was, as indulgence of nostalgia for the past," confirming that it had been up till that point.[46] An article in *Historic Preservation,* the magazine of the American National Trust, argued emphatically that preservationists, far from "making futile, reactionary gestures," represented the "cutting edge of a true cultural revolution."[47] Such self-confidence would have been hard to find a decade before.

A peak moment in Europe was the 1975 European Architectural Heritage Year (EAHY). An initiative of the Council of Europe, it acknowledged how important—and, indeed, how popular—an issue conservation had become, further promoting it through exhibitions and films and, most importantly, by making new public funds available.[48] Coming hardly eight years after Wilson had called for doing away with the built remains of the Victorian age, it was a powerful signal that politicians now favored conservation over renewal—or, at the very least, took it more seriously. It also made *heritage* a household term in Britain.[49]

The reasons for conservation's transformation into a popular movement were manifold. For one, there was a growing dissatisfaction with modern architecture and urban planning. As early as 1955, the British architectural critic Ian Nairn had bemoaned "the annihilation of the site, the steamrollering of all individuality of place to one uniform and mediocre pattern."[50] None other than the urbanist Jane Jacobs picked up on Nairn's critique, as it chimed with her own thinking. In *The Death and Life of Great American Cities* (1961), perhaps the most influential book about the city in the second half of the twentieth century, she also tore into the "monotony, sterility and vulgarity" of modern architecture and planning.[51] It sent her back to rediscover the chaotic, organically grown city of the past, but to Jacobs wallowing in "nostalgic memories" was simply a "waste of time"—which, however, did not keep her critics from accusing her of doing just that.[52]

What, in 1961, sounded heretical had become mainstream by the 1970s. In 1968, hardly a year after Wilson's attack on Victorian architecture, the collapse of Ronan Point, a twenty-two-story tower block in East London, following a gas explosion, spelled the end of high-rise developments in Britain.[53] Everywhere the "grandiose urban renewal schemes of the 1950s were beginning to emerge as conspicuous failures," prompting architects to "take a second look at what we already had," as *Progressive Architecture* noted in 1976.[54] "Modern architecture is dead," declared *Der Spiegel* a year later, also observing a yearning for old city centers.[55]

In parallel with these critical assessments of urban renewal, a stream of books evaluating what had vanished began to appear, such as *Lost New York* (1964), by architect and architectural critic Nathan Silver, incidentally a neighbor of Jacobs's, and *Lost London* (1971), by Hermione Hobhouse.[56] Other authors chose more violent metaphors, like the German writer and publisher Wolf Jobst Siedler with *Die gemordete Stadt* (1961), literally "the murdered city"; Colin Amery and Dan Cruickshank with *The Rape of Britain* (1975); and Louis Chevalier with *L'assassinat de Paris* (1977), to name just a few better-known examples of the genre.[57]

These books testify to the ongoing reevaluation of Victorian architecture. Indeed, architecture was subject to similar changes in taste as fashion and design. Although most preservationists claimed to want to save buildings because of their historical importance, aesthetics certainly played a part in the process. As the star of modern architecture burned itself out, that of the Victorian age gradually began to shine brighter again. "By comparison with our post-war monsters, Victorian and even Edwardian buildings now impress us by their gusto," observed a British critic in 1972.[58] In fact, this process had been going on since the late 1950s, with the Victorian Society a pioneer. As early as 1966, the architectural correspondent of the *Times* had noted how "the until recently, widely held notion that everything Victorian is to be despised" was on the wane.[59] By the 1970s it was all but gone.

Consequently, the transformation of historic preservation from an elitist into a popular concern was driven by three parallel and intersecting developments: First, people felt dissatisfied and disillusioned with modernist architecture, which often was unable to deliver on its ambitious promises—or rather whose promises had turned sour. Second, people realized that the more organically grown cities and traditional architecture that modernist renewal programs wanted to do away with had their advantages. And third, greater historical distance led people to recognize as beautiful what previously seemed hideous to them. As the call for historic preservation grew louder, so did its critics, not a few of whom accused it, like Douglas Johnson, of nostalgia.

Hardly anyone discussed the relationship between conservation and nostalgia more extensively than the German art historian and Hessian state conservator Reinhard Bentmann. An outspoken critic of the popular interest in historic preservation, he understood it in the context of a nostalgia wave indicative of a society that longed to regress into the "womb of history."[60] Across Germany, he complained, agencies responsible for the protection of historic buildings—like the one he presided over—were flooded with petitions to save and preserve a jumble of old buildings and objects that he and his colleagues obviously did not deem worthy of preservation. Already, he continued, people were discussing mass-produced everyday items of the twentieth century with as much connoisseurship as experts did medieval objets d'art. And who could blame them, really, he concluded: living as they did in "ahistorical concrete fortresses of today's satellite cities or the poisonous monotony of sterile suburbs," no wonder they craved the warmth and intimacy of the historical city or village.[61]

What may sound like a critique of modernist architecture was not. Rather, Bentmann blamed provincialism, profiteering, petty bourgeoisie tastes, and Americanism for the failure of modern architecture, which, to him, still offered the best solutions in terms of housing and planning. As a result of its debasement by outside forces, modernist architecture now stood for an inhospitable and calamitous world, and historic architecture, in contrast, for an idyllic one, one image just as false as the other. In passing, Bentmann also criticized the EAHY, which, he claimed, had both responded to and ennobled the nostalgia wave.[62] Dieter Baacke and Lübbe, too, both mentioned conservation and the EAHY as evidence for a growing sense of nostalgia.[63]

In effect, then, Bentmann used nostalgia to explain the popular interest in the past—here the architectural past—and simultaneously to dismiss it. For Bentmann, as for other critics, the recourse to the past was mistaken, constituting a flight from the present. While he did not deny that there were problems, the way to solve them was through better modern architecture, not through preserving that of the past. Insofar as his attack on nostalgia and his defense of modern architecture were two sides of the same coin, Bentmann's article throws a spotlight on the critique more generally. It also shows that conservationism and modernism did not necessarily cancel each other out.

The same kind of logic underlay the critique of conservation in Britain, which could be even more outspoken and polemical at times. "They wish to stop things happening," Johnson wrote about conservationists; "they wish to prevent old buildings from being pulled down and new buildings from being put up. And all this, because they fear the future, they dislike the present, and they think things were better in the past."[64] In short, because they idealized the past, nostalgic conservationists were unable or unwilling to shape the present and the future or were simply antimodernist and anachronistic.

By the mid-1980s, this view had become mainstream among British historians. David Cannadine saw the public mood of the country as "nostalgic and escapist, disenchanted with the contemporary scene, preferring conservation to development, the country to the town, and the past to the present."[65] "Preservation has deepened our knowledge of the past but dampened creative use of it," Lowenthal wrote, also noting that it had developed into a "ubiquitous crusade."[66] For Hewison, the "nostalgic impulse" constituted "an important part of the conservationist frame of mind."[67] Even Raphael Samuel, normally the voice of moderation, lost his patience when it came to the "preservation mania," chiding it for trading on "regressive fantasies."[68]

But did conservationists really wish to stop all old buildings from being pulled down and new buildings from being put up? What did they cite as their motivations? And what, if anything, did nostalgia mean to them? Unsurprisingly, conservationists tended to avoid the term. If they used it all, then it was usually to defend themselves against the charge. A rare exception was Silver, whose book *Lost New York* could be said to evoke the specter of nostalgia in its very title. Wondering to himself in the introduction why someone would defend an old building, he concluded, "All we have to account for and describe it is that unsatisfactory word 'nostalgia.'" Feeling that the term "disparaged" what it described, he nevertheless felt thrown back to it and was unwilling to surrender it because it contained a "most important and useful component" (though he did not explain which that was).[69]

Mostly, however, when conservationists mentioned nostalgia, it was only to reject it. When EAHY chairman Duncan Sandys, a conservative British politician who had founded the Civic Trust and been instrumental in steering the 1967 Civic Amenities Act through Parliament, explained why it was important to protect old buildings, he thought it necessary to clarify: "It is certainly not just a love of old stones. Nor is it simply a nostalgic attachment to the past."[70] Likewise, many German newspaper articles on the EAHY brought up nostalgia only to refute it.[71]

Usually, conservation advocates preferred to speak about the future. Choosing "A future for our past" as its motto, the EAHY argued for the importance of safeguarding built heritage for generations to come, as most conservationists did generally.[72] For Hobhouse the "most important reason for retaining older buildings is not the antiquarian one but the improvement of the lives of present and future citizens."[73] An article in *Historic Preservation* called conservationists "citizens of the future, not the past."[74] The insistence on the future-looking character of conservation shows how aware conservationists were of being seen as antiquarian and nostalgic, while in their own eyes their advocacy for preservation was not driven by an opposition to new buildings or modern architecture but instead by a desire to save the remains of the past for the future.

Even when it comes to someone as associated with nostalgia as Betjeman, things were more complicated. As we have seen, when he was a young man, he did not shy away from proposing the razing of Euston Station and its arch. "Much Victorian architecture is really bad and shoddy," he still acknowledged once he had come to value it, saying of the Euston Arch, "If it were just *old*, I would not be so anxious to plead for its preservation."[75] Instead, it was its architectural as well as its symbolic importance that compelled him. Decades before the heritage critics, Betjeman had already polemicized against what he called the "antiquarian prejudice": the belief that whatever is older is better.[76] His book on the topic has even been called "one of the earliest attacks on what we would call the 'heritage industry.'"[77]

Pevsner also sounded like a heritage critic when he bemoaned "the return of historicism" in the late 1960s: an "alarming recent phenomenon" that threatened "to choke original action and replace it by action which is inspired by period precedent."[78] Before he became one of the most prominent spokespeople for conservationism as chairman of the Victorian Society, Pevsner had been known mostly as a champion of modernism. To him this was not at all contradictory, because he traced back the modernist movement to, mostly British, pioneers of the nineteenth century such as William Morris.[79] In their own view, Pevsner and Betjeman wanted to preserve buildings like the Euston Arch and St. Pancras not for sentimental reasons but because of their historical significance.

Nostalgia also did not come up when the young architects campaigning for the survival of Penn Station were interviewed decades later as part of the New York Preservation Archive Project. The architect Diana Goldstein, who started AGBANY, remembered feeling that her "profession owed it to their own history" to stand up for Penn Station because "if they didn't do something about it, what was the future for all other great buildings."[80] "We thought it was very important to maintain the counterpoint of history, expressed so beautifully at Penn Station between the steel and glass train shed, which was a very modern thing," her colleague Norval White concurred.[81] In fighting for Penn, AGBANY also fought the idea that "preservation was a thing for old people yearning for the past," architect Peter Samton recalled.[82] Hence, their partisanship for Penn Station was also taking a stand against the association of preservation with nostalgia. And looking back, they felt they had succeeded in this, despite losing their first big battle. Their campaign marked, according to AGBANY member Herbert Oppenheimer, the "beginning of the recognition that old buildings have a place in the modern city."[83] For the members of AGBANY, then, there was no conflict between urban modernism and conservation. The same was true for others participating in their protests such as Jane Jacobs; Philip Johnson, one of the United States' foremost modernist architects; and the architectural critic Aline Saarinen.[84]

Not only were railway stations, despite seeming anachronistic by the 1960s, part of modernism's heritage, conservation itself was a modern phenomenon: originating in the nineteenth century as a reaction to the destruction wrought on the historical fabric by urbanization and industrialization, it reappeared as a reaction to postwar urban renewal.[85] Conservationists' "concepts of history and cultural value and their methods of pursuing their goals" were "intrinsically modern."[86]

The idea at the heart of the critique of conservation as nostalgic was that conservation and modernity constituted irreconcilable opposites. This collapsed when the cut-off date for buildings to be preserved from demolition moved yet again to include modern architecture itself in the late 1970s. In 1979 a group of British enthusiasts of interwar modernism, following the example of the Victorian Society, found the Thirties Society, which gradually embraced postwar modernism as well, rechristening itself the Twentieth Century Society in 1992.[87] As modernist buildings of the postwar era began to be listed, it looked as if conservation had had the last laugh over the modernist program of renewal. In truth, however, the two ideals coexisted side by side—and continued to.

The same year that the Thirties Society was formed, British Rail decided to raze Broad Street Station in the north of the City of London. Conservationists managed to delay but not prevent the inevitable. In the summer of 1985, the bulldozers rolled in. For the benefit of the TV cameras, one of them was operated by none other than Prime Minister Margaret Thatcher herself. Speaking to the press afterward, she celebrated the postmodernist Broadgate office and shopping complex meant to replace the station as an "architectural monument to the future built during the technological revolution"—an allusion to the Industrial Revolution whose remains now had to make way for the next revolution.[88] Overseeing the destruction work from the top of a bulldozer did not keep Thatcher, ironically, from using the occasion to bemoan that "we live in an era of conservation."[89]

This episode is highly revealing: while Thatcher acknowledged the power of conservation, the destruction of Broad Street Station nevertheless clearly demonstrated its limits. It also demonstrated that the contradiction between conservation and modernism and the idea that the latter hampered the former persisted well into the 1980s and beyond. And, finally, it casts an interesting light on the debate about how Thatcher used the past: publicly embracing the values of the Victorians, she obviously did not care much for their built heritage. Designed to show her as a woman of action who mercilessly bulldozed through all resistance—the Miners' Strike three months earlier, now that of the conservationists—this image of Thatcher rebuts those who sought to portray her as nostalgic and backward-looking and who saw heritage as a Thatcherite project. As her comment shows, she was nothing if not a heritage critic.

It also sheds some light on the politics of conservation—namely, that "Conservatives are by no means always conservationists."[90] Thatcher certainly was not, and neither was Ronald Reagan, whose administration abolished the Heritage Conservation and Recreation Service and cut back on funds for preservation schemes.[91] Nor were liberal or left-wing politicians necessarily against conservation. Britain's first conservation association, the Society for the Protection of Ancient Buildings, had been cofounded by the Socialist William Morris, while in the United States the conservation movement emerged during and as part of the Progressive Era.[92] Conservation, then, cannot be aligned with one political camp: it had defenders and detractors on both sides of the aisle.

Behind the clashes over whether a certain building was to be demolished or to be preserved, and historic preservation more generally, stood a bigger and more abstract conflict about the place of the past in the present and, ultimately, the understanding of time. Looking at the use of nostalgia in this debate not only illuminates the meanings of the term but also brings this conflict out into the open. In the context of historic preservation, nostalgia primarily signified a backward-looking attitude. Like the critics of nostalgia, those equating conservation with nostalgia operated within a modernist understanding of time that did not allow for alternatives or nuances: for most of them, conservationists had opted against modernism and, thereby, modernity, trying to solve the problems of the present with recipes from the past, if not escaping to it altogether.

However, for many if not most preservationists, the dichotomy between modernism and preservation, or past and present, was a false one: they neither wanted to save every old building nor prevent new ones from being built. Conservationists' conception of the city was different from the modernists', one that was not exclusively subject to the requirements of the day but in which the best of old and new coexisted side by side. If the critics espoused a modernist understanding of time, preservationists could be said to work within a more complex postmodernist temporality, in which past and present intersected and overlapped, as they often do in the material fabric of a city. In short, from the debate over conservation, nostalgia emerges once again as an accusation of a wrong attitude toward the past and a wrong understanding of time. It also shows how the thinking about both was changing.

The Way We Were: The Museum Boom

From Euston Station it takes just a little over two hours by train to get to Wigan in Lancashire—not that the former industrial town attracts a lot of tourists or day-trippers. If it is at all known outside Britain, it is for George Orwell's 1937 book *The Road to Wigan Pier,* an investigation into unemployment, as well as the working and living conditions of the English working class.[93] Its title derives from an old music hall joke—there never was a pier in Wigan, only an industrial wharf—and the mixture of being the butt of a joke and the epitome of industrial toil has continued to define the image of Wigan long after it ceased to be a center of industry.

Between the hardships of the depression of the 1930s and the hardships of the present, Wigan has been one of Britain's cities most affected by deindustrialization. By the mid-1980s, 30 percent of its land area was classified as derelict, and unemployment had risen to over 18 percent.[94] In this more than difficult situation, the Wigan Metropolitan Borough Council decided to try something new: it established a heritage center, a new type of local history museum, hoping that it would create jobs, attract tourists, and promote local pride. Opened by Queen Elizabeth II in 1986, it quickly became one of the most talked-about museums in the country, partly because it experimented with new presentation techniques and partly because Robert Hewison picked on it as the epitome of the heritage industry.[95] Soon it appeared in many other studies on heritage, museums, and tourism as well as all over the national press.[96]

The local history museum was not the only type of museum attracting critical attention at that time. The open-air museum—especially Britain's first and, to this day, biggest open-air museum, Beamish in County Durham in the north of England—was also a potent sign of the growth and the changes in the museum sector and how it presented the past to the public. Beamish and Wigan Pier, therefore, serve as case studies for examining how museums transformed themselves in the 1970s and 1980s and why and how they were seen as drawing on and evoking nostalgia in their visitors, as well as the meaning of nostalgia in this context. However, before we set out on the road to Wigan Pier itself and the discussion of nostalgia, it is necessary to look at the bigger picture.

"How dead is a museum? 'Musty,' 'fusty,' 'old-fashioned,' 'moth-eaten' are all adjectives with which we are familiar and which we expect to find in almost any journalistic passage in which the word 'museum' occurs."[97] Sir Frank Francis, director of the British Museum, was anything but buoyant about the state of museums when he gave his presidential address to the Museums Association in 1966. Like conservation, like history in general, museums were in crisis—or at least were often said to be—in the 1960s, and not only in Britain. Contributors to a German book on the future of the museum from 1970 were almost uniformly pessimistic, complaining, like Francis, that for the public the word *museum* was synonymous with "outdated, dusty, uninteresting."[98]

In the United States, by comparison, there was little sense of crisis in the museum world. Americans had, a historian complained as early as 1966, "more historic houses and museums than we need," institutions that, besides, presented "some pretty dubious nostalgia disguised as 'history.'"[99] If anything, museums were too popular. "Our museums are everywhere flourishing— which is to say, they are active, prosperous and crowded," reported *New York Times* art critic Hilton Kramer in 1967, continuing, "Museums have ceased to be pious repositories of an exalted past. They are now energetic arbiters in the values of the present, and they often give the impression of casting a hungry eye on the future."[100] Apparently, American museums had already achieved the level of popularity and relevance their European cousins were perceived to be lacking.

By the 1980s, the situation had changed completely. Now European observers also wondered whether museums were too popular; they were certain that there were too many. "Is Britain becoming one big museum?" an article in *New Society* asked in 1983.[101] This was the question that drove Hewison to investigate the place of the past in contemporary Britain: his book *The Heritage Industry* "grew out of hearing it regularly asserted that every week or so, somewhere in Britain, a new museum opens. The statistic seemed so astonishing that it needed checking. When it turned out to be more or less accurate, it seemed appalling. How long would it be before the United Kingdom became one vast museum?"[102] For Hewison, as for many others, the growth in museums signaled nothing so much as the "imaginative death of this country," a "country obsessed with its past, and unable to face its future."[103] "New museums open . . . at a rate of one a fortnight," Samuel said, echoing Hewison's observation, albeit rejecting his conclusion that they transformed the "country into a gigantic museum."[104]

West German intellectuals observed similar developments at their own doorstep: formerly beset by critics, museums were now besieged by masses of visitors. The "process of musealization had accelerated dramatically" as well, Lübbe noted in the mid-1980s, in terms of both the number of museums and what they collected.[105] "Not a day goes by that the erection of a new museum or the extension of an existing one is not reported," the ethnologist Gottfried Korff—not only an important museum theorist but also an influential curator—echoed the heritage critics, mocking the "windmill and coffee mill nostalgia."[106]

Such observations were not completely inaccurate. The number of museums had, indeed, increased enormously over the course of the preceding decades and continued to do so throughout the 1980s. Before the Second

World War, there were just about 530 museums in Britain—most of them, 428, in England, 43 of which were located in the capital and nearly all of them established after the middle of the nineteenth century.[107] By the 1980s there were so many museums, no one really knew how many there were: Hewison estimated 3,500, a calculated exaggeration that turned out not to be very far off the mark.[108] A 1987 report counted 3,537 museums in total, three-quarters of which had been established since the Second World War—nearly half of them since 1971—together attracting over sixty-eight million visits every year.[109] Most of these museums either were maintained by local authorities or were independent, both of which suggests that a sizable portion of them were local history museums.[110]

In the United States the National Endowment for the Arts surveyed 1,821 museums in 1975: 683 of them were history museums, and only one-fifth had existed before 1900.[111] The total number of history museums in the United States, however, was much higher. A 1980 report estimated it at around 5,500, with the greatest growth in the 1960s, when, on average, 100 new museums opened every year.[112] Again a huge percentage, if not the majority, of these museums were local history museums.[113]

In West Germany, too, the number of museums and museum visits rose constantly: from 346 museums and eight million visits in 1958 to 438 museums and ten million visits in 1963; 501 museums and fourteen million visits in 1970; 658 museums and twenty-five million visits in 1976; 805 museums and thirty-five million visits in 1981; and 1,326 museums and fifty-one million visits in 1987.[114] In other words, around 1,000 museums—or three-fourths of the total—had been founded between the late 1950s and the late 1980s.

A new museum may not have opened every week, as Hewison and others claimed, but looking back from the vantage point of the mid-1980s, their number had indeed risen quite spectacularly. Looking for an explanation for the museum boom, critics drew on nostalgia, which also served to characterize the new types of museums emerging from it. Neither the open-air museum nor the local history museum was an invention of the postwar era. One of the earliest open-air museums, and certainly the most influential one, Skansen, near Stockholm, had opened in 1891, followed, in the United States, by Henry Ford's Greenfield Village in 1928 and Colonial Williamsburg in 1934, but it was after the war that open-air museums really started to proliferate.[115] By the early 1980s, there were fifty-three open-air museums in West Germany, most of them established in the 1960s and the 1970s, attracting over

880,000 visitors a year.[116] In France, roughly two to three *eco musées* opened every year between the late 1970s and the late 1980s, their overall number rising from five in the late 1960s to almost forty in the late 1980s.[117]

Beamish was established in the 1960s by Frank Atkinson, who came to the museum world through volunteering at a local museum. At twenty-five he was running it, as the youngest museum director in Britain. After visiting Skansen and other Scandinavian folk museums, Atkinson decided to bring the concept to Britain and immediately started collecting. From there it was a long way to the museum of today. Opening with a small exhibition in 1972, Beamish grew slowly but steadily into the surrounding area, as more and more translocated buildings were reassembled on its grounds. Quickly Beamish itself became something of a model, not least because it was one of the first open-air museums to present both the rural and the industrial past, winning the Museum of the Year Award and the European Museum of the Year Award in 1986 and 1987, respectively.[118]

Much more common than the expansive open-air museums were the small local history museums that could be found in big cities as well as small villages. In West Germany the next *Heimatmuseum* usually was never very far away. Like the open-air museum, these museums devoted to local history sprang up in the latter half of the nineteenth century; in Germany they were closely connected to the *Heimat* movement, a reaction to urbanization and environmental destruction.[119] By the turn of the century, already around 100 existed on the territory later forming West Germany, to which the interwar period added another 153, followed by 99 between 1948 and 1959, 163 between 1960 and 1969, and 211 between 1970 and 1979, so that by the early 1980s there were around 870 *Heimatmuseums* in total.[120]

In the United States and Britain, the overall growth in museums was also largely driven by local history museums, which began to proliferate after the Second World War. The "heritage center" was originally a brainchild of the journalist and architectural writer Malcolm MacEwen, who, however, had imagined it as an "Architectural Interpretation Center" to stimulate public debate in response to the "crisis in architecture" of the 1970s.[121] Town councils looking for new purposes for historic buildings they had taken over to save them from demolition picked up his idea during the EAHY, which also led to the use of the term *heritage*. At least this is how it was in the case of St. Mary's Church Castlegate in York and St. Michael's Church in Chester, both disused medieval churches, which housed the first two heritage centers financed

Figure 4.4　From eyesore to museum: The former warehouse alongside the Leeds and Liverpool Canal after it became the Wigan Pier Heritage Centre. Archives: Wigan & Leigh

partly with EAHY funds.[122] Encouraged by the success of these pioneers—the center in York attracted eighty thousand visitors in the early 1980s and twice as many in the mid-1980s—another thirty-eight heritage centers had opened in Britain by the mid-1980s.[123]

None of them attracted as much attention as the Wigan Pier Heritage Centre, the biggest and most ambitious of them all (see Figures 4.4 and 4.5). Comprising several former industrial buildings alongside the Leeds and Liverpool Canal and costing 3.86 million pounds, it was funded by the Wigan Metropolitan Borough Council, the Greater Manchester Council, the Tourist Board, the North West Museums Service, and the European Regional Development Fund.[124] The rhetoric matched the investment: the Wigan Metropolitan Borough Council lauded the Wigan Pier Heritage Centre as nothing less than "one of Britain's best-known sites" and a "national monument," and the

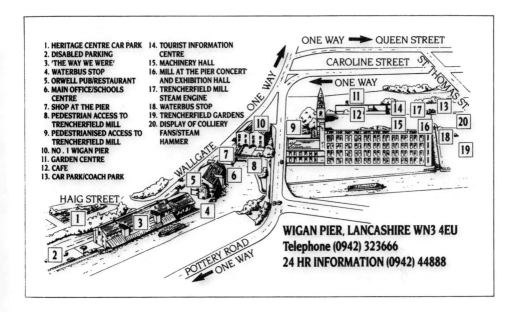

1. HERITAGE CENTRE CAR PARK
2. DISABLED PARKING
3. 'THE WAY WE WERE'
4. WATERBUS STOP
5. ORWELL PUB/RESTAURANT
6. MAIN OFFICE/SCHOOLS CENTRE
7. SHOP AT THE PIER
8. PEDESTRIAN ACCESS TO TRENCHERFIELD MILL
9. PEDESTRIANISED ACCESS TO TRENCHERFIELD MILL
10. NO . 1 WIGAN PIER
11. GARDEN CENTRE
12. CAFE
13. CAR PARK/COACH PARK
14. TOURIST INFORMATION CENTRE
15. MACHINERY HALL
16. MILL AT THE PIER CONCERT AND EXHIBITION HALL
17. TRENCHERFIELD MILL STEAM ENGINE
18. WATERBUS STOP
19. TRENCHERFIELD GARDENS
20. DISPLAY OF COLLIERY FANS/STEAM HAMMER

ONE WAY ➡ QUEEN STREET
CAROLINE STREET
ONE WAY
ST. THOMAS ST
ONE WAY
WALLGATE
HAIG STREET
POTTERY ROAD ONE WAY

WIGAN PIER, LANCASHIRE WN3 4EU
Telephone (0942) 323666
24 HR INFORMATION (0942) 44888

Figure 4.5   Map of the site of Wigan Pier Heritage Centre. Archives: Wigan & Leigh

planned renovation project as "a statement of faith and confidence for the future of the whole town and its people."[125] Like Beamish, the Wigan Pier Heritage Centre became something of a model for a new type of museum as well as a new approach to presentation.

But what made the open-air museum and the local history museum (or heritage center), and Beamish and Wigan Pier, nostalgic in the eyes of their critics? The past on display certainly was an important factor. Both types of museums were primarily concerned with local history, the history of the town or the region where they were located, as well as with social history, the everyday working and living conditions of "common" people and thereby aspects most museums still tended to disregard at the time. With its colliery, mine, and miner's cottage, Beamish, for instance, addressed the industrial past, with its farm the rural past, and with its Victorian town topics like social differences, living conditions, consumer behavior, leisure, religion, and gender. Taking inspiration from this, the designers of the exhibition at Wigan tried to cram all these different aspects into a former warehouse alongside the Leeds and Liverpool Canal.

When Atkinson began to line up support for his plans for Beamish in the 1960s, he was faced with a lot of opposition. In an episode reminiscent of Harold Wilson's comment on the "grime, muddle and decay" of Victorian heritage, Atkinson's superior in the local bureaucracy "despised [Atkinson's] concern for the industrial past of the County, believing that the 'old black image' should be destroyed and anything which looked as though it might perpetuate this was an anathema."[126] While this critique did not amount to the charge of nostalgia, it certainly implied that the past should be left behind on the road to a better future.

On top of their concern with social and everyday history on regional and local levels, the new museums also focused on the most recent past. As sociologist and museum scholar Tony Bennett noted in 1988, Beamish "works on the ground of popular memory": "In evoking past ways of life of which the visitor is likely to have had either direct or, through parents and grandparents, indirect knowledge and experience, the overwhelming effect is one of an easy-going at-homeness and familiarity."[127] Dealing with a past with which most visitors had a personal relationship, Beamish could not but trigger memories and emotions, the objects on display acting "as vehicles for the nostalgic remembrance of sentimentalized pasts."[128] It was the same for Wigan. By deciding to focus on "a time close enough to be within living memory," it provided "a link with our own day" in the eyes of the people running it—or mere nostalgia in those of its critics.[129] The decision to focus on the comparatively prosperous 1900s rather than the miserable 1930s of Orwell's time and to call it the Way We Were exacerbated such accusations.[130]

Yet what these critics really took issue with was not so much the content, but the way museums presented it. "Its significance consists," Bennett wrote about Beamish, "as much in how it is told as what is said." Leaving out labor unrest, trade unions, and women's history, Bennett was convinced, Beamish presented the past "through the cracked looking-glass of the dominant culture." It transformed "industrialism from a set of ruptural events into a moment in the unfolding of harmonious relations between rulers and ruled."[131] In short, it offered a distorted and nostalgic image of the past as a golden age by overlooking or downplaying social disparities and class conflicts.

Critics of Wigan Pier made the same point. Inspired by Hewison, art critic Waldemar Januszczak launched into a polemic of his own against the "sophisticated museum double-talk" that enabled a "society to present an era of such abject misery, squalor, dirt, disease, exploitation, child-cruelty in so rosy a light," culminating in the rhetorical questions, "What kind of fantasy past are we actually creating in our heritage centres? . . . Simple nostalgia or sinister obfuscation?"[132] In this context, nostalgia was first and foremost a way of accusing museums of presenting a distorted, whitewashed, and sentimentalized version of the past.

As the critics never explained how exactly the museums did this, one needs to read between the lines. One issue clearly stood out: costumed interpretation. Scandinavian open-air museums had long put their guides in period costumes to people the museum grounds without evoking much critique.[133] Beamish adopted this practice almost from the beginning, relying on twelve (at low season) to twenty-five (at high season) interpreters who engaged with the visitors, answering their questions and demonstrating tasks from the period.[134] These interpreters were expected to "assume the thoughts, feelings and emotions of an historical personage," as well as to possess "an in-depth knowledge of history."[135]

Wigan went a step further. Whereas at Beamish the interpreters remained "firmly in the here and now at all times," Wigan employed actors who researched and portrayed one or more particular historical characters, performing scenes ranging "from the death of a miner, complete with coffin laid out in the parlour, to clog dancing and temperance society marches," with the aim being to "enliven the exhibits" and to re-create the "atmosphere of Wigan at the turn of the century" (see Figure 4.6).[136] Subsequently picked up by other museums, this was a new practice in Britain, and one that attracted considerable critical scrutiny. Both Hewison's and Januszczak's accusations of nostalgia were aimed against the performative and immersive approach, which turned the museum into an "amusement park," a "theme park," or, worst of all, a kind of Disneyland, all comparisons frequently cropping up in the literature.[137] "The new Wigan Pier's Cousin is not the museum but the fairground," Januszczak declared.[138] In this context, nostalgia not only meant distorting the past but also turning it into an entertainment.

It was also code for emotions more generally. As the Beamish guide for its interpreters implied, the performance was meant to engage audiences not merely on a cerebral but also on an experiential and emotional level. Critics recognized this. The "main purpose of Wigan Pier is to create, not so much an informative, as an emotional experience," Hewison observed.[139] "Heritage culture's interest in the past," Januszczak seconded, "is subjective and emotional, a nostalgic longing for non-existent better days."[140]

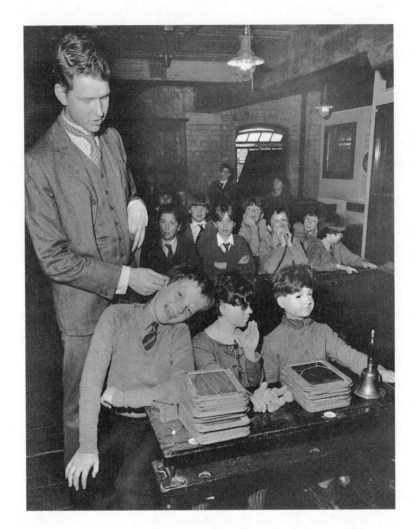

Figure 4.6   History as performance: the Edwardian classroom at Wigan Pier Heritage Centre.
Archives: Wigan & Leigh

Yet the term *nostalgia* also served to attack the commercialization of the
past, its transformation into a "heritage industry." Hewison went to Wigan
because it represented to him the worst of the museum boom, showcasing
how "look[ing] back in nostalgia has become an economic enterprise."[141] In his
1988 documentary *The Heritage Business,* he interviewed Terry Jones from the
Wigan Borough Council, who obliged him by confirming his worst suspicions.

"We are in the nostalgia business," Jones openly admitted, "we are using the artefacts, the site, the actors, a whole range of things to create the atmosphere of the turn of the century. Something that's just in living memory . . . that's what we are after."[142] And that was exactly what Hewison and other critics rejected.

Finally, nostalgia also appeared, if more obliquely, as synonymous with presentism. In Beamish, Bennett lamented, everything "is frozen at the same point in time."[143] The museum, historian Colin Sorensen criticized, denied "the realities of time, this artificial omission of any interval between then and now," implying "that then and now are very similar, and that we and they are, except for a few superficial differences, very similar also."[144] This accusation was perhaps the hardest to refute but also the hardest to avoid: buildings and objects from the past exhibited in a museum context are necessarily exhibited in the present, and so every museum, every exhibition is unavoidably presentist: it is much easier for them to show a moment in time than the passing of it. However, while Beamish and Wigan related the past to the present, they never claimed that they were identical. Rather, as the Wigan Pier guidebook declared, "The way we are, the way we will be, is the direct result of the way we were."[145]

The sociologist Adrian Mellor had just visited Wigan Pier when he chanced upon Januszczak's review. Agreeing with him insofar as he, too, detected an unmistakable whiff of nostalgia, he ultimately defended the exhibition. Far from making him "want to return to some authentic 'golden age' of working class life," it reminded him "of the back-breaking and dangerous toil which had been the experience of recent generations of my own family, and . . . the number of people still subject to such degradations."[146] Mellor understood the exhibition not as affirming but as challenging dominant cultural beliefs—after all, it addressed the working conditions in the coal mines at length, devoting one exhibit to the Maypole Disaster in 1908, when an explosion in a colliery near Wigan killed seventy-six miners.[147] "Desperately long hours in cramped, unpleasant and hazardous conditions were commonplace," the guidebook read. "Low pay, poor housing and disease led to short life expectancy and an infant mortality rate as high as thirty percent."[148] Such remarks did not exactly sound as if the display concealed or downplayed hardships and squalor.

In an extended version of his article, Mellor emphasized visitors' ability to derive their own interpretation from the exhibition.[149] Later studies, taking issue with Hewison's account, drew similar conclusions. "The acting was not intended to be nostalgic," concluded Patricia Mary Sterry in a 1994 analysis of heritage centers, "but to illustrate a message of what mining conditions were like."[150] For sociologist Gaynor Bagnall, the idea "that visitors simplistically accept a nostalgic re-enactment of the past does not capture the reality of the work of the actors at the Pier," as she wrote in a study on performance at heritage sites in 2003.[151]

Unlike critical accounts, these studies engaged directly with the museum's visitors, researching how they reacted to its displays and performative elements. This led them to see the visitors not so much as passive consumers but instead as active and resistant, fashioning their own understandings from what the museum offered. Finally, and most importantly, they did not view experience and emotion as inherently disadvantageous for museum work. In Bagnall's eyes the "emotional response" Wigan Pier evoked in its visitors enabled them "to feel as if they had experienced a realistic version of the past," and she argued that "meaning is achieved through constructing a plausible experience, rather than presenting a series of facts."[152] In other words, far from thwarting the educational mission of the museum, the interactive and performance-based experiential and emotional approach favored by Beamish and Wigan was conducive to it.

So prevalent was the nostalgia charge, museum practitioners could not but react to it. "We're not trying to be biased in any direction," Atkinson declared when interviewed by Hewison for a documentary in 1986. "We're not trying to say, for instance, these were the good old days any more than we're trying to say these were the bad old days. I mean they were both in a sense that it depended on who you were and where you were at any point. So, what we're trying to say in a sense is these were the days, this is how it was, take it or leave it, draw your own conclusions."[153] Neither accepting nor rejecting the nostalgia charge, Atkinson stressed instead how Beamish represented the multifaceted past as neutrally as possible to enable visitors to make up their own minds. He himself took an ambivalent position toward nostalgia. In 1968, at a time when the term was not yet as pejorative as it would later become, Atkinson foresaw that "nostalgia is going to be bigger and bigger business in the next few years" and that it was an important factor in drawing people in, even going so far as to admit that "'regional heritage' and 'nostalgia' is a necessity and is indeed the full justification for Beamish."[154] In an interview from the early 2000s, he compared nostalgia to the "sugar on the pill" that made history more palatable to the public.[155]

When Hewison returned to Beamish for his documentary *The Heritage Business,* Atkinson had just retired. Now, Hewison interviewed Jim Perry, the president of the Durham Mechanics, a local working-class association, quizzing him about the role of nostalgia at Beamish. "Yeah, yeah, when I come here, others, too, we do feel nostalgic," Perry admitted. "One can't help but remember, you know, some of the things that happened to you, things that do stick in your memory, which are probably stuck with you for the rest of your life." That did not mean, however, that Perry believed the past was a better place. Asked by Hewison whether he was glad not to live in one of the houses on display, he agreed emphatically: "Oh yeah, this is progress, obviously. As we go on things must get better for people who work, for working-class people and no one would want to go back to those days."[156] For Perry, then, nostalgia and progress did not cancel each other out: touched by the display of the old times, as a working-class person, he definitely did not wish to return to them. Which shows that visitors did indeed come up with their own interpretation of the past and that Beamish allowed for different and contrasting readings by its visitors.

Peter Lewis, Wigan Pier's first director, took an even more ambivalent view vis-à-vis nostalgia. Clearly irked by Hewison's critique, Lewis rebuffed his accusation that Wigan Pier's primary aim was to create an "emotional experience."[157] Rather, he clarified, the intention had been to improve the quality of life of and provide employment for people in the area and to educate them about their past, thereby instilling a sense of local pride, as well as to attract tourists.[158] "Nostalgia was once a perfectly good word," Lewis claimed, then went on the offensive: "Now it's a stick used by those who consider themselves superior to beat the emotions or experiences of others. Of all the words we use, however, it is the one which, properly understood, conveys most. It means to look back—to seek a return but with a sense of pain. It is not sentimental or cloying. If anything it is what we most want our visitors to experience."[159] Instead of rebuffing the nostalgia charge, Lewis embraced it, even going so far as to elevate it to "what we most want our visitors to experience." Dismissing the negative association of nostalgia with sentimentalism, he stressed the aspect of pain. Again and again, Lewis returned to his point, reiterating that he used "the word nostalgically deliberately" to convey "remembrance with pain," that it was "about sentiment, not sentimentality."[160]

In this way, Lewis imbued the concept with his own meaning. But what did *nostalgia* mean, in clear contradiction to how he had started his talk, except "emotions and experiences"? Like the studies quoted earlier, Lewis's response to Hewison suggests that the quarrel over nostalgia in museums—and, by extension, in popular history—was really about whether it was permissible to use experiential and immersive approaches and to appeal to visitors' emotions to lure them into museums and to educate them about the past. This is what Lewis intended and, if contemporary studies were correct, realized at Wigan Pier and later at Beamish, when he became Atkinson's successor.

In the debate about museums, then, *nostalgia* took on several different but related and overlapping meanings: first, as distorting the past; second, as commercializing the past; third, as turning it from a place of education into one of entertainment by drawing on performative elements associated with theater and theme parks; and finally, and most importantly, as a stand-in for emotions. In all these meanings, *nostalgia* fulfilled one central function, and that was to dismiss the new museums and new museum displays, which, in the eyes of their critics, were incompatible with, undermining even, their educational mission.

Much like the debate about conservation, the one about museums carried a hidden political subtext. Because the growth of the museum sector in Britain became apparent during the premiership of Margaret Thatcher and because heritage centers like Wigan Pier were also motivated by commercial deliberations—and therefore seemed to fit in with Thatcher's neoliberal agenda—and because they often looked back on the Victorian and Edwardian past as Thatcher had done in the debate about "Victorian values," heritage came to be associated with Thatcherism. On closer inspection, however, associating these new museums with Thatcherism is more than doubtful. Beamish and Wigan certainly did not celebrate "Victorian values." And although there were some private, commercial heritage centers, most were, like Wigan Pier, financed by local, regional, and national authorities and thus represented exactly the sort of cultural policy Thatcher renounced.[161]

In fact, Thatcher had as little love for museums as she had for conservation. As Roy Strong noted in his diary, she held an "*idée fixe* about museums, that they were dead things, piled-up lumber from Britain's past which was now holding the country back."[162] In September 1984, one year before posing on a bulldozer at the former site of Broad Street Station and at the height of the Miners' Strike, Thatcher unwittingly reinforced Strong's point when, during a visit to the National Railway Museum in York, she warned, once again sounding like a heritage critic, against the dangers of Britain becoming a "museum society."[163]

If something like a "heritage industry," a commercialized museum landscape, emerged under Thatcher, this was not because she took an interest in museums but rather the opposite: by cutting expenses, she forced museums to seek funding elsewhere and to become more entrepreneurial. For museums in London, with its millions of inhabitants and tourists, this may have been a difficult task but it was not impossible. In a 1980s advertisement campaign—designed by Saatchi & Saatchi, the biggest advertising agency in the world at the time, which also ran Thatcher's election campaigns—the Victoria and Albert Museum presented itself as "an ace caff, with quite a nice museum attached," making fun of the old image of museums as elite, aloof, and austere.[164] The joke seemed to have escaped the heritage critics, who instead focused on publicly funded local museums in economically deprived areas, for which it was much harder to cope in the new cultural climate. While Beamish was "shorn of a substantial part of its revenue and capital funding" in the 1980s, Wigan Pier quickly fell on hard times and had to close in 2007.[165]

Since then, its buildings have stood empty and unused, as they did before the heritage center moved in, which, by the late 2010s, itself could be said to have become a source of local nostalgia.[166] It is not hard to see why. Today, visiting its abandoned former site and recalling a time when ambitious public authorities were ready to invest heavily in such projects, when thousands of visitors came here each year and the national press, for once, had something positive to report about Wigan, it is tempting to wonder whether a more sympathetic portrayal by intellectuals would perhaps have helped it to survive—or at least made it more difficult to shut down.

Time Warp: Historical Reenactments

Roughly a hundred miles southeast of Wigan lies Newark-on-Trent. Situated alongside the river Trent, Newark is a scenic little town with the domineering spire of St. Mary Magdalene, its cobbled marketplace, its castle, and Sconce and Devon Park, named after the remains of the Queen's Sconce, a leftover from the English Civil War, when Newark, a Royalist fort, was repeatedly besieged by Parliamentary troops. This history is still present today and never more so than when the reenactors of the Sealed Knot, dressed as Cavaliers and Roundheads, descend on the town, as they did on a sunny May weekend in 2015. While the Sealed Knot regularly re-creates the siege—and surrender—of Newark in 1646, the reenactment in 2015 marked a special occasion: the opening of the National Civil War Centre, the first museum in Britain devoted entirely to the history of the English Civil War.[167]

Today such a collaboration between a museum and reenactors is far from unusual. Whereas reenactors are thankful for any opportunity to ride their hobby horse—let alone real ones—and especially when they can do so on original battle sites like the Queen's Sconce, museums appreciate the drawing power of reenactments. Indeed, it is in battle reenactments—the "iconic form of reenactment"—that the origins of costumed interpretation, later adopted by museums like Wigan Pier and Beamish, lie, and perhaps this illustrious ancestry is partly responsible for its dubious reputation.[168] If interpreters in a museum context attracted accusations of nostalgia, it stands to reason that battle reenactors, appearing to glorify war as well as historical ideas about masculinity, heroism, and nationalism, attract even more scrutiny.

Nearly all the heritage critics of the 1980s took at least passing swipes at historical reenactments. Kammen mentions the popularity of battle reenactments together with the museum boom and historic preservation as evidence of the increasing nostalgia in the second half of the twentieth century.[169] "Reenactments enliven history for millions who turn a blind or bored eye on ancient monuments, not to mentioned history books," Lowenthal acknowledged in *The Past Is a Foreign Country,* immediately adding that they could also transport people "into a fictitious yesterday purged of historical guilt, where people act out fantasies denied them in the contemporary world."[170] Hewison also noted the "vogue for historical re-enactments."[171] Another commentator saw them as "nothing but mere titillation, meaningless amateur dramatics promoting the post-modern simulacrum, a hazy image of a manipulated and trivialized past."[172]

Not just the heritage critics but historians overall tend to display an "intense hostility to reenactment," which, in no small measure, informs its characterization as nostalgic.[173] The fact that the *Handbook on Reenactment Studies* includes an article on the topic shows how much the practice of reenacting and the concept of nostalgia are connected. "When detractors describe reenactors as 'nostalgic,'" Jonathan D. Schroeder argues here, "what they are usually doing is casting doubt upon a core premise of historical reenactment," insinuating that "the reenactor is not in control of her production but is controlled by it"; it is not a "rational act" but portrayed as an "obsession." At the same time, Schroeder notes, "little attention has been paid to the role of nostalgia in reenactment": scholars "use the term to moralize" rather than analyze their relationship.[174] To such an analysis this section wants to contribute.

The oldest and still largest reenactment society in Britain, the Sealed Knot, serves as its primary example. It was founded by Brigadier Peter Young, an officer, veteran of the Second World War, and professor of history at the Royal Military Academy Sandhurst, together with some of his colleagues and friends in 1968.[175] From its very beginnings, the "compulsive neurotics of the Sealed Knot, who like dressing up in old ironmongery and firing caps at one another," as *Punch* mocked them in 1985, attracted a good deal of derision.[176] It can even boast of having been satirized by Terry Pratchett in his Discworld novels as the "Ankh-Morpork Historical Re-creation Society," nicknamed "the Peeled Nuts": "Those clowns who dress up and pretend to fight old battles with blunt swords."[177]

To get a better sense of historical reenactments in general, the Sealed Knot's activities are compared to Civil War reenactments in the United States—not so much because they both revolve around military conflicts within a nation, but because this was where the "birth of modern-day battle reenactment" took place, without which a British reenactment scene might not exist.[178] Such a comparison is all the more necessary because there is still relatively little scholarship on reenactments in Britain—the Sealed Knot's carefully archived papers were virtually untouched when they were consulted for this study— or, for that matter, in continental Europe, whose reenactment scene is much smaller and even less researched.[179]

Depending on how the practice is defined, battle reenactment could have begun in antiquity, when the Romans restaged battles as part of their triumphs. In their modern incarnation, reenactments could—like historic preservation and museums—well be blamed on the Victorians. The Eglinton Tournament of 1839 at Eglinton Castle in Ayrshire, Scotland, for instance, would make for a decent enough starting point—apart from the fact that it presented a fictitious medieval joust. From the Edwardian to the interwar period, Britain saw a succession of pageants, many of which featured performers dressed in historical uniforms.[180] The Sealed Knot both recognized and rejected this tradition: on the one hand it sought to "produce pageants"; on the other, there was a "very apparent reluctance within the SK membership to participate in any event which bore the name of pageant."[181] This suggests the American example may have been more influential than the homegrown tradition, given that pageants were primarily festive parades to boost local patriotism with little concern for historical authenticity, which would become a central concept for reenacting in the second half of the twentieth century.

When exactly Americans began to reenact their Civil War is equally contested, with some claiming that the practice started right after if not even during the war itself.[182] The fiftieth anniversary of the Battle of Gettysburg in 1913 was marked with a reenactment—the last in which veterans of the actual battle took part—as were anniversaries of the battles of Manassas, Antietam, and Gettysburg in 1936, 1937, and 1938, all of which attracted audiences in the tens of thousands.[183] But it was during the Civil War centennial in the 1960s that reenacting truly came into its own, with a reenactment of the Battle of Manassas in 1961 drawing one hundred thousand spectators.[184] In the context of the civil rights movement, reenactments also became highly contentious—though they were criticized even more for presenting the war as elaborate, commercial spectacles.[185]

In the aftermath of the Manassas reenactment, many "deplored the intrusions of commercialism and a carnival atmosphere which . . . were an affront to good taste and an abuse to history," and no one more so than the members of the Civil War Centennial Commission.[186] "If the National Commission tries to reenact a battle," the historian Allan Nevins announced after becoming its chairman, "my dead body will be the first found on the field."[187] Nevins survived, if barely. As executive director Karl S. Betts told members of the House of Representatives, the commission had "done a great deal to discourage re-enactments on many, many occasions. But the local people want to do it, and there is very little you can do to prevent that."[188] The National Park Service was also anxious about completely prohibiting reenactments on battlefields in its care, making exceptions for reenactments of the battles of Antietam and Gettysburg in 1962 and 1963. Clearly, historians and officials were extremely critical of reenactments from the outset.[189]

With the next big national anniversary, the bicentennial of the Declaration of Independence in 1976, reenacting returned with a vengeance.[190] The 1980s became a peak time with 6,500 reenactors—the whole scene was estimated to comprise around 50,000 people—turning out for the 125th anniversary of the Battle of Manassas, which *Time* described as "noisy, nostalgic fun."[191] And this was nothing in comparison to the 125th and 135th anniversary reenactments of the Battle of Gettysburg in 1988 and 1998, which saw more than twice that number.[192] Although Gettysburg's 150th in 2018 attracted 15,000 reenactors and 200,000 onlookers, some believed the hobby was in decline, its politics more problematic than ever at a time when alt-right groups assembled under the Confederate flag to defend Confederate monuments.[193]

It is possible that the English Civil War would not be reenacted at all today had it not been for these American examples. The Sealed Knot may be the oldest existing reenactment society in Britain, but it was not the first. Indeed, as cofounder David Chandler, a historian and colleague of Young at Sandhurst, reports, the first reenactments on British soil were not of the English but of the American Civil War. In 1962 the enthusiasts of the Confederate High Command (UK) regularly re-created battles from the American Civil War in the Thames valley.[194] While the society seems to have vanished fairly quickly, interest in the Civil War did not. By 1975, a new group, the American Civil War Society, had come into being and, gathering some nine hundred members by the 2000s, today it is one of the largest reenactment societies in Britain after the Sealed Knot.[195]

Whatever role the American Civil War reenactments may have played, the Sealed Knot was born out of a publicity stunt. When, in 1967, Peter Young's publisher put some soldiers in period costumes to launch his latest book, a history of the 1642 Battle of Edgehill, the event was so well received that Young and his colleagues saw this as proof, correctly as it turned out, that there was enough popular interest to sustain a reenactment society. The following year they founded the Sealed Knot. Its first-ever muster, as it calls its reenactments, took place at Frimley Park in July 1968.[196] By the time of the reenactment of the Battle of Cropredy in 1970, membership had swollen to 1,200.[197] It continued to grow from 2,000 in the early 1970s, to 5,270 in the mid-1980s, to over 6,000 in the early 2000s and, with its membership, its reenactments also grew in number and size (Figure 4.7 shows a reenactment of 1643 siege of Reading in 1980).[198]

Over this period the Sealed Knot became more and more concerned with historical authenticity—something even the Cavaliers were rather cavalier about in the beginning, as John Tucker, a founding member, recalled: "My first appearance as a Cavalier was in a chopped-up duffle-coat and a plastic doily."[199] Still, almost from the beginning, newspaper articles were commending the Knot for its "considerable concern for authenticity" and the

Figure 4.7   History as performance: the 1643 siege of Reading as re-created by the Sealed Knot in 1980. Trinity Mirror / Mirrorpix / Alamy

"great effort" it took "to stage battles as authentically as possible."[200] For some, these efforts at verisimilitude were not going nearly far enough. In 1980 a group of disgruntled Knotters, appalled by what they saw as Young's "'Hollywood' showmanship"—"all Bri-Nylon and plastic lace," as one of them put it—split from the Sealed Knot to form the English Civil War Society.[201] By the early 1990s, it had collected three thousand members of its own.[202] For a while, the two English Civil War reenactment societies viewed each other much like one might have expected Cavaliers and Roundheads did in times of yore. Gradually, however, these rivalries subsided to the point where they started to collaborate regularly on larger reenactments like the one in Newark in 2015. At the same time, museums and heritage sites started to welcome reenactors on their premises to reach out to new audiences. When English Heritage established a special events unit in the early 1980s, it made Howard Giles, a member of the English Civil War Society, its director.[203]

Yet what motivated a growing number of people to participate in reenactments—mere nostalgia? Probably there are "as many individual rea-

sons for reenacting Civil War battles as there were reasons to fight the origi-
nals," historian Stephen Cushman assumes.[204] One reason mentioned frequently by practitioners is to educate oneself, as well as the public, about
the past. "The aim of the Sealed Knot is to create and revive interest in a for-
mative period of British history," its *Members Compendium* declared. "People
join for many different reasons," it went on, listing as the most important ones
"excitement, friendship, interest and enjoyment of an unusual way."[205] For
Young the prime motivation for the Sealed Knot's existence was "fun," a word
many other members also used when asked about their motivation for
joining.[206] For the Knotters, there was no contradiction, as they saw no reason
"why fun should not also be educational, in fact, education hurts less if it is
made amusing."[207] A large part of the fun was the social aspect of reenacting,
which was often a hobby for the whole family that fostered lasting friendships,
a point a lot of Knotters, as well as American reenactors, emphasized.[208]

For many reenactors these motivations probably were more decisive than
nostalgia, however defined. For many, but not all: insofar as nostalgia was
understood as the wish to escape the present, some reenactors, far from denying the charge, happily pleaded guilty to it. When a journalist asked Young
in 1971 why people joined the Sealed Knot, he replied bluntly: "It enables
people to escape from their bloody dull lives."[209] "Perhaps there is also a tendency to escape from the mundane realities of late 20th Century everyday
life," his lieutenant David Chandler too reflected.[210] "This escape into the past
is fundamentally what the Sealed Knot is all about. You can get away from
the pressures of work, meet new friends and forget for a brief period the frus-
trations of daily life," one Knotter wrote.[211] "An important appeal of the
Sealed Knot is that it offers a complete escape from modern life," a female
member confirmed when interviewed by a newspaper.[212]

American reenactors provided similar reasons. In *Time Machines*, a now-
classic survey of the field of public history from 1984, Jay Anderson, an academic historian as well as living history practitioner, found a "nostalgic
preference for the past" born out of a "need to escape . . . from the late
twentieth-century world of digital watches and omnipresent computers,"
from the "rat race where everything has to be delivered overnight by air
express, and time is measured in nanoseconds." Living historians, he continued, wanted "desperately to slow down the pace of life and regain a
sense . . . of rootedness."[213] Randal Allred, also a historian and a reenactor,
noted, "The hobby is certainly a kind of escape: a flight from an age of isolation

and fragmentation into an age of community and shared values."[214] Other re-enactors interviewed over time confirm this picture either by explicitly mentioning "escape" or "escapism" or by implying as much.[215]

For Anderson living history offered a chance to "escape from the present into the timeless world of the past." Sounding like Alvin Toffler here, who, incidentally, had characterized open-air museums as "enclaves of the past," Anderson goes on to describe reenactors as "future-shocked" and living history as an "oasis of eternity in the desert of modern abstract time."[216] In short, he understood nostalgia—or rather the nostalgic charge of reenacting—much in the same way Toffler, Fred Davis, and Lübbe defined it: by providing an escape from the accelerated change of the contemporary world into a slower past, reenactments and living history offer a way to cope with modern life.

Having acknowledged the role of nostalgia in living history, Anderson launched into a defense of it. "Nostalgia," he concluded his book, "was once a good, tough word for the deadly disease of homesickness. Two centuries ago, people died from nostalgia. I often wish we could strip the word of its sentimental accretions; it would be a useful tool in the years to come."[217] Only a few years later, Peter Lewis would characterize *nostalgia* with almost the same words: both wanted to save the term by ridding it of its "sentimental" connotation and by reintroducing that of "pain." Adopting a term their critics had brought up, practitioners defined it in their own way.

But what does escape mean given that neither living historians nor re-enactors ever really leave the present? "Self-descriptions of re-enactors," historian John Brewer notes, "seem to collapse the distance between past and present, reducing it to zero so that the re-enactor inhabits a sort of overwhelming timelessness in which the present self and past other merge into a single identity, a unique individual experience."[218] What Brewer calls "timeless" could also be characterized as presentist.

Other studies, adopting the language of reenactors, speak of "time warp" or "period rush."[219] If we believe them, this "time warp" is what all reenactors are ultimately after—even if they rarely achieve it. It is also what motivates their attempts at historical authenticity. What critics portray as a misplaced obsession with the superficial serves an important function for reenactors: by altering their appearance and comportment, by wearing and carrying often uncomfortable and heavy period clothes and armor, reenactors change how they perceive and experience themselves to access how someone in the past, a soldier or a farmer, may have felt.

"Re-living really *is* the right word," a member of the Sealed Knot wrote; "in 17th century costume you feel transported back 350 years, especially as all around you people are dressed in a similar manner."[220] "As soon as you don the uniform," confirmed another, a computer programmer in real life, "you immediately feel transported back 350 years."[221] An experience that began with changing one's clothes continued with the physical process of re-enacting. "We took a cannon down a scarp," recalls Sealed Knot cofounder John Tucker. "There were about 30 people on the trail ropes and it was very misty. There was no noise at all except for the clinking of spurs and the rattle of side-arms and the slithering of the horses. It was exactly as it would have been at the time and we suddenly realized then that it was no longer just dressing up—we were actually reliving the period."[222] "I marched abreast of more than a hundred men up the long green field in the hot June sun, the first row sent to the slaughter," reports the sociologist Rory Turner about a similar experience. "It was hard to think clearly about anything in the tumult, until I lay dead and still on the ground and the lines pushed forward and past me. Later I thought, 'So that's what it was like.' There is a kind of knowledge that can only be gained by living through something."[223]

These reports of two time-warp experiences are highly revealing. First, they show that what reenactors describe in this way is triggered by physical exertion and the concomitant suspension of thought: losing oneself in the experience instead of trying to experience something. Second, it shows that the time warp is an extremely short-lived experience that only becomes apparent after the fact. And finally, and most importantly, it becomes clear that a time warp is not an experience of the past at all but of its distance: the brief illusion of being in the past only accentuates the fact that reenactors can never truly access it and that the best they can hope for is to "relive" it—that is, to reenact it in the present: "that's what it was like" as opposed to "that is what it was." Far from collapsing past and present, the time warp in fact emphasizes the impossibility of recapturing the past. Turner's and Tucker's experience, and, by extension, those of reenactors generally, is not one of synchronicity but of anachronism. As in the passages quoted here, reenacting means constantly comparing the period reenacted with the period in which the reenactment takes place, recognizing how different they are and, thereby, how unbridgeable the gap between them really is.

Indeed, reenactments are nothing if not machines for producing anachronism. "This summer I had the faintly surreal experience of waiting to use a portable urinal at a British history re-enactment festival," *Times* journalist Ben Macintyre reported in 2019, "and witnessing a First World War Tommy in khaki, a Viking with horned helmet and a Napoleonic soldier in a plumed tricorn hat, all peeing side by side, as if this anachronistic historical assembly was the most normal thing in the world."[224] Anyone who has ever visited a reenactment will have had similar experiences: reenactors in period dress getting out of cars, sitting in cafés and restaurants, or waiting for the bus—much as the stuntman Max Diamond did at a London bus stop in 1971, on this occasion as a member not of the Sealed Knot but of the British Jousting Society (see Figure 4.8). With his arm around the model Gail Miller dressed in late 1960s style, Diamond, in medieval gear, and his fellow knight Nosher Powell, halberd raised to attract a taxi, replicate the clash of times that is also present in the material fabric of London in the background, with the Gothic revival tower of the Houses of Parliament—a nineteenth-century building riffing off the Middle Ages—and the modern-day car traffic. Therefore, while nostalgia, when it comes to historical reenactments, mostly signified escapism, it can also be understood as presentist in the Ankersmitian sense: not as collapsing past and present but as making manifest the difference and distance between them.

As in the case of conservation, characterizing reenactors as nostalgic also had a political component. In the United States, reenacting the Civil War was, from the very beginning, associated with a longing for an imaginary and largely fictitious old South and with resentment against the North and the civil rights movement in particular. In the 1960s, reenactments "bore an uncomfortable resemblance to white resistance, and some guys seemed only to be there because there was no Klan event that weekend," as one participant admitted when interviewed decades later.[225] Tony Horwitz, who traveled the South extensively for his 1998 book *Confederates in the Attic* and took part in reenactments as a participant observer, noted that for many people in the South, the past had become a "talisman against modernity, an emotional lever for . . . reactionary politics" made apparent in the reenactments, which were "blindingly white affairs."[226] More recently, the writer Ta-Nehisi Coates has remarked on the "near-total absence of African-American visitors" at the battlefields, noting how the Civil War is "a story for white people—acted out by white people, on white people's terms—in which blacks feature strictly as stock characters and props."[227]

The English Civil War, by contrast, did not resonate with contemporary sensibilities in nearly the same way. Three hundred years after its conclusion,

Figure 4.8 Clashing times: two knights in jousting armor and a fashion model in London in 1971.

PA Images / Alamy

this conflict between king and Parliament and its underlying religious rivalries appeared reassuringly old-fashioned, and reenactments of its battles
consequently lacked the "intensely felt partisanship" of American reenactments, as Stephen Cushman, one of the very few historians to compare reenactments of the two civil wars, has noted.[228] The fact that most reenactors
preferred to embody Cavaliers had less to do with any deep-seated Royalist
sympathies than with their glamorous attire and demeanor: "Who wanted
to be a Roundhead when you could be a Cavalier!" complained a founding
member of the Sealed Knot, who had to resort to putting an ad—"Roundheads
Urgently Wanted"—in the *Times* to marshal a parliamentary force for the
Cavaliers to fight.[229]

Underlying the "fun" of reenactment, however, was a darker, more serious
side. In the interview quoted earlier, Young called reenacting, in a remark soon
to become something of a motto for the Sealed Knot, a "rebellion against the
times in which we live."[230] For Chandler reenacting was closely associated
"with a sense of growing nostalgia for the dimly-understood but sorely-missed
splendours of great power status of the past, linked to an often subconscious
revolt against the all-too-often gaudy, tasteless and raucous features of so-
called 'modern western civilization.'" Warming to his theme, he went on, "It
is a rejection of the drug-cult, the gurus, the 'beautiful people' and all the rest of
what seems to have more in common with Sodom and Gomorrah than with contemporary democracy and the 'age of common man'—in favour of the quieter,
less frenetic attitudes of earlier times."[231] In the context of such remarks—or
rants, rather—it was perhaps no coincidence that the Sealed Knot was founded in
1968 of all years, when the student and countercultural movements, to which
Chandler alludes here, were at their height. Revolted by a present he con-
demns as "gaudy," "tasteless," "raucous," and "frenetic," that he even likens to
"Sodom and Gomorrah," Chandler revolts by withdrawing into a "sorely-missed"
past at once "quieter" and more glorious. And, as if this were not enough to
confirm the critics' claims about nostalgia, he uses the term himself!

If such remarks suggest at least a small-*c* conservative bent, the Sealed Knot
always took great care to emphasize that it was "not Political and never intended to be," that it "never made any distinction between men, or women
for that matter, as regards their creed, colour, sex or politics," that there were
"voters of every persuasion in the Knot, from virulent Marxists to genuine
fascists."[232] Yet the continued emphasis on its political neutrality may well

be read as evidence that the Sealed Knot was not as neutral as it made itself out to be—or that it certainly felt under pressure to divorce itself from the public image of being reactionary. A journalist visiting one of its musters in the early 1990s remarked on the "Conservative prejudices" in evidence.[233] In both cases, the United States and the United Kingdom, the perception of reenactments as conservative may well have contributed to their being viewed as nostalgic affairs—or *nostalgia* may have stood in for *conservative* here.

Which does not mean that reenactments are inherently conservative. Not only is there a comparatively small but influential Black reenactment scene in the United States, the actor Azie Dungey turned her experiences portraying a slave at George Washington's Mount Vernon into the show *Ask a Slave,* educating audiences about slavery and racism and the lack of knowledge thereof in present-day America.[234] If "to speak as the slave would . . . is to rupture the narrative," as Coates writes, that is exactly what Dungey and the Black reenactors do.[235] In so doing, they also demonstrate that reenacting is not necessarily a conservative, affirmative practice but can also be put to subversive uses, challenging people's ideas about the past.

The British artist Jeremy Deller drew on the practice in a similar way when, in 2001, he initiated a reenactment of the "Battle of Orgreave." The original "battle" took place at the height of the Miners' Strike, when five thousand miners picketing a steelworks found themselves across from six thousand police officers in riot gear, with dogs and on horseback, resulting in a violent altercation, more reminiscent of a battle from the Civil War than a modern-day labor conflict.[236] The police presence was a calculated show of force by Thatcher, who, a month later, drawing a parallel between the Falklands War and the striking miners, called them the "enemy within."[237] Taking part in the reenactment were former miners who had been present at the original event, as well as many members of the Sealed Knot and other reenactment societies from across the country. Howard Giles directed the reenactment.[238] When Deller's book about the event was published, it bore the title *The English Civil War Part II.*[239] Scholars writing about the reenactment have found both that "nostalgia came rushing back in" and that it dismantled "nostalgia for sentimental class unity," which underscores, once again, the differing and contrasting meanings the concept inhabits when it comes to reenactments: it can mean to distort and to sentimentalize the past, to abolish its distance from the present, and to make the past present as different from the present.[240]

The *Roots* Phenomenon

Museum visitors, reenactors, and their spectators are not the only ones who take to the road to seek out the past. For family historians, too, traveling is indispensable—whether to access records in local or national archives or to see where their ancestors once lived—to the extent that "genealogical tourism" has long been a recognized subcategory of "heritage tourism."[241] In 2004 the British comedian David Baddiel went on such a journey to search for his Jewish ancestors, some of whom had been murdered in the Holocaust. It took him from his home in London to Warsaw and Kaliningrad and back to London again. Baddiel was only one of many people embracing family history research at this time, but he did so under special circumstances: aided by expert researchers and on camera as part of the first season of the television series *Who Do You Think You Are?* Initially a special interest program on BBC2, its surprise success, followed by its subsequent move to BBC1 in 2006, demonstrated just how popular a hobby genealogy had become.[242]

Despite—or maybe because of—its popularity, *Who Do You Think You Are?* and, through it, family history research met with sharp criticism. "It seems a senseless waste of a life to interrogate the dead in search of an off-the-peg identity," a journalist wrote in the *Times,* implying that genealogical research was not about exploring the past at all but a way of fashioning an identity for oneself in the present. Slightly contradicting himself, he went on to claim that the whole endeavor seemed "less about discovering how we lived then than distracting us from how we live now," in this way portraying family history as both presentist, driven by the search for a present-day identity, and nostalgic, an escape from the present.[243] "At the moment when so many of us have become generally hopeless at maintaining family life," an article in the *Independent* noted similarly, "a connection with kith and kin safely dead offers a welcome refuge," hence implying an escapist dimension as well.[244] While avoiding the term *nostalgia,* both articles suggested that this was what family history research was primarily about.

Indeed, like the conservation movement, the museum boom, and historical reenactments, the transformation of genealogy into a vast popular hobby has often been understood in terms of nostalgia. As in the case of reenactments, the heritage critics noted the development without taking much interest in it. For Lowenthal, the "ancestor-hunters" displayed an "obsessive concern with rooted legacies" that was "more backward- than forward-looking."[245] Family history societies mushroomed, Samuel noted, their members filling the record offices and local history libraries.[246] "During the early and mid-1970s abundant evidence appeared to indicate that interest in family history is running high," Kammen likewise observed for the United States.[247]

As with the other examples discussed in this chapter, the increasing interest in genealogical research, while certainly prodigious in the 1970s, predated the decade and the genealogically themed television programs and genealogy websites with which it is so often associated. As a modern hobby it spread out, like historical reenactments, from the United States. The biggest single influence was Alex Haley's novel *Roots: The Saga of an American Family* (1976) and, even more so, the two miniseries adapted from it, *Roots* (1977) and *Roots: The Next Generations* (1979), both of which ran in thirty-two countries.[248] Its lasting legacy can be gleaned from the fact that the book has been constantly reissued and the series remade as recently as 2016.[249] *Roots: The Next Generations* ended, like the book, by showing Haley—played by the actor James Earl Jones—interviewing his relatives, reading microfilms in the archive, and traveling to Africa for research. In an epilogue, Haley himself addressed the viewers directly, calling on them to follow his example.[250]

For Haley, who, after all, had ghostwritten the autobiography of Malcolm X, *Roots* was a political as well as a personal quest. He saw family history as a way for Black Americans to claim a place in a history they were so often written out of. Many heeded Haley's invitation to explore their own roots. The same year *Roots* ran on television, two guides for Black genealogy appeared, *Ebony* published the article "How to Trace Your Family Tree," and the Afro-American Historical and Genealogical Society was founded.[251] "Among many blacks," *Time* noted, "*Roots* has kindled an intense desire to search out their genealogies," albeit admitting that "blacks' interest in their African heritage began years ago." The article also acknowledged that, as Haley's research had shown, reconstructing their family's past was particularly hard and, in many cases, simply impossible for those whose ancestors had been enslaved, as the federal census omitted their names up to 1870.[252] The new interest in roots therefore often meant "White Roots," to quote the title of a 1977 article in *Time*.[253] Indeed, the overwhelming majority of Americans taking up genealogy were not of African but of white European descent.[254] When *Newsweek* devoted a cover to "Everybody's Search for Roots" in July 1977, it conspicuously showed a white family. "The irony of the watershed cultural moment surrounding 'Roots' was that a book about slavery and the African diaspora became a catalyst for a largely white ethnic revival," as the *Washington Post* put it succinctly in 2019.[255]

The impact of *Roots* was so extensive that many publications have called the boom in popular genealogy the "*Roots* phenomenon."[256] Still, its rise preceded Haley's book by more than a decade. "Hordes of amateur ancestor hunters are on the prowl nowadays, sallying into musty courthouses and old cemeteries to compile their own genealogies," *Life* reported as early as 1963.[257] Librarians and archivists all over the United States noted the increasing interest in genealogy as well as the broader makeup of genealogists since the 1960s.[258] In Britain, too, the "awakening interest, on a popular level, in genealogical research" of the late 1950s had become an "enormous increase of interest in genealogy" by the end of the next decade.[259]

With *Roots*, family historians finally could no longer be ignored, especially as it brought in countless new recruits. At the Mormon Church Family History Library in Salt Lake City, the biggest of its kind in the world, traffic almost doubled after its broadcast.[260] In the early 1980s, a conservative estimate put the number of people participating in genealogical studies in the United States and Canada at five hundred thousand, half of whom were organized in over 750 genealogical societies.[261] In 1977, 29 percent of Americans polled said they were "very interested" in family history; the number rose to 45 percent in 1995, 60 percent in 2000, 73 percent in 2005, and 87 percent in 2009.[262] Surveys conducted of the users of genealogical libraries and the membership of genealogical societies in the United States concluded that family historians tended to be middle aged, white collar, with above-average income and education, and slightly more female.[263] A Canadian study reported similar findings.[264]

The "*Roots* effect" also made itself felt in other countries, particularly in Britain, where a survey from 1986 reported that the series was one of respondents' main reasons for becoming interested in genealogy.[265] The BBC got in on the trend in 1979 with a documentary of its own—soon nicknamed "English roots"—in which the newscaster Gordon Honeycombe provided the audience with a do-it-yourself guide by tracing his own family history.[266] The media's interest in genealogy both reflected its popularity and further stimulated it. By the early 1980s, roughly half the users of the Public Records Office (renamed the National Archives in 2003) were conducting family tree research; by the late 1990s, they made up 94 percent.[267] The Family Records Centre, a branch office of the National Archives geared especially to family historians, received 140,000 visitors in 1997, the year it opened, and 200,000 annual visitors by the early 2000s.[268] The readership of *Family Tree Magazine,* the United Kingdom's biggest genealogical magazine, doubled from 30,000 in the mid-1980s to 60,000 in the 1990s.[269] According to a 2008 YouGov poll, a third of Britons had made attempts to trace their family history—a sizable percentage, though still low compared with the United States.[270]

Another major boost was technology. Many hobby genealogists were early adopters when it came to computers, which they used for compiling, storing, and indexing the information and documents they collected.[271] Then the internet arrived. "Powering the phenomenon are the new tools of the digital age," *Time* noted in 1999, "computer programs that turn the search for family trees into an addiction; websites that make it easy to find and share information; and chat rooms filled with folks seeking advice and swapping leads."[272] Few texts on family history research neglect to mention that it is the third most common use of the internet after shopping and pornography.[273] Ancestry.com, the biggest and best-known genealogical website, claims to hold over thirty million records, to have more than twenty million users, and to make over $1 billion in revenue.[274] Together with other websites, it has greatly simplified the search for ancestors, functioning as a sort of gateway drug for many.

As a result, family history research became even more widely popular, which resulted in more media attention and new genealogical television shows like *Who Do You Think You Are?* Running incessantly in the United Kingdom since 2004, it has also been adapted for the United States, Australia, Canada, and many other countries.[275] In the United States, scholar Henry Louis Gates Jr. has hosted a succession of similar programs since 2006, such as *African American Lives* and *Finding Your Roots,* whose own roots can be traced to Haley, whom Gates repeatedly cited as an inspiration. For him, too, family history was a political project, a way to understand the contemporary situation and history of African Americans and Americans in general. His aim was, "first, to show that we're all immigrants, and secondly, that we're all mixed."[276] Technology transformed genealogy yet again, this time by the comparatively cheap availability of DNA sequencing. In addition to—or sometimes instead of—painstakingly researching their ancestry through archival research, family historians began to explore their ethnic backgrounds by having their DNA tested.[277]

Never quite achieving the popularity it commands in the United States and Britain, family history research has taken root in other countries, too.

"Not long ago most Europeans would have stared blankly if asked to give their great-grandmother's name. Outside the ranks of titled aristocracy, climbing the family tree was mainly a hobby for aristocrats, maiden aunts, and eccentrics," reported *Newsweek* in 1988 in an article titled "Europe's Genealogy Craze."[278] At about the same time, Pierre Nora complained—with more than a hint of exaggeration—that "there is hardly a family today in which some member has not recently sought to document as accurately as possible his or her ancestors' furtive existences," with 43 percent of visitors to French archives carrying out genealogical research.[279] "Genealogy was all the rage," Annie Ernaux, too, remembers. "People went to the town halls in their native regions and collected birth and death certificates."[280] Nora also included an article on genealogy in *Les lieux de mémoire* that claimed that France's three hundred genealogists of the past had grown to twenty thousand and, with them, genealogy had developed into a widespread, democratic hobby.[281] By 2002 their number was estimated at around forty thousand, half of them professionals.[282] Compared with Britain, let alone the United States, this was still a small number. Taking his cue from Nora, François Hartog notes how "a nonspecialist public, concerned or curious about genealogy, began visiting the archives" in the 1980s.[283] In this way, the rise of genealogy informed both the critique of commemoration and presentism.

In Germany, family history research first attracted public attention in the 1990s. By then the number of genealogists had doubled since 1978 and the membership of genealogical societies risen to fifteen thousand, not including the many occasional hobbyists who never went as far as joining one.[284] If that was little even compared with France, there was a reason for it: as a handbook for genealogists complained in 1972, genealogy was still tainted in Germany because, during the time of National Socialism, people who wanted to study or work for the state had to prove their "Aryan" ancestry.[285] Revealingly, the German spin-off of *Who Do You Think You Are?* only achieved a meagre four episodes, and this although—or perhaps precisely because—such a format would have lent itself to discussing ordinary citizens' involvement with National Socialism.[286] As the German case illustrates, genealogy television programs may have fueled the interest in the subject, but they would not have been successful without it being popular in the first place.

Not everyone was pleased that genealogy had become so popular: professional historians, librarians, and archivists were more than skeptical. When a British journalist noted in 1962 that "the patronising attitude of academics that genealogy is something not quite respectable is dying," he was too opti-mistic.[287] "Virtual battle lines have been drawn between genealogists and archivists, as each group has seen the other as the major obstacle to accom-plishing mutually exclusive goals," noted the archivist Phebe R. Jacobsen in 1981.[288] While a librarian in the early 1980s welcomed that the "'hands-off' policy that was so typical among libraries just a decade or two ago has been largely transformed into one of 'open arms,'" one archivist still wrote of a "love-hate relationship" at the end of the decade.[289]

While archivists and librarians increasingly made peace with genealogists, recognizing their importance in terms of visitor numbers and funds, historians remained unconvinced. In the mid-1970s, the American historian Samuel P. Hays noted the "mutual disdain" with which the two groups generally viewed each other.[290] "For many years professional historians had little time for a field they saw as amateurish, insufficiently rigorous and lacking context," com-plained the family historian Michael Sharpe as late as 2011.[291] Confirms Alison Light in 2014, "Professional historians have generally given family history short shrift."[292] If popular genealogy has been the subject of research at all, it has come mainly from sociology and anthropology. Except for François Weil's his-tory of genealogy in the United States, and public historians like Tanya Evans trying to bridge the gap between academic and amateur historians, family his-tory research—whether as a hobby, as part of popular culture, or as a historical practice—has met with little interest by historians.[293]

More usually historians understood family history research as a nostalgic practice. While, for Jay P. Anglin, writing in 1975, the "current craze for nostalgia has had the effect of stimulating public interest in ancestry with a consequent boon in amateur genealogy," for Jonathan D. Sarna, writing in 1980, "the current genealogical obsession" contained "a puzzling undertone of nostalgia."[294] A year earlier the historian David A. Gerber warned his col-leagues not to "dismiss the popular trend as little more than a fad, or as mere nostalgia," suggesting that this was exactly what many of them did.[295] More recently, Evans has argued that most of her colleagues still tend to view ge-nealogists "as sentimental, nostalgic and unanalytical": "Academics have been quick to distance themselves from genealogists in their desire to set them-selves apart from and above those 'amateur' family historians; from those who supposedly 'wallow in self-indulgent nostalgia.'"[296] Here, as in other contexts, nostalgia primarily denoted both a backward-looking attitude and distortion: family historians, the term implies, are amateurs, who neither know how to handle the archive nor are interested in the bigger historical picture, but confine themselves instead to the smallest possible unit: their own family.

Some genealogists—even some professionals—could be said to prove them right. Anthony Wagner, for instance, the foremost British authority on genealogy in the 1960s and 1970s and Garter Principal King of Arms—that is, the Queen's principal adviser on all things ceremony and heraldry—held the "great political and social changes" that cut off "great numbers of people from their historical roots" responsible for genealogy's flourishing, which he, consequently, understood as a "reaction against the confusion and rootlessness of modern life." Writing in 1970, he noted that for him genealogy was a way to revive these roots and to reconnect with the "pre-industrial England" that had acquired the "quality of a lost home," inadvertently alluding to nostalgia's original meaning.[297]

Wagner explained the popularity of genealogy just as others did that of nostalgia: as a yearning to recapture a past from which modern people felt disconnected due to continued accelerated change.[298] He was not the only one to think so. In the "jet-stream of the still accelerating Industrial-cum-Technological Revolutions" of the present, genealogy provided "help to increase historical awareness and social consciousness," family historian Leo Derrick-Jehu believed in 1968.[299]

Accelerated change may have resulted in people feeling disconnected from the past, but it simultaneously compelled them to seek the past out as an antidote to or a refuge from it. In the "increasing rush and pressures of today's world," family history research, one of its practitioners explained in 1998, provided a sort of rest: "We are happy for a few hours a week to escape into those times again."[300] If family historians emerge here as escapist, what they escape to, however, is not the past but the research that provides them with an autonomy they experience nowhere else in their daily lives.

Other observers focused less on accelerated change than on what they saw as the alienation of modern life. From a "defense of genealogy," the archivist Patrick M. Quinn in 1991 launched into an attack against the "cultural vacuity of American life": "Adrift in a sea of instant culture with dubious meanings," family historians "yearned for genuine heritage. Faced with an unrewarding present and a precarious future, they seek refuge, comfort, certainty—a cultural anchor in a knowable past." As a more specific example, he mentions the "breakup of the nuclear family," another frequent explanation for the rise of popular genealogy.[301]

In his inaugural address at a conference of the London family history societies in 1978, John Rayment spoke about "the increasing deterioration of
family unity," which he saw "at the bottom of a great many of the evils of
modern life," recommending genealogy as a remedy.[302] "At a time when the
structure of family life is being threatened," noted a 1979 genealogical handbook, "it is no exaggeration to claim that the study of family history is the
single most important antidote to this trend," adding quickly, "provided, of
course, that it is not undertaken in a spirit of regretful nostalgia."[303] "Perhaps
nostalgia for the past and a search for 'roots' are a reaction to the loosening of
family ties today and uncertainty for the future," mused one practitioner in
1981.[304] Yet the idea of the decline of the traditional, close-knit family due to the
onslaught of the ills of modern life—sexual promiscuity and divorce mainly—
has itself been characterized as nostalgic.[305] Meanwhile, the widespread cliché
that most people are drawn to genealogy because they are lonely or experience
their own family life as deficient has also been debunked.[306]

Surveys conducted of family historians over the years have not established
nostalgia as a dominant motivating factor. A study of Canadian genealogists
from the early 1990s, for instance, found "little indication of nostalgic
yearning."[307] Likewise, two British surveys of the members of the Birmingham
and Midland Society for Genealogy and Heraldry in 1974 and 1981 revealed
few responses displaying any overt or hidden traces of nostalgia, however
defined. If, for a few respondents, genealogy had been a long-standing interest since childhood, the majority started following the death of a relative,
or after inheriting papers or objects, which prompted them to investigate
their family's past.[308] For a third group, family history research was a part
of their general interest in history.[309] Two members compared it to a cross-
word puzzle, like "detective work" a frequent comparison.[310]

These findings are further substantiated by the responses to a directive
that sociologist Anne-Marie Kramer sent to 525 participants of the Mass Observation Project in 2008 in which she asked them why, in their view, family
history research was so popular, whether and why they participated in it
themselves, and what larger roles and functions it fulfilled.[311] Of the 224 respondents, none expressed doubt about its popularity, many putting it down
to the sustained media attention and *Who Do You Think You Are?* in particular.[312] While some found genealogy "silly," "rubbish," or "indescribably
boring," the overwhelming majority viewed it positively, with many having
dabbled in it themselves.[313]

A few respondents—mainly those who were not practitioners—mentioned nostalgia as a possible explanation: "So maybe this creates some sense of nostalgia for times that were simpler, not racing along so fast," one respondent mused.[314] Another commented, "In my opinion FHR [family history research] is so popular, partly as a result of nostalgia, a desire to know whether the past was better or worse than the here and now."[315] Some did not use the term *nostalgia* but could be said to allude to it. "I think researching family history is so popular because many people have become rootless," pondered a retired teacher.[316] "In this rushing mad world of today, maybe people have lost their way and have nothing solid to hold on to, to give them their identity," concurred a forty-eight-year-old housewife from Finchingfield, concluding, "FHR makes them feel safe and worthwhile."[317] Apart from accelerated change, some respondents also mentioned the "diminishing role of the family" or that "family ties have loosened enormously."[318] Apparently, not only historians but also parts of the public viewed family history as a nostalgic practice. Practitioners did so much more rarely. "Living in the world today is complex, often uncertain and in some ways disorienting. The pace of change is fast," wrote a forty-two-year-old male mental health worker from Eastbourne. "So maybe this creates some sense of nostalgia for times that were simpler, not racing along so fast. I'm sure it also creates a need to feel rooted in something beyond this hectic time. That certainly is true of me."[319]

Like the participants in the Birmingham and Midland survey of the 1970s and 1980s, however, most respondents to the Mass Observation directive gave other reasons for their interest in family history research. For a forty-five-year-old travel guide from Nantwich, it made "history not an academic dusty, boring thing of dates and people, but vibrant and interconnecting with each individual."[320] A thirty-four-year-old research and information officer admitted that she "learnt so much more about English history in the time I have been researching my family history . . . than I ever did at school. . . . It has also opened my eyes to the social and economic conditions that my ancestors lived through."[321] Likewise, a middle-aged male respondent from Aberdeen, and "big fan of FHR," saw it as "a great link to wider social, economic and political—I would say 'real history.' I've been really impressed by the amount of people who got involved and were not that interested in deeper history, developed a wider interest in the social conditions of various periods. It can humanize and illustrate history."[322] A thirty-six-year-old woman from Bolsover, too, professed her "deep interest in social history."[323]

While some historians reject genealogy as "identity-driven history" as opposed to—as well as undermining—social history, such responses suggest the opposite.[324] Family history research, an Australian study has found, "often leads people to become interested in social history."[325] In another study "all the participants . . . shared a concern with putting ancestors into historical context."[326] As early as 1981, the Labour member of Parliament and left-wing local historian Stan Newens emphasized that "research into family origins here in Britain is helping to create a new awareness of the past among people who previously knew very little, if anything, of their forefathers and not all that much more about the environment in which they lived and the events of their times."[327] For Newens, family history was a way for people who, like himself, had been born into humble circumstances to find out about their own past as members of the working class and to do so by researching it themselves, thereby acquiring new skills as well as an independent perspective: it raised the "level of historical consciousness" and encouraged "people to study their own history."[328]

Not only is family history not nostalgic, its defenders argue, it can also dispel nostalgic ideas about the past. "The vast majority of family historians whom I have come across," reports British historian David Hey, "are only too well aware that their ancestors had a harder life than most of us have today." Learning about the past, the living and working conditions of their ancestors, "shatters the myth of 'the good old days.'"[329] "While it is often argued that family historians love seeking out Golden Ages," Tanya Evans writes, "the family historians I have worked with . . . are primarily keen to overturn assumptions and oft-told stories they remain suspicious of."[330] Rather than affirming present-day ideas of self and society, family history research here emerges as a potentially subversive practice.

Whether this is accurate or not, genealogy itself has certainly transformed from the most elitist branch of history to a "democratic hobby."[331] According to the Canadian study, most family historians experience their research as a "leveler," emphasizing the common ancestry across backgrounds.[332] For others, the democratization of genealogy has resulted in a "democratization of history."[333] Indeed, for many people family history is both the most obvious and the easiest way to take an interest in history and to research it themselves. If family historians are amateurs when accessing libraries and archives, historiography, and methodology, they are, after all, experts when it comes to the history of their own family. In this way, family history research demonstrates, in the words of historian Jerome de Groot, that "armed with some few skills and the time to investigate the mass of information, anyone can produce a narrative of the past which explains and textualizes it," thereby challenging "the role of the academic or professional historian as gatekeeper of knowledge."[334]

If this may be too optimistic a view, it may at least partly explain why many professional historians tend to be so ill-disposed toward family historians: they may perceive them not only as amateurs dabbling in things they know little about but also as intruding on their turf. Nostalgia here again takes on many different shades: it signifies a yearning for roots in a rapidly changing world that turned the past into a slower and simpler version of the present or, more positively, a compensatory space. Ultimately, however, by invoking it, academic historians defend their own interpretative authority over the past.

In recent years such critical attitudes toward family history have become all the more questionable, as some historians have taken to the practice themselves: Ivan Jablonka and Mark Mazower, for instance, have both written books about their Jewish grandparents in the turmoil and persecution of twentieth-century Europe.[335] In *Common People,* the English historian Alison Light traced her working-class roots, which prompted her to reflect on—and to defend—the practice of family history and those who participate in it.[336] By embedding personal histories in the wider social and political history, these books achieve what family history more generally is often said to be lacking. Whether they also change how historians view the practice remains to be seen.

Conclusion

Historians have adopted the concept of nostalgia since the 1970s in specific situations and for specific reasons: to explain why ever-larger parts of the population not only took an unprecedented interest in the past but also engaged with it more directly, by campaigning on behalf of historic buildings threatened by demolition, by frequenting in ever-growing numbers an ever-growing number of museums, by taking part in or visiting historical reenactments, and by doing historical research themselves through amateur genealogy. At the same time, the accusation of nostalgia was a way to call these practices into question. First, it implied distorting the past rather than exploring it to better understand it and, through it, the present. Second, nostalgia meant turning the past into a golden age superior to the present, thus violating the modernist understanding of time into the bargain. Third, it suggested entertaining instead of educating, to appeal to audiences' hearts rather than their brains. And finally, it was used to attack the commodification and commercialization of the past.

Overall, however, the case studies assembled here have found only limited evidence for nostalgia, however understood, at least when it comes to the charges of distortion and sentimentalization. Practitioners cited many reasons for engaging with the past, from education, fun, and socializing with like-minded people to the desire to pass something—whether material or immaterial—on to their children or future generations. Finally, there were more banal reasons for the popularity of these practices: not only did more people have more money and leisure time at their disposal than ever before, they were also better educated.

Focusing on nostalgia, the heritage critics neglected to cast their net wider and to investigate other aspects. Yet if their critique was flawed, it was not without merit, as without it we would know far less about popular history in the 1970s and 1980s than we do. Despite overlooking important aspects and motivations, the heritage critics at least took popular history seriously, which cannot be said of all historians at the time.

But if nostalgia carried such pejorative connotations and if it led to important aspects being overlooked, would it not be better to give up the term altogether and to replace it with other, more neutral terms? Arguing that what "was described by some as the 'nostalgic impulse' actually bound up diverse perspectives and resulted in multiple types of historymaking that cannot be defined simply as wistfulness for a lost past," historian M. J. Rymsza-Pawlowska has drawn just this conclusion.[337] And insofar as nostalgia does not accurately capture the transformation of the landscape of public history in the 1970s and 1980s but disparages it, it may well be the right conclusion to draw.

Yet if we want to understand how public history was debated as well as the opposition and critique it faced in this period, we need to take the nostalgia charge seriously: it simply was too widespread and prominent to be ignored. Ignoring it would disregard how the new practices were perceived at the time and what obstacles conservationists, museum professionals, reenactors, and family historians faced. By putting nostalgia center stage, we not only gain clearer insights into these struggles—struggles that, after all, continue to this day—we also better understand how and why the term *nostalgia* was employed at the time.

What makes it even harder to get rid of nostalgia is the fact that, while it was often introduced by critics, at least some practitioners used the term themselves. Peter Lewis and Jay Anderson, for instance, a museum practitioner and a living historian, tried to rescue and redefine the concept to suit their own purposes. Other practitioners, as well as many later studies, also employed the term but, unlike the heritage critics, not as a universal explanation for the popularity of history or to attack it; rather, they used it in a much more limited and neutral fashion. Finally, even if *nostalgia* retrospectively appears to be a problematic term, it played a useful role: it facilitated a discussion of new approaches to the past that differed from traditional ones, approaches that did not so much present history in a cerebral, text-based, top-down way but instead allowed people to engage with it in ways that were more personal, immersive, experiential, and bottom-up.

In the end, the heritage critics seem to have been correct at least in one regard: nostalgia may not have been "everywhere," as Lowenthal wrote, but "American culture in the 1970s was flooded with history," as Rymsza-Pawlowska writes.[338] While this chapter by and large corroborates this view, it expands on it in two ways. First, history was popular not only in the United States but across Europe (and probably other parts of the world as well), and there was a considerable transnational traffic. While American preservationists looked to Europe as a model, historical reenactments and family history spread there from the United States. Second, while these developments became apparent in the 1970s, they originated in the preceding decade: whether the conservation movement, the museum boom, historical reenactments, or family history, all these practices had already gained momentum and followers in the immediate postwar era. Consequently, they had less to do with the depression—economic and otherwise—of the 1970s than with the prosperity of the preceding years that allowed more people to participate in them, thus making history more democratic. If, as Samuel has famously insisted, history is "not the prerogative of the historian" but the "work of a thousand hands," there were now more hands involved than ever before.[339]

In summary, the new landscape of popular and public history taking shape since the 1960s was far too complex and diverse to be reduced to nostalgia, and reducing it to nostalgia was something of a knee-jerk reaction. We therefore need to treat contemporary analyses with a good dose of skepticism. At the same time, because the nostalgia argument was so widespread and common, because it was so integral to the debate at the time and applied to so many different examples, it enables us to examine the history of public history in a comprehensive way and to inquire about peoples' motivations behind and reasons for engaging with the past. Once used to dismiss such questions, nostalgia retrospectively makes for a good starting point to pose them.

Conclusion

You want a timeless song, I wanna change the game
Like modern architecture, John Lautner coming your way
I know you like this beat 'cause Jeff been doing the damn thing
You wanna turn it up loud, future nostalgia is the name.

—Dua Lipa, "Future Nostalgia"[1]

Dua Lipa's song "Future Nostalgia," released in 2019 as a single announcing the album of the same name, can be read as a comment on nostalgia and even as a rejoinder to the antinostalgia pop culture critique. Twenty-four when she wrote it, she was a bare two years older than Paul McCartney when he wrote "Yesterday." The two songs, the one from 1964 and the other from 2019, make perfect bookends for this study. While McCartney expressed the sentiments often associated with nostalgia without using the term in the same year its new meaning entered British dictionaries, Dua Lipa used the term in a way that shows both how prominent and, with—or perhaps due to—this prominence, how broad and blurred it had become in the intervening fifty-five years, reaching far beyond the dictionary definition.

Like the term *nostalgia* itself, Dua Lipa's song can be read in different ways. Instead of producing the "timeless song" that critics, and maybe her audiences, too, expect from her, she declares she wants to "change the game," comparing her songwriting to modern architecture and herself to the modernist architect John Lautner. A student of Frank Lloyd Wright, Lautner is best remembered for his futuristic designs of the 1950s and 1960s, some of which—not coincidentally—have featured in science-fiction films. Yet while Dua Lipa explicitly takes up and professes to aspire to the modernist ethic of creation ex nihilo in her lyrics (ironically by referring to the modernist past), she simultaneously diverts it through her music: incorporating influences from the 1960s to the 1990s, her album *Future Nostalgia* had, as critics across the board noted, a very retro sound and feel to it. Far from inaugurating a new style or challenging its audiences in the way modernism strove to do, it was universally celebrated as a feel-good album during the first wave of the COVID-19 pandemic: *Rolling Stone* called it "the perfect balm for a stressful time"; "Dua Lipa reminds us how to feel care-free," declared NPR.[2]

As in the contrast between modernist ethic and retro practice, what "future nostalgia" meant was open to debate, if not a contradiction in terms: it could signify a longing for the future, or for a past modernist-futurist way of looking to the future, or an anticipated future nostalgia for the present of 2019. It could mean all three or nothing at all: a cryptic phrase everyone can understand how they see fit, filling it with their own meaning. Dua Lipa herself professed to wanting to make "something that felt nostalgic but had something fresh and futuristic about it too," thus squaring the circle—or rather bending the arrow pointing from past to future.[3] Even without the epithet "future," nostalgia had, by the 2010s, become such a hazy concept that it threatened to lose meaning altogether, especially when it came to the critique of pop culture, politics, and popular history to which it was central. As the previous chapters have shown, nostalgia could take on many different meanings, stand in for different concepts, and carry different connotations, most of which, however, tended to be critical if not polemical.

In the literature expressly dealing with it, nostalgia did not start out as an entirely negative concept. For some commentators, mostly from sociology and philosophy, it fulfilled, at least potentially, positive functions, particularly as compensation for the stress of accelerated change in modernity. Beginning in the 2000s, psychologists have expanded on this understanding of nostalgia as a coping mechanism.[4] *Yesterday* has somewhat sidelined this more positive take interpretation because predominantly nostalgia was perceived not as beneficial in terms of individuals but as a collective phenomenon pertaining to and crippling societies' ability to navigate the present and the future. This was how almost all the major contributions to the debate about nostalgia understood it—and, to a large extent, how it is still understood today. Starting with the critics of heritage and postmodernity, there was a notable turn from the diagnosis of nostalgia to one of presentism: instead of finding too much past in the present, critics now saw the past as being swallowed up by a present increasingly unable to view the past as distinct from itself. Confusingly, they nevertheless used the term *nostalgia* to characterize this development.

While presentism gradually replaced nostalgia as a major concern for historians particularly, the broader discourse has remained fixated on nostalgia. More books on the subject are coming out now than ever before, and most of them tend to understand it in the existing tradition, a tradition they are often only partially aware of. *Yesterday* has pieced together this tradition to show its inherent ideological assumptions, its contradictions, and its shortfalls, to contribute to more critical awareness.

One area in which the literature on nostalgia has massively expanded in recent years is politics. Nowhere has nostalgia attracted more heated criticism. Still, theorists of nostalgia have paid so little attention to politics that the regularly erupting debate about nostalgia in politics can be seen almost as a separate discourse. As there was little attempt even by political thinkers to define what they meant by "the politics of nostalgia," *Yesterday* had to extract what this phrase conveyed from how it was employed in a political context. As politics is commonly seen as being about solving the problems of the present and planning for the future, it is hardly surprising that nostalgia figures primarily as an insult here. What makes the term perfectly suited for accusing a person, a group, a camp, or an idea of holding or exhibiting, variously, regressive, reactionary, or anachronistic ideas and attitudes makes it simultaneously unsuitable for political analysis, especially if its underlying ideological connotations are overlooked.

When it comes to pop culture, *nostalgia* is also a loaded term, mostly invoked to dismiss certain pop cultural artifacts, if not a whole style or period, as uncreative and derivative. Whether pop culture critics employ *nostalgia* in an emotional, aesthetic, or temporal sense, they predominantly use it in a pejorative way to characterize artifacts and styles drawing on the past as inferior to ones that, supposedly, inaugurate new beginnings. As we have seen, this does not do justice to the complexities of pop culture. For one, many of the examples quoted as evidence of nostalgia do not bear out the charge on closer examination. Even those artifacts critics see as quintessentially nostalgic often engage with the past in much more complicated and ambiguous ways. Similarly, audiences react to representations of the past in diverse ways. In both regards, playfulness, irony, and shock have been as much in evidence as yearning or sentimentality, if not more. Here again, *Yesterday* prompts us to move beyond the existing critique and recognize how looking back can be a stimulus for creativity rather than a sign of its absence.

Finally, nostalgia plays an important role in the critique of popular representations of the past. In this area as well, it occupies different, though again usually adverse, meanings, implying that these representations were distorting the past, particularly by sentimentalizing it. This already points to another frequent function of the term: to dismiss emotional and experiential representations of or engagements with the past. However, as in politics and pop culture, nostalgia can also imply backward-looking attitudes, an antiquarian interest in the past motivated not by the desire to understand it—and through it the present—but by the desire to engage with it for its own sake, thus denoting the opposite of history as historians understand it. Consequently, here, too, instead of speaking about nostalgia in a broad and unspecific sense, it would make more sense to use narrower, clearly defined terms.

As different as these fields may be in other respects, how nostalgia is applied within them is overall similar: as a pejorative concept implying an incorrect attitude toward or use of the past. As *Yesterday* has shown, this understanding of nostalgia is grounded in underlying temporal assumptions that are usually not openly addressed or discussed. Nostalgia is seen as a wrong attitude toward the past because it does not adhere to an understanding of time that views it as linear, dynamic, and homogeneous, with a closed-off past and open future. Nostalgia, in the eyes of its critics, does not subscribe to the idea of progress but contradicts it by putting, as Maurice Halbwachs phrased it, the golden age not in the future but in the past.[5] Even though fewer intellectuals may have been willing to defend progress in the face of its mounting costs and critique, that does not mean they were willing to relinquish it; instead, they defended it indirectly—by attacking nostalgia.

By teasing out the usually unaddressed temporal assumptions underlying the critique of nostalgia, *Yesterday* contributes not only to historicizing and conceptualizing nostalgia but also to the history of temporality in general. It shows that concepts of time are not limited to debates expressly about time, past, present, and future but that the understanding of time influences how practically everything is interpreted. Exactly because time is so essential, it is often essentialized: seen as self-evident and natural, it is taken as a given that does not warrant further attention.

More specifically, *Yesterday* questions the common cliché of the future-oriented postwar era, the nostalgic 1970s, and the corresponding transition from a modern-futurist-historical to a postmodern-presentist regime of historicity. The idea of progress was never undisputed: as soon as it emerged, it was followed by a critique of progress that became increasingly louder. But even though the idea of progress was contested, it never vanished: as the sustained critique of nostalgia shows, it lingered on and persisted. Politics, whether progressive or conservative, that do not promise a contribution to making the future better in some ways are as unimaginable as politics not drawing on the past—whether as a negative foil or as a model, as something to conserve or to overcome, or both at the same time. Likewise, pop culture constantly operates between the poles of innovation and repetition, between striving for newness and drawing on the past—as *Future Nostalgia,* both album and song, aptly illustrate.

Much as progress did not suddenly become suspect in the 1970s, many if not most of the examples quoted as evidence of the 1970s "nostalgia wave" were much older: whether the "politics of nostalgia," retro trends in pop culture and fashion, or the history boom, the beginnings of all these phenomena are to be found in the 1950s and 1960s if not earlier. Rather, it was in the 1970s that they came to be understood in the context of nostalgia, which simultaneously took on much more negative meanings.

The idea of a 1970s nostalgia wave also seems questionable in the light of the following decades. Although the 1980s are frequently portrayed as a more optimistic decade compared with the preceding one, the diagnoses of nostalgia expanded. With the critique of heritage and postmodernity, its meanings became yet broader. While it may be possible to point to various moments when nostalgia was especially prominent, it is much harder to say when nostalgia was *not* an issue of discussion. In fact, it has been an unceasing intellectual and public concern from the 1960s to the present.

Just as viewing nostalgia as a characteristic of one period can skew the findings, so does viewing it in a national framework. By placing the nostalgia discourse and the phenomena and practices it pertains to in a transnational framework, *Yesterday* questions existing explanations and raises new questions. This does not, however, mean that it promotes an understanding of nostalgia as a universal, pancultural, or even global emotion. Rather, because nostalgia is so often understood as a concept linked to Western modernity, extreme care and an awareness of local concepts are called for when applying it to other regions of the world. Instead, future research would do well to follow the reverse approach by, first, seeking out local concepts for engaging with the past and subsequently contrasting them with Western concepts of nostalgia, thereby also throwing new critical light on them. By showing the extent to which the thinking about nostalgia is rooted in implicit Western and modern assumptions, *Yesterday* hopes to have prepared the ground for this research.

At the same time, it raises questions for the study of memory and emotions. While nostalgia frequently appears as synonymous with memory or emotion (or both), how exactly memory and nostalgia relate to each other is underconceptualized and underresearched. In the nostalgia critique, the question hardly comes up at all, as it seems to acknowledge only one form of memory: nostalgia. Is it possible to define nostalgic memories if all memory is nostalgic and if the term *nostalgia* is used to dismiss memory as a subject of investigation?

For the history of emotions, nostalgia poses a similar problem: How is it possible to historicize an emotion as fraught and contested as nostalgia? What happens if the emotion that is to be investigated cannot be found in the sources? Or put differently, what if the term denoting the emotion is ascribed from the outset and the outside and not reflected in or even outright rejected by the people, phenomena, and practices it is ascribed to? To give an example: If nostalgia is, as Simon Reynolds argues, "one of the great pop emotions," how can we explore its emotional quality in pop when Reynolds also uses nostalgia to criticize pop generally or when many of the examples he and others quote as evidence of pop's nostalgia do not meet this description?[6] Similarly, how can we investigate the role of nostalgia in politics when nostalgia simultaneously serves to denounce certain brands of politics?

As these questions show, the critique of nostalgia, or to be exact, its failure to distinguish between analytical and polemical uses of the term, has brought us to a dead end. Is there any way to get out of it, to apply the concept in a (more) meaningful way? The results of this study are not exactly promising in this regard. Precisely because *nostalgia* has become such a widespread and universal, as well as vague and ambiguous, term that has been applied to basically any representation, use of, or engagement with the past someone else disagrees with or wants to contest, it is highly unlikely that it can be employed in an analytical manner. Indeed, it may well be lost for use in an academic context altogether.

And yet the unspecific and tendentious way *nostalgia* is employed does not mean that it is completely impossible to recover it—at least when it comes to intellectual discourse. To achieve this, however, it is necessary to change how we are using it. Here are some recommendations that, simple as they are, could help to lay a more solid foundation for future research on nostalgia.

First, such research would use the term much more sparingly and carefully than previous research and literature, especially when it comes to politics and pop culture.

Second, it would acknowledge that *nostalgia* has, for most of its career, carried overwhelmingly negative connotations and that these connotations have been based on an understanding of nostalgia as a modern condition, a result of and a reaction to modernity, as well as on the modern understanding of time.

Third, such research would need to distance itself from this ideological background and define exactly what it means by the term *nostalgia,* how it uses it, and how it relates to the existing research, acknowledging that people use and define *nostalgia* in different ways.

Fourth, instead of introducing nostalgia from the outset and applying it in a top-down manner, as is usually the case, such research would begin by investigating how the past is used and discussed and to what extent these uses correspond—or do not correspond—to nostalgia as defined beforehand.

Fifth, as this approach suggests, it is advisable to consider alternative terms (*retro, presentism,* and so on) and to distinguish between different ways to represent, use, or engage with the past (personal, collective, educational, emotional, experiential, immersive, performative, and so on) without understanding them as mutually exclusive and to clarify how they relate to nostalgia, if at all.

This process is, sixth, especially advisable when dealing with regions outside the English-speaking world or times before the modern era, where research should start by looking for local and contemporary concepts for engaging with the past instead of further universalizing and essentializing nostalgia.

Whether or not nostalgia is—or can become—a useful concept, it certainly appears as if we are stuck with it. If the magical term *nostalgia* did not fulfill a function, it would not have had such a long and productive career since the middle of the twentieth century. Despite—or precisely because—it is so deeply entangled with the thinking about time, modernity, and history, it remains an interesting problem to ponder. "I know you're dying trying to figure me out," Lipa sings in "Future Nostalgia"—implying that we never will, and the same might be said for nostalgia. But perhaps whether or not we figure it out is less important than continuing to try.

Notes

Introduction

1. Beatles, "Yesterday," Genius, https://genius.com/The-beatles-yesterday-lyrics; "Yesterday by the Beatles," SecondHandSongs, https://secondhandsongs.com /performance/1409.

2. Giles Smith, "Yesterday," in *The Beatles: 40 Years of Classic Writing,* ed. Mike Evan (London: Plexus, 2009), 111–114.

3. Johannes Hofer, "Dissertatio Medica De Nostalgia, Oder Heimwehe" (medical diss., Bertschius, Basel, 1688); Johannes Hofer, "Medical Dissertation on Nostalgia (1688)," trans. Carolyn Kiser Anspach, *Bulletin of the History of Medicine* 2 (1934): 376–391.

4. On the medical history of nostalgia, see Jean Starobinski, "The Idea of Nostalgia," trans. William S. Kemp, *Diogenes* 14 (1966): 81–103; Michael Roth, "Remembering Forgetting: Maladies de la Memoire in 19th-Century France," *Representations* 26 (1989): 49–68; Michael Roth, "Dying of the Past: Medical Studies of Nostalgia in Nineteenth-Century France," *History and Memory* 3 (1991): 5–29; Michael Roth, "The Time of Nostalgia: Medicine, History and Normality in 19th-Century France," *Time and Society* 1 (1992): 271–286; Lisa Gabrielle O'Sullivan, "Dying for Home: The Medicine and Politics of Nostalgia in Nineteenth Century France" (PhD diss., Queen Mary University of London, 2006); and Thomas Dodman, *What Nostalgia Was: War, Empire and the Time of a Deadly Emotion* (Chicago: University of Chicago Press, 2018).

5. Achim Landwehr, "Nostalgia and the Turbulence of Times," *History and Theory* 57, no. 2 (2018): 251–268; Dodman, *What Nostalgia Was;* Susan J. Matt,

Homesickness: An American History (Oxford: Oxford University Press, 2011), 130, 174.

6. *The Concise Oxford Dictionary of Current English* (Oxford: Oxford University Press, 1964), s.v. "nostalgia."

7. *Oxford English Dictionary Online* (Oxford: Oxford University Press, June 2022), s.v. "nostalgia," https://www.oed.com/view/Entry/128472?redirectedFrom=nostalgia.

8. See, for instance, Andrew Gordon, *The Rise and Fall of the Future: America's Changing Vision of Tomorrow, 1939–1986* (Jefferson, NC: McFarland, 2020); Rüdiger Graf, "Totgesagt und nicht gestorben: Die Persistenz des Fortschritts im 20. und 21. Jahrhundert," *Traverse: Zeitschrift für Geschichte* 23, no. 3 (2016): 91–102; Elke Seefried, "Reconfiguring the Future? Politics and Time from the 1960s to the 1980s—Introduction," *Journal of Modern European History* 13, no. 3 (2015): 306–316; and Helga Nowotny, *Time: The Modern and Postmodern Experience,* trans. Neville Plaice (London: Polity, 1996). On progress more generally, see Peter Wagner, *Progress: A Reconstruction* (Cambridge, UK: Polity, 2016); and Reinhart Koselleck, "Fortschritt," in *Geschichtliche Grundbegriffe: Historisches Lexikon zur politisch-sozialen Sprache in Deutschland,* ed. Otto Brunner, Werner Conze, and Reinhart Kosellck (Stuttgart: Klett-Cotta, 1975), 351–423.

9. Alvin Toffler, *Future Shock* (London: Pan Books, 1970), 407.

10. Raphael Samuel, *Theatres of Memory: Past and Present in Contemporary Culture* (London: Verso, 1994), 17.

11. John Tosh, *The Pursuit of History: Aims, Methods and New Directions in the Study of History,* 6th ed. (London: Routledge, 2015), 16.

12. Charles S. Maier, "The End of Longing? Notes toward a History of Postwar German National Longing," in *The Postwar Transformation of Germany,* ed. John S. Brady, Beverly Crawford, and Sarah Elise Williarty (Ann Arbor: University of Michigan Press, 1999), 271–285, here 273.

13. Christopher Lasch, *The True and Only Heaven: Progress and Its Critics* (New York: Norton, 1991), 83.

14. David Lowenthal, "Nostalgia Tells It Like It Wasn't," in *The Imagined Past: History and Nostalgia,* ed. Christopher Shaw and Malcolm Chase (Manchester: Manchester University Press, 1989), 18–32.

15. Michael Kammen, *Mystic Chords of Memory: The Transformation of Tradition in American Culture* (New York: Alfred A. Knopf, 1991), 688.

16. Malcolm Chase and Christopher Shaw, "The Dimensions of Nostalgia," in Shaw and Chase, *Imagined Past,* 1–17, here 1; Dipesh Chakrabarty, "Postcoloniality and the Artifice of History: Who Speaks for 'Indian' Pasts?," *Representations* 37 (1992): 1–26, here 1.

17. See Fred Davis, *Yearning for Yesterday: A Sociology of Nostalgia* (New York: Free Press, 1979), 16–26; Svetlana Boym, *The Future of Nostalgia* (New York: Basic

Books, 2001), 41–55; and Paul Grainge, *Monochrome Memories: Nostalgia and Style in Retro America* (Westport, CT: Praeger, 2002), 19–65.

18. Starobinski, "Idea of Nostalgia," 82.

19. Starobinski, 101.

20. Maurice Halbwachs, *On Collective Memory,* ed., trans., and with an introduction by Lewis A. Coser (Chicago: University of Chicago Press, 1992), 49.

21. Boym, *Future of Nostalgia,* xvi.

22. Starobinski, "Idea of Nostalgia," 82.

23. Starobinski, 82. Also see Ute Frevert et al., *Emotional Lexicons: Continuity and Change in the Vocabulary of Feeling, 1700–2000* (Oxford: Oxford University Press, 2014).

24. See Matt, *Homesickness;* Dodman, *What Nostalgia Was;* Juliane Brauer, "Heidi's Homesickness," in *Learning How to Feel: Children's Literature and Emotional Socialization, 1870–1970,* by Ute Frevert et al. (Oxford: Oxford University Press, 2014), 209–227; and Kyra Giorgi, *Emotions, Language and Identity on the Margins of Europe* (Basingstoke, UK: Palgrave Macmillan, 2014).

25. See Jan Plamper, *The History of Emotions: An Introduction,* trans. Keith Tribe (Oxford: Oxford University Press, 2015), 257–269.

26. See Boym, *Future of Nostalgia;* Peter Fritzsche, "Specters of History: On Nostalgia, Exile and Modernity," *American Historical Review* 106, no. 5 (2001): 1587–1618; and Peter Fritzsche, *Stranded in the Present: Modern Time and Melancholy of History* (Cambridge, MA: Harvard University Press, 2004). This theory, which relies on the work of Reinhart Koselleck, is discussed in Chapter 1.

27. See Koselleck, "Fortschritt." For premodern concepts of time, see G. J. Whitrow, *Time in History: Views of Time from Prehistory to the Present Day* (Oxford: Oxford University Press, 1988); and Arno Borst, *The Ordering of Time: From the Ancient Computus to the Modern Computer* (Cambridge, UK: Polity, 1993). For a more detailed discussion of these issues, see the conclusion of Chapter 1.

28. See Fernando Esposito, "Zeitenwandel: Transformationen geschichtlicher Zeitlichkeit nach dem Boom: Eine Einführung," in *Zeitenwandel: Transformationen geschichtlicher Zeitlichkeit nach dem Boom,* ed. Fernando Esposito (Göttingen: Vandenhoeck & Ruprecht, 2017), 7–62. See also Reinhart Koselleck, *Futures Past: On the Semantics of Historical Time,* trans. Keith Tribe (Cambridge, MA: MIT Press, 1985); Reinhart Koselleck, *Sediments of Time: On Possible Histories,* trans. and ed. Sean Franzel and Stefan-Ludwig Hoffmann (Stanford, CA: Stanford University Press, 2018); Nowotny, *Time;* Achim Landwehr, *Geburt der Gegenwart: Eine Geschichte der Zeit im 17. Jahrhundert* (Frankfurt am Main: S. Fischer, 2014); Achim Landwehr, *Die anwesende Abwesenheit der Vergangenheit: Essays zur Geschichtstheorie* (Frankfurt am Main: S. Fischer, 2016); François Hartog, *Regimes of Historicity: Presentism and the Experience of Time* (New York: Columbia University Press, 2015); Chris Lorenz and Berber Bevernage, eds., *Breaking Up Time: Negotiating the Borders*

between Present, Past and Future (Göttingen: Vandenhoeck & Ruprecht, 2013); Marek Tamm and Laurent Olivier, eds., *Rethinking Historical Time: New Approaches to Presentism* (London: Bloomsbury, 2019); and Aleida Assmann, *Is Time Out of Joint? On the Rise and Fall of the Modern Time Regime,* trans. Sarah Clift (Ithaca, NY: Cornell University Press, 2020).

29. Erica G. Hepper et al., "Pancultural Nostalgia: Prototypical Conceptions across Cultures," *Emotion* 14 (2014): 733–747.

30. David Lowenthal, *The Past Is a Foreign Country—Revisited* (Cambridge: Cambridge University Press, 2015), 38.

31. See Makoto Harris Takao, "Beyond Nostalgia and the Prison of English: Positioning Japan in a Global History of Emotions," *Zeithistorische Forschungen / Studies in Contemporary History* 18, no. 1 (2021): 21–43.

32. Boym, *Future of Nostalgia,* 13. See also Giorgi, *Emotions, Language and Identity.*

33. The French debate about *la mode rétro* is discussed in Chapter 3; see there for further references.

34. Simon Reynolds, *Retromania: Pop Culture's Addiction to Its Own Past* (New York: Faber and Faber, 2011), xxiii.

35. See, for instance, M. J. Rymsza-Pawlowska, *History Comes Alive: Public History and Popular Culture in the 1970s* (Chapel Hill: University of North Carolina Press, 2017).

36. Katharina Niemeyer, "Introduction: Media and Nostalgia," in *Media and Nostalgia: Yearning for the Past, Present and Future,* ed. Katharina Niemeyer (Basingstoke, UK: Palgrave Macmillan, 2014), 1–23. For an overview of the emerging interdisciplinary field of "nostalgia studies," see Michael Hviid Jacobsen, ed., *Nostalgia Now: Cross-Disciplinary Perspectives on the Past in the Present* (London: Routledge, 2020); and Michael Hviid Jacobsen, ed., *Intimations of Nostalgia: Multidisciplinary Explorations of an Enduring Emotion* (Bristol: Bristol University Press, 2022).

1. Revisiting

1. Alex Grasshoff, dir., *Future Shock,* narrated by Orson Welles (1972), video, 42:11, here 1:56–2:38, https://www.dailymotion.com/video/xp1tiz.

2. Grasshoff, 4:22–4:25.

3. Alvin Toffler, *Future Shock* (London: Pan Books, 1970), 12.

4. Toffler, 20.

5. Toffler, 432.

6. Toffler, 407.

7. Toffler, 18.

8. Toffler, 361.

9. Toffler, 25; see also 21–26.

10. Toffler, 327.

11. Toffler, 407.

12. Grasshoff, *Future Shock,* 26:54–27:12.

13. Toffler, *Future Shock,* 409.

14. Toffler, 353.

15. Toffler, 354.

16. Toffler, 12.

17. Richard Hofstadter, *The American Political Tradition and the Men Who Made It,* foreword by Christopher Lasch (1948; New York: Vintage, 1989), xxxiii.

18. C. P. Snow, *The Two Cultures and the Scientific Revolution* (Cambridge: Cambridge University Press, 1959), 42–43.

19. Egbert de Vries, *Man in Rapid Social Change* (London: SCM Press Ltd., 1961), 95.

20. Toffler, *Future Shock,* 328.

21. Marshall McLuhan, *The Mechanical Bride: Folklore of Industrial Man* (1951; London: Routledge, 1967), 156.

22. Marshall McLuhan and Quentin Fiore, *The Medium Is the Massage: An Inventory of Effects,* coordinated by Jerome Angel (1967; London: Penguin, 1996), 74–75.

23. Alvin Toffler, "The Future as a Way of Life," *Horizon Magazine* 7 (1965): 108–115.

24. Robert Jay Lifton, "Protean Man," *Partisan Review* 35, no. 1 (1968): 13–33, here 26. See also Robert Jay Lifton, *History and Human Survival: Essays on the Young and Old, Survivors and the Dead, Peace and War, and on Contemporary Psychohistory* (New York: Random House, 1971), 311–331.

25. J. H. Plumb, *The Death of the Past* (London: Macmillan, 1969), 13.

26. Plumb, 14.

27. Arthur P. Dudden, "Nostalgia and the American," *Journal of the History of Ideas* 22, no. 4 (1961): 515–530, here 517.

28. Dudden, 528–529.

29. Dudden, 530.

30. Jean Starobinski, "The Idea of Nostalgia," trans. William S. Kemp, *Diogenes* 14 (1966): 81–103, here 101.

31. *Oxford English Dictionary Online,* s.v. "nostalgia" (Oxford: Oxford University Press, September 2016), http://www.oed.com/view/Entry/128472?redirectedFrom =nostalgia&. See also Susan J. Matt, *Homesickness: An American History* (Oxford: Oxford University Press, 2011), 102–103, 174.

32. See the *Times* Digital Archive; the *New York Times* Digital Archive; Christopher Lasch, *The True and Only Heaven: Progress and Its Critics* (New York: Norton, 1991), 106–108; and David Lowenthal, *The Past Is a Foreign Country* (Cambridge: Cambridge University Press, 1985), 11.

33. *Webster's New International Dictionary of the English Language* (Springfield, MA: G. & C. Merriam, 1957), s.v. "nostalgia"; *Webster's Third New International Dictionary of the English Language* (Springfield, MA: G. & C. Merriam, 1961), s.v. "nostalgia."

34. *The Concise Oxford Dictionary of Current English* (Oxford: Oxford University Press, 1964), s.v. "nostalgia." The popularity of this new meaning also can be seen via a search in Google Ngram Viewer for "nostalgia" and *nostalgie,* 1900–2010.

35. See Thomas Dodman, *What Nostalgia Was: War, Empire and the Time of a Deadly Emotion* (Chicago: University of Chicago Press, 2018), 126.

36. Maurice Halbwachs, *Les cadres sociaux de la mémoire* (Paris: Félix Alcan, 1925), 140–154.

37. *Dictionnaire de la langue française* (Paris: Gallimard, 1958), s.v. "nostalgie," 801.

38. "Tristesse vague cause par l'éloignment de ce que l'on a connu, par le sentiment d'un passé révolu, par un désir insatisfait": *Dictionnaire du français contemporain* (Paris: Librairie La Rousse, 1966), s.v. "nostalgie." Unless otherwise noted, all translations are my own.

39. The current online edition of *Le Grand Robert de la langue française* lists three different definitions of *nostalgia:* first, as homesickness; second, as a melancholic regret for a thing in the past, a desire to go back, to return to the past; and third, as boredom, melancholy, and sadness: "mal du pays": "Regret mélancolique (d'une chose révolue); désir de revenir en arrière, de retrouver le passé," "Ennui, mélancolie, spleen, tristesse," *Le Grand Robert de la langue française,* s.v. nostalgie (Paris: Le Robert, 2008), https://dictionnaire.lerobert.com/definition/nostalgie.

40. Theodor W. Adorno, "Jene zwanziger Jahre," *Merkur* 16, no. 167 (1962): 46–51, here 47.

41. Maurice Halbwachs, *Das Gedächtnis und seine sozialen Bedingungen* (Berlin: Luchterhand, 1966), 149.

42. Stephen Spender, *The Struggle of the Modern* (London: Hamish Hamilton, 1963), 208–209, here 212.

43. Spender, 209.

44. Ralph Harper, *Nostalgia: An Existential Longing and Fulfilment in the Modern Age,* foreword by Richard A. Macksey (Cleveland: Press of Western Reserve University, 1966), 27.

45. Harper, 26–27, 29.

46. Spender, *Struggle of the Modern,* 209, 212.

47. Harper, *Nostalgia,* 28.

48. Lasch, *True and Only Heaven,* 116.

49. See Edwin McDowell, "Publishing: Alvin Toffler '72 report on A.T.&T.," *New York Times,* October 5, 1984, C29.

50. See the first page of the 1971 paperback edition.

51. "Nostalgia," *Newsweek,* December 28, 1970, 30–34.

52. Gerald Clarke, "The Meaning of Nostalgia," *Time,* May 3, 1971, 37; Frank Heath, "Nostalgia Shock," *Saturday Review,* May 29, 1971, 18.

53. Clarke, "Meaning of Nostalgia," 37.

54. Howard F. Stein, "American Nostalgia," *Columbia Forum* 3, no. 3 (1974): 20–23, here 20.

55. Milton Singer, "On the Symbolic and Historic Structure of an American Identity," *Ethos* 5 (1977): 431–455, here 431.

56. Jim Hougan, *Decadence: Radical Nostalgia, Narcissism, and Decline in the Seventies* (New York: William Morrow, 1975), 196.

57. Ronald Inglehart, *The Silent Revolution: Changing Values and Political Styles among Western Publics* (Princeton, NJ: Princeton University Press, 1977), 371.

58. Anthony Brandt, "A Short Natural History of Nostalgia," *Atlantic,* December 1978, 58–63, here 60.

59. Fred Davis, *Yearning for Yesterday: A Sociology of Nostalgia* (New York: Free Press, 1979), 104–108.

60. Davis, 106.

61. Davis, 122.

62. See, for instance, Lowenthal, *Past Is a Foreign Country,* 10, 12, 195; Robert Hewison, *The Heritage Industry: Britain in a Climate of Decline* (London: Methuen, 1987), 45–46; Janelle L. Wilson, *Nostalgia: Sanctuary of Meaning* (Lewisburg, PA: Bucknell University Press 2005), 25, 30–31, 34, 82; Peter Fritzsche, "How Nostalgia Narrates Modernity," in *The Work of Memory: New Directions in the Study of German Society and Culture,* ed. Peter Fritzsche and Alon Confino (Urbana: University of Illinois Press, 2002), 62–85, here 64; and Alastair Bonnett, *The Geography of Nostalgia: Global and Local Perspectives on Modernity and Loss* (London: Routledge, 2016), 20, 41.

63. "The Nifty Fifties," *Life,* June 16, 1972, 38–46; Johnathan Rodgers, "Back to the '50s," *Newsweek,* October 16, 1972, 78–82; "Back to the Unfabulous '50s," *Time,* May 8, 1974, 60.

64. Thomas Meehan, "Must We Be Nostalgic about the Fifties?," *Horizon* 9, no. 1 (1972): 4–17, here 5.

65. Michael Wood, "Nostalgia or Never: You Can't Go Home Again," *New Society* 7, no. 631 (1974): 343–346, here 343. See also Ray Connolly, "The Fascinating '50s," *Evening Standard,* March 4, 1972, 13; "Benny Green, Forward—into the

Fifties!," *Daily Mirror,* May 30, 1972, 14–15; and Simon Jenkins, "The Return of the Foggy Fifties," *Evening Standard,* January 2, 1973, 21.

66. Horst-Dieter Ebert, "'Jene Sehnsucht nach den alten Tagen . . . ,'" *Der Spiegel,* January 29, 1973, 86–99, here 86.

67. *Der große Brockhaus in zwölf Bänden* (Wiesbaden: Brockhaus, 1955), s.v. "Nostalgie."

68. *Brockhaus-Enzyklopädie in zwanzig Bänden* (Wiesbaden: Brockhaus, 1971), s.v. "Nostalgie."

69. Ebert, "'Jene Sehnsucht,'" 87; Ina-Maria Greverus, *Auf der Suche nach Heimat* (Munich: Beck, 1979), 171.

70. *Der Grosse Brockhaus in zwölf Bänden* (Wiesbaden: F. A. Brockhaus, 1979), s.v. "Nostalgie."

71. *Meyers Enzyklopädisches Lexikon in 25 Bänden* (Mannheim: Bibliographisches Institut, 1976), s.v. "Nostalgie"; Dieter Baacke, "Nostalgie: Zu einem Phänomen ohne Theorie," in *Meyers Enzyklopädisches Lexikon* (Mannheim: Lexikonverlag, 1976), s.v. "Nostalgie."

72. See Margot Dietrich, "Nostalgie: Vom Fachwort zum Modewort," *Der Sprachdienst* 18, no. 1 (1974): 2–4. The Google Ngram Viewer data for *Nostalgie,* 1900–2010, reflect this increase in the 1970s.

73. Wolfgang Schivelbusch, "Das nostalgische Syndrom: Überlegungen zu einem neueren antiquarischen Gefühl," *Frankfurter Hefte: Zeitschrift für Kultur und Politik* 28, no. 4 (1973): 270–276, here 270, 276; Dieter Baacke, "Nostalgie: Ein Phänomen ohne Theorie," *Merkur* 30 (1976): 442–452, here 445, 452.

74. Baacke, "Nostalgie," 448.

75. Gerhard Zwerenz, *Die Westdeutschen: Erfahrungen, Beschreibungen, Analysen* (Munich: Bertelsmann, 1977), 302, 299. Also see Davis, *Yearning for Yesterday,* 42–44, 56–64; and Meehan, "Must We Be Nostalgic?," 5, 13.

76. Arnold Gehlen, "Das entflohene Glück: Eine Deutung der Nostalgie," *Merkur* 30 (1976): 432–442, here 438, 439.

77. Hermann Lübbe, *Geschichtsbegriff und Geschichtsinteresse: Analytik und Pragmatik der Historie* (Basel: Schwabe, 1977), 254; Hermann Lübbe, *Zeit-Erfahrungen: Sieben Begriffe zur Beschreibung moderner Zivilisationsdynamik* (Stuttgart: Franz Steiner, 1996), 12–16; Reinhart Koselleck, "'Space of Experience' and 'Horizon of Expectation': Two Historical Categories," in *Futures Past: On the Semantics of Historical Time,* trans. Keith Tribe (Cambridge, MA: MIT Press, 1985), 255–275.

78. Reinhart Koselleck, "Historical Criteria of the Modern Concept of Revolution," in *Futures Past,* 43–57, here 50.

79. Lübbe, *Geschichtsbegriff und Geschichtsinteresse,* 304–335; Hermann Lübbe, *Zwischen Trend und Tradition: Überfordert uns die Gegenwart?* (Zurich: Edition Interfrom, 1981), 7–22.

80. Lübbe, *Geschichtsbegriff und Geschichtsinteresse,* 318; Lübbe, *Zwischen Trend und Tradition,* 12.

81. Lübbe, *Geschichtsbegriff und Geschichtsinteresse,* 318.

82. Lübbe, *Zwischen Trend und Tradition,* 13.

83. Davis, *Yearning for Yesterday,* 109.

84. Toffler, *Future Shock,* 407.

85. See Baacke, "Nostalgie."

86. On Nazi nostalgia, see Chapter 2; on *la mode rétro,* see Chapter 3.

87. For the United States, see Daniel T. Rodgers, *Age of Fracture* (Cambridge, MA: Belknap Press of Harvard University Press, 2011), 221; Thomas Hine, *The Great Funk: Falling Apart and Coming Together (on a Shag Rug) in the Seventies* (New York: Farrar, Straus and Giroux, 2007), 89–92; Andreas Killen, *1973 Nervous Breakdown: Watergate, Warhol, and the Birth of Post-Sixties America* (New York: Bloomsbury 2006), 177; and Philip Jenkins, *Decade of Nightmares: The End of the Sixties and the Making of the Eighties America* (Oxford: Oxford University Press, 2006), 68–70. For Britain, see Dominic Sandbrook, *State of Emergency: The Way We Were: Britain, 1970–1974* (London: Penguin, 2011), 190–199, 337; Christopher Booker, *The Seventies: Portrait of a Decade* (Harmondsworth, UK: Penguin, 1980), 5–7; and Norman Shrapnel, *The Seventies: Britain's Inward March* (London: Constable, 1980), 15, 79–84.

88. Quoted in Clarke, "Meaning of Nostalgia," 37.

89. Douglas Johnson, "Not What It Used to Be," *Vole* 5 (1978): 42–43, here 42.

90. Patrick Wright, *On Living in an Old Country: The National Past in Contemporary Britain* (1985; Oxford: Oxford University Press, 2009), 1, 3.

91. David Lowenthal and Marcus Binney, eds., *Our Past before Us: Why Do We Save It?* (London: Temple Smith, 1981). For more on the movement, see Chapter 4.

92. Hewison, *Heritage Industry,* 9.

93. *A Future for the Past,* BBC Radio 4, aired June 26, 1986; *The Man Who Made Beamish,* BBC2, aired November 26, 1986; *The Heritage Business,* BBC2, aired March 16, 1988. I am grateful to Robert Hewison for making the last documentary available to me.

94. Robert Lumley, "The Debate on Heritage Reviewed," in *Towards the Museum of the Future: New European Perspectives,* ed. Roger Miles and Lauro Zavala (London: Routledge 1994), 57–70; Peter Mandler, "The Heritage Panic of the 1970s and 1980s in Great Britain," in *The Invention of Industrial Pasts: Heritage, Political Culture and Economic Debates in Great Britain and Germany, 1850–2010,* ed. Peter Itzen and Christian Müller (Augsburg: Wißner: 2013), 58–69.

95. Lowenthal, *Past Is a Foreign Country,* 4; Hewison, *Heritage Industry,* 10. See also Wright, *On Living,* 20–22.

96. See, for instance, David Cannadine, "Brideshead Re-revisited," *New York Review of Books,* December 19, 1985, 17–20; Neal Ascherson, "Why 'Heritage' Is Right-Wing," *Observer,* November 8, 1987, 9; Neal Ascherson, "'Heritage' as Vulgar English Nationalism," *Observer,* November 29, 1987, 9; and Waldemar Januszczak, "Romancing the Grime," *Guardian,* September 2, 1987, 9.

97. Raphael Samuel, *Theatres of Memory: Past and Present in Contemporary Culture* (London: Verso, 1994), 259–273, 17.

98. Samuel, xlvii.

99. See *Oxford English Dictionary Online,* s.v. "heritage" (Oxford: Oxford University Press, September 2016), https://www.oed.com/view/Entry/86230?rskey =ckc8ZA&result=1&isAdvanced=false#eid.

100. Patrick Cormack, *Heritage in Danger,* 2nd ed. (1976; London: Quartet Books, 1978), 14.

101. Wright, *On Living,* 77; Lowenthal, *Past Is a Foreign Country,* 36; Hewison, *Heritage Industry,* 32.

102. Cormack, *Heritage in Danger,* 15, 13.

103. For more on this, see Miles Glendinning, *The Conservation Movement: A History of Architectural Preservation, Antiquity to Modernity* (London: Routledge, 2013), 329–331, 402–408; and Michael Falser and Winfried Lipp, eds., *A Future for Our Past: The 40th Anniversary of European Architectural Heritage Year (1975–2015)* (Berlin: Hendrik Bäßler Verlag, 2015), as well as Chapter 4.

104. E. R. Chamberlin, *Preserving the Past* (London: Dent, 1979), xi.

105. Wright, *On Living,* 66; Hewison, *Heritage Industry,* 9.

106. Richard Vinen, *Thatcher's Britain: The Politics and Social Upheaval of the Thatcher Era* (London: Simon and Schuster, 2009), 54, 187–190.

107. Martin Wiener, *English Culture and the Decline of the Industrial Spirit, 1850–1980,* new ed. (1981; Cambridge: Cambridge University Press, 2004).

108. "Is Britain's Decline a Myth? Lincoln Allison Talks to Martin Wiener about Interpretations of History," *New Society,* November 17, 1983, 274–275, here 274. See also Vinen, *Thatcher's Britain,* 187–188.

109. See Wright, *On Living,* 120, 240–241; Lowenthal, *Past Is a Foreign Country,* 9, 104; Hewison, *Heritage Industry,* 141. See also Mandler, "Heritage Panic," 58.

110. Wright, *On Living,* 37–44.

111. Robert Hewison, interview by the author, December 7, 2015.

112. Lowenthal, *Past Is a Foreign Country,* xv, xvii; similarly, Wright, *On Living,* 131–132, 198–199.

113. Hewison, *Heritage Industry,* 24.

114. Lowenthal, *Past Is a Foreign Country,* 3.

115. David Lowenthal, *The Heritage Crusade and the Spoils of History* (Cambridge: Cambridge University Press, 1989), 1.

116. Paul Addison, "Getting On," *London Review of Books,* October 9, 1986, 3.

117. David Lowenthal, "Nostalgia Tells It Like It Wasn't," in *The Imagined Past: History and Nostalgia,* ed. Christopher Shaw and Malcolm Chase (Manchester: Manchester University Press, 1989), 18–32, here 28.

118. Lowenthal, 27, 30.

119. Patrick Wright, "Sneering at the Theme Parks: An Encounter with the Heritage Industry—Patrick Wright in Conservation with Tim Putnam," in *On Living,* 238–256, here 240 (first published in *Block* 15 [1989]: 48–55).

120. Lowenthal, "Nostalgia Tells It," 18.

121. Lesley M. Smith, introduction to *The Making of Britain: Echoes of Greatness,* ed. Lesley M. Smith (Basingstoke, UK: Macmillan, 1988), 1–7, here 1; Adrian Mellor, "Enterprise and Heritage in the Dock," in *Enterprise and Heritage: Crosscurrents of National Culture,* ed. John Corner and Sylvia Harvey (London: Routledge, 1991), 93–115, here 95.

122. Julian Barnes, *England, England* (London: Picador, 1998), 70, 71.

123. Johnson, "Not What It Used," 42.

124. Samuel, *Theatres of Memory,* 307.

125. Lowenthal, *Past Is a Foreign Country,* xv.

126. Michael Kammen, *Mystic Chords of Memory: The Transformation of Tradition in American Culture* (New York: Alfred A. Knopf, 1991), 625, 626.

127. Kammen, 618.

128. Kammen, 628.

129. See Ian Tyrell, *Historians in Public: The Practice of American History, 1890–1970* (Chicago: University of Chicago Press, 2005), 154.

130. Cormack, *Heritage in Danger,* 165.

131. Annie Ernaux, *The Years,* trans. Alison L. Strayer (London: Fitzcarraldo Editions, 2018), 96.

132. Tony Judt, *Postwar: A History of Europe since 1945* (New York: Penguin, 2005), 772.

133. Barnes, *England, England,* 53.

134. Quoted in Philippe Poirrier, "Heritage and Cultural Policy in France under the Fifth Republic," *International Journal of Cultural Policy* 9, no. 2 (2003): 215–225, here 219.

135. Pierre Nora, "The Era of Commemoration," in *Realms of Memory: Construction of the French Past,* ed. Pierre Nora and Lawrence D. Kritzman, trans. Arthur Goldhammer (New York: Columbia University Press, 1998), 3:609–637, here 625.

136. Nora, 625.

137. Philippe Hoyau, "Heritage and 'the Conserver Society': The French Case," trans. Chris Turner, in *The Museum Time-Machine: Putting Cultures on Display,* ed. Robert Lumley (London: Routledge, 1988), 25–34, here 26. See, for instance, Françoise Choay, *The Invention of the Historic Monument,* trans. Lauren M. O'Connell (1992; Cambridge: Cambridge University Press, 2001), 140–143.

138. Hoyau, "Heritage," 32; Choay, *Invention of the Historic Monument,* 169.

139. Marc Guillaume, *La politique du patrimoine* (Paris: Galilée, 1980), 71; on nostalgia, see also 69–72.

140. Judt, *Postwar,* 773.

141. See Peter Davis, *Ecomuseums: A Sense of Place* (London: Continuum, 2011).

142. Pêr-Jakez Helias, *Le cheval d'orgueil: Mémoires d'un Breton du pays bigouden* (Paris: Plon, 1975); Émilie Carles, *Une soupe aux herbes sauvages* (Paris: Jean-Claude Simoën, 1977). See also Sarah Farmer, *Rural Inventions: The French Countryside after 1945* (Oxford: Oxford University Press, 2020), 79–97.

143. See Cannadine, "Brideshead Re-revisited"; Lowenthal, *Past Is a Foreign Country,* 6; Samuel, *Theatres of Memory,* 66, 298.

144. Emanuel Le Roy Ladurie, *Montaillou, village occitan de 1294 à 1324* (Paris: Gallimard, 1975).

145. See, for instance, Jean Borreil, "Des politiques nostalgiques," *Les Révoltes Logiques* 3 (1976): 87–105; and François Furet, "Beyond the Annales," *Journal of Modern History* 55, no. 3 (1983): 389–410, here 404–405.

146. See Martin Burlage, *Große Historische Ausstellungen in der Bundesrepublik Deutschland 1960–2000* (Münster: LIT, 2005), 21–91.

147. Ulrich Müller, review of *Oswald von Wolkenstein: Eine Biographie,* by Anton Schwob, and *Ich Wolkenstein: Eine Biographie,* by Dieter Kühn, *Zeitschrift für deutsches Altertum und deutsche Literatur* 108, no. 3 (1979): 89–94, here 89.

148. Peter Wapnewski, "Ein neues Mittelalter?," *Der Spiegel,* July 25, 1977, 137–139.

149. See Louisa Ermelino, "Open Book: When in Milan," *Publishers Weekly,* July 7, 2017, https://www.publishersweekly.com/pw/by-topic/international/international -book-news/article/74199-open-book-when-in-milan.html.

150. Umberto Eco, "Dreaming of the Middle Ages," in *Travels in Hyperreality: Essays,* trans. William Weaver (London: Picador, 1987), 61–72, here 61. For his claim to have triggered the wave, see Thomas Stauder, *Gespräche mit Umberto Eco aus drei Jahrzehnten* (Berlin: Lit, 2012), 71.

151. Martin Croucher, "Latter-Day Knights Battle for Imaginary Kingdoms," *Epoch Times,* March 17, 2008, https://web.archive.org/web/20080515192325/http://en .epochtimes.com/news/8-3-17/67686.html. On the Society for Creative Anachronism, see also Jay Anderson, *Time Machines: The World of Living History* (Nashville:

American Association for State and Local History, 1984), 186; Lowenthal, *Past Is a Foreign Country,* 363; and Michael A. Cramer, *Medieval Fantasy as Performance: The Society for Creative Anachronism and the Current Middle Ages* (Lanham, MD: Scarecrow, 2010).

152. Cullen Murphy, "Nostalgia for the Dark Ages," *Atlantic,* May 1984, 12–16.

153. See Hermann Lübbe, *Der Fortschritt und das Museum: Über den Grund unseres Vergnügens an historischen Gegenständen* (London: Institute of Germanic Studies, University of London, 1982); and Gottfried Korff, "Musealisierung total? Notizen zu einem Trend, der die Institution, nach der er benannt ist, hinter sich gelassen hat," in *Historische Faszination Geschichtskultur heute,* ed. Klaus Fußmann, Heinrich Theodor Grütter, and Jorn Rüsen (Cologne: Böhlau, 1994), 129–144.

154. See Jens Jäger, "Heimat, Version: 1.0," Docupedia-Zeitgeschichte, August 13, 2018, http://docupedia.de/zg/Jaeger_heimat_v1_en_2018; and Celia Applegate, *A Nation of Provincials: The German Idea of* Heimat (Berkeley: University of California Press, 1990).

155. Walter Schmiele, "Wallfahrt zu entbehrten Glücksgefühlen," *Frankfurter Allgemeine Zeitung,* February 11, 1978, BuZ1.

156. Siegfried Lenz, *Heimatmuseum* (Hamburg: Hoffmann & Campe, 1978); Siegfried Lenz, *The Heritage,* trans. Krishna Winston (London: Methuen, 1981).

157. Greverus, *Auf der Suche nach Heimat,* 171–181, 177.

158. "Heimat—unter grüner Flagge," *Der Spiegel,* July 23, 1979, 134–136, here 134. See also Dieter Tiemann, "Heimat, deine Sterne: Analyse eines mißbrauchten Begriffs," *Frankfurter Allgemeine Zeitung,* November 26, 1981, 29.

159. See, for instance, Timothy Garton Ash, "The Life of Death," *New York Review of Books,* December 19, 1985, 26–39; and Miriam Hansen, "Dossier on *Heimat,*" *New German Critique* 36 (1985): 3–24.

160. Anton Kaes, *From Hitler to Heimat: The Return of History as Film* (Cambridge, MA: Harvard University Press, 1989), 164; Alon Confino, "Edgar Reitz's *Heimat* and German Nationhood: Film, Memory, and Understandings of the Past," *German History* 16, no. 2 (1998): 185–208. See also Michael E. Geisler, "'Heimat' and the German Left: The Anamnesis of a Trauma," *New German Critique* 36 (1985): 25–66; and Alexandra Ludewig, *Screening Nostalgia: 100 Years of German Heimat Film* (Bielefeld, Germany: Transcript, 2011), 261–293.

161. Applegate, *Nation of Provincials,* 10; see also 9, 14, 62.

162. Lowenthal, "Nostalgia Tells It," 19.

163. Barnes, *England, England,* 55, 54.

164. Malcolm Chase and Christopher Shaw, "The Dimensions of Nostalgia," in Shaw and Chase, *Imagined Past,* 1–17, here 15.

165. Frank Ankersmit, *History and Tropology: The Rise and Fall of a Metaphor* (Berkeley: University of California Press, 1994), 197; Svetlana Boym, *The Future of Nostalgia* (New York: Basic Books, 2001), 30.

166. See Jean Baudrillard, *Simulacra and Simulation,* trans. Sheila Faria Glaser (1981; Ann Arbor: University of Michigan Press, 1994), 1–42.

167. Jean-François Lyotard, *The Postmodern Condition: A Report of Knowledge,* trans. Geoff Bennington and Brian Massumi, foreword by Fredric Jameson (Minneapolis: University of Minnesota Press, 1984), 41.

168. Baudrillard, *Simulacra and Simulation,* 6.

169. Baudrillard, 43, 44.

170. Baudrillard, 10.

171. Fredric Jameson, *Postmodernism, or, The Cultural Logic of Late Capitalism* (London: Verso, 1991), 19.

172. Fredric Jameson, "Postmodernism and the Cultural Logic of Late Capitalism," *New Left Review* 146, no. 1 (1984): 53–92, here 69, 71; Jameson, *Postmodernism,* 286.

173. Jameson, *Postmodernism,* 286, 79, 27.

174. Jameson, 19, 286.

175. Linda Hutcheon, "Irony, Nostalgia, and the Postmodern," in *Methods for the Study of Literature as Cultural Memory,* ed. Raymond Vervliet and Annemarie Estor (Amsterdam: Rodopi, 2000), 189–207, here 203.

176. Elizabeth Wilson, "These New Components of the Spectacle: Fashion and Postmodernism," in *Postmodernism and Society,* ed. Roy Boyne and Ali Rattansi (Basingstoke, UK: Macmillan Education, 1990), 209–234, here 227.

177. See Baudrillard, *Simulacra and Simulation;* and Jameson, *Postmodernism,* 67–96.

178. Tom Shales, "The Re Decade," *Esquire,* March 1986, 67–69, here 68.

179. Shales, 67.

180. Baudrillard, *Simulacra and Simulation,* 10, 8. Jameson, ironically, given that he first commented on postmodernism in a museum, does not mention museums at all; see Fredric Jameson, "Postmodernism and the Consumer Society," in *The Anti-aesthetic: Essays on Postmodern Culture, Seattle,* ed. Hal Foster (Port Townsend, WA: Bay Press, 1983), 111–125.

181. Samuel, *Theatres of Memory,* 95, 266.

182. David Harvey, *The Condition of Postmodernity: An Enquiry into the Origins of Cultural Change* (London: Blackwell, 1989), 62–63, 85–87.

183. Harvey, 54–58.

184. Harvey, 240.

185. Bruno Latour, *We Have Never Been Modern,* trans. Catherine Porter (Cambridge, MA: Harvard University Press, 1993), 68.

186. Latour, 69.

187. Baudrillard, *Simulacra and Simulation,* 10.

188. Latour, *We Have Never Been Modern,* 75, 69, 72.

189. Bruno Latour, *An Inquiry into Modes of Existence: An Anthropology of the Moderns* (Cambridge, MA: Harvard University Press, 2013), 9. See also Achim Landwehr, *Die anwesende Abwesenheit der Vergangenheit: Essays zur Geschichtstheorie* (Frankfurt am Main: S. Fischer, 2016).

190. Lasch, *True and Only Heaven,* 82, 92; Christopher Lasch, "The Politics of Nostalgia: Losing History in the Mists of Ideology," *Harper's,* November 1984, 65–70, here 65.

191. Lasch, *True and Only Heaven,* 118.

192. Lasch, "Politics of Nostalgia," 69.

193. Ankersmit, *History and Tropology,* 197.

194. Ankersmit, 201.

195. Ankersmit, 205, 206.

196. Ankersmit, 206.

197. Ankersmit, 206.

198. Ankersmit, 202.

199. Maurice Halbwachs, *On Collective Memory,* ed., trans., and with an introduction by Lewis A. Coser (Chicago: University of Chicago Press, 1992), 48. See also Halbwachs, *Les cadres sociaux,* 140–154.

200. Halbwachs, *On Collective Memory,* 49. See also Suzanne Vromen, "Maurice Halbwachs and the Concept of Nostalgia," in *Knowledge and Society: Studies in the Sociology of Culture Past and Present: A Research Annual* (Greenwich, CT: JAI, 1986), 6:55–66.

201. Pierre Nora, "La memoire collective," in *La nouvelle histoire,* ed. Jacques Le Goff, Roger Chartier, and Jacques Revel (Paris: Éditions Complexe, 1978), 398–401.

202. See Richard Terdiman, *Present Pasts: Modernity and the Memory Crisis* (Ithaca, NY: Cornell University Press, 1993); and Jay Winter, "Notes on the Memory Boom: War, Remembrance and the Uses of the Past," in *Memory, Trauma and World Politics: Reflections on the Relationship between Past and Present,* ed. Duncan Bell (Basingstoke, UK: Palgrave Macmillan, 2006), 54–73.

203. Pierre Nora, "General Introduction: Between Memory and History," in *Realms of Memory: Construction of the French Past,* ed. Pierre Nora and Lawrence D. Kritzman, trans. Arthur Goldhammer (New York: Columbia University Press, 1993), 1:1–20, here 6–7.

204. Nora, 1.

205. Ernaux, *Years,* 129.

206. Nora, "General Introduction," 12.

207. See Nora, 3.

208. Nora, 2.

209. Nora, 17.

210. Nora, 2.

211. Ernaux, *Years,* 127.

212. Lasch, *True and Only Heaven,* 112.

213. Nora, "General Introduction," 12.

214. See Steven Englund, "The Ghost of Nation Past," *Journal of Modern History* 64, no. 2 (1992): 299–320; Nancy Wood, "Memory's Remains: *Les lieux de mémoire,*" *History and Memory* 6, no. 1 (1994): 123–149; Stephen Legg, "Contesting and Surviving Memory: Space, Nation, and Nostalgia in *Les Lieux de Mémoire,*" *Environment and Planning D: Society and Space* 23 (2005): 481–504; and Michael Rothberg, "Introduction: Between Memory and Memory: From *Lieux de mémoire* to *Noeuds de mémoire,*" *Yale French Studies,* no. 118/119 (2010): 3–12.

215. Frank Ankersmit, *Sublime Historical Experience* (Stanford, CA: Stanford University Press, 2005), 262.

216. Nora, "Era of Commemoration," 609, 618, 634.

217. See Patrick H. Hutton, "Reconsiderations of the Idea of Nostalgia in Contemporary Historical Writing," *Historical Reflections* 39, no. 3 (2013): 1–9, here 1. See also Patrick H. Hutton, *The Memory Phenomenon in Contemporary Historical Writing: How the Interest in Memory Has Influenced Our Understanding of History* (New York: Palgrave Macmillan, 2016), 129–148.

218. Winter, "Notes on the Memory Boom," 55.

219. Fritzsche, "Specters of History," 1589.

220. Fritzsche, "How Nostalgia Narrates Modernity," 65, 64. See also Peter Fritzsche, *Stranded in the Present: Modern Time and Melancholy of History* (Cambridge, MA: Harvard University Press, 2004).

221. Fritzsche, "How Nostalgia Narrates Modernity," 66.

222. Fritzsche, 81.

223. See also Charles S. Maier, "The End of Longing? Notes toward a History of Postwar German National Longing," in *The Postwar Transformation of Germany,* ed. John S. Brady, Beverly Crawford, and Sarah Elise Williarty (Ann Arbor: University of Michigan Press, 1999), 271–285; and Paul Betts, "The Twilight of Idols: East German Memory and Material Culture," *Journal of Modern History* 72 (2000): 731–765.

224. For more on this, see Chapter 2.

225. Boym, *Future of Nostalgia,* xiv, xvi.

226. Boym, 41–55.

227. Boym, xiv.

228. See Lowenthal, *Past Is a Foreign Country,* 50; Jameson, *Postmodernism,* 285, 377; Harvey, *Condition of Postmodernity,* 286, 291; and Lasch, *True and Only Heaven,* 117.

229. Martin Kaste, "Futurist 40 Years Later: Possibilities Not Predictions," NPR, July 26, 2010, https://www.npr.org/templates/story/story.php?storyId =128719212&t=1591281702230; Greg Lindsay, "Future Shock at 40: What the Tofflers Got Right (and Wrong)," *Fast Company,* October 15, 2010, https://www .fastcompany.com/1695307/future-shock-40-what-tofflers-got-right-and-wrong; Richard Stoker, "50 Years of Future Shock and Adapting to New Technologies," *Startup,* June 9, 2019, https://medium.com/swlh/50-years-of-future-shock-and -adapting-to-new-technologies-e8978f1436dc; John Schroeter, ed., *After Shock: The World's Foremost Futurists Reflect on 50 Years of Future Shock and Look Ahead to the Next 50* (Bainbridge Island, WA: John August Media, 2020).

230. Douglas Rushkoff, *Present Shock: When Everything Happens Now* (New York: Current, 2013), 4, 2; on Toffler, see 9–10, 14–16.

231. Rushkoff, 10; see also 3, 9.

232. Rushkoff, 3.

233. The last chapter is entitled "Apocalypto": Rushkoff, 243–266.

234. See, for instance, James Gleick, *Faster: The Acceleration of Just about Everything* (New York: Pantheon Books, 2000); Judy Wajcman, *Pressed for Time: The Acceleration of Life in Digital Capitalism* (Chicago: University of Chicago Press, 2015); and J. R. McNeill and Peter Engelke, *The Great Acceleration: An Environmental History of the Anthropocene since 1945* (Cambridge, MA: Harvard University Press, 2016).

235. Hartmut Rosa, *Social Acceleration: A New Theory of Modernity* (New York: Columbia University Press, 2013), originally published as *Beschleunigung: Die Veränderung der Zeitstrukturen in der Moderne* (Frankfurt am Main, 2005).

236. See Rosa, *Social Acceleration,* 401n65.

237. Rosa, 21.

238. Rosa, 26, 76–77, 113–118, 259–276.

239. Rosa, 270, 271.

240. Rosa, 293 (emphasis in the original).

241. Rosa, 41, 83.

242. Rosa, 83.

243. François Hartog, *Regimes of Historicity: Presentism and the Experience of Time* (New York: Columbia University Press, 2015), xvi, 9, 17.

244. Hartog, 107, 17, 201 (emphasis in the original); see also 104–120.

245. Hartog, 190, 196, 201.

246. Hartog, 149; for the two case studies, see 120–131, 141–148, 149–191.

247. Hartog, 125, 241n100.

248. Hartog, 150.

249. Hartog, xvii. Also see Chris Lorenz, "Out of Time? Some Critical Reflections on François Hartog's Presentism," in *Rethinking Historical Time: New Approaches to Presentism,* ed. Marek Tamm and Laurent Olivier (London: Bloomsbury, 2019), 43–56.

250. Hans Ulrich Gumbrecht, *Our Broad Present* (New York: Columbia University Press, 2014), xiv.

251. Gumbrecht, xiii.

252. Aleida Assmann, *Is Time Out of Joint? On the Rise and Fall of the Modern Time Regime,* trans. Sarah Clift (Ithaca, NY: Cornell University Press, 2020).

253. Wright, *On Living;* David Lowenthal, *The Past Is a Foreign Country—Revisited* (Cambridge: Cambridge University Press, 2015).

254. See Wright, *On Living,* xviii–xix; and Lowenthal, *Past Is a Foreign Country—Revisited,* 588n15.

255. Lowenthal, *Past Is a Foreign Country—Revisited,* 595.

256. Simon Reynolds, *Retromania: Pop Culture's Addiction to Its Own Past* (New York: Faber and Faber, 2011), xi.

257. Reynolds, xiv, x–xi.

258. Reynolds, x–xi; Mark Fisher, *Ghosts of My Life: Writings on Depression, Hauntology and Lost Futures* (Winchester, UK: Zero Books, 2014), 9; Owen Hatherley, *The Ministry of Nostalgia* (London: Verso, 2016), 3.

259. Reynolds, *Retromania,* 5.

260. See Reynolds, chaps. 2, 3, and 10.

261. Ernaux, *Years,* 209–210.

262. Rodgers, *Age of Fracture,* 221.

263. Rodgers, 221, 223.

264. Rodgers, 224, 255.

265. Alex Walsham, "Past and . . . Presentism," *Past and Present* 234 (2017): 213–217, here 214. See also Carlos Spoerhase, "Presentism and Precursorship in Intellectual History," *Culture, Theory and Critique* 49, no. 1 (2008): 49–72.

266. On anachronism, see Achim Landwehr, "Über Anachronismus," in *Diesseits der Geschichte: Für eine neue Historiographie* (Göttingen: Wallstein, 2020), 209–236.

267. On the history of the experience of time, particularly in the premodern period, see G. J. Whitrow, *Time in History: Views of Time from Prehistory to the Present Day*

(Oxford: Oxford University Press, 1988); Arno Borst, *The Ordering of Time: From the Ancient Computus to the Modern Computer* (Cambridge, UK: Polity, 1993); Achim Landwehr, *Geburt der Gegenwart: Eine Geschichte der Zeit im 17. Jahrhundert* (Frankfurt am Main: S. Fischer, 2014); and Landwehr, *Die anwesende Abwesenheit der Vergangenheit.*

268. See Reinhart Koselleck, "Fortschritt," in *Geschichtliche Grundbegriffe: Historisches Lexikon zur politisch-sozialen Sprache in Deutschland,* ed. Otto Brunner, Werner Conze, and Reinhart Kosellck (Stuttgart: Klett-Cotta, 1975), 351–423.

269. See, for instance, Andrew Gordon, *The Rise and Fall of the Future: America's Changing Vision of Tomorrow, 1939–1986* (Jefferson, NC: McFarland, 2020); Rüdiger Graf, "Totgesagt und nicht gestorben: Die Persistenz des Fortschritts im 20. und 21. Jahrhundert," *Traverse: Zeitschrift für Geschichte* 23, no. 3 (2016): 91–102; and Elke Seefried, "Reconfiguring the Future? Politics and Time from the 1960s to the 1980s—Introduction," *Journal of Modern European History* 13, no. 3 (2015): 306–316.

270. J. H. Plumb, "The Historian's Dilemma," in *Crisis in the Humanities,* ed. J. H. Plumb (London: Penguin, 1964), 24–44, here 34 (emphasis in the original).

271. Boym, *Future of Nostalgia,* 355. The same notion is also implicit in her view of what she calls reflective nostalgia.

272. Landwehr, *Geburt der Gegenwart,* 38; Landwehr, *Die anwesende Abwesenheit der Vergangenheit,* 156.

273. Walter Benjamin, "Theses on the Philosophy of History," in *Illuminations,* trans. Harry Zohn, ed. Hannah Arendt (New York: Harcourt, Brace and World, 1968), 253–264, here 257.

2. Regressing

1. Alvin Toffler, *Future Shock* (London: Pan Books, 1970), 327–328; Robert Jay Lifton, *History and Human Survival: Essays on the Young and Old, Survivors and the Dead, Peace and War, and on Contemporary Psychohistory* (New York: Random House, 1971), 329.

2. Fred Davis, *Yearning for Yesterday: A Sociology of Nostalgia* (New York: Free Press, 1979), 109.

3. Christopher Lasch, *The True and Only Heaven: Progress and Its Critics* (New York: Norton, 1991), 117.

4. Robert Hewison, *The Heritage Industry: Britain in a Climate of Decline* (London: Methuen, 1987), 47.

5. Dieter Baacke, "Nostalgie: Ein Phänomen ohne Theorie," *Merkur* 30 (1976): 442–452, here 450.

6. Arthur M. Schlesinger, "The New Conservatism: The Politics of Nostalgia," *Report,* June 16, 1955, 9–12.

7. Mark Lilla, *The Shipwrecked Mind: On Political Reaction* (New York: New York Review of Books, 2016); Zygmunt Bauman, *Retrotopia* (Cambridge, UK: Polity, 2017); Pippa Norris and Ronald Inglehart, *Cultural Backlash: Trump, Brexit, and Authoritarian Populism* (New York: Cambridge University Press, 2019). See also Sophie Gaston and Sacha Hilhorst, *At Home in One's Past: Nostalgia as a Cultural and Political Force in Britain, France and Germany* (Cambridge, UK: Demos, 2018), 23; Catherine E. de Vries and Isabell Hoffmann, *The Power of the Past: How Nostalgia Shapes European Public Opinion* (Gütersloh: Bertelsmann, 2018); Edoardo Campanella and Marta Dassù, *Anglo Nostalgia: The Politics of Emotion in a Fractured West* (London: Hurst, 2019); Robert Gildea, *Empires of the Mind: The Colonial Past and the Politics of the Present* (Cambridge: Cambridge University Press, 2019); Colin Crouch, *Post-democracy after the Crisis* (Cambridge, UK: Polity, 2020); and Anne Applebaum, *The Twilight of Democracy: The Seductive Lure of Authoritarianism* (New York: Doubleday, 2020).

8. Michael Kenny, "Back to the Populist Future? Understanding Nostalgia in Contemporary Ideological Discourse," *Journal of Political Ideologies* 22, no. 3 (2017): 256–273, here 258.

9. See, for instance, Christopher Clark, *Time and Power: Visions of History in German Politics, from the Thirty Years' War to the Third Reich* (Princeton, NJ: Princeton University Press, 2019).

10. Lionel Trilling, *The Liberal Imagination* (New York: Viking, 1950), ix.

11. Peter Viereck, *Conservatism Revisited: The Revolt against Revolt* (London: John Lehmann, 1949), viii.

12. See Jonathan M. Schoenwald, *A Time for Choosing: The Rise of Modern American Conservatism* (Oxford: Oxford University Press, 2001), 5.

13. See Stephen P. Depoe, *Arthur M. Schlesinger, Jr., and the Ideological History of American Liberalism* (Tuscaloosa: University of Alabama Press, 1994), 44.

14. Arthur M. Schlesinger, "Stevenson and the American Liberal Dilemma," *Twentieth Century* 153 (1953): 28–29, here 28, On his life, see Depoe, *Arthur M. Schlesinger Jr.*

15. Arthur M. Schlesinger Jr., "The Need for an Intelligent Opposition," *New York Times,* April 2, 1950, 164.

16. Arthur M. Schlesinger, "The New Conservatism in America: A Liberal Comment," *Confluence* 2 (1953): 61–71, here 61.

17. Schlesinger, "New Conservatism: The Politics of Nostalgia."

18. Schlesinger, 9.

19. Schlesinger, 10.

20. Schlesinger, 12.

21. On Viereck's life and thought, see Claes G. Ryn, "Peter Viereck: Unadjusted Man of Ideas," *Political Science Reviewer* 7 (1977): 325–366; Irving Louis Horowitz, "Peter Viereck: European-American Conscience, 1916–2006," *Society* 44, no. 2 (2007): 60–63; and Jay Patrick Starliper, *Aesthetic Origins: Peter Viereck and the Imaginative Sources of Politics,* with a foreword by Claes G. Ryn (New York: Routledge, 2017).

22. George H. Nash, *The Conservative Intellectual Movement in America since 1945* (Wilmington, DE: Intercollegiate Studies Institute, 1996), 68.

23. Tom Reiss, "The First Conservative," *New Yorker,* October 24, 2005.

24. See Ryn, "Peter Viereck," 325–326; and Reiss, "First Conservative."

25. George H. Sabine, review of *Conservatism Revisited,* by Peter Viereck, *Annals of the American Academy of Political and Social Science* 267, no. 1 (1950): 207.

26. Viereck, *Conservatism Revisited,* 21.

27. Peter Viereck, *The Unadjusted Man: A New Hero for Americans: Reflections on the Distinction between Conforming and Conserving* (Boston: Beacon, 1956), 98. See also Peter Viereck, *Conservatism Revisited,* rev. ed. (New York: Free Press, 1962), 124–125.

28. Viereck, *Conservatism Revisited* (1962), 99.

29. Viereck, 125. On Viereck's critique of the new conservatism, see Starliper, *Aesthetic Origins,* 11–12, 163–166.

30. Viereck, *Unadjusted Man,* 99.

31. Peter Viereck, "The Philosophical 'New Conservatism'" (1962), in *The Radical Right: The New American Right,* expanded ed., ed. Daniel Bell (New York: Anchor Books, 1964), 185–207, here 188.

32. On Kirk's biography, see Bradley J. Birzer, *Russell Kirk: American Conservative* (Lexington: University Press of Kentucky, 2015); and John M. Pafford, *Russell Kirk* (New York: Continuum, 2010).

33. Pafford, *Russell Kirk,* 95; Russell Kirk, *Confessions of a Bohemian Tory: Episodes and Reflections of a Vagrant Career* (New York: Fleet, 1963), 150; Rossiter quoted the line to ridicule Kirk: see Clinton Rossiter, *Conservatism in America: The Thankless Persuasion,* 2nd ed. (New York: Alfred A. Knopf, 1966), 221.

34. Kirk, *Confessions of a Bohemian Tory,* 23.

35. Clinton Rossiter, *Conservatism in America* (Melbourne: Heinemann, 1955), 177.

36. Rossiter, *Conservatism in America* (1955), 211.

37. Viereck, *Conservatism Revisited* (1962), 140.

38. Walter Berns, review of *A Program for Conservatives,* by Russell Kirk, *Journal of Politics* 17 (1955): 683–686, here 686.

39. Francis Biddle, "The Blur of Mediocrity," *New Republic,* August 24, 1953, 17–19, here 18.

40. Gordon K. Lewis, "The Metaphysics of Conservatism," *Western Political Quarterly* 6, no. 4 (1953): 728–741, here 731; William V. Shannon, "The New Conservatism," *Commonweal,* December 31, 1954, 360–364, here 362.

41. Russell Kirk, *A Program for Conservatives* (Chicago: Henry Regnery, 1954), 23.

42. Russell Kirk, *The Conservative Mind from Burke to Santayana* (Chicago: Henry Regnery, 1953), 7–8.

43. Kirk, 8.

44. Kirk, *Program for Conservatives,* 294.

45. Russell Kirk, "Ex Tenebris," *Queen's Quarterly* 64 (1957): 186–201, here 188.

46. Kirk, 189.

47. Kirk, *Program for Conservatives,* 295.

48. Kirk, 297.

49. Barry Goldwater, *Goldwater,* with Jack Casserly (New York: Doubleday, 1988), 110.

50. See Birzer, *Russell Kirk,* 245–246, 273–282.

51. Russell Kirk, "To the Point," *Western Kansas Press,* August 28, 1963, 4, quoted in Birzer, *Russell Kirk,* 274. On his view of Goldwater, see also Russell Kirk, "The Mind of Barry Goldwater," in *Confessions of a Bohemian Tory* (New York: Fleet, 1963), 185–192.

52. Viereck, *Conservatism Revisited* (1962), 147. Rossiter called him Goldwater's "favorite political theorist": Rossiter, *Conservatism in America* (1966), 220.

53. Richard Hofstadter, "Goldwater and His Party: The True Believer and the Radical Right," *Encounter* 23, no. 4 (1964): 3–13, here 11.

54. Irving Howe, "The Goldwater Movement," *Dissent,* Autumn 1964, 374–381, here 375–376.

55. Toffler, *Future Shock,* 327.

56. Quoted in Schoenwald, *Time for Choosing,* 144.

57. See Matthew D. Lassiter, *The Silent Majority: Suburban Politics in the Sunbelt South* (Princeton, NJ: Princeton University Press, 2006).

58. Joseph Epstein, "The New Conservatives: Intellectuals in Retreat," *Dissent,* Spring 1973, 151–162, here 151.

59. See Murray Friedman, *The Neoconservative Revolution: Jewish Intellectuals and the Shaping of Public Policy* (Cambridge: Cambridge University Press, 2012).

60. Irving Kristol, *Reflections of a Neoconservative: Looking Back, Looking Ahead* (New York: Basis Books, 1983), xii.

61. Irving Kristol, "The Neoconservative Persuasion" (2003), in *The Neoconservative Persuasion: Selected Essays, 1942–2009,* ed. Gertrude Himmelfarb, foreword by William Kristol (New York: Basic Books, 2011), 190–194, here 192.

62. See Birzer, *Russell Kirk,* 346–347; and W. Wesley McDonald, *Russell Kirk and the Age of Ideology* (Columbia: University of Missouri Press, 2004), 202–205.

63. Quoted in William H. Honan, "Russell Kirk Is Dead at 75," *New York Times,* April 30, 1994, L13.

64. Donald Atwell Zoll, "The Social Thought of Russell Kirk," *Political Science Reviewer* 2, no. 1 (1972): 112–136, here 134.

65. James Combs, *The Reagan Range: The Nostalgic Myth in American Politics* (Bowling Green, OH: Bowling Green State University Popular Press, 1993), 144.

66. Daniel Marcus, *Happy Days and Wonder Years: The Fifties and the Sixties in Contemporary Cultural Politics* (Piscataway, NJ: Rutgers University Press, 2004), 60, 51.

67. Sean Wilentz, *The Age of Reagan: A History, 1974–2008* (New York: HarperCollins, 2008), 136.

68. Quoted in Hedrick Smith, "Carter Wins Nomination for a Second Term," *New York Times,* August 14, 1980, A1.

69. See, for instance, David M. Alpern, James Doyle, John Walcott, and Christopher Arterton, "The Republican Landslide," *Newsweek,* November 17, 1980, 27–32, here 27; and Elizabeth Drew, "A Reporter at Large," *New Yorker,* March 16, 1980, 49–74, here 65. See also Elizabeth Drew, *Portrait of an Election* (London: Routledge & Kegan Paul, 1981), 116.

70. Richard Reeves, "Why Reagan Won't Make It," *Esquire,* May 8, 1979, 6–7, here 6.

71. Drew, "Reporter at Large," 65.

72. Lou Cannon, "Reagan," in *The Pursuit of the Presidency 1980,* ed. Richard Harwood (New York: Berkley Books, 1980), 251–272, here 253.

73. See Doug Rossinow, *The Reagan Era: A History of the 1980s* (New York: Columbia University Press, 2015), 11–15.

74. Ronald Reagan, "The Value of Understanding the Past," in *A Time for Choosing: The Speeches of Ronald Reagan, 1961–1982* (Chicago: Regnery Gateway, 1983), 73–84, here 75.

75. Ronald Reagan, *My Early Life or Where's the Rest of Me?,* with Richard G. Hubler (London: Sidgwick and Jackson, 1981), 13.

76. Ronald Reagan, "Address at Commencement Exercises at the University of Notre Dame," May 17, 1981, https://www.reaganlibrary.gov/archives/speech/address-commencement-exercises-university-notre-dame.

77. Ronald Reagan, "Remarks at a Reagan-Bush Rally in Sacramento, California," November 5, 1984, https://www.reaganlibrary.gov/archives/speech/remarks-reagan-bush-rally-sacramento-california.

78. Ronald Reagan, "Remarks at a White House Reception for Kennedy Center Honorees," December 4, 1988, https://www.reaganlibrary.gov/archives/speech/remarks-white-house-reception-kennedy-center-honorees-3.

79. See, for instance, Ronald Reagan, "Remarks at a Louisiana Republican Fundraising Reception in New Orleans, Louisiana," September 28, 1981, https://www .reaganlibrary.gov/archives/speech/remarks-louisiana-republican-fundraising -reception-new-orleans-louisiana; Ronald Reagan, "Remarks at a White House Luncheon Celebrating the Centennial of the Birth of Franklin Delano Roosevelt," January 28, 1982, https://www.reaganlibrary.gov/archives/speech/remarks-white -house-luncheon-celebrating-centennial-birth-franklin-delano-roosevelt; and Ronald Reagan, "Remarks at a White House Reception Commemorating the 50th Anniversary of the Folger Shakespeare Library," April 22, 1982, https://www .reaganlibrary.gov/archives/speech/remarks-white-house-reception-commemorating -50th-anniversary-folger-shakespeare.

80. Ronald Reagan, "Remarks at a Conservative Political Action Conference Dinner," February 26, 1982, https://www.reaganlibrary.gov/archives/speech/remarks -conservative-political-action-conference-dinner-0.

81. Reagan, "Birth of Franklin Delano Roosevelt," January 28, 1982.

82. See, for instance, Ronald Reagan, "Eureka College Commencement Address: President Reagan's Commencement Address, 1982," May 9, 1982, Reagan Foundation, YouTube video, 29:01, https://www.youtube.com/watch?v=dT _H0ZREQQU.

83. See Jeffrey K. Tulis, *The Rhetorical Presidency* (Princeton, NJ: Princeton University Press, 1987), 189.

84. Reed L. Welch, "The Great Communicator: Rhetoric, Media, and Leadership Style," in *A Companion to Ronald Reagan,* ed. Andrew L. Johns (Chichester, UK: Wiley Blackwell, 2015), 74–95, here 77.

85. Lee Edwards, *Reagan: A Political Biography* (San Diego: Viewpoint Books, 1967), 68.

86. Reagan, *My Early Life,* 28.

87. See Paul D. Erickson, *Reagan Speaks: The Making of an American Myth* (New York: New York University Press, 1985), 12–20.

88. On this concept, see Jan Assmann, *Cultural Memory and Early Civilization: Writing, Remembrance, and Political Imagination* (Cambridge: Cambridge University Press, 2011).

89. I'm using Barbara Rosenwein's term here but in a more literal sense, to characterize the community between Reagan and his audience. See Barbara H. Rosenwein, "Worrying about Emotions in History," *American Historical Review* 107, no. 3 (2002): 821–845.

90. See Janelle L. Wilson, *Nostalgia: Sanctuary of Meaning* (Lewisburg, PA: Bucknell University Press 2005), 85–87; Tim Wildschut et al., "Collective Nostalgia: A Group-Level Emotion That Confers Unique Benefits on the Group," *Journal of Personality and Social Psychology* 107, no. 5 (2014): 844–863; and Clay Routledge, *Nostalgia: A Psychological Resource* (New York: Psychology Press, 2016), 51–68.

91. Ronald Reagan, "Address at Commencement Exercises at Eureka College, Eureka, Illinois," May 9, 1982, https://www.reaganlibrary.gov/archives/speech/address-commencement-exercises-eureka-college-eureka-illinois.

92. Reagan, "Conservative Political Action Conference Dinner," February 26, 1982.

93. Reagan, "Value of Understanding the Past," 83.

94. Erickson, *Reagan Speaks,* 45.

95. Erickson, 49.

96. Francis L. Loewenheim, "Reaganscribing History," *New York Times,* March 23, 1981, A17.

97. Marcus, *Happy Days,* 64, 67.

98. Garry Wills, *Reagan's America: Innocents at Home* (New York: Penguin, 2000), 459. On Reagan's rhetoric and use of the past, see also Daniel T. Rodgers, *Age of Fracture* (Cambridge, MA: Belknap Press of Harvard University Press, 2011), 222–224.

99. Ronald Reagan, "Address before a Joint Session of Congress on the State of the Union," January 25, 1988, https://www.presidency.ucsb.edu/documents/address-before-joint-session-congress-the-state-the-union-0. On Reagan's use of the 1960s, see Bernard von Bothmer, *Framing the Sixties: The Use and Abuse of a Decade from Ronald Reagan to George W. Bush* (Amherst: University of Massachusetts Press, 2010), 28–44.

100. Ronald Reagan, "Remarks and a Question-and-Answer Session with Reporters on the Second Anniversary of the Inauguration of the President," January 20, 1983, https://www.reaganlibrary.gov/archives/speech/remarks-and-question-and-answer-session-reporters-second-anniversary-inauguration; Ronald Reagan, "Remarks to Employees at the Ivorydale Soap Manufacturing Plant in St. Bernard, Ohio," October 3, 1985, https://www.reaganlibrary.gov/archives/speech/remarks-employees-ivorydale-soap-manufacturing-plant-st-bernard-ohio; Ronald Reagan, "Remarks at a White House Ceremony Honoring the National Teacher of the Year," April 9, 1984, https://www.reaganlibrary.gov/archives/speech/remarks-white-house-ceremony-honoring-national-teacher-year; Ronald Reagan, "Remarks at a White House Ceremony Honoring Law Enforcement Officers Slain in the War on Drugs," April 19, 1988, https://www.reaganlibrary.gov/archives/speech/remarks-white-house-ceremony-honoring-law-enforcement-officers-slain-war-drugs; Ronald Reagan, "Remarks at the Annual Convention of the Lions Club International in Dallas, Texas," June 21, 1985, https://www.reaganlibrary.gov/archives/speech/remarks-annual-convention-lions-club-international-dallas-texas.

101. Ronald Reagan, "Remarks to Women Administration Appointees on Women's Equality Day," August 26, 1984, https://www.reaganlibrary.gov/archives/speech/remarks-women-administration-appointees-womens-equality-day; Ronald Reagan, "Letter Accepting the Resignation of Richard G. Darman as Assistant to the

President and Deputy to the Chief of Staff," February 1, 1985, https://www
.reaganlibrary.gov/archives/speech/letter-accepting-resignation-richard-g-darman
-assistant-president-and-deputy-chief.

102. Ronald Reagan, "Remarks about Federal Tax Reduction Legislation at a Meeting of
the House Republican Conference," July 24, 1981, https://www.reaganlibrary.gov
/archives/speech/remarks-about-federal-tax-reduction-legislation-meeting-house
-republican-conference; Ronald Reagan, "Remarks to Reporters following a
Meeting with Representative Eugene V. Atkinson of Pennsylvania," October 14,
1981, https://www.reaganlibrary.gov/archives/speech/remarks-reporters-following
-meeting-representative-eugene-v-atkinson-pennsylvania.

103. Ronald Reagan, "Inaugural Address," January 20, 1981, in *Actor, Ideologue,
Politician: The Public Speeches of Ronald Reagan,* ed. Davis W. Houck and Amos
Kiewe (Westport, CT: Greenwood, 1993), 176–180, here 178.

104. See Marcus, *Happy Days,* 72; and von Bothmer, *Framing the Sixties,* 35.

105. Ronald Reagan, "Republican National Convention, 17 July 1980," in *Actor,
Ideologue, Politician,* 158–166, here 158, 159.

106. George F. Will, *The Pursuit of Virtue and Other Tory Notions* (New York: Simon and
Schuster, 1982), 200.

107. Cannon, "Reagan," 253; Cannon, *President Reagan: The Role of a Lifetime* (New
York: Simon and Schuster, 1991), 23.

108. Wills, *Reagan's America,* 447.

109. See Public Papers of the President: Ronald Reagan, 1981–1989, Ronald Reagan
Presidential Library and Museum, https://www.reaganlibrary.gov/archives/public
-papers-president-ronald-reagan.

110. See, for instance, Ronald Reagan, "Remarks and a Question-and-Answer Session
with Regional Editors and Broadcasters on Domestic and Foreign Policy Issues,"
February 9, 1983, https://www.reaganlibrary.gov/archives/speech/remarks-
and-question-and-answer-session-regional-editors-and-broadcasters-domestic;
Ronald Reagan, "Remarks at a Reagan-Bush Rally in Decatur, Illinois," August 20,
1984, https://www.reaganlibrary.gov/archives/speech/remarks-reagan-bush-rally
-decatur-illinois; and Ronald Reagan, "The President's News Conference,"
December 20, 1983, https://www.reaganlibrary.gov/archives/speech/presidents
-news-conference-10.

111. Ronald Reagan, "Remarks at Georgetown University's Bicentennial Convocation,"
October 1, 1988, https://www.reaganlibrary.gov/archives/speech/remarks
-georgetown-universitys-bicentennial-convocation.

112. Ronald Reagan, "Remarks at the National Convention of the American Legion in
Louisville, Kentucky," September 6, 1988, https://www.reaganlibrary.gov/archives
/speech/remarks-national-convention-american-legion-louisville-kentucky; Ronald
Reagan, "Remarks at the Annual Republican Congressional Fundraising Dinner,"

May 11, 1988, https://www.reaganlibrary.gov/archives/speech/remarks-annual
-republican-congressional-fundraising-dinner-0.

113. See Kurt Ritter, "Ronald Reagan," in *U.S. Presidents as Orators: A Bio-critical Sourcebook,* ed. Halford Ryan (Westport, CT: Greenwood, 1995), 316–343; and Andrew R. Murphy, "Longing, Nostalgia, and Golden Age Politics: The American Jeremiad and the Power of the Past," *Perspectives on Politics* 7, no. 1 (2009): 125–141.

114. Ronald Reagan, "Inaugural Address, January 21, 1985," in *Actor, Ideologue, Politician,* 268–272, here 268.

115. See Walter E. Williams, "What's Wrong with Turning Back the Clock?," *Anthem Syndicate,* September 2, 1980, reprinted in Walter E. Williams, *America: A Minority View* (Stanford, CA: Hoover Institution Press, 1982), 91–92, here 91; and Rowland Evans and Robert D. Novak, *The Reagan Revolution* (New York: E. P. Dutton, 1981), xiii.

116. Drew S. Days, "Turning Back the Clock: The Reagan Administration and Civil Rights," *Harvard Civil Rights–Civil Liberties Law Review* 19 (1984): 309–347.

117. See Hugh Davis Graham, "Civil Rights Policy," in *The Reagan Presidency: Pragmatic Conservatism and Its Legacies,* ed. W. Elliot Brownlee and Hugh Davis Graham (Lawrence: University of Kansas Press, 2003), 283–292; Wilentz, *Age of Reagan,* 180–187; Lilia Fernandez, "Ronald Reagan, Race, Civil Rights, and Immigration," in *A Companion to Ronald Reagan,* ed. Andrew L. Johns (Chichester, UK: Wiley Blackwell, 2015), 185–203; and Rossinow, *Reagan Era,* 8–12, 222.

118. See Gareth Davies, "The Welfare State," in Brownlee and Graham, *Reagan Presidency,* 209–232.

119. See Matthew Avery Sutton, "Reagan, Religion and the Culture Wars of the 1980s," in Johns, *Companion to Ronald Reagan,* 204–220; and Andra Scanlon, "Ronald Reagan and the Conservative Movement," in Johns, *Companion to Ronald Reagan,* 585–607.

120. Ross K. Baker, "The Diplomacy of Nostalgia," *Worldview* 25, no. 12 (1982): 13–14.

121. On Reagan's foreign policy, see Michael V. Paulauskas, "Reagan, the Soviet Union and the Cold War," in Johns, *Companion to Ronald Reagan,* 276–294; and Wilentz, *Age of Reagan,* 151–175.

122. Quoted in Katharine Q. Seelye, "Gingrich Looks to Victorian Age to Cure Today's Social Failings," *New York Times,* March 14, 1995.

123. Quoted in Seelye.

124. Gertrude Himmelfarb, *The De-moralization of Society: From Victorian Virtues to Modern Values* (London: Institute of Economic Affairs, Health and Welfare Unit, 1995).

125. Stefan Collini, "Speaking with Authority: The Historian as Social Critic," in *English Pasts: Essays in Culture and History* (New York: Oxford University Press, 1999), 85–102, here 91, 88. See also David Cannadine, "Gilding Victoria," *Prospect,* December 20, 1995; Elaine Hadley, "The Past Is a Foreign Country: The Neoconservative Romance with Victorian Liberalism," *Yale Journal of Criticism* 10, no. 1 (1997): 7–38; and Simon Joyce, *The Victorians in the Rearview Mirror* (Athens: Ohio University Press, 2007), 111–114.

126. Hadley, "Past Is a Foreign Country," 9.

127. "Mr. Clinton's Future and the G.O.P.," *New York Times,* December 6, 1994. On Gingrich, the 1950s, and Norman Rockwell, see Marcus, *Happy Days,* 171–203.

128. Himmelfarb, *De-moralization of Society,* 3.

129. "TV Interview for London Weekend Television *Weekend World* ('Victorian Values')," January 16, 1983, Margaret Thatcher Foundation, https://www .margaretthatcher.org/document/105087.

130. "Radio Interview for IRN Programme *The Decision Makers,*" April 15, 1983, Margaret Thatcher Foundation, https://www.margaretthatcher.org/document /105291.

131. "TV Interview for Mexican TV," June 10, 1985, Margaret Thatcher Foundation, https://www.margaretthatcher.org/document/105885.

132. "Radio Interview for IRN," January 23, 1987, Margaret Thatcher Foundation, https://www.margaretthatcher.org/document/106731.

133. Commons Sitting of Thursday 17 February 1983, *Hansard,* https://hansard .parliament.uk/Commons/1983-02-17/debates/762ffc71-975f-462e-8163 -ceb71b2c3b77/Engagements.

134. Commons Sitting of Friday 25 March 1983, *Hansard,* https://hansard.parliament .uk/commons/1983-03-25/debates/4b08d22d-ce81-4023-9db0-0144f70b0d1d /WelfareState.

135. Commons Sitting of Tuesday 26 April 1983, *Hansard,* https://hansard.parliament .uk/Commons/1983-04-26/debates/255447b1-c69c-4a79-a0e2-8f8eab7f2bc5 /CommonsChamber.

136. See also Philip Maughan, "Peter Kennard: From Maggie Regina to Blue Murder," *New Statesman,* April 17, 2013, http://www.newstatesman.com/art-and-design /2013/04/peter-kennard-maggie-regina-blue-murder.

137. Raphael Samuel, "Soft Focus Nostalgia," *New Statesman,* May 27, 1983, ii–iv, here ii.

138. See Eric M. Sigsworth, ed., *In Search of Victorian Values* (Manchester: Manchester University Press, 1988); James Walvin, *Victorian Values* (London: Cardinal, 1988); Gordon Marsden, introduction to *Victorian Values: Personalities and Perspectives in Nineteenth-Century Society,* ed. Gordon Marsden (London: Longman, 1990),

2–12; and T. C. Smout, ed., *Victorian Values: A Joint Symposium of the Royal Society of Edinburgh and the British Academy, December 1990* (Oxford: Oxford University Press, 1992).

139. Paul Preston, "Paperback History," *History Today,* August 1985 59.

140. Bernard Porter, "'Though Not an Historian Myself . . .': Margaret Thatcher and the Historians," *Twentieth Century British History* 5, no. 2 (1994): 246–256, here 249.

141. "House of Commons PQs," March 15, 1979, Margaret Thatcher Foundation, https://www.margaretthatcher.org/document/103972.

142. Margaret Thatcher, "Speech to Australian Institute of Directors," October 2, 1981, Margaret Thatcher Foundation, https://www.margaretthatcher.org/document/104711.

143. "Conservative Party Election Broadcast," June 7, 1983, Margaret Thatcher Foundation, https://www.margaretthatcher.org/document/105382.

144. Raphael Samuel, "Mrs. Thatcher's Return to Victorian Values," in Smout, *Victorian Values,* 9–29, here 10, 11.

145. See Peter Jenkins, *Mrs. Thatcher's Revolution: The Ending of the Socialist Era* (London: Jonathan Cape, 1987), 67; Sigsworth, *In Search of Victorian Values;* John Gardiner, *The Victorians: An Age in Retrospect* (London: Hambledon and London, 2002), 87; and Joyce, *Victorians in the Rearview Mirror,* 111–114.

146. Samuel, "Soft Focus Nostalgia," ii; similarly, Marsden, introduction to *Victorian Values,* 4.

147. Samuel, "Mrs. Thatcher's Return," 14.

148. Stuart Hall, *The Hard Road to Renewal: Thatcherism and the Crisis of the Left* (London: Verso, 1988), 2.

149. See Jenkins, *Mrs. Thatcher's Revolution,* 30; Jim Tomlinson, *The Politics of Decline: Understanding Post-war Britain* (Harlow, UK: Longman, 2000); and Richard English and Michael Kenny, "Public Intellectuals and the Question of British Decline," *British Journal of Politics and International Relations* 3, no. 3 (2001): 259–283.

150. Margaret Thatcher, "Speech at Kensington Town Hall," January 19, 1976, Margaret Thatcher Foundation, https://www.margaretthatcher.org/document/102939; Margaret Thatcher, "Speech to Finchley Conservatives (Association AGM)," March 8, 1976, Margaret Thatcher Foundation, https://www.margaretthatcher.org/document/102977.

151. Correlli Barnett, *The Audit of War: The Illusion and Reality of Britain as a Great Nation* (London: Macmillan, 1986); Andrew Gamble, *Britain in Decline: Economic Policy, Political Strategy and the British State* (London: Macmillan, 1981); Martin Wiener, *English Culture and the Decline of the Industrial Spirit, 1850–1980,* new ed.

(1981; Cambridge: Cambridge University Press, 2004). On the influence of these books on Thatcher, see Jenkins, *Mrs. Thatcher's Revolution*, xiii–xviii, 30–49; Shirley Robin Letwin, *The Anatomy of Thatcherism* (London: Fontana, 1992), 250–255; and Richard Vinen, *Thatcher's Britain: The Politics and Social Upheaval of the Thatcher Era* (London: Simon and Schuster, 2009), 186–190.

152. Porter, "'Though Not an Historian,'" 251.

153. Asa Briggs, "Victorian Values," in Sigsworth, *In Search of Victorian Values*, 10–26, here 11.

154. Walvin, *Victorian Values*, 3.

155. Jenkins, *Mrs. Thatcher's Revolution*, 67. See also Vinen, *Thatcher's Britain*, 281.

156. Vinen, *Thatcher's Britain*, 281.

157. See Charles Moore, *Margaret Thatcher: The Authorized Biography* (London: Allen Lane, 2013), 1:656–704.

158. Anthony Barnett, *Iron Britannia: Time to Take the Great out of Britain* (1982; London: Faber, 2012), 65–66, 67. On the Falklands War, see Vinen, *Thatcher's Britain*, 134–153.

159. Thomas Pakenham, "Behind the Falklands Victory," *New York Times Magazine*, July 11, 1982, 60.

160. Stuart Hall, "The Empire Strikes Back," *New Socialist*, July / August 1982, 7.

161. E. P. Thompson, *The Heavy Dancers* (New York: Pantheon, 1985), vii, 103, first published as *The Defence of Britain: A Sequel to Protest and Survive* (London: European Nuclear Disarmament and Campaign for Nuclear Disarmament, 1983). On the perception of the Falklands War on the left generally, see Clive J. Christie, *Nationalism and Internationalism: Britain's Left and Policy towards the Falkland Islands, 1982–1984* (Hull, UK: University of Hull, Department of Politics, 1985).

162. Barnett, *Iron Britannia*, xxii.

163. Jonathan Raban, *Coasting* (London: Collins Harvill, 1986), 102.

164. Paul Theroux, *The Kingdom by the Sea: A Journey around Great Britain* (Boston: Houghton Mifflin, 1983), 213. On the coverage of the Falklands War by Raban and Theroux, see David Monaghan, *The Falklands War: Myth and Countermyth* (Basingstoke, UK: Macmillan, 1998), 117–149.

165. Letwin, *Anatomy of Thatcherism*, 37.

166. See Kenny, "Back to the Populist Future?"

167. See Monaghan, *Falklands War*, 15.

168. Margaret Thatcher, *Complete Public Statements 1945–1990*, CD-ROM (Oxford: Oxford University Press, 1999), interview no. 87_021, January 1987, TV interview for ABC.

169. "House of Commons PQs," February 17, 1983, Margaret Thatcher Foundation, https://www.margaretthatcher.org/document/105255.

170. "TV Interview for ABC," June 16, 1983, Margaret Thatcher Foundation, https://www.margaretthatcher.org/document/105178.

171. Margaret Thatcher, "Speech to Conservative Rally at Cheltenham," July 2, 1982, Margaret Thatcher Foundation, https://www.margaretthatcher.org/document /104989.

172. Eric Hobsbawm, "Falklands Fallout," in *The Politics of Thatcherism,* ed. Stuart Hall and Martin Jacques (London: Lawrence and Wishart, 1983), 257–270, here 260, 269.

173. Bryan Appleyard, "She Picked Her Ground as Champion of a Besieged Bourgeoisie," *Sunday Times,* November 25, 1990, 3.

174. Stefan Collini, "Victorian Values: From the Clapham Sect to the Clapham Omnibus," in *English Pasts: Essays in History and Culture* (Oxford: Oxford University Press, 1999), 103–115, here 106.

175. Samuel, "Mrs. Thatcher's Return," 28.

176. See his autobiography, Karl Heinz Bohrer, *Jetzt: Geschichte meines Abenteuers mit der Phantasie* (Berlin: Suhrkamp, 2017), 241.

177. Karl Heinz Bohrer, "Die weiße Riesin: Englands neuer Premier ist kein Tory," *Merkur* 33, no. 6 (1979): 611–615. See also Bohrer, *Jetzt,* 226, 227.

178. Karl Heinz Bohrer, "Falkland und die Deutschen," *Frankfurter Allgemeine Zeitung,* May 15, 1982, 25. See also Jan Müller, "Karl Heinz Bohrer on German National Identity: Recovering Romanticism and Aestheticizing the State," *German Studies Review* 23, no. 2 (2000): 297–316; Perry Anderson, "A New Germany?," *New Left Review* 57 (May–June 2009): 5–40; and Paul Graham, "The Avant-Garde of Decline: Karl Heinz Bohrer's Essays on England," *Journal of European Studies* 44, no. 2 (2014): 134–150.

179. Karl Heinz Bohrer, "Die letzte Armada," *Frankfurter Allgemeine Zeitung,* April 13, 1982, 25.

180. Gertrude de Alencar, "Gefährliche 'Prinzipien,'" *Frankfurter Allgemeine Zeitung,* May 24, 1982, 11; Reiner Schmidt, "Ästhetische Verzückung," *Frankfurter Allgemeine Zeitung,* May 27, 1982, 9; Gerd Laschefski, "Fragwürdige Verhaltungsmuster," *Frankfurter Allgemeine Zeitung,* May 28, 1982, 8; Martin Steder, "Falkland und alle Deutschen?," *Frankfurter Allgemeine Zeitung,* June 8, 1982, 9.

181. Bohrer, "Die letzte Armada," 25.

182. Karl Heinz Bohrer, "Ein wunderbarer Krieg?," *Frankfurter Allgemeine Zeitung,* July 27, 1982, 17.

183. See his autobiographical novel, Karl Heinz Bohrer, *Granatsplitter: Erzählung einer Jugend* (Munich: Hanser, 2012).

184. Reprinted as Karl Heinz Bohrer, "Ein bisschen Lust am Untergang," in *Ein bisschen Lust am Untergang: Englische Ansichten* (Frankfurt: Suhrkamp, 1982), 11–22, here 13.

185. Karl Heinz Bohrer, "Die Stadt des Poeten," reprinted in Bohrer, *Ein bisschen Lust am Untergang,* 86–95, here 92.

186. See Bohrer, *Ein bisschen Lust am Untergang;* Bohrer, *Jetzt,* 232–234.

187. On Bohrer's changing views on decadence, see Graham, "Avant-Garde of Decline."

188. Bohrer, *Ein bisschen Lust am Untergang,* 166.

189. See Martina Steber, *Die Hüter der Begriffe: Politische Sprachen des Konservativen in Großbritannien und der Bundesrepublik Deutschland, 1945–1980* (Berlin: De Gruyter Oldenbourg, 2017), 108–115.

190. Steber, 214–220, 240–271.

191. Baacke, "Nostalgie," 449.

192. See Axel Schildt, "'Die Kräfte der Gegenreform sind auf breiter Front angetreten': Zur konservativen Tendenzwende in den Siebzigerjahren," *Archiv für Sozialgeschichte* 44 (2004): 449–478; and Steber, *Die Hüter der Begriffe,* 245–246.

193. See Rolf Zundel, "Man trägt wieder konservativ," *Die Zeit,* March 29, 1974; and Rolf Zundel, "Tendenzwende—mehr als Einbildung," *Die Zeit,* December 13, 1974, 1.

194. Paul Widmer, "Konservatismus als intellektuelle Alternative: Theoretische Ansätze in der neu entfachten Konservatismusdebatte," *Schweizer Monatshefte* 54, no. 11 (1975): 849–855, here 849.

195. Christoph Burgauner, "Die ästhetische Melancholie," *Neue Deutsche Hefte* 21, no. 1 (1974): 104–111, here 104–105, 111.

196. George Tabori, "Staats-Theater: Oder das satte Lächeln vom Tiger," *Kursbuch* 70 (1982): 33–49, here 49.

197. Gerd-Klaus Kaltenbrunner, "Vorwort des Herausgebers," in *Konservatismus international* (Stuttgart: Seewald, 1973), 8–11, here 9.

198. Armin Mohler, *Tendenzwende für Fortgeschrittene* (Munich: Criticon, 1978), 83.

199. Nikolaus Lobkowicz, "Was verspricht der Konservatismus?," in *Demokratie in Anfechtung und Bewahrung,* Festschrift für Johannes Broermann, ed. Joseph Listl and Herbert Schambeck (Berlin: Duncker & Humblot, 1982), 85–105, here 103.

200. See Steber, *Die Hüter der Begriffe,* 328.

201. Hans-Jochen Vogel, "Über das Staatsverständnis der CDU: Zum V. Abschnitt des CDU-Grundsatzprogramms," *Die Neue Gesellschaft* 26, no. 7 (1979): 623–626, here 626.

202. "Hitler 73," *Der Spiegel,* April 2, 1973, 38–44, here 38.

203. Horst Krüger, "Hitlers Wiederkehr: Eine Mode, NS-Nostalgie oder mehr?," *Frankfurter Allgemeine Zeitung,* May 17, 1973, 22.

204. "Springtime for Hitler," *Newsweek,* April 30, 1973, 16–17, here 16.

205. Erich Fried, "Die Halbwahrheiten über Hitler: Zur Hitlernostalgie der westlichen Welt," in *Gedanken in und an Deutschland: Essays und Reden,* ed. Michael Lewin (Vienna: Europaverlag, 1988), 57–63, here 57, 58 (first published in *Deutsche Volkszeitung,* August 8, 1973); Heinrich Böll, "Vorwort zu 'Nacht über Deutschland,'" in *Essayistische Schriften und Reden,* ed. Bernd Balzer (Cologne: Kiepenheuer & Witsch, 1979), 3: 304–306; Günter Wallraff and Eckart Spoo, "Nostalgie. Fünf Karikaturen," in *Unser Faschismus nebenan: Griechenland gestern—ein Lehrstück für morgen* (Cologne: Kiepenheuer & Witsch, 1975), 142–158, here 142.

206. Joachim C. Fest, *Hitler: Eine Biographie* (Frankfurt am Main: Propyläen, 1973). See also Heinrich Schwendemann, "Zwischen Abscheu und Faszination: Joachim C. Fests Hitler-Biographie als populäre Vergangenheitsbewältigung," in *50 Klassiker der Zeitgeschichte,* ed. Jürgen Danyel, Jan-Holger Kirsch, and Martin Sabrow (Göttingen: Vandenhoeck & Ruprecht, 2007), 127–131.

207. Joachim C. Fest, *Ich nicht: Erinnerungen an eine Kindheit und Jugend* (Reinbek bei Hamburg: Rowohlt, 2008).

208. See Fest, *Hitler,* 1039.

209. Karl-Heinz Janssen, "High durch Hitler: NS-Nostalgie auf Großleinwand mit Stereoeffekt," *Die Zeit,* July 8, 1977.

210. See Jörg Berlin, ed., *Was verschweigt Fest? Analysen und Dokumente zum Hitler-Film von J.C. Fest* (Cologne: Pahl-Rugenstein, 1978).

211. For an overview, see Rudolph Binion, "Foam on the Hitler Wave," *Journal of Modern History* 46 (1974): 522–528; Eberhard Jäckel, "Rückblick auf die sogenannte Hitler-Welle," *Geschichte in Wissenschaft und Unterricht* 28 (1977): 695–710; Gitta Sereny, "Facing Up to the New 'Hitlerwave' in Germany," *New Statesman,* May 19, 1978, 666–669; and William Carr, "Historians and the Hitler Phenomenon," *German Life and Letters* 34 (1980/81): 260–272.

212. See "Schalen, Leuchter und Humpen," *Die Zeit,* October 11, 1974; Dietmar Polaczek, "Mit deutschem Gruß," *Frankfurter Allgemeine Zeitung,* March 23, 1977, 23; and "Mal was nettes über die Nazi-Zeit," *Der Spiegel,* December 5, 1977, 214–220, here 218.

213. *Verhandlungen des Deutschen Bundestages: Stenographische Berichte,* 8. Wahlperiode, 46. Sitzung, October 5, 1977, 3497.

214. *Verhandlungen des Deutschen Bundestages: Stenographische Berichte,* 8. Wahlperiode, 47. Sitzung, October 6, 1977, 3614.

215. *Verhandlungen des Deutschen Bundestages: Stenographische Berichte,* 8. Wahlperiode, 46. Sitzung, October 5, 1977, 3483–3485.

216. See Barbara Manthe, "On the Pathway to Violence: West German Right-Wing Terrorism in the 1970s," *Terrorism and Political Violence* 33, no. 1 (2021): 49–70; Uffa Jensen, *Ein antisemitischer Doppelmord: Die vergessene Geschichte des Rechtsterrorismus in der Bundesrepublik* (Berlin: Suhrkamp, 2022).

217. *Verhandlungen des Deutschen Bundestages: Stenographische Berichte,* 8. Wahlperiode, 47. Sitzung, October 6, 1977, 3614.

218. Joachim C. Fest, "Thinking about Hitler," *Encounter* 45, no. 3 (1975): 81–87, here 81.

219. See Habbo Knoch, "Die Serie 'Holocaust': Geschichtsvermittlung als Fernsehunterhaltung," *Indes* 1 (2016): 62–73; and Frank Bösch, "Versagen der Zeitgeschichtsforschung? Martin Broszat, die westdeutsche Geschichtswissenschaft und die Fernsehserie 'Holocaust,'" *Zeithistorische Forschungen / Studies in Contemporary History* 6 (2009): 477–482.

220. Helmut Kohl, "Das Erbe von Ahlen: Rede zum 30. Jahrestag des Ahlener Programms am 26. Februar 1977 in Ahlen," in *Der Kurs der CDU: Reden und Beiträge des Bundesvorsitzenden 1973–1993* (Stuttgart: DVA, 1993), 175–188, here 176.

221. *Verhandlungen des Deutschen Bundestages: Stenographische Berichte,* 9. Wahlperiode, 26. Sitzung, March 19, 1981, 1259.

222. Helmut Kohl, "Aufbruch in die Zukunft: Rede auf dem 21. Bundesparteitag der CDU in Bonn am 12. Juni 1973," in *Der Kurs der CDU,* 37–55, here 42.

223. Kohl, 37–38.

224. See Christian Wicke, *Helmut Kohl's Quest for Normality: His Representation of the German Nation and Himself* (New York: Berghahn, 2015), 7, 75–78.

225. See *Verhandlungen des Deutschen Bundestages: Stenographische Berichte,* 9. Wahlperiode, 121. Sitzung, Regierungserklärung, October 13, 1982, 7229.

226. *Verhandlungen des Deutschen Bundestages: Stenographische Berichte,* 9. Wahlperiode, 127. Sitzung, November 11, 1982, 7759.

227. "Das haben die glänzend pariert," *Der Spiegel,* February 14, 1983, 24–32, here 29.

228. Hans-Peter Riese, "Das große Behagen: Anmerkungen zur Rhetorik der Wende," in *Halbzeit in Bonn: Die Bundesrepublik zwei Jahre nach der Wende,* ed. Karsten Schröder and Günter Verheugen (Cologne: Kiepenheuer & Witsch, 1985), 250–260, here 254, 255–256.

229. *Verhandlungen des Deutschen Bundestages: Stenographische Berichte,* 12. Wahlperiode, 32. Sitzung, June 14, 1991, 2505–2507, here 2507.

230. See, for instance, Henry M. Broder, "'Wir lieben die Heimat,'" *Der Spiegel,* July 2, 1995, 54–64. On Ostalgie generally, see Paul Betts, "Remembrance of Things Past: Nostalgia in West and East Germany, 1980–2000," in *Pain and Prosperity. Reconsidering Twentieth Century German History,* ed. Paul Betts and Greg Eghigian

(Stanford, CA: Stanford University Press, 2003), 178–207; Anna Saunders and Debbie Pinfold, eds., *Remembering and Rethinking the GDR: Multiple Perspectives and Plural Authenticities* (Basingstoke, UK: Palgrave Macmillan, 2013); and Stephan Ehrig, Marcel Thomas, and David Zell, eds., *The GDR Today: New Interdisciplinary Approaches to East German History, Memory and Culture* (Oxford: Peter Lang, 2018).

231. Lothar Fritze, "'Ostalgie'—Das Phänomen der rückwirkenden Verklärung der DDR-Wirklichkeit und seine Ursachen," in *Materialien der Enquete-Kommission "Überwindung der Folgen der SED-Diktatur im Prozeß der deutschen Einheit,"* ed. Deutscher Bundestag (Baden-Baden: Nomos, 1999), 5:479–510, here 498; Winfried Gebhardt and Georg Kamphausen, "'Ostalgie'—Das Phänomen der rückwirkenden Verklärung der DDR-Wirklichkeit und seine Ursachen," in Deutscher Bundestag, *Materialien der Enquete-Kommission,* 5:511–539.

232. One of the few contemporary voices to criticize *Westalgie* was the historian Christian Meier, "Am Ende der alten Bundesrepublik," *Merkur* 48, no. 7 (1994): 561–572. On *Westalgie,* see also Betts, "Remembrance of Things Past"; Tobias Dürr, "On 'Westalgia': Why West German Mentalities and Habits Persist in the Berlin Republic," in *The Spirit of the Berlin Republic,* ed. Dieter Dettke (New York: Berghahn, 2003), 37–47; Andrew Plowman, "*Westalgie*? Nostalgia for the 'Old' Federal Republic in Recent German Prose," *Seminar* 40, no. 3 (2004): 249–261; and Linda Shortt, "Reimagining the West: West Germany, Westalgia, and the Generation of 1978," in *Debating German Cultural Identity since 1989,* ed. Anke Fuchs and Linda Shortt (Rochester, NY: Camden, 2011), 156–169.

233. Dominic Boyer, "Ostalgie and the Politics of the Future in Eastern Germany," *Public Culture* 18, no. 2 (2006): 361–381, here 373.

234. Sara Abbasi, "Nostalgic Elderly Brexiters Have Stolen My Future," *Guardian,* June 26, 2016.

235. See, for instance, Volker Wagner, "In Brexit Vote, UK Nostalgia Beat EU Dreams," *Deutsche Welle,* June 27, 2016, https://www.dw.com/en/opinion-in-brexit-vote-uk -nostalgia-beat-eu-dreams/a-19361035; and Anne Applebaum, "Amid Brexit, British Citizens Are Suddenly Gripped by Nostalgia," *Washington Post,* April 3, 2017.

236. Pankaj Mishra, "Brexiteers Are Pining for Empire," Bloomberg, April 29, 2016, https://www.bloomberg.com/view/articles/2016-04-29/brexit-supporters-are -pining-for-the-days-of-empire.

237. Kehinde Andrews, "Colonial Nostalgia Is Back in Fashion, Blinding Us to the Horrors of Empire," *Guardian,* August 24, 2016.

238. Tom Whyman, "Theresa May's Empire of the Mind," *New York Times,* February 15, 2017; David Olusoga, "Empire 2.0 Is Dangerous Nostalgia for Something That Never Existed," *Guardian,* March 19, 2017; Ishaan Tharoor, "Brexit and Britain's Delusions of Empire," *Washington Post,* March 31, 2017; Gary Younge, "Britain's Imperial Fantasies Have Given Us Brexit," *Guardian,* February 3, 2018. Because Robert Saunders analyzes and critiques this trope, I am focusing here on nostalgia

more generally: see Robert Saunders, "Brexit and Empire: 'Global Britain' and the Myth of Imperial Nostalgia," *Journal of Imperial and Commonwealth History* 48, no. 6 (2020): 1140–1174.

239. Ed Kilgore, "Donald Trump and the Religion of White Nostalgia," *New York Magazine,* October 26, 2016; Sarah Pulliam Bailey, "How Nostalgia for White Christian America Drove So Many Americans to Vote for Trump," *Washington Post,* January 5, 2017; Neil Irwin, "Donald Trump's Economic Nostalgia," *New York Times,* June 28, 2016. See also Chris Arnade, "Nostalgia: The Yearning That Will Continue to Carry the Trump Message Forward," *Guardian,* March 24, 2017.

240. Gregory Rodriguez and Dawn Nakagawa, "Looking Backward and Inward: The Politics of Nostalgia and Identity," *Huffington Post,* July 28, 2016, https://www.huffingtonpost.com/gregory-rodriguez/political-nostalgia_b_11199804.html?guccounter=1. See also Cathal Kelly, "The New Age of Nostalgia," *Globe and Mail,* December 28, 2016; and Samuel Earle, "The Politics of Nostalgia," *Jacobin,* January 20, 2017, https://www.jacobinmag.com/2017/01/donald-trump-inauguration-nationalism.

241. Cas Mudde, "Can We Stop the Politics of Nostalgia That Have Dominated 2016?," *Newsweek,* December 15, 2016.

242. Lilla, *Shipwrecked Mind,* 15.

243. Bauman, *Retrotopia.*

244. De Vries and Hoffmann, "Power of the Past"; Gaston and Hilhorst, *At Home in One's Past.*

245. Gaston and Hilhorst, *At Home in One's Past,* 193–195, 273–275.

246. De Vries and Hoffmann, "Power of the Past," 3, 9–11, 17.

247. Norris and Inglehart, *Cultural Backlash,* 52.

248. Campanella and Dassú, *Anglo Nostalgia,* 3, 13.

249. Crouch, *Post-democracy,* 91–117.

250. Applebaum, *Twilight of Democracy,* 55–104.

251. Danny Dorling and Sally Tomlinson, *Rule Britannia: Brexit and the End of Empire* (London: Biteback, 2019), see particularly 10, 63–64, 143; Gildea, *Empires of the Mind,* 231–237. See also Robert Saunders, "Brexit and Empire."

252. Boris Johnson, "The EU Wants a Superstate, Just as Hitler Did," *Telegraph,* May 15, 2016.

253. Jack Maidment, "Jacob Rees-Mogg Compares Brexit to Battles of Agincourt, Waterloo and Trafalgar," *Telegraph,* October 3, 2017.

254. Richard J. Evans, "How the Brexiteers Broke History," *New Statesman,* November 14, 2018, https://www.newstatesman.com/politics/uk/2018/11/how-brexiteers-broke-history.

255. Applebaum, *Twilight of Democracy,* 63.

256. Tim Stanley, "Brexit Isn't about Nostalgia. It's about Ambition. Trust Me, I'm a Historian," *Telegraph,* June 21, 2016.

257. Peter Apps, "EU Referendum: Michael Gove's Full Statement on Why He Is Backing Brexit," *Independent,* February 20, 2016.

258. "David Davis's Speech on Brexit at the Institute of Chartered Engineers," UKPOL, February 4, 2016, http://www.ukpol.co.uk/david-davis-2016-speech-on-brexit/.

259. Vote Leave, http://www.voteleavetakecontrol.org.

260. Andrea Leadsom, "The Choice the UK Now Faces Is to Accept a Largely Unreformed EU, or Choose the Route of Freedom and Democracy," Vote Leave, May 17, 2016, http://www.voteleavetakecontrol.org/andrea_leadsom_the_choice _the_uk_now_faces_is_to_accept_a_largely_unreformed_eu_or_choose_the_route _of_freedom_and_democracy.html.

261. Apps, "EU Referendum."

262. David Cameron, "PM Speech on the UK's Strength and Security in the EU," May 9, 2016, https://www.gov.uk/government/speeches/pm-speech-on-the-uks-strength -and-security-in-the-eu-9-may-2016.

263. Cameron, "PM Speech."

264. Andrew Roberts, "Cameron's Travesty of History: The PM Must Know It's Bunkum to Say Brexit Raises the Threat of War. It Just Shows the Panic at No 10," *Daily Mail,* May 10, 2016.

265. Fintan O'Toole, "The Paranoid Fantasy behind Brexit," *Guardian,* November 16, 2018.

266. See Robert Saunders, *Yes to Europe! The 1975 Referendum and Seventies Britain* (Cambridge: Cambridge University Press, 2018), 11–14.

267. Michael Gove, Boris Johnson, and Gisela Stuart, "Letter to the Prime Minister and Foreign Secretary: Getting the Facts Clear on Turkey," Vote Leave, June 16, 2016, http://www.voteleavetakecontrol.org/letter_to_the_prime_minister_and_foreign _secretary_getting_the_facts_clear_on_turkey.html. See also "The Misrepresenta- tions and Misleading Statements Made by Vote Leave on Turkey Being Fast Tracked for Full EU Membership," European Law Monitor, July 20, 2016, https://www.europeanlawmonitor.org/eu-referendum-topics/vote-leave -misrepresentations-on-turkey-and-migration.html.

268. See Michael Oswald, "In Zukunft zurück in die Vergangenheit: Nostalgie als politische Rhetorik," in *Die gespaltenen Staaten von Amerika: Die Wahl Donald Trumps und die Folgen für Politik und Gesellschaft,* ed. Michael Oswald and Winand Gellner (Wiesbaden: Springer, 2018), 141–157, here 142.

269. See Donald J. Trump, "Inaugural Address, January 20, 2017," GovInfo, https://www .govinfo.gov/content/pkg/DCPD-201700058/pdf/DCPD-201700058.pdf.

270. Gaston and Hilhorst, *At Home in One's Past,* 23; De Vries and Hoffmann, "Power of the Past," 5; Campanella and Dassú, *Anglo Nostalgia,* ix.

271. Justin Gest, *The New Minority: White Working Class Politics in an Age of Immigration and Inequality* (Oxford: Oxford University Press, 2016), 10.

272. "*The New Minority: White Working Class Politics in an Age of Immigration and Inequality,*" Oxford University Press, https://global.oup.com/academic/product/the-new-minority-9780190632540?cc=gb&lang=en&#.

273. Owen Jones, *Chavs: The Demonisation of the Working Class* (London: Verso, 2012), xv. See also Gurminder K. Bhambra, "Brexit, Trump, and 'Methodological Whiteness': On the Misrecognition of Race and Class," *British Journal of Sociology* 68, no. S1 (2017): S214–S232; Satnam Virdee and Brendan McGeever, "Racism, Crisis, Brexit," *Ethnic and Racial Studies* 41, no. 10 (2018): 1802–1819; Aurelien Mondon and Aaron Winter, "Whiteness, Populism and the Racialisation of the Working Class in the United Kingdom and the United States," *Identities* 26, no. 5 (2019): 510–528.

274. David Goodhart, *The Road to Somewhere: The Populist Revolt and the Future of Politics* (London: Hurst, 2017), 24.

275. See, for instance, Jonathan Freedland, "The Road to Somewhere by David Goodhart: A Liberal's Rightwing Turn on Immigration," *Guardian,* March 22, 2017; and Bhambra, "Brexit, Trump."

276. *The Mass Observation Project: Spring 2016 Directive* (Brighton, UK: Mass Observation Archive, 2016), http://www.massobs.org.uk/images/Spring_2016_final.pdf.

277. University of Sussex, Mass Observation Archive, Spring Directive 2016, SxMOA2/1/105/3/1, B5725, F3641, F5620, H1543, H1745, H2639, B5342.

278. University of Sussex, Mass Observation Archive, Spring Directive 2016, C2579, R1025, R1418, F3409.

279. "In Full: Vince Cable's Speech to Conference," *Liberal Democrat Voice,* March 11, 2018, https://www.libdemvoice.org/in-full-vince-cables-speech-to-conference-56902.html.

280. See "Sir Vince Cable Denies Branding Older Brexit Voters Racist," BBC, March 12, 2018, https://www.bbc.com/news/uk-politics-43367204. See also Duncan Geddis, "Vince Cable in Brexit Racism Row over 'White Faces' Speech," *Times* (London), March 12, 2018.

281. On the role of nostalgia in the struggles within the Labour Party, see Richard Jobson, *Nostalgia and the Post-war Labour Party: Prisoners of the Past* (Manchester: Manchester University Press, 2018).

282. See Clark, *Time and Power.*

283. Hartmut Rosa, *Social Acceleration: A New Theory of Modernity* (New York: Columbia University Press, 2013), 258 (emphasis in the original).

284. Martina Steber, "A Better Tomorrow: Making Sense of Time in the Conservative Party and the CDU/CSU in the 1960s and 1970s," *Journal for Modern European History* 13, no. 3 (2003): 317–337, here 318. See also Steber, *Die Hüter der Begriffe.*

285. See Emily Robinson, *History, Heritage and Tradition in Contemporary British Politics: Past Politics and Present Histories* (Manchester: Manchester University Press, 2012); and Steber, "Better Tomorrow."

286. See Johannes Fabian, *Time and the Other: How Anthropology Makes Its Object* (New York: Columbia University Press, 1983). For a general critique of this thinking, see Achim Landwehr, "Von der 'Gleichzeitigkeit des Ungleichzeitigen,'" *Historische Zeitschrift* 295 (2012): 1–34.

287. Reinhart Koselleck, *Futures Past: On the Semantics of Historical Time,* trans. Keith Tribe (Cambridge, MA: MIT Press, 1985), 95, 99, 160, 239, 246, 266.

288. Ernst Bloch, *Heritage of Our Times,* trans. Neville and Stephen Plaice (Berkeley: University of California Press, 1991), 97. See also Frederic J. Schwartz, "Ernst Bloch and Wilhelm Pinder: Out of Sync," *Grey Room* 2, no. 3 (2001): 54–89.

3. Reviving

1. See Simon Reynolds, *Retromania: Pop Culture's Addiction to Its Own Past* (New York: Faber and Faber, 2011), ix–xxiii.

2. Elizabeth Guffey, *Retro: The Culture of Revival* (London: Reaktion, 2006), 131.

3. See James Laver, *Taste and Fashion* (London: Harrap, 1937), 255.

4. Reynolds, *Retromania,* xxix, x.

5. Raphael Samuel, *Theatres of Memory: Past and Present in Contemporary Culture* (London: Verso, 1994), 110.

6. Elizabeth Wilson, "These New Components of the Spectacle: Fashion and Postmodernism," in *Postmodernism and Society,* ed. Roy Boyne and Ali Rattansi (Basingstoke, UK: Macmillan Education, 1990), 209–234, here 226.

7. Frank Heath, "Nostalgia Shock," *Saturday Review,* May 29, 1971, 18.

8. "The Nifty Fifties," *Life,* June 16, 1972, 38–46, here 39.

9. Jonathan Rodgers, "Back to the '50s," *Newsweek,* October 16, 1972, 78–82, here 79.

10. Rodgers, 78; similarly, Richard R. Lingeman, "Proms and Liking Ike: There Was Another Fifties," *New York Times Magazine,* June 17, 1973, 26–39.

11. Thomas Meehan, "Must We Be Nostalgic about the Fifties?," *Horizon* 9, no. 1 (1972): 4–17, here 5.

12. Ray Connolly, "The Fascinating '50s," *Evening Standard,* March 4, 1972, 13; Simon Jenkins, "The Return of the Foggy Fifties," *Evening Standard,* January 2, 1973, 21.

13. Wolfgang Schivelbusch, "Das nostalgische Syndrom: Überlegungen zu einem neueren antiquarischen Gefühl," *Frankfurter Hefte: Zeitschrift für Kultur und Politik* 28, no. 4 (1973): 270–276, here 270.

14. "Der Mythos der 50er Jahre: Die Sehnsucht nach den Wunderjahren," *Der Spiegel,* April 9, 1978, cover.

15. See Gene Busnar, *It's Rock 'n' Roll* (New York: Julian Messner, 1979); and Reynolds, *Retromania,* 286.

16. Otto Fuchs, *Bill Haley: The Father of Rock and Roll* (Gelnhausen, Germany: Wagner, 2011), 585.

17. See Fuchs, 602–612.

18. Quoted in John Swenson, *Bill Haley* (London: W. H. Allen, 1983), 137.

19. See, for instance, Busnar, *It's Rock 'n' Roll,* 3.

20. See Richard Nader, "Oldies' Biggest Fan, Dies at 69," *New York Times,* December 9, 2009; Busnar, *It's Rock 'n' Roll,* 3; and Reynolds, *Retromania,* 286–87.

21. Quoted in Reynolds, *Retromania,* 286.

22. The film is available online: "The London Rock and Roll Show 1972," YouTube video, 2:19:48, https://www.youtube.com/watch?v=uC4Z62aqG60.

23. See Ray Foulk and Caroline Foulk, *When the World Came to the Isle of Wight,* 2 vols. (Surbiton, UK: Medina, 2015).

24. Quoted in Fuchs, *Bill Haley,* 230.

25. Robin Denslow, "Rock Concert at Wembley," *Guardian,* August 7, 1972, 8; Antony Thorncroft, "Rock 'n' Roll Revival," *Financial Times,* August 7, 1971, 3.

26. Jane Mulvagh, *Vivienne Westwood: An Unfashionable Life* (London: HarperCollins, 1998), 52.

27. Mulvagh, 52; Fred Vermorel, *Fashion and Perversity: A Life of Vivienne Westwood and the Sixties Laid Bare* (London: Bloomsbury, 1996), 59.

28. Vermorel, *Fashion and Perversity,* 61. See also Vivienne Westwood and Ian Kelly, *Vivienne Westwood* (London: Picador, 2014), 135.

29. Connolly, "Fascinating '50s," 13.

30. Rodgers, "Back to the '50s," 79.

31. Vermorel, *Fashion and Perversity,* 61.

32. Reynolds, *Retromania,* 240.

33. Quoted in Simon Reynolds, *Rip It Up and Start Again: Postpunk 1978–1984* (London: Penguin, 2006), 50.

34. Rodgers, "Back to the '50s," 79.

35. "Sha-Na-Na Live @ Woodstock 1969 at the Hop," YouTube video, 2:23, https://www.youtube.com/watch?v=HXLsMszmQpA.

36. Busnar, *It's Rock 'n' Roll,* 3.

37. Busnar, 4.

38. See Philip Auslander, "Good Old Rock and Roll: Performing the 1950s in the 1970s," *Music Studies* 15, no. 2 (2003): 166–194, here 170.

39. Jan Hodenfield, "Sha Na Na Na Yip Yip Mum Mum Get a Job: Is '50s Nostalgia behind the Popularity of These Columbia and Brooklyn College Undergrads?," *Rolling Stone*, October 18, 1969, 30.

40. Hodenfield, 31.

41. Hodenfield, 31.

42. Steve Turner, "Moving History with Sha Na Na," *Beat Instrumental*, November 1972, 6–9, here 8.

43. Turner, 8.

44. Hodenfield, "Sha Na Na Na," 30.

45. See, for instance, Carl Belz, *The Story of Rock* (New York: Oxford University Press, 1969); Nik Cohn, *Awopbopaloobop Alopbamboom: Pop from the Beginning* (London: Paladin, 1970); Jonathan Eisen, ed., *The Age of Rock: Sounds of the American Cultural Revolution* (New York: Random House, 1969); and Charlie Gillett, *The Sound of the City: The Rise of Rock and Roll* (London: Souvenir Press, 1970).

46. Rodgers, "Back to the '50s," 82.

47. Richard Hasbany, "Irene: Considering the Nostalgia Sensibility," *Journal of Popular Culture* 9 (1976): 816–826, here 825.

48. See Marcus Hearn, *The Cinema of George Lucas*, foreword by Ron Howard (New York: Harry N. Abrams, 2005), 52–55.

49. Fredric Jameson, *Postmodernism, or, The Cultural Logic of Late Capitalism* (London: Verso, 1991), 19.

50. Michael D. Dwyer, *Back to the Fifties: Nostalgia, Hollywood Film, and Popular Music of the Seventies and Eighties* (Oxford: Oxford University Press, 2015), 75.

51. Larry Sturhahn, "The Filming of *American Graffiti* (1974)," in *George Lucas: Interviews*, ed. Sally Kline (Jackson: University Press of Mississippi, 1999), 14–32, here 22.

52. Roger Ebert, "American Graffiti (11 August 1973)," in *Roger Ebert's Four-Star Reviews 1967–2007* (Kansas City, MO: Andrew McMeel, 2007), 25–26.

53. See, for instance, Paul Newland, *British Films of the 1970s* (Manchester: Manchester University Press, 2015), 93; and David Allen, "British Graffiti: Popular Music and Film in the 1970s," in *British Film Culture in the 1970s: The Boundaries of Pleasure*, ed. Sue Harper and Justin Smith (Edinburgh: Edinburgh University Press: 2012), 99–111.

54. Kevin Donnelly, *Pop Music in British Cinema: A Chronicle* (London: BFI, 2007), 56.

55. See Andrew Yule, *Enigma: David Puttnam: The Story So Far* (Edinburgh: Mainstream, 1988), 85.

56. Yule, 86.

57. See Stephen Glynn, *The British Pop Music Film: The Beatles and Beyond* (New York: Palgrave Macmillan, 2013), 165–166.

58. "That'll Be the Day," *Cinema TV Today*, April 28, 1973, 14; "That'll Be the Day," *Variety*, November 28, 1973, 14.

59. Quoted in Alexander Walker, *National Heroes: British Film in the Seventies and Eighties* (London: Harrap, 1985), 71; Vermorel, *Fashion and Perversity*, 60. See also Mulvagh, *Vivienne Westwood*, 57; Westwood and Kelly, *Vivienne Westwood*, 147.

60. Quoted in Walker, *National Heroes*, 71.

61. Julian Fox, "That'll Be the Day," *Films and Filming*, July 10, 1973, 53–54, here 53.

62. Fox, 53.

63. Yule, *Enigma*, 94–95.

64. See Dick Hebdige, *Subculture: The Meaning of Style* (London: Routledge, 1988), 52–54.

65. Dave Smith, "Mods v Rockers in the Who's Quadrophenia," *Photoplay*, March 1979, 20–21.

66. Jan Dawson, "Reverse Gear," *Listener*, August 23, 1979, 248.

67. Tom Forester, "The Return of the Mods," *New Society*, May 24, 1979, 437–438; Peter York, "Mods: The Second Coming," *Harpers and Queen*, September 1979, 158–163.

68. Arnd Schirmer, "Exotische Wesen," *Der Spiegel*, April 9, 1979, 261–263, here 261.

69. Schirmer, 263.

70. "Heimweh nach den falschen Fünfzigern," *Der Spiegel*, April 3, 1978, 90–111, here 90.

71. "Heimweh nach den falschen Fünfzigern," 92, 97–111.

72. Christian Rathke, *Die Fünfziger Jahre: Aspekte und Tendenzen: Katalog der Ausstellung des Kunst- und Museumsvereins Wuppertal 23.9.–13.11.77* (Wuppertal, Germany: Kunst- und Museumsvereins Wuppertal, 1977), 4.

73. For an overview, see Christian Rathke, "Politik, Design und Bildende Kunst der Fünfziger Jahre in Deutschland: Vorstellung einiger Neuerscheinungen," *Kunstforum International* 59, no. 3(1983): 148–159.

74. See Ulrich Greiner, "Froh geniessen," *Frankfurter Allgemeine Zeitung*, December 30, 1978, 23.

75. *Bravo*, June 8, 1978, cover.

76. Pierre Yves Guillen, "Saint Laurent: L'Apprentie sorcier," *Combat*, February 1, 1971; Alison Adburgham, "Saving the Worst for Last," *Guardian*, January 30, 1971; and Eugenia Sheppard, "Saint-Laurent: Truly Hideous," *International Herald Tribune*, January 30, 1971, all quoted in Alexander Samson, "Chronicle of a

Scandal," in *Yves Saint Laurent: The Scandal Collection, 1971,* trans. Elizabeth Heard, ed. Alexander Samson, Olivier Saillard, and Dominique Veillon (New York: Abrams, 2017), 41–46, here 42.

77. "Yves St. Debacle," *Time,* February 15, 1971, 2.

78. Roland Barthes, *The Fashion System* (New York: Hill and Wang, 1983), 300.

79. Yves Saint Laurent, interview by Claude Berhold, *Elle,* March 1, 1971, 62, quoted in Olivier Saillard, "The Collection That Created a Scandal: Yves Saint Laurent Spring-Summer 1971 Haute Couture," in Samson, Saillard, and Veillon, *Yves Saint Laurent,* 13–23, here 19.

80. Farid Chenoune, "Spring-Summer 1971: Anatomy of a Scandal," in *Saint Laurent,* ed. Pierre Bergé (New York: Abrams, 2010), 198–205, here 198.

81. Pierre-Yves Guillen, *Combat,* February 1, 1971, quoted in Chenoune, "Spring-Summer 1971," 202; M.-A. Dabadie, "Saint Laurent: Une triste occupation," *Le Figaro,* January 30–31, 1971, quoted in Saillard, "Collection That Created a Scandal," 14.

82. *Vogue Paris,* March 1971, quoted in Saillard, "Collection That Created a Scandal," 19.

83. "Deux filles à la mode choisissent leur mode," *Elle,* March 1, 1971, 124, quoted in Saillard, "Collection That Created a Scandal," 17.

84. Quoted in Saillard, 18.

85. See also Angela McRobbie, "Second-Hand Dresses and the Role of the Ragmarket," in *Zoot Suits and Second-Hand Dresses,* ed. Angela McRobbie (Boston: Unwin Hyman, 1988), 23–49.

86. See Valerie Steele, "Anti-fashion: The 1970s," *Fashion Theory* 1, no. 3 (1997): 279–295; and Jennifer Le Zotte, *From Goodwill to Grunge: A History of Second-Hand Styles and Alternative Economies* (Chapel Hill: University of North Carolina Press, 2017).

87. *Women's Wear Daily,* March 12, 1971, quoted in Chenoune, "Spring-Summer 1971," 198.

88. Pascal Bonitzer and Serge Toubiana, "Anti-rétro: Entretien avec Michel Foucault, *Cahiers du cinema,*" in *Cahiers du Cinéma,* vol. 4, *1973–1978: History, Ideology and Cultural Struggle, An anthology from* Cahiers du Cinéma *nos 248–292, September 1973–September 1978,* ed. David Wilson (London: Routledge, 2000), 159–172.

89. On *la mode rétro* and its political and historical context, see Henry Rousso, *The Vichy Syndrome: History and Memory in France* (Cambridge, MA: Harvard University Press, 1991); Alan Morris, *Collaboration and Resistance Reviewed: Writers and the Mode Rétro in Post-Gaullist France* (New York: Berg, 1992); Bertram M. Gordon, "The 'Vichy Syndrome' Problem in History," *French Historical Studies* 19, no. 2

(1995): 495–518; Richard J. Golsan, "Collaboration and Context: Lacombe Lucien, the Mode Rétro, and the Vichy Syndrome," in *Identity Papers: Contested Nationhood in Twentieth-Century France,* ed. Steven Ungar and Tom Conley (Minneapolis: University of Minnesota Press, 1996), 139–155; and Margaret Atack, "Performing the Nation in the Mode Rétro," *Journal of War and Culture Studies* 9, no. 4 (2016): 335–347.

90. Bonitzer and Toubiana, "Anti-rétro," 161.

91. Saul Friedländer, *Where Memory Leads: My Life* (New York: Other Press, 2016), 192. He first commented on the subject in Saul Friedländer, *Reflections of Nazism: An Essay on Kitsch and Death,* trans. the French by Thomas Weyr (New York: Harper and Row, 1984).

92. *Oxford English Dictionary,* s.v. "retro, *adj.*" (Oxford: Oxford University Press, September 2016), https://www.oed.com/view/Entry/241735?rskey=QlFSwS&result=2&isAdvanced=false#eid.

93. Clara Pierre, *Looking Good: The Liberation of Fashion* (New York: Reader's Digest Press, 1976), 175.

94. Bernardine Morris, "Will the 'Retro' Look Make It?," *New York Times,* January 1, 1979, 18.

95. Bonitzer and Toubiana, "Anti-rétro," 159.

96. See Rousso, *Vichy Syndrome,* 127–131.

97. Jean Baudrillard, *Simulacra and Simulation,* trans. Sheila Faria Glaser (1981; Ann Arbor: University of Michigan Press, 1994), 44.

98. Baudrillard, 196, 47.

99. Jameson, *Postmodernism,* 19. See also Fredric Jameson, "Postmodernism and the Cultural Logic of Late Capitalism," *New Left Review* 146, no. 1 (1984): 53–92, here 66.

100. Samuel, *Theatres of Memory,* 112, 113.

101. Guffey, *Retro,* 20.

102. James Laver, *Victoriana* (London: Ward Lock, [1966]), 9.

103. See Jules Lubbock, "Victorian Revival," *Architectural Review* 163 (1978): 161–167; and Anthony Burton, "The Revival of Interest in Victorian Decorative Art and the Victoria and Albert Museum," in *The Victorians since 1901: Histories, Representations and Revisions,* ed. Miles Taylor and Michael Wolff (Manchester: Manchester University Press, 2004), 121–137.

104. Becky E. Conekin, *"The Autobiography of a Nation": The 1951 Festival of Britain* (Manchester: Manchester University Press, 2003), 85.

105. Quoted in Bevis Hillier, introduction to *A Tonic to the Nation: The Festival of Britain 1951,* ed. Mary Banham and Bevis Hillier, with a prologue by Roy Strong (London: Thames and Hudson, 1976), 10–17, here 12.

106. Conekin, *"Autobiography of a Nation,"* 85.

107. Lubbock, "Victorian Revival," 161.

108. See C. H. Gibbs-Smith, *The Great Exhibition of 1851: A Commemorative Album* (London: Victoria and Albert Museum, 1950).

109. See V&A Archive, MA/28/85/1, Exhibition of Victorian and Edwardian Decorative Arts.

110. Reyner Banham, "Here's Richness," *Art News,* November 15, 1952, 3.

111. Barbara Morris, "The 1952 Exhibition of Victorian and Edwardian Decorative Arts at the Victoria and Albert Museum: A Personal Recollection," *Journal of the Decorative Arts Society 1850–the Present* 25 (2001): 11–24, here 24.

112. Anthony Burton, *Vision and Accident: The Story of the Victoria and Albert Museum* (London: V&A Publications, 1999), 214.

113. *Victoriana: An Exhibition of the Arts of the Victorian Era in America, Brooklyn Institute of Arts and Sciences, April 7–June 5, 1960* (New York: Brooklyn Museum, 1960), unpaginated.

114. Charles Platten Woodhouse, *The Victoriana Collector's Handbook* (London: George Bell and Sons, 1970), 1.

115. Quoted in Nik Cohn, *Today There Are No Gentlemen: The Changes in Englishmen's Clothes since the War* (London: Weidenfeld and Nicolson, 1971), 22.

116. Cohn, 22.

117. Cohn, 31; see 27–32 on the Teddy Boys.

118. Alvin Toffler, *Future Shock* (London: Pan Books, 1970), 407.

119. Bevis Hillier, *The Style of the Century* (London: Herbert, 1983), 206.

120. See *Um 1900: Art Nouveau und Jugendstil: Kunst und Kunstgewerbe aus Europa und Amerika zur Zeit der Stilwende, 28 Juni bis 28 September 1952* ([Zurich]: n.p., [1952]). See also Jost Hermand, "Vorwort," in *Jugendstil,* ed. Jost Hermand (Darmstadt, Germany: Wissenschaftliche Buchgesellschaft, 1971), ix–xvi, here x; Robert Schmutzler, "Nachwort," in *Art Nouveau—Jugendstil* (Teufen, Switzerland: Arthur Niggli, 1962), 279; and *Exhibition of Victorian and Edwardian Decorative Arts* (London: Victoria and Albert Museum, 1952).

121. "Modern Art and Art Nouveau: The Spook School," *Times* (London), November 19, 1952, 2.

122. See *München 1869–1958: Aufbruch zur modernen Kunst: Rekonstruktion der ersten Internationalen Kunstausstellung 1869* (Munich: Haus der Kunst, 1958); Peter Selz and Mildred Constantine, eds., *Art Nouveau: Art and Design at the Turn of the Century* (New York: Doubleday, 1960); and Jean Cassou and Albert Châtelet, eds., *Les sources du XXe siècle: Les arts en Europe de 1884 à 1914* (Paris: Musée national d'art moderne, 1960).

123. Peter Selz, introduction to Selz and Constantine, *Art Nouveau,* 7–17, here 6.

124. Selz, 17.

125. See K. A. Citroen, ed., *Jugendstil: Sammlung K. A. Citroen, Amsterdam; Ausstellung im Hessischen Landesmuseum, Darmstadt, 31. August bis 28. Oktober 1962* (Darmstadt, Germany: Hessisches Landesmuseum, 1962); Schmutzler, *Art Nouveau;* Mario Amaya, *Art Nouveau* (London: Studio Vista, 1966); and Martin Battersby, *The World of Art Nouveau* (London: Arlington Books, 1968).

126. "New Look at Art Nouveau," *Time,* August 21, 1964, 38.

127. Brian Edmund Reade, *Art Nouveau and Alphonse Mucha* (London: Victoria and Albert Museum, 1963); V&A Archive, MA/28/125 and MA/29/43.

128. Reyner Banham, "First Master of the Mass Media?," *Listener,* June 27, 1963, 1080–1081, here 1080.

129. Brian Edmund Reade, *Aubrey Beardsley* (London: Victoria and Albert Museum, 1966); V&A Archive, MA/28/148/1 and 2.

130. Lawrence Gowing, "Switched On by Beardsley," *Observer,* December 24, 1967, 19; David Piper, "Most Cool Cat," *Guardian,* October 20, 1967, 7; "Beardsley Drawings Seized," *Guardian,* August 10, 1966, 1.

131. George Melly, "Poster Power," *Observer,* December 3, 1967, 13–17, here 13.

132. Quoted in Dominic Lutyens and Kirsty Hislop, *70s Style and Design* (London: Thames and Hudson, 2009), 70. See also Guffey, *Retro,* 11–12.

133. See Lucy Fischer, *Cinema by Design: Art Nouveau, Modernism, and Film History* (New York: Columbia University Press, 2017), 211–216.

134. See Le Zotte, *From Goodwill to Grunge,* 140–148.

135. See Valerie Steele, *Fifty Years of Fashion: New Look to Now* (New Haven, CT: Yale University Press, 1997), 56.

136. Jennie Dingemans, "Gown Perfect for Ball—or Bed," *Daily Express,* June 20, 1966, 7. See also Barbara Hulanicki and Martin Pel, *The Biba Years, 1963–1975* (London: V&A, 2014), 94.

137. Quoted in Hulanicki and Pel, *Biba Years,* 44.

138. See Alwyn W. Turner, *The Biba Experience* (Woodbridge, UK: Antique Collectors' Club, 2004), 20–22; and Hulanicki and Martin, *Biba Years,* 75.

139. "My Kind of Book," *Petticoat,* July 30, 1966, 9.

140. Quoted in Turner, *Biba Experience,* 22.

141. Quoted in Le Zotte, *From Goodwill to Grunge,* 143.

142. Piri Halasz, "You Can Walk across It on the Grass," *Time,* April 15, 1966, 30–34. On this and Swinging Sixties London generally, see Felix Fuhg, *London's Working-Class Youth and the Making of Post-Victorian Britain, 1958–1971* (Basingstoke, UK: Palgrave Macmillan, 2021), 3, 126–130.

143. See Le Zotte, *From Goodwill to Grunge,* 148–152.

144. Hermand, "Vorwort," xii, x.

145. "New Look at Art Nouveau," 38.

146. See "New Look at Art Nouveau"; and Dieter Baacke, "Jugendstil um 1900 und Hippiebewegung: Zwischen historischer Bewegung und bleibenden Strukturen," in *Jugend 1900–1970: Zwischen Selbstverfügung und Deutung,* ed. Dieter Baacke (Opladen, Germany: Leske + Budrich, 1991), 106–124.

147. Guffey, *Retro,* 63.

148. Bevis Hillier, *Art Deco of the 20s and 30s* (London: Studio Vista, 1968), 158. See also Hillier, *Style of the Century,* 210.

149. See Guffey, *Retro,* 67; and Paul Maenz, *Art Deco: Formen zwischen zwei Kriegen* (Cologne: Dumont Schauberg, 1974), 1.

150. *Les Années 25: Art Déco / Bauhaus / Stijl: Esprit Nouveau* (Paris: Musée des arts décoratifs, 1966), 14.

151. See Bevis Hillier, *The World of Art Deco: An Exhibition Organized by the Minneapolis Institute of Arts, July–September 1971* (London: Studio Vista, 1971); Judith Applegate, *Art Deco* (New York: Finch College Museum of Art, 1971); Erika Billeter, *Die zwanziger Jahre: Kontraste eines Jahrzehnts* (Bern: Benteli Verlag, 1973); *Art Deco 1925: Exhibition Catalogue, 30 September to 31 October 1975* (Brussels: Société Generale de Banque, 1975); Yvonne Brunhammer, *The Nineteen Twenties Style* (London: Paul Hamlyn, 1969); Martin Battersby, *The Decorative Twenties* (London: Studio Vista, 1969); and Giulia Veronesi, *Into the Twenties: Style and Design, 1909–1929* (London: Thames and Hudson, 1968).

152. Roy Strong, introduction to *The Collector's Encyclopedia: Victoriana to Art Deco,* ed. Ian Cameron (London: Collins, 1974), 7–8, here 8.

153. Deborah Stratton, "Art Deco? It's All Cubes of Course or Is It Triangles?," *Art and Antiques Weekly,* November 21, 1970, 22.

154. Hillier, *World of Art Deco,* 48.

155. See David Bourdon, "Stacking the Deco," *New York Magazine,* November 11, 1974, 64–66.

156. Quoted in Lawrence Alloway, "Roy Lichtenstein's Period Style: From the 'Thirties to the 'Sixties and Back," *Arts Magazine* 42, no. 1 (1967): 24–29, here 25.

157. Alloway, 25. See also Nicolas Calas, "Insight through Irony," *Arts Magazine* 44, no. 1 (1969): 29–33; and Hillier, *World of Art Deco,* 48.

158. Katherine Morrison McClinton, *Art Deco: A Guide for Collectors* (New York: C. N. Potter, 1972), 3.

159. Pierre, *Looking Good,* 167.

160. On Big Biba, see V&A Archive of Art and Design AAD/1996/6/5/145, AAD/2014/1/1/ 1–11; Kennedy Fraser, "Feminine Fashions," *New Yorker,* February 18, 1974, 92–97; Barbara Hulanicki, *From A to Biba* (London: Hutchinson, 1983); Turner, *Biba*

Experience; Steven Thomas and Alwyn W. Turner, *Welcome to Big Biba* (Woodbridge, UK: Antique Collectors' Club, 2006); and Lutyens and Hislop, *70s Style and Design,* 70–74.

161. Quoted in Thomas and Turner, *Welcome to Big Biba,* 72.

162. Quoted in Thomas and Turner, 72.

163. Helmuth Plessner, "Die Legende von den zwanziger Jahren," *Merkur* 16, no. 167 (1962): 33–46; Theodor W. Adorno, "Jene zwanziger Jahre," *Merkur* 16, no. 167 (1962): 46–51.

164. Bosley Crowther, "Run, Bonnie and Clyde," *New York Times,* September 3, 1967; "Screen: 'Bonnie and Clyde' Arrives," *New York Times,* April 14, 1967, 36.

165. See Robert Brent Toplin, *History by Hollywood: The Use and Abuse of the American Past* (Urbana: University of Illinois Press, 1996), 127–153.

166. Charles Marowitz, "Bonnie & Clyde Symptom and Cause," *Village Voice,* December 21, 1967, 98.

167. Pauline Kael, "Bonnie and Clyde," *New Yorker,* October 21, 1967, 147–171, here 158.

168. Paul Monaco, *Ribbons in Time: Movies and Society since 1945* (Bloomington: Indiana University Press, 1987), 102, 101.

169. David Newman and Robert Benton, "Lightning in a Bottle," in *The Bonnie and Clyde Book,* ed. Sandra Wake and Nicola Hayden (London: Lorrimer, 1972), 13–31, here 19.

170. Peter Biskind, *Easy Riders, Raging Bulls: How the Sex-Drugs-and-Rock 'n' Roll Generation Saved Hollywood* (London: Bloomsbury, 1998), 49; Toplin, *History by Hollywood,* 127–153.

171. On these films, see Peter Lev, *American Films of the '70s: Conflicting Visions* (Austin: University of Texas Press, 2000); and Monaco, *Ribbons in Time,* 93–125.

172. Monaco, *Ribbons in Time,* 102.

173. Lutyens and Hislop, *70s Style and Design,* 73.

174. Ula Lukszo, "Noir Fashion and Noir *as* Fashion," in *Fashion in Film,* ed. Adrienne Munich (Bloomington: Indiana University Press, 2011), 54–81, here 68.

175. Lev, *American Films of the '70s,* xxi.

176. See Hillier, *Art Deco,* 165.

177. Prudence Blac and Karen de Perthuis, "Postwar Hollywood, 1947–1967," in *Costume, Makeup, and Hair,* ed. Adrienne L. McLean (New Brunswick, NJ: Rutgers University Press, 2016), 75–98, here 95.

178. "Bonnie Comes on with a Stylish Band: Faye Dunaway in a '30s Revival," *Life,* January 12, 1968, 69–73.

179. See Donald Scoggins and Jay Jorgensen, *Creating the Illusion: A Fashionable History of Hollywood Costume Designers* (Philadelphia: Running Press, 2015), 303.

180. Angela Carter, "Notes for a Theory of Sixties Style," *New Society,* December 14, 1967, 866–867.

181. Quoted in Timothy Scott, *West Germany and the Global Sixties: The Antiauthoritarian Revolt, 1962–1978* (Cambridge: Cambridge University Press, 2013), 292.

182. See Hulanicki and Pel, *Biba Years,* 164.

183. Ellen Stock, "The Gatsby Look: Suitable for Spring," *New York Magazine,* March 18, 1974, 58–60.

184. Stock, 60.

185. See Robert Polito, "*Highway 61 Revisited* (1965)," in *The Cambridge Companion to Bob Dylan,* ed. Kevin J. H. Dettmar (Cambridge: Cambridge University Press, 2009), 137–142.

186. See Ron Everyman and Scott Barretta, "From the 30s to the 60s: The Folk Music Revival in the United States," *Theory and Society* 25, no. 4 (1996): 501–543.

187. Derek B. Scott, "The Britpop Sound," in *Britpop and the English Musical Tradition,* ed. Andy Bennett and Jon Stratton (Surrey, UK: Ashgate, 2010), 103–122; Jon Savage, *The Kinks: The Official Biography* (London: Faber and Faber, 1984), 90.

188. Dave Davies, *Kink: An Autobiography* (London: Boxtree, 1996), 107.

189. Quoted in Andy Miller, *The Kinks' "The Kinks Are the Village Green Preservation Society"* (New York: Continuum, 2003), 46.

190. Terry Gilliam and Michael Palin, *Time Bandits: The Movie Script* (New York: Dolphin Books, 1981), 36.

191. David Lowenthal, *The Past Is a Foreign Country* (Cambridge: Cambridge University Press, 1985), 69.

192. Michael J. Gaughan, "Time Bandits," *Film Quarterly* 36, no. 1 (1982): 41–46, here 41.

193. See Andrew Gordon, "Back to the Future: Oedipus as Time Traveller," *Science-Fiction Studies* 14, no. 3 (1987): 372–385, here 372.

194. Robert Palmer, "The Evolution of Rock, a Long and Winding Road," *New York Times,* August 22, 1985, C14.

195. Julie Burchill, "Back to the Future," *New Society,* January 3, 1986, 25.

196. P. J. O'Rourke, "LSD: Let the Sixties Die," *Rolling Stone,* September 24, 1987, 115–116, here 115.

197. Todd Gitlin, "The Uses of Nostalgia," *Tikkun* 2, no. 4 (1987): 13–15, here 13.

198. Peter Collier and David Horowitz, *Destructive Generation: Second Thoughts about the Sixties* (New York: Summit Books, 1989), 217.

199. James Collins, "Time-Warp: Led Zeppelin, Goatees, Harry Connick, Film Noir, Go-Go Boots, Disco, Plaid—Nostalgiamania Takes Us into the Past! Now, How Do We Get Back?," *Spy,* November 1991, 62–67, here 62, 63.

200. Holly Brubach, "Retroactivity," *New Yorker,* December 31, 1990, 74–81, here 75, 76.

201. Brubach, 76. See also "Fashion: On the Street; Gee, Mom, What Were the 60's Like?," *New York Times,* September 9, 1990, 64; and Anne-Marie Schiro, "60's Style: Who's Teeny Now?," *New York Times,* December 5, 1990, C1.

202. O'Rourke, "LSD," 116.

203. Burchill, "Back to the Future," 25.

204. David Farber, introduction to *The Sixties: From Memory to History,* ed. David Farber (Chapel Hill: University of North Carolina Press, 1994), 1–10, here 1.

205. Richard Horn, *Fifties Style: Then and Now* (Bromley: Columbus, 1985), 8.

206. Brenda Polan, "Circling the Square," *Guardian,* February 17, 1983, 11.

207. Victor Bondi, ed., *American Decades, 1980–1989* (Detroit: Gale, 1996), 221, 231.

208. Michiko Kakutani, "What Is Hollywood Saying about the Teen-age World Today," *New York Times,* April 22, 1984, 2/1.

209. See Daniel Marcus, *Happy Days and Wonder Years: The Fifties and the Sixties in Contemporary Cultural Politics* (Piscataway, NJ: Rutgers University Press, 2004), 106–108.

210. See Kristen Hoerl, *The Bad Sixties: Hollywood Memories of the Counterculture, Antiwar, and the Black Power Movement* (Jackson: University Press of Mississippi, 2018), 3–5, 53–54, 61–91.

211. See Vivian Sobchack, *Screening Space: The American Science Fiction Film* (New Brunswick, NJ: Rutgers University Press, 1987), 274; and Dwyer, *Back to the Fifties,* 18–44.

212. Janet Maslin, "In 'Future,' Boy Returns to the Past," *New York Times,* July 3, 1985, C18.

213. Dwyer, *Back to the Fifties,* 26. On Reagan, see Mark Weinberg, *Movie Nights with the Reagans* (New York: Simon and Schuster, 2018), 138–151.

214. Sobchack, *Screening Space,* 274.

215. Tom Shales, "The Re Decade," *Esquire,* March 1986, 67–69, here 67.

216. Jameson, *Postmodernism,* 19.

217. Tana Wollen, "Over Our Shoulders: Nostalgic Screen Fictions for the 1980s," in *Enterprise and Heritage: Crosscurrents of National Culture,* ed. John Corner and Sylvia Harvey (London: Routledge, 1991), 173–188, here 180.

218. Higson refers to Patrick Wright and Robert Hewison in a footnote: Andrew Higson, "Re-presenting the National Past: Nostalgia and Pastiche in Heritage Film," in *British Cinema and Thatcherism: Fires Were Started,* ed. Lester Friedman (London: University College London Press, 1993), 109–112, here 112. On its origin in the heritage debate, see also Claire Monk, "The British 'Heritage Film' and Its Critics," *Critical Survey* 7, no. 2 (1995): 116–124.

219. David Cannadine, "Brideshead Revered," *London Review of Books,* March 17, 1983, 12–13; David Cannadine, "Brideshead Re-revisited," *New York Review of Books,* December 19, 1985, 17–23; Peter Conrad, "Don't Look Back," *Tatler,* April 1986, 98–105, 148–150; Lowenthal, *Past Is a Foreign Country,* 6, 307n148; Robert Hewison, *The Heritage Industry: Britain in a Climate of Decline* (London: Methuen, 1987), 53; Samuel, *Theatres of Memory,* 58, 89, 233, 260, 281; Dominic Sandbrook, *Who Dares Wins: Britain, 1979–1982* (London: Penguin, 2019), 615–618.

220. John Heilpern, "English Nostalgia Conquers America," *Times* (London), January 1, 1982, 13.

221. Quoted in Michiko Kakutani, "Waugh's Brideshead Coming to TV," *New York Times,* January 14, 1982, C17.

222. Tom Shales, "Waugh-Be-Gone Evening," *Washington Post,* March 29, 1982.

223. See Weinberg, *Movie Nights with the Reagans,* 55–68.

224. James Chapman, *Past and Present: National Identity and the British Historical Film* (London: I. B. Tauris, 2005), 13–14; Sandbrook, *Who Dares Wins,* 621–625.

225. Wollen, "Over Our Shoulders," 178; Cairns Craig, "Rooms without a View," *Sight and Sound,* June 1991, 10–13, here 10; Higson, "Re-presenting the National Past," 109.

226. Alison Light, "Englishness," *Sight and Sound,* July 1991, 63.

227. See John Hill, *British Cinema in the 1980s: Issues and Themes* (Oxford: Clarendon, 1999), 84–96.

228. See Robert Emmet Long, *The Films of Merchant Ivory* (New York: Harry N. Abrams, 1997).

229. See Claire Monk, *Heritage Film Audiences: Period Films and Contemporary Audiences in the UK* (Edinburgh: Edinburgh University Press, 2012).

230. See Phil Powrie, *French Cinema in the 1980s: Nostalgia and the Crisis of Masculinity* (Oxford: Clarendon, 1997); and Danya Oscherwitz, *Past Forward: French Cinema and the Post-colonial Heritage* (Carbondale: Southern Illinois University Press, 2010), 1–2.

231. Oscherwitz, *Past Forward,* 2–3, 33–63.

232. See Lutz Koepnick, "'Amerika gibt's überhaupt nicht': Notes on the German Heritage Film," in *German Pop Culture: How "American" Is It?,* ed. Agnes Mueller (Ann Arbor: University of Michigan Press, 2004), 47–82.

233. See Paul Cooke and Rob Stone, eds., *Screening European Heritage: Creating and Consuming History on Film* (Basingstoke, UK: Palgrave Macmillan, 2016).

234. Higson, "Re-presenting the National Past"; Wollen, "Over Our Shoulders"; Monk, "British 'Heritage Film.'"

235. Dwight Macdonald, "Masscult and Midcult," in *Masscult and Midcult: Essays against the American Grain,* ed. John Summers, introduction by Louis Menand (New York: New York Review Books, 2011), 3–71, here 35.

236. Sandbrook, *Who Dares Wins*, 617.

237. Ann Boyd, "The Wilder Shores of Fashion," *Observer*, January 25, 1981, 35.

238. Jane Mulvagh, *Vogue History of 20th Century Fashion*, foreword by Valerie D. Mendes (London: Viking, 1988), 342.

239. Mulvagh, *Vivienne Westwood*, 144.

240. Quoted in Laird Borrelli-Persson, "Why the Swagger of Vivienne Westwood's 1981 Pirate Collection Resonates 40 Years On," *Vogue*, May 17, 2021.

241. See Westwood and Kelly, *Vivienne Westwood*; and Mulvagh, *Vivienne Westwood*.

242. See Mulvagh, *Vivienne Westwood*; and Jon Savage, "Viv Westwood: After Let It Rock, Sex and Seditionaries, Her New Collection Is World's End," *Face*, January 1981, 25–27.

243. See Dave Rimmer, *New Romantics: The Look* (London: Omnibus, 2003).

244. Suzy Menkes, "Post Punk," *Times* (London), February 24, 1982, 11.

245. Quoted in Alistair O'Neill, "Fashion in the 1980s: A Time of Revival," in *The Fashion History Reader: Global Perspectives*, ed. Giorgio Riello and Peter McNeil (London: Routledge, 2011), 525–527, here 525.

246. Rimmer, *New Romantics*, 10.

247. Caroline Rennolds, *New York Fashion: The Evolution of American Style* (New York: Abrams, 1989), 264.

248. Bondi, *American Decades*, vii.

249. Caroline Evans and Minna Thornton, *Women and Fashion: A New Look* (London: Quartet Books, 1989), 59.

250. McRobbie, "Second-Hand Dresses," 23–24.

251. McRobbie, 41–42.

252. Jon Savage, "The Age of Plunder," *Face*, January 1983, 45–49, here 45, 49.

253. Elizabeth Wilson, *Adorned in Dreams: Fashion and Modernity* (London: I. B. Tauris, 2003), 172.

254. Suzy Menkes, "The Shock of the Old," *New York Times*, March 21, 1993, 9/8.

255. Tony Hendra, "The 1970s: A Dynamite Spy Boogie-Down Celebration of the Decade of the Twentieth Century," *Spy*, December 1988, 70–74, here 72.

256. Nick Ravo, "The 70's (Stayin' Alive) Won't Die (Stayin' Alive)," *New York Times*, November 13, 1991, C1.

257. See David Sillitoe, "Flashback to the Future," *Guardian*, October 10, 1992, 29; McConnell, ed., *American Decades, 1990–1998*, 205–208; and Nicky Gregson, Kate Brooks, and Louise Crewe, "Bjorn Again? Rethinking 70s Revivalism through the Reappropriation of 70s Clothing," *Fashion Theory* 5, no. (2001): 3–27.

258. Michael Bracewell, *The Nineties: When Surface Was Depth* (London: Flamingo, 2003), 203.

259. Chuck Klosterman, *The Nineties* (New York: Penguin, 2022), 23, 3; see also 103–106.

260. See Liz Smith, "Swinging into the Future," *Times* (London), March 21, 1989, 14; "Fashion: On the Street," 64; and Schiro, "60's Style," C1; Brubach, "Retroactivity."

261. Harriet Quick, "In a Mod Mood," *Guardian*, September 6, 1995, A10.

262. David Kamp, "London Swings! Again!," *Vanity Fair,* March 1997. See on this Daniel Rachel, *Don't Look Back in Anger: The Rise and Fall of Cool Britannia, Told by Those Who Were There* (London: Trapeze, 2019), 237–261.

263. Simon Reynolds, "Reasons to Be Cheerful: The Case against Britpop," *Frieze,* September 11, 1995, https://www.frieze.com/article/reasons-be-cheerful-0.

264. Scott, "Britpop Sound," 111.

265. See Rachel, *Don't Look Back in Anger.*

266. John Storey, "The Sixties in the Nineties: Pastiche of Hyperconsciousness?," in *Culture and Power in Cultural Studies: The Politics of Signification* (Edinburgh: Edinburgh University Press, 2010), 58–70; M. Keith Booker, *Postmodern Hollywood: What's New in Film and Why It Makes Us Feel So Strange* (Westport, CT: Praeger, 2007), 71.

267. Bracewell, *Nineties,* 19, 14.

268. Roger Tredre, "Gurus Say Retro Here to Stay," *Observer,* January 22, 1995, 10.

269. See Susannah Frankel, "Remembrance of Padded: Still Trying to Forget the Eighties? Don't Bother. They're Back," *Guardian,* March 12, 1997, A10; Caroline Sullivan, "Eighty Reasons to Forget the Eighties," *Guardian,* December 4, 1998, A16; and Sam Taylor, "Deadly Synths: The Eighties Revival Starts Here," *Observer,* December 13, 1998, C9.

270. Michiko Kakutani, "Get Out Your Shoulder Pads: The 80's Are Here," *New York Times,* April 25, 2001, E1.

271. Simon Reynolds, "The 70's Are So 90's. The 80's Are the Thing Now," *New York Times,* May 5, 2002, 2/1.

272. Jeff Leeds, "We Hate the '80s," *New York Times,* February 13, 2005.

273. Lisa Armstrong, "Back to the Nineties," *Times* (London), May 13, 2006, 61.

274. Lisa Armstrong, "Eighties Revival," *Times* (London), July 15, 2006, 50–51.

275. Lauren Cochrane, "The 90s Are Back: How to Get the Look Right," *Guardian,* March 11, 2016.

276. Matthew Schneier, "Don't You Forget about Me! The Formerly Irredeemable '80s Return," *New York Times,* April 20, 2016, D1; Alexander Fury, "The Return of the '90s," *New York Times,* July 13, 2016, M217.

277. Hadley Freeman, "From Black Mirror to Stranger Things, Why Do We Keep Going Back to the 80s?," *Guardian,* February 18, 2017.

278. Vanessa Friedman, "Help! The '80s Are Back," *New York Times,* March 15, 2018.

279. Josh Duboff, "Why Is Pop Music Suddenly Obsessed with the Late 90s?," *Vanity Fair,* November 15, 2018.

280. Rob Sheffield, "Things That Make You Go Hmmm: Why 2018 Was a Year of Nineties Obsessions," *Rolling Stone,* December 14, 2018.

281. Rhiannon Picton-James, "Is Vintage Clothing Over?," *New York Times,* December 26, 2018.

282. Vanessa Friedman, "Should We Really Embrace '90s Fashion?," *New York Times,* May 15, 2021.

283. Susan Sontag, "Notes on 'Camp,'" in *Against Interpretation and Other Essays* (New York: Dell, 1969), 277–293, here 280–281.

284. Theodor W. Adorno, "Kitsch," in *Essays on Music,* ed. Richard Leppert, new translations by Susan H. Gillespie (Berkeley: University of California Press, 2002), 501–505, here 501.

285. Lowenthal, *Past Is a Foreign Country,* 13.

286. Charles S. Maier, "The End of Longing? Notes toward a History of Postwar German National Longing," in *The Postwar Transformation of Germany,* ed. John S. Brady, Beverly Crawford, and Sarah Elise Williarty (Ann Arbor: University of Michigan Press, 1999), 271–285, here 273.

287. Frank Heath, "Nostalgia Shock," *Saturday Review,* May 29, 1971, 18.

288. Strong, introduction to *The Collector's Encyclopedia,* 7.

289. Jamie Wolf, "Retro Babble," *New West,* January 14, 1980, 41–45, here 42; similarly Pierre, *Looking Good,* 184.

290. Picton-James, "Is 'Vintage' Clothing Over?"

291. Reynolds, "70's Are So 90's." See also Armstrong, "Back to the Nineties."

292. Kennedy Fraser, *The Fashionable Mind: Reflections on Fashion, 1970–1981* (New York: Knopf, 1981), 241.

293. Shales, "Re Decade," 67.

294. Collins, "Time-Warp," 65.

295. Bracewell, *Nineties,* 204.

296. Reynolds, *Retromania,* x.

297. Reynolds, ix–xxiii.

298. Fisher, *Ghosts of My Life,* 9; Hatherley, *The Ministry of Nostalgia.*

299. Angela McRobbie, *Postmodernism and Popular Culture* (London: Routledge, 1995), 3.

300. Jonathan Lethem, "The Ecstasy of Influence," in *The Ecstasy of Influence: Nonfictions, Etc.* (New York: Doubleday, 2011), 93–120, here 97.

301. Jonathan Lethem, "The Afterlife of Ecstasy," in *Ecstasy of Influence,* 121–124, here 122.

302. Gilles Deleuze and Félix Guattari, *A Thousand Plateaus: Capitalism and Schizo-phrenia,* translation and foreword by Brian Massumi (Minneapolis: University of Minnesota Press, 2005).

303. Ted Polhemus's map of subcultures, which also includes revivals, is an example of what that could look like: see Ted Polhemus, *Streetstyle: From Sidewalk to Catwalk* (London: PYMCA, 2010).

4. Reliving

1. C. Vann Woodward, "The Future of the Past," *American Historical Review* 75, no. 3 (1970): 711–726, here 725.

2. Reinhart Koselleck, "Wozu noch Historie? Vortrag auf dem Deutschen Historikertag in Köln am 4. April 1970," *Historische Zeitschrift* 212 (1971): 1–18, here 1.

3. See Hermann Lübbe, *Geschichtsbegriff und Geschichtsinteresse: Analytik und Pragmatik der Historie* (Basel: Schwabe, 1977), 321; and Hermann Lübbe, *Zwischen Trend und Tradition: Überfordert uns die Gegenwart?* (Zurich: Edition Interfrom, 1981), 8.

4. David Lowenthal, *The Past Is a Foreign Country* (Cambridge: Cambridge University Press, 1985), xv.

5. Robert Hewison, *The Heritage Industry: Britain in a Climate of Decline* (London: Methuen, 1987), 83; David Lowenthal, *The Heritage Crusade and the Spoils of History* (Cambridge: Cambridge University Press, 1989), 11.

6. See Michael Kammen, *Mystic Chords of Memory: The Transformation of Tradition in American Culture* (New York: Alfred A. Knopf, 1991), 531–703.

7. Daniel T. Rodgers, *Age of Fracture* (Cambridge, MA: Belknap Press of Harvard University Press, 2011), 221.

8. See Ian Tyrrell, *Historians in Public: The Practice of American History, 1890–1970* (Chicago: University of Chicago Press, 2005), 153–154; M. J. Rymsza-Pawlowska, *History Comes Alive: Public History and Popular Culture in the 1970s* (Chapel Hill: University of North Carolina Press, 2017); and Peter Mandler, *History and National Life* (London: Profile Books, 2002), 100–102.

9. On the turn to a more reenactive and affective approach to the past since the 1970s, see Rymsza-Pawlowska, *History Comes Alive,* 6. See also Vanessa Agnew, "History's Affective Turn: Historical Reenactment and Its Work in the Present," *Rethinking History* 11, no. 3 (2007): 299–312.

10. See Gavin Stamp, "The Art of Keeping One Jump Ahead: Conservation Societies in the Twentieth Century," in *Preserving the Past: The Rise of Heritage in Modern Britain,* ed. Michael Hunter (Stroud, UK: Alan Sutton, 1996), 77–98; and Miles Glendinning, *The Conservation Movement: A History of Architectural Preservation, Antiquity to Modernity* (London: Routledge, 2013), 317.

11. See Eric J. Plosky, "The Fall and Rise of Pennsylvania Station: Changing Attitudes toward Historic Preservation in New York City" (MA thesis, Massachusetts Institute of Technology, 1999); and Anthony C. Wood, *Preserving New York: Winning the Right to Protect a City's Landmarks* (New York: Routledge, 2008).

12. See Elain Harwood and Alan Powers, eds., *The Heroic Period of Conservation* (London: Twentieth Century Society, 2004); and William J. Murtagh, "Jesus Never Sleeps," in *Past Meets Future: Saving America's Historic Environments,* ed. Antoinette J. Lee (Washington, DC: National Trust for Historic Preservation, 1992), 51–58. See also David Pearce, *Conservation Today* (London: Routledge, 1989), 2–4; and John Pendlebury, *Conservation in the Age of Consensus* (Abingdon, UK: Routledge, 2009), 63. For Germany, see Rudy Koshar, *Germany's Transient Pasts: Preservation and National Memory in the Twentieth Century* (Chapel Hill: University of North Carolina Press, 1998).

13. Douglas Johnson, "Not What It Used to Be," *Vole* 5 (1978): 42–43, here 42.

14. Quoted in Mark Clapson and Peter J. Larkham, *The Blitz and Its Legacy: Wartime Destruction to Post-war Reconstruction* (Farnham, UK: Ashgate, 2013), 78.

15. Christopher Klemek, *The Transatlantic Collapse of Urban Renewal: Postwar Urbanism from New York to Berlin* (Chicago: University of Chicago Press, 2011), 13.

16. Nikolaus Pevsner, *Studies in Art, Architecture and Design,* vol. 2, *Victorian and After* (London: Thames and Hudson, 1968), 243.

17. See Melissa S. Ragain, *Domesticating the Invisible: Form and Environmental Anxiety in Postwar America* (Oakland: University of California Press, 2021), 66.

18. Quoted in Jane Fawcett, ed., *The Future of the Past: Attitudes to Conservation, 1174–1974* (London: Thames and Hudson, 1976), 64.

19. See Dominic Sandbrook, *Never Had It So Good: A History of Britain from Suez to the Beatles* (London: Abacus, 2005), 122.

20. See John Betjeman, "Dictating to Railways," *Architectural Review* 74 (1933): 83–84, here 84.

21. John Betjeman, "Heritage of the Rail Age," *Daily Telegraph,* February 8, 1960, reprinted as "The Demolition of Euston Arch," in *Coming Home: An Anthology of His Prose, 1920–1977,* selected and introduced by Candida Lycett Green (London: Methuen, 1997), 412–415, here 412.

22. Derek Stanford, *John Betjeman* (London: Neville Spearman, 1961), 35, see also 53; "Major Minor Poet," *Time,* February 2, 1959, 70–71; Alastair Buchan, "A Nostalgia for Steam Engines," *Reporter,* April 30, 1959, 39.

23. See "Societies' Concern for Monuments," *Times* (London), November 7, 1961, 5. On the Victorian Society, see Glendinning, *Conservation Movement,* 122–128, 234, 315–317; Paul Thompson, "The Victorian Society," *Victorian Studies* 7, no. 4 (1964): 387–392; and London Metropolitan Archives, LMA 4460 (Victorian

Society), B09/072 (Victorian Society AGM minutes and papers), B10/173 (Victorian Society Main committee minutes).

24. "The Battle of Euston Arch," *Daily Mail,* October 17, 1961.

25. "Euston Portico Fate Inevitable Says Mr. Macmillan," *Times* (London), November 4, 1961, 5; "The Euston Murder," *Architectural Review,* April 1962, 235–238.

26. See Simon Bradley, *St Pancras Station* (London: Profile, 2007), 157–160. On the development of listing, see Simon Thurley, *Men from the Ministry: How Britain Saved Its Heritage* (New Haven, CT: Yale University Press, 2013).

27. Rowan Moore, "St Pancras Renaissance Hotel: The Rebirth of a Gothic Masterpiece," *Guardian,* February 13, 2011.

28. "'62 Start Is Set for New Garden: Penn Station to Be Razed to Street Level in Project," *New York Times,* July 27, 1961, 15. On this and the following, see also Plosky, "Fall and Rise."

29. See Gregory F. Gilmartin, *Shaping the City: New York and the Municipal Art Society* (New York: Clarkson Potter, 1994), 370–371; and Plosky, "Fall and Rise," 35–36. On the National Trust, see Elizabeth D. Mulloy, *The History of the National Trust for Historic Preservation, 1963–1973* (Washington, DC: Preservation Press, 1976); Lee, *Past Meets Future;* and William J. Murtagh, *Keeping Time: The History and Theory of Preservation in America,* rev. ed. (New York: John Wiley and Sons, 1997). On the British National Trust as a model, see "Minutes of Informal Conference Preliminary to Organisation of a National Council on Historic Sites and Buildings," February 5, 1947, 130-82-1-2, Box 1, National Trust for Historic Preservation: Correspondence and Administrative Records relating to Annual Meetings, 1952–1981, National Archives, College Park, MD.

30. See "Penn Station Ruin Protested," *Progressive Architecture,* September 1962, 63; Foster Hailey, "Battle over Future of Penn Station Continues," *New York Times,* September 23, 1962, 78; and Martin Tolchin, "Demolition Starts at Penn Station, Architects Picket," *New York Times,* October 29, 1963, 1, 24. On AGBANY, see also Gilmartin, *Shaping the City,* 370–371; and Plosky, "Fall and Rise," 42–45.

31. "AGBANY vs. Apathy at Penn Station," *Architectural Forum,* September 1962, 5.

32. Ada Louise Huxtable, "Despair of Demolition," *New York Times,* September 17, 1964, 8.

33. See Joseph B. Rose, "Landmarks Preservation in New York," *Public Interest* 74 (1984): 132–145.

34. Rose.

35. Rose. See also Murtagh, "Jesus Never Sleeps."

36. See Wood, *Preserving New York,* 1–20; and Randall Mason, *The Once and Future New York: Historic Preservation and the Modern City* (Minneapolis: University of Minnesota Press, 2009), ix.

37. See Mulloy, *National Trust for Historic Preservation,* 259–263; and James A. Glass, *The Beginning of a New National Historic Preservation Program, 1957 to 1969,* foreword by Charles B. Hosmer Jr. (Washington, DC: National Conference of State Historic Preservation Officers, 1990), 17–22.

38. See John Delafons, *Politics and Preservation: A Policy History of the Built Heritage, 1882–1996* (London: Spon, 1997), 92–94.

39. National Trust for Historic Preservation, ed., *Historic Preservation Today: Essays Presented to the Seminar on Preservation and Restoration, Williamsburg, Virginia, September 8–11, 1963* (Charlottesville: University Press of Virginia, 1966), vi.

40. Margot Gayle, interview by Anthony C. Wood, April 26, 1984, New York Preservation Archive Project, https://www.nypap.org/oral-history/margot-gayle/. See also Mary Anne Ostrom, "A Champion of Cast Iron," *Historic Preservation* 40, no. 4 (1988): 18–22; and Gilmartin, *Shaping the City,* 393–394.

41. United States Conference of Mayors, ed., *With Heritage So Rich: A Report of a Special Committee on Historic Preservation under the Auspices of the United States Conference of Mayors* (New York: Random House, 1966), 207.

42. "Local Amenity Societies," *Civic Trust News,* July/August 1977, 7–10, here 7. On the Civic Trust, see Pearce, *Conservation Today,* 4; Harwood and Powers, *Heroic Period of Conservation,* 9; Pendlebury, *Conservation,* 68; and National Archives AN 111/1075 (Civic Trust), EW 11/9 (Civic Trust), HLG 71/2468 (Civic Trust), Work 14/2252 (Ministry of Works representation on the Civic Trust).

43. See Rodney Harrison, *Heritage: Critical Approaches* (Abingdon, UK: Routledge, 2013), 70.

44. Delafons, *Politics and Preservation,* 1.

45. Karl Korn, "Nur Denkmalschutz?," *Frankfurter Allgemeine Zeitung,* June 7, 1978, 1.

46. John Morris Dixon, "Ring in the Old," *Progressive Architecture,* November 1976, 7; John Morton, "Introduction: Looking for the Past," *Progressive Architecture,* November 1976, 45.

47. Clem Labine, "Preservationists Are Un-American!," *Historic Preservation* 31, no. 1 (1979): 18–20.

48. On the EAHY, see the contributions to Michael Falser and Winfried Lipp, eds., *A Future for Our Past: The 40th Anniversary of European Architectural Heritage Year (1975–2015)* (Berlin: Hendrik Bäßler Verlag, 2015); Delafons, *Politics and Preservation,* 107–112; and Glendinning, *Conservation Movement,* 329–331, 402–408.

49. See Hewison, *Heritage Industry,* 31.

50. Ian Nairn, "Outrage," *Architectural Review* 117 (1955): 361–460, here 365.

51. Jane Jacobs, *The Death and Life of Great American Cities* (New York: Vintage, 1961), 3, 7.

52. Jacobs, 114; see also 267, 374. See, for instance, Lloyd Rodwin, "Neighbors Are Needed," *New York Times,* November 5, 1961, 10.

53. See Dominic Sandbrook, *White Heat: A History of Britain in the Swinging Sixties* (London: Abacus: 2006), 620–622.

54. Morton, "Introduction," 45.

55. "Architekten: Kistenmacher im Büßerhemd," *Der Spiegel,* September 19, 1977, 206–223, here 206. See also "Eine Zukunft für die Vergangenheit: SPIEGEL-Report über die Sanierung deutscher Altstädte," *Der Spiegel,* June 17, 1974, 44–55.

56. Nathan Silver, *Lost New York* (Boston: Houghton Mifflin, 1967); Hermione Hobhouse, *Lost London: A Century of Demolition and Decay* (London: Macmillan, 1971).

57. Wolf Jobst Siedler with photographs by Elisabeth Niggemeyer, *Die gemordete Stadt: Abgesang auf Putte und Straße, Platz und Baum* (1961; Berlin: Siedler, 1993); Colin Amery and Dan Cruickshank, *The Rape of Britain* (London: Elek, 1975); Louis Chevalier, *L'assassinat de Paris* (Paris: Calmann-Lévy, 1977).

58. Raymond Mortimer, "The Decline of Architecture," *Sunday Times* (London), July 16, 1972, 31.

59. James Richard, "All Change of King's Cross and St. Pancras?," *Times* (London), September 3, 1966, 9.

60. Reinhard Bentmann, "Der Kampf um die Erinnerung: Ideologische und methodische Konzepte des modernen Denkmalkultes," in *Denkmalräume—Lebensräume,* ed. Ina-Maria Greverus (Giessen: Schmitz, 1976), 213–246, here 213. On Bentmann, see also Koshar, *Germany's Transient Pasts,* 289.

61. Bentmann, "Der Kampf um die Erinnerung," 217.

62. Bentmann, 218, 219.

63. See Dieter Baacke, "Nostalgie: Zu einem Phänomen ohne Theorie," in *Meyers Enzyklopädisches Lexikon* (Mannheim: Lexikonverlag, 1976), 17:449–452, here 451; and Lübbe, *Geschichtsbegriff und Geschichtsinteresse,* 306; see also 316, 318, 323, 330–331.

64. Johnson, "Not What It Used," 42.

65. David Cannadine, "Brideshead Re-revisited," *New York Review of Books,* December 19, 1985, 17–20, here 17.

66. David Lowenthal, *The Past Is a Foreign Country* (Cambridge: Cambridge University Press, 1985), xvii, 387; see also xv–xvii, 384–406.

67. Hewison, *Heritage Industry,* 28; see also 98.

68. Raphael Samuel, *Theatres of Memory: Past and Present in Contemporary Culture* (London: Verso, 1994), 139, xlix.

69. Silver, *Lost New York,* xiii.

70. Duncan Sandys, "European Architectural Heritage Year," *European Yearbook* 23 (1975): 124–137, here 125. On Sandys, see Delafons, *Politics and Preservation*, 85–96.

71. See, for instance, Clara Menck, "Beginnt eine neue Epoche der Denkmalpflege," *Frankfurter Allgemeine Zeitung*, August 7, 1974, 19; Helene Rahms, "Die Hochhäuser möchten sie am liebsten abreißen," *Frankfurter Allgemeine Zeitung*, January 23, 1975, 19; and Karl Korn, "Nur Denkmalschutz?," *Frankfurter Allgemeine Zeitung*, June 7, 1978, 1. On the EAHY in Germany, see Koshar, *Germany's Transient Pasts*, 323–327.

72. See the contributions in Falser and Lipp, *Future for Our Past.*

73. Hobhouse, *Lost London*, 1.

74. Clem Labine, "Preservationists Are Un-American!," *Historic Preservation* 31, no. 1 (1979): 18–20, here 20.

75. John Betjeman, *First and Last Loves* (London: John Murray, 1952), 132; Betjeman, "Demolition of Euston Arch," 413.

76. John Betjeman, *Antiquarian Prejudice* (London: Hogarth, 1939).

77. John Gardiner, *The Victorians: An Age in Retrospect* (London: Hambledon and London, 2002), 93.

78. Pevsner, *Studies in Art*, 243.

79. Nikolaus Pevsner, *Pioneers of the Modern Movement from William Morris to Walter Gropius* (London: Faber and Faber, 1936).

80. Diana Goldstein, interview by Anthony C. Wood, October 25, 2003, New York Preservation Archive Project, https://www.nypap.org/oral-history/diana-goldstein/.

81. "Reminiscences of Norval White," New York Preservation Archive Project, April 20, 2006, https://www.nypap.org/wp-content/uploads/2016/03/White_Norval _20060420.pdf.

82. Peter Samton, interview by Annette Rosen, 2004, New York Preservation Archive Project, https://www.nypap.org/oral-history/peter-samton-2/.

83. Herbert Oppenheimer, interview by Annette Rosen, 2003, New York Preservation Archive Project, https://www.nypap.org/oral-history/herbert-oppenheimer/.

84. See "AGBANY vs. Apathy at Penn Station," *Architectural Forum*, September 1962, 5; and Wood, *Preserving New York*, 298.

85. For its beginnings in the nineteenth century, see Glendinning, *Conservation Movement*; Murtaugh, *Keeping Time*; and Mason, *Once and Future New York*.

86. Pendlebury, *Conservation*, 21.

87. Its first president was Bevis Hillier, whom we met in Chapter 3: see Alan Powers and Gavin Stamp, "The Twentieth Century Society: A Brief History," in *The Heroic Period of Conservation*, ed. Elain Harwood and Alan Powers (London: Twentieth

Century Society, 2004), 157–160, here 159. On the conservation of modern architecture more generally, see Glendinning, *Conservation Movement,* 358.

88. "Margaret Thatcher Bulldozes Broad Street Station," *Thames News,* July 31, 1985, YouTube video, 1:13, https://www.youtube.com/watch?v=biYzLrmZCqo.

89. "Dulwich Vulgarity," *Spectator,* August 10, 1985, 5.

90. Pearce, *Conservation Today,* 12.

91. Glass, *Beginning,* 60; Murtaugh, *Keeping Time,* 70.

92. See Chris Miele, "The First Conservation Militants: William Morris and the Society for the Protection of Ancient Buildings," in Hunter, *Preserving the Past,* 17–37; Mason, *Once and Future New York,* xiii–xv.

93. George Orwell, *The Road to Wigan Pier* (1937; London: Penguin, 2014).

94. Hewison, *Heritage Industry,* 19. On Wigan and northern England in the 1980s more generally, see Beatrix Campbell, *Wigan Pier Revisited: Poverty and Politics in the Eighties* (London: Virago, 1985).

95. *The Heritage Business,* Up North, BBC2, March 16, 1988; Hewison, *Heritage Industry,* 21–31.

96. See John Urry, *The Tourist Gaze: Leisure and Travel in Contemporary Societies* (London: Sage, 1990), 94–98, 102, 106. See also Samuel, *Theatres of Memory,* 244, 262–264; Adrian Mellor, "Enterprise and Heritage in the Dock," in *Enterprise and Heritage: Crosscurrents of National Culture,* ed. John Corner and Sylvia Harvey (London: Routledge, 1991), 93–115; Margaret Drabble, "The North beyond the Grit," *New York Times,* July 26, 1987, XX 15; Waldemar Januszczak, "Romancing the Grime," *Guardian,* September 2, 1987, 9; Edward Welch, "Heritage Hot Spots Bring Past to Life," *Sunday Times* (London), July 10, 1988, F6–F7; Desmond Balmer, "Wigan's Last Laugh," *Observer,* April 30, 1989, 51; Liz Gill, "Presenting the Past Imperfect," *Times* (London), October 4, 1989, 23; and Mike Gerrard, "Pier into the Past: Nostalgia Is Wigan's Main Industry," *Daily Telegraph,* January 14, 1991.

97. Frank Francis, "Presidential Address," *Museums Journal* 66, no. 2 (1966–1967): 85–91, here 85.

98. Paul Ludwig, "Das Museum heute und morgen," in *Das Museum der Zukunft: 43 Beiträge zur Diskussion über die Zukunft des Museums,* ed. Gerhard Bott (Köln: DuMont Schauberg, 1970), 175–177, here 175.

99. Walter Muir Whitehill, "The Right of Cities to Be Beautiful," in United States Conference of Mayors, *With Heritage So Rich,* 45–55, here 55.

100. Hilton Kramer, "The Crisis of Our Museums: From Dusty Corners to the Discotheque," *New York Times,* December 3, 1967, D37.

101. David White, "Is Britain Becoming One Big Museum?," *New Society,* October 20, 1983, 95.

102. Hewison, *Heritage Industry,* 9. See also Robert Hewison, "Museums Are One of Our Few Growth Industries," *Listener,* June 26, 1986, 11–12, here 12.

103. Hewison, *Heritage Industry,* 9.

104. Samuel, *Theatres of Memory,* 139, 260.

105. Hermann Lübbe, *Der Fortschritt und das Museum: Über den Grund unseres Vergnügens an historischen Gegenständen* (London: Institute of Germanic Studies, University of London, 1982), 1. See also Lübbe, *Zwischen Trend und Tradition,* 7; and Lübbe, *Geschichtsbegriff und Geschichtsinteresse,* 319.

106. Gottfried Korff, "Die Popularisierung des Musealen und die Musealisierung des Popularen," in *Museum als soziales Gedächtnis? Kritische Beiträge zur Museumswissenschaft und Museumspädagogik,* ed. Gottfried Fliedl (Klagenfurt, Austria: Kärntner Druck- und Verlagsgesellschaft, 1988), 9–23, here 9, 19.

107. Henry Miers, *A Report on the Public Museums of the British Isles (Other than the National Museums)* (Edinburgh: Constable, 1928), 14.

108. Hewison, "Museums Are One," 11.

109. David R. Prince and Bernadette Higgins-McLoughlin, *Museums UK: The Findings of the Museums Data-Base Project* (London: Museums Association, 1987), 10, 26, 106, 135.

110. See Prince and Higgins-McLoughlin.

111. See National Endowment for the Arts, *Museums USA: A Survey Report* (Washington, DC: National Endowment for the Arts, 1975), xi, 3.

112. See Lee Kimche, "American Museums: The Vital Statistics," *Museum News* 59, no. 2 (1980): 52–57, here 54.

113. See American Association for State and Local History, *A Culture at Risk: Who Cares for America's Heritage?* (Nashville: American Association for State and Local History, 1984), 27.

114. See *Statistisches Jahrbuch Deutscher Gemeinden* 52 (1964): 259–261; 64 (1977): 287–291; 68 (1981): 188; and 75 (1988): 243; and *Gesellschaftliche Daten: Bundesrepublik Deutschland* 4 (1982): 324.

115. See Kenneth Hudson, *Museums of Influence* (Cambridge: Cambridge University Press, 1987), 120–131; and Sten Rentzhog, *Open Air Museums: The History and Future of a Visionary Idea,* trans. Skans Victoria Airey (Kristianstad, Sweden: Carlssons, 2005).

116. Joachim Eisleb, *Freilichtmuseen und ihre Besucher: Eine sozialgeographische Analyse unter besonderer Berücksichtigung des Museumsdorfs Cloppenburg, Niedersächsisches Freilichtmuseum* (Vechta, Germany: Vechtaer Druckerei, 1987), 23–40.

117. See Peter Davis, *Ecomuseums: A Sense of Place* (London: Continuum, 2011), 100–101. See also Hudson, *Museums of Influence,* 160–166.

118. Frank Atkinson, *The Man Who Made Beamish: An Autobiography* (Gateshead, UK: Northern Books, 1999). See also *The Man Who Made Beamish,* BBC2, December 9,

1986; and Gary S. Cross and John K. Walton, *The Playful Crowd: Pleasure Places in the Twentieth Century* (New York: Columbia University Press, 2005), 205–236.

119. See Martin Roth, *Heimatmuseum: Zur Geschichte einer deutschen Institution* (Berlin: Gebrüder Mann, 1990).

120. Numbers compiled from Hanswilhelm Haefs, *Die deutschen Heimatmuseen: Ein Führer zu mehr als 900 Museen und Sammlungen in der Bundesrepublik Deutschland und West-Berlin* (Frankfurt am Main: Krüger, 1984).

121. See Malcolm MacEwen, "Taking the Profession to the Public to Provoke Them," *RIBA Journal* 80, no. 5 (1973): 220–221. See also Michael Gee, *Heritage Centres Report: A National Survey* (Manchester: Manchester Polytechnic, 1985), 1; and Patricia Mary Sterry, "An Analysis of Heritage Centres with Special Reference to the Role of Design" (PhD diss., Manchester Metropolitan University, 1994), 77–78.

122. See "Britain's First Heritage Centres: Study Centres Come to Town," *Civic Trust News* 47 (1975): 5–6; "First Heritage Centre Opens in Chester," *Civic Trust News* 51 (1975): 3–4; "Making History Come Alive," *Country Life,* November 20, 1975, 1381; Gee, *Heritage Centres Report,* 12–16; Sterry, "Analysis of Heritage Centres," 78–82; and Cheshire Archives and Local Studies, 2115961 (Chester Heritage City Conservation News), 228515 (Cyrill Morris, Leading the Way: Celebrating Chester's Unique Role in European Architectural Year 1975), ZCR 251/2E (Chester Civic Trust 1947–78), and ZDPU/20 (Correspondence European Architectural Heritage Year).

123. See Gee, *Heritage Centres Report,* 16, 6.

124. Wigan Metropolitan Borough, "The Wigan Pier Project," March 1984, Wigan Archives and Local Studies, SR3\36\C SB9. See also Hewison, *Heritage Industry,* 20; and Sterry, "Analysis of Heritage Centres," 153–190.

125. Wigan Metropolitan Borough Council, ed., *Wigan* (Wigan, UK, 1984), 1, 5, 1.

126. Atkinson, *Man Who Made Beamish,* 92.

127. Tony Bennett, "Museums and 'the People,'" in *The Museum Time-Machine: Putting Cultures on Display,* ed. Robert Lumley (London: Routledge, 1988), 63–84, here 73.

128. Bennett, 67.

129. *The Way We Were,* museum brochure, 3, Wigan Archives and Local Studies, SR3\36\C.

130. See Hewison, *Heritage Industry,* 21; and Mellor, "Enterprise and Heritage," 95.

131. Bennett, "Museums and 'the People,'" 65, 72.

132. Januszczak, "Romancing the Grime," 9.

133. See Jane Malcolm-Davies, "Borrowed Robes: The Educational Value of Costumed Interpretation at Historic Sites," *International Journal of Heritage Studies* 10, no. 3 (2004): 277–293, here 280. See also Cross and Walton, *Playful Crowd;* and Rentzhog, *Open Air Museums.*

134. See Christopher Martin Ford, "The 'Theatre-in-Museum' Movement in the British Isles" (PhD diss., University of Leeds, 1998), 74; and Cross and Walton, *Playful Crowd,* 229–232.

135. Quoted in Cross and Walton, *Playful Crowd,* 231.

136. Ford, "'Theatre-in-Museum' Movement," 71. See also Peter Lewis, "Illustrations and Observations from Wigan and Beamish," in *Manual of Heritage Management,* ed. Richard Harrison (Oxford: Butterworth-Heinemann, 1994), 333–334; Sterry, "Analysis of Heritage Centres," 165; Terry Stevens, "Wigan Pier Back to Reality," *Leisure Management,* June 1987, 31–34, here 32; *Way We Were,* 3; and Hewison, *Heritage Industry,* 18.

137. See Colin Sorensen, "Theme Parks and Time Machines," in *The New Museology,* ed. Peter Vergo (London: Reaktion Books, 1989), 60–73; Christopher Lasch, "The Politics of Nostalgia: Losing History in the Mists of Ideology," *Harper's,* November 1984, 65–70, here 69; Christopher Lasch, *The True and Only Heaven: Progress and Its Critics* (New York: Norton, 1991), 118; David Lowenthal, "Nostalgia Tells It Like It Wasn't," in *The Imagined Past: History and Nostalgia,* ed. Christopher Shaw and Malcolm Chase (Manchester: Manchester University Press, 1989), 18–32, here 23–24; and Michael Kammen, *Mystic Chords of Memory: The Transformation of Tradition in American Culture* (New York: Alfred A. Knopf, 1991), 635–639. For an analysis of this comparison, see Cross and Walton, *Playful Crowd.*

138. Januszczak, "Romancing the Grime," 9.

139. Hewison, *Heritage Industry,* 21.

140. Januszczak, "Romancing the Grime," 9.

141. Hewison, *Heritage Industry,* 29; on Wigan Pier, see 15–29.

142. *Heritage Business,* 11:42–12:03.

143. Bennett, "Museums and 'the People,'" 68.

144. Sorensen, "Theme Parks and Time Machines," 64.

145. *Way We Were,* 3.

146. Adrian Mellor, "Where There's Grime, There's Sense," *Guardian,* September 5, 1987, 12.

147. See *Way We Were,* 6–9.

148. *Way We Were,* 3.

149. Mellor, "Enterprise and Heritage," 97.

150. Sterry, "Analysis of Heritage Centres," 177.

151. Gaynor Bagnall, "Performance and Performativity at Heritage Sites," *Museum and Society* 1, no. 2 (2003): 87–103, here 94.

152. Bagnall, 90.

153. *Man Who Made Beamish,* 13:00–13:21.

154. Frank Atkinson, "Regional Museums," *Museums Journal* 68, no. 2 (1968): 74–77, here 74; Atkinson quoted in Cross and Walton, *Playful Crowd,* 225.

155. Quoted from a 2003 interview with Atkinson in Rentzhog, *Open Air Museums,* 233.

156. *Heritage Business,* 16:02–16:32.

157. Peter Lewis, "Wigan Pier Strikes Back," in *The Dodo Strikes Back,* ed. John Iddon (London: Strawberry Fair, 1988), 10–13, here 11.

158. See Lewis, 11.

159. Lewis, 13.

160. Peter Lewis, "Dependence or Independence," in *Money, Money, Money and Museums,* ed. Timothy Ambrose (Edinburgh: HMSO, 1991), 39–49, here 43; Peter Lewis, "Illustrations and Observations from Wigan and Beamish," in Harrison, *Manual of Heritage Management,* 333–334; Peter Lewis, "Making or Mocking?," *Museums Journal* 91, no. 7 (1991): 33–35.

161. On commercial heritage centers, see Louise Zarmati, "A Positive View of 'the Heritage Industry': A Study of Seven Private Heritage Centres in Britain" (MPhil thesis, University of Cambridge, 1991).

162. Roy Strong, *The Roy Strong Diaries, 1967–1987* (London: Weidenfeld and Nicolson, 1997), 231.

163. "Press Conference in York, 26 September 1984," Margaret Thatcher Foundation, https://www.margaretthatcher.org/document/105510. See also Peter Davenport, "Thatcher Warning of Museum Society," *Times* (London), September 27, 1984, 1; and R. W. Apple Jr., "The Coal Strike: A Struggle against 'Mrs. Thatcher's Britain,'" *New York Times,* October 7, 1984, E5.

164. See Fiona McLean, *Marketing the Museum* (London: Routledge, 1997), 54, 151.

165. Lewis, "Making or Mocking," 35; "Last Chance to See 'The Way We Were,'" *Past Forward* 47 (2007/20008): 9.

166. "Wigan Pier Museum Remembered in New Film 10 Years after Closing," *Wigan Today,* December 13, 2017, https://www.wigantoday.net/news/wigan-pier-museum -remembered-new-film-10-years-after-closing-720053. For the full film, see "Wigan Pier Museum Highlights," posted December 6, 2017, YouTube video, 10:40, https://www.youtube.com/watch?v=wI1D0A5bMwI.

167. "Civil War Centre Opens in Newark," BBC News, May 3, 2015, https://www.bbc .com/news/uk-england-nottinghamshire-32485012; Sophie Campbell, "Inside Newark's New National Civil War Centre," *Daily Telegraph,* May 3, 2015.

168. Mads Daugbjerg, "Battle," in *The Routledge Handbook of Reenactment Studies,* ed. Vanessa Agnew, Jonathan Lamb, and Juliane Tomann (Abingdon, UK: Routledge, 2020), 25–28. See also Malcolm-Davies, "Borrowed Robes."

169. See Kammen, *Mystic Chords of Memory,* 533.

170. Lowenthal, *Past Is a Foreign Country,* 301; on reenactment, see also 295–301.

171. Hewison, *Heritage Industry,* 83.

172. Kevin Walsh, *The Representation of the Past: Museums and Heritage in the Post-modern World* (London: Routledge, 1992), 103.

173. Mike Crang, "Magic Kingdom or Quixotic Quest for Authenticity?," *Annals of Tourism Research* 23, no. 2 (1996): 415–431, here 422. See also R. Lee Hadden, *Reliving the Civil War: A Reenactor's Handbook* (Mechanicsburg, PA: Stackpole Books, 1999), 5–6; Tom Dunning, "Civil War Re-enactments: Performance as a Cultural Practice," *Australasian Journal of American Studies* 21, no. 1 (2002): 63–73, here 68; and Christopher Bates, "What They Fight For: The Men and Women of Civil War Reenactment" (PhD diss., University of California, Los Angeles, 2016), 87, 103, 111–112, 152.

174. Jonathan D. Schroeder, "Nostalgia," in Agnew, Lamb, and Tomann, *Routledge Handbook of Reenactment Studies,* 156–159, here 156, 159.

175. See Alison Michelli, *Commando to Captain-Generall: The Life of Brigadier Peter Young* (Barnsley, UK: Pen and Sword Military, 2007).

176. "Bargepole," *Punch,* July 3, 1985, 51.

177. Terry Pratchett, *Feet of Clay* (New York: Corgi Books, 1996), 99.

178. Daugbjerg, "Battle," 26.

179. The papers of the Sealed Knot are held at the University of Nottingham, Manuscript and Special Collections, SKO and SKU. All archival material quoted in this section comes from there. See also Mario Carretero, Everardo Perez-Manjarrez, and Brady Wagoner, eds., *Historical Reenactment: New Ways of Experiencing History* (New York: Berghahn, 2022); Agnew, Lamb, and Tomann, eds., *The Routledge Handbook of Reenactment Studies;* Ulrike Jureit, *Magie des Authentischen: Das Nachleben von Krieg und Gewalt im Reenactment* (Göttingen: Wallstein, 2020); and Iain McCalman and Paul A. Pickering, eds., *Historical Reenactment from Realism to the Affective Turn* (Basingstoke, UK: Palgrave Macmillan, 2010).

180. See Tom Hulme, "'A Nation of Town Criers': Civic Publicity and Historical Pageantry in Inter-war Britain," *Urban History* 44, no. 2 (2017): 270–292.

181. *The Sealed Knot Members Compendium,* 1973, S. 1; Philip O. Stearns, "The Tower of London," *Orders of the Day,* August 15, 1974, SKU25/6.

182. See Dunning, "Civil War Re-enactments."

183. See Dunning, 64–65.

184. See Ward Allan Howe, "Bull Run Prepares for Tourist Onslaught," *New York Times,* May 29, 1960, X, 23; Robert F. Whitney, "Manassas—100 Years Later," *New York Times,* December 11, 1960, XX, 1; and Philip R. Smith Jr., "Manassas Girds for Third Bull Run Battle," *New York Times,* June 4, 1961, XX, 21.

185. On the Civil War centennial, see John Bodnar, *Remaking America: Public Memory, Commemoration and Patriotism in the Twentieth Century* (Princeton, NJ: Princeton University Press, 1992), 206–226; Jon Wiener, "Civil War, Cold War, Civil Rights:

The Civil War Centennial in Context, 1960–1965," in *The Memory of the Civil War in American Culture*, ed. Alice Fahs and Joan Waugh (Chapel Hill: University of North Carolina Press, 2004), 237–257; and Robert J. Cook, *Troubled Commemoration: The American Civil War Centennial, 1961–1965* (Baton Rouge: Louisiana State University Press, 2007).

186. Civil War Centennial Commission, ed., *The Civil War Centennial: A Report to the Congress* (Washington, DC: Government Printing Office, 1968), 45.

187. Civil War Centennial Commission, 14. See also Cook, *Troubled Commemoration*.

188. "Centennial of War Is Found Popular," *New York Times*, April 6, 1961, L34.

189. See Bodnar, *Remaking America*, 215, 226; and Bates, "What They Fight For," 88, 97.

190. See Milton Singer, "On the Symbolic and Historic Structure of an American Identity," *Ethos* 5 (1977): 431–455, here 437–438; David Lowenthal, "The Bicentennial Landscape: A Mirror Held Up to the Past," *Geographical Review* 67, no. 3 (1977): 253–267; Bodnar, *Remaking America*, 226–243; Hadden, *Reliving the Civil War*, 5; and Bates, "What They Fight For," 5.

191. John Skow, Beth Austin, and Joseph J. Kane, "Bang, Bang! You're History, Buddy," *Time*, August 11, 1986, 58–60, here 59. See also Hadden, *Reliving the Civil War*, 5.

192. See Randal Allred, "Catharsis, Revision, and Re-enactment: Negotiating the Meaning of the American Civil War," *Journal of American Culture* 19, no. 4 (1996): 1–13, here 2; Bates, "What They Fight For," 5; Michael E. Ruane, "Reenactors Swarm Gettysburg for Tributes of Civil War's Turning Point," *Washington Post*, June 30, 2013; and Victoria Benning and Peter Slevin, "A Brush with the Real Thing at Gettysburg," *Washington Post*, July 9, 1998.

193. See Bryn Stole, "The Decline of the Civil War Re-enactor," *New York Times*, July 28, 2018. See also Gigi Douban, "Fewer People Participate in Civil War Reenactments," NPR, July 4, 2011, https://www.npr.org/2011/07/04/137609367/fewer-people -participate-in-civil-war-reenactments?t=1607595217791.

194. David Chandler, "Pageantry & Tradition: The Re-enactment Scene in England," *Living History*, Summer 1984, 23–28, here 25.

195. See Stephen Hunt, "Acting the Part: 'Living History' as a Serious Leisure Pursuit," *Leisure Studies* 23, no. 4 (2004): 387–403.

196. "Testimony of Peter Bentham Hill," in Sandra Costello, *In the Beginning: The Formation of the Sealed Knot* (2008), SKO 1/2/1. See also Michelli, *Commando to Captain-Generall*, 228–229.

197. See Tom Picton, "The Cavaliers Take to the Field Again," *Illustrated London News*, June 27, 1970, 18–19; and Crux, "London Diary," *New Statesman*, July 10, 1970, 9.

198. See Michelli, *Commando to Captain-Generall*, 232; James Corall, "The King and the Cause," *In Britain*, May 1992, 37–42, here 40; Minutes of the Inner Council,

August 26, 1985, SKO1/1/4; and "Déjà New: Historical Re-enactment," *Economist,* April 27, 2002, 32.

199. John Tucker, "Men Who Go to War in Plastic Doilies," *Mayfair,* September 12–13, 1970, 46–49, 80. See also Malcolm-Davies, "Borrowed Robes."

200. Richard Cox, "Only Damaged Dignity at the Battle of Newbury 1969," *Daily Telegraph Magazine,* November 21, 1969, 34–40, here 35; Picton, "Cavaliers Take to the Field," 18–19.

201. Tom Forester, "Weekend Warriors," *New Society,* September 10, 1981, 418.

202. See Kirsty Milne, "Fighting a Very Civil Civil War," *New Statesman and Society,* August 20, 1993, 12–13.

203. See Milne; and "Déjà New," 32.

204. Stephen Cushman, *Bloody Promenade: Reflections on a Civil War Battle* (Charlottesville: University Press of Virginia, 1999), 52.

205. *The Sealed Knot Members Compendium,* 1973, 1, SKO2/4/1.

206. "Valedictory Address by the Captain-General," February 13, 1973, SKO1/1/1. See also "Manifesto of the Field-Marshall to ye Sealed Knot," *Orders of the Day,* March 15, 1972, SKU25/6; Russell Miller, "About Men Joins the Roundheads in Battle," *Evening Standard,* September 1, 1971, 19; and Mary McCormack, "The Tallents Go to War!," unidentified magazine article, SKU26/4.

207. "Manifesto of the Field-Marshall."

208. Malcolm Davison, "Into Battle," *Spread Eagle* 48, no. 4 (1973): 128–131; McCormack, "Tallents Go to War!," 22; Forester, "Weekend Warriors," 418; Chandler, "Pageantry & Tradition," 28; Nigel Bradley, "Very Civil War," *In Britain,* April 1972, 25–26, 51; "Déjà New." On the United States, see Hadden, *Reliving the Civil War,* 4; and Tony Horwitz, *Confederates in the Attic: Dispatches from the Unfinished Civil War* (New York: Vintage, 1998), 134.

209. Miller, "About Men," 19.

210. Chandler, "Pageantry & Tradition," 28.

211. Bradley, "Very Civil War," 51.

212. David Robinson, "Oh What a Lovely Civil War," *Daily Post,* September 30, 1986, 15.

213. Jay Anderson, *Time Machines: The World of Living History* (Nashville: American Association for State and Local History, 1984), 183.

214. Allred, "Catharsis, Revision, and Re-enactment," 7.

215. See, for instance, Horwitz, *Confederates in the Attic,* 16, 61, 139, 558; and Bates, "What They Fight For," 177–181.

216. Alvin Toffler, *Future Shock* (London: Pan Books, 1970), 353–354; Anderson, *Time Machines,* 183–185.

217. Anderson, *Time Machines,* 186.

218. John Brewer, "Reenactment and Neo-realism," in *Historical Reenactment from Realism to the Affective Turn,* ed. Iain McCalman and Paul A. Pickering (Basingstoke, UK: Palgrave Macmillan, 2010), 79–89, here 81.

219. See Anderson, *Time Machines,* 133, 183; Rory Turner, "Bloodless Battles: The Civil War Reenacted," *The Drama Review* 34, no. 4 (1990): 123–136, here 126; Allred, "Catharsis, Revision, and Re-enactment," 6; and Horwitz, *Confederates in the Attic,* 7.

220. Bradley, "Very Civil War," 26.

221. Malcolm Davison, "From Computers to Cavaliers," *Spread Eagle* 48, no. 3 (1973): 87–89, here 88.

222. Miller, "About Men," 19.

223. Turner, "Bloodless Battle," 126.

224. Ben Macintyre, "Ultimate Summer of Mud, Sweat and Tears," *Times* (London), August 17, 2019, 27.

225. Quoted in Bates, "What They Fight For," 73.

226. Horwitz, *Confederates in the Attic,* 386, 137. See also Dunning, "Civil War Re-enactments," 70.

227. Ta-Nehisi Coates, *We Were Eight Years in Power: An American Tragedy* (London: Hamish Hamilton, 2017), 141, 152.

228. Cushman, *Bloody Promenade,* 59. See also Diane Purkiss, "Why the British Don't Remember Their Civil War and Americans Do Remember Theirs," History News Network, 2006, https://historynewsnetwork.org/article/28872.

229. "Reminiscences of John Adair," 2007, SKU1/2/1-9; "Roundheads Urgently Wanted," *Times* (London), May 9, 1969, 20.

230. Miller, "About Men"; Chandler, "Pageantry & Tradition," 28. See also *The Sealed Knot Members Compendium,* 1973, 1, SKO2/4/1; and Picton, "Cavaliers Take to the Field," 18–19.

231. Chandler, "Pageantry & Tradition," 24.

232. "Valedictory Address by the Captain-General," 20. See also Chandler, "Pageantry & Tradition," 27; and James Delingpole, "Band of Heroes, or Sad's Army," *Times* (London), December 27, 2003, 26–27.

233. Milne, "Fighting a Very Civil," 13.

234. See Cathy Stanton and Stephen Belyea, "'Their Time Will Yet Come': The African American Presence in Civil War Reenactment," in *Hope and Glory: Essays of the Legacy of the Fifty-Fourth Massachusetts Regiment,* ed. Martin H. Blatt, Thomas J. Brown, and Donald Yacovone (Amherst: University of Massachusetts Press, 2000), 253–274. See also Dunning, "Civil War Re-enactments," 70; Soraya Nadia McDonal, "'Ask a Slave' Talks Race and Gender Issues in the Age of YouTube," *Washington Post,* November 12, 2013; and "A Conversation with Azie Dungey," *American*

Historian, August 2014, https://www.oah.org/tah/issues/2014/august/a-conversation-with-azie-dungey/.

235. Coates, *We Were Eight Years,* 141.

236. See Tristram Hunt, "The Charge of the Heavy Brigade," *Guardian,* September 4, 2006; and David Conn, "The Scandal of Orgreave," *Guardian,* May 18, 2017.

237. Margaret Thatcher, "Speech to the 1922 Committee, 19 July 1984," Margaret Thatcher Foundation, https://www.margaretthatcher.org/document/105563.

238. See Jonathan Jones, "Missiles Fly, Truncheons Swing, Police Chase Miners as Cars Burn. It's All Very Exciting. But Why Is It Art?," *Guardian,* June 19, 2001; Katie Kitamura, "'Recreating Chaos': Jeremy Deller's *The Battle of Orgreave,*" in McCalman and Pickering, *Historical Reenactment,* 39–49.

239. Jeremy Deller, *The English Civil War Part II: Personal Accounts of the 1984–85 Miner's Strike* (London: Artangel, 2001).

240. Kitamura, "'Recreating Chaos,'" 45; Claire Bishop, *Artificial Hells: Participatory Art and the Politics of Spectatorship* (London: Verso, 2012), 33.

241. See, for instance, Carla Almeida Santos and Grace Yan, "Genealogical Tourism: A Phenomenological Examination," *Journal of Travel Research* 49, no. 1 (2010): 56–67.

242. *Who Do You Think You Are?,* season 1, episode 4, BBC2, November 23, 2004, http://www.bbc.co.uk/whodoyouthinkyouare/past-stories/david-baddiel.shtml. See also Gemma Romain, "*Who Do You Think You Are?* Journeys and Jewish Identity in the Televisual Narrative of David Baddiel," *Jewish Culture and History* 11, no. 1–2 (2009): 283–296; Amy Holdsworth, "*Who Do You Think You Are?* Family History and Memory on British Television," in *Televising History: Mediating the Past in Postwar Europe,* ed. Erin Bell and Ann Gray (Basingstoke, UK: Palgrave Macmillan 2010), 234–247; and Jerome de Groot, *Consuming History: Historians and Heritage in Contemporary Popular Culture* (London: Routledge, 2009), 201–202.

243. Mick Hulme, "Root Around for Your Family Tree If You Must, but Then Get Your Own Life," *Times* (London), December 17, 2004, 15.

244. Terence Black, "A Family Tree Is So Much Less Trouble Than a Family," *Independent,* October 1, 2004. See also Leo McKinstry, "Sorry, but Family History Really Is Bunk," *Spectator,* April 30, 2008, 22.

245. Lowenthal, *Past Is a Foreign Country,* 11; Lowenthal, *Heritage Crusade,* 13.

246. Raphael Samuel, "Introduction: Exciting to Be English," in *Patriotism: The Making and Unmaking of British National Identity,* vol. 1: *History and Politics,* ed. Raphael Samuel (London: Routledge, 1989), xviii–lxvii, here xlv. See also Samuel, *Theatres of Memory,* 25, 150, 159.

247. Kammen, *Mystic Chords of Memory,* 642.

248. See Matthew F. Delmont, *Making Roots: A Nation Captivated* (Oakland: University of California Press, 2016).

249. See Stephane Dunn, "Why the *Roots* Remake Is So Important," *Atlantic,* May 29, 2016.

250. *Roots: The Next Generations,* episode 7, "The 1960s," ABC, February 24, 1979.

251. Michele Burgen, "How to Trace Your Family Tree," *Ebony,* June 1977, 52–62; François Weil, *Family Trees: A History of Genealogy in America* (Boston: Harvard University Press, 2013), 199; Charles L. Blockson and Ron Fry, *Black Genealogy* (Englewood Cliffs, NJ: Prentice-Hall, 1977); and James D. Walker, *Black Genealogy: How to Begin* (Athens: University of Georgia, 1977).

252. William Marmon, "Why 'Roots' Hit Home," *Time,* February 14, 1977, 45–49, here 49.

253. "White Roots: Looking for Great-Grandpa," *Time,* March 28, 1977, 55–56.

254. See Weil, *Family Trees.*

255. Honor Sachs, "The Dark Side of Our Genealogy Craze," *Washington Post,* December 13, 2019.

256. See, for instance, David A. Gerber, "Haley's Roots and Our Own: An Inquiry into the Nature of a Popular Phenomenon," *Journal of Ethnic Studies* 5, no. 3 (1978): 87–111, here 105; Anthony J. Camp, *Everyone Has Roots: An Introduction to Genealogy* (London: W. H. Allen, 1978); Kammen, *Mystic Chords of Memory,* 618, 641–645; and Delmont, *Making Roots,* 191.

257. "Life Guide: Helpful Hints for Genealogy Hunters," *Life,* January 18, 1963, 13.

258. See Richard J. Cattani, "The Boom in Ancestor Hunting," *Christian Science Monitor,* March 21, 1977, 3; Rick J. Ashton, "Curators, Hobbyists, and Historians: Genealogy at the Newberry Library," *Library Quarterly* 47, no. 2 (1977): 149–162, here 160; and Russell E. Bidlack, "Genealogy Today," *Library Trends* 32, no. 1 (1983): 7–23, here 10.

259. "Looking for Roots in the Family," *Manchester Guardian,* January 21, 1958, 5; Peter Spufford, "Recent Developments in Genealogy," *Amateur Historian* 7, no. 6 (1967): 178–181, here 181. See also Samuel, *Theatres of Memory,* 148.

260. See David Gelman, "Everybody's Search for Roots," *Newsweek,* July 4, 1977, 26–35, here 30.

261. Robert M. Taylor, "Summoning the Wandering Tribes: Genealogy and Family Reunions in American History," *Journal of Social History* 16, no. 2 (1982): 21–37, here 32.

262. See Jackie Hogan, *Roots Quest: Inside America's Genealogy Boom* (London: Rowman and Littlefield, 2019), 1–2.

263. See Peggy Tuck Sinko and Scott N. Peters, "A Survey of Genealogists at the Newberry Library," *Library Trends* 32, no. 1 (1983): 97–110; Ashton, "Curators,

Hobbyists, and Historians"; and Cardell K. Jacobson, Phillip R. Kunz, and Melanie W. Conlin, "Extended Family Ties: Genealogical Researchers," in *Aging and the Family,* ed. Stephen J. Bahr and Evan T. Peterson (Lexington, MA: Lexington Books, 1989), 193–206.

264. See R. D. Lambert, "The Family Historian and Temporal Orientations towards the Ancestral Past," *Time and Society* 5 (1996): 115–143.

265. Simon Michael Titley-Bayes, "Family History in England, c. 1945–2006: Culture, Identity and (Im)mortality" (PhD diss., University of York, 2006), 145.

266. See *Family History,* BBC2, 5 episodes, March 17–21, 1979. See also Gordon Honeycombe, "Root and Branch," *Radio Times,* March 17–23, 1979, 7–8; Peter Fiddick, "Family History," *Guardian,* April 20, 1979, 12; and Titley-Bayes, "Family History in England," 170.

267. See Stan Newens, "Family History Societies," *History Workshop Journal* 11, no. 1 (1981): 154–159, here 155.

268. See Titley-Bayes, "Family History in England," 45–46, 216, 225.

269. See Titley-Bayes, 44.

270. See "Have You Ever Traced or Looked into Your Family History (Genealogy)?," YouGov, June 6, 2018, https://yougov.co.uk/topics/education/survey-results/daily /2018/06/06/76b82/3; and Titley-Bayes, "Family History in England," 70, 101.

271. See Weil, *Family Trees,* 203; Titley-Bayes, "Family History in England," 92; and Michael Sharpe, *Family Matters: A History of Genealogy* (Barnsley, UK: Pen and Sword, 2011), 200–231.

272. Margot Hornblower, "Roots Mania," *Time,* April 19, 1999, 54–67.

273. See McKinstry, "Sorry"; Gregory Rodriguez, "How Genealogy Became Almost as Popular as Porn," *Time,* May 30, 2014; Alison Light, "A Visit to the Dead: Genealogy and the Historian," in *History after Hobsbawm: Writing the Past for the Twenty-First Century,* ed. John H. Arnold, Matthew Hilton, and Jan Rüger (Oxford: Oxford University Press, 2018), 292–305; and Hogan, *Roots Quest.*

274. See "Company Facts," Ancestry.com, https://www.ancestry.com/corporate/about -ancestry/company-facts. See also Jerome de Groot, "The Genealogy Boom: Inheritance, Family History and Popular Historical Imagination," in *The Impact of History? Histories at the Beginning of the Twenty-First Century,* ed. Pedro Ramos Pinto and Bertrand Taithe (Abingdon, UK: Routledge, 2015), 21–33, here 29.

275. See Holdsworth, *"Who Do You Think You Are?"*; and de Groot, *Consuming History,* 201–202.

276. See "Henry Louis Gates Jr.: A Life Spent Tracing Roots," NPR, May 8, 2012, https://www.npr.org/2012/05/08/152273032/henry-louis-gates-jr-a-life-spent -tracing-roots. See also Henry Louis Gates Jr., "Forty Acres and a Gap in Wealth," *New York Times,* November 18, 2007; and Tambay Obenson, "'Finding Your

Roots': Henry Louis Gates, Jr. on the Political Importance of His PBS Series," IndieWire, October 26, 2020, https://www.indiewire.com/2020/10/finding-your -roots-henry-louis-gates-jr-interview-1234592979/.

277. See Matthew Stallard and Jerome de Groot, "'Things Are Coming Out That Are Questionable, We Never Knew About': DNA and the New Family History," *Journal of Family History* 45, no. 3 (2020): 274–294.

278. Jacob Young and Meggan Dissly, "Europe's Genealogy Craze," *Newsweek,* March 7, 1988, 58–59, here 58.

279. Pierre Nora, "General Introduction: Between History and Memory," in *Realms of Memory: Construction of the French Past,* ed. Pierre Nora and Lawrence D. Kritzman, trans. Arthur Goldhammer (New York: Columbia University Press, 1993), 1:1–20, here 15.

280. Annie Ernaux, *The Years,* trans. Alison L. Strayer (London: Fitzcarraldo Editions, 2018), 144.

281. André Burguière, "La genealogie," in *Les lieux de mémoire,* vol. 3, *Les France,* pt. 3, *De l'archive à l'emblème,* ed. Pierre Nora (Paris: Gallimard, 1992), 20–51, here 20.

282. Martine Segalen and Claude Michelat, "L'amour de la généalogie," in *Jeux de familles,* ed. Martine Segalen (Paris: CNRS Editions, 2002), 193–208.

283. François Hartog, *Regimes of Historicity: Presentism and the Experience of Time* (New York: Columbia University Press, 2015), 6; see also 116, 139.

284. "Vorfahren: Fleisch am Knochen," *Der Spiegel,* July 4, 1990, 83–84. See also "Ahnenforschung: Mein Ur-Ur-Ur-Ur-Ur-Opa und ich," *Der Spiegel,* May 24, 2017; "Wenn Ahnenforschung zur Leidenschaft wird," *Frankfurter Allgemeine Zeitung,* May 3, 1985, 49; and "Die Geschichte von unten schreiben: Auf der Suche nach den Ahnen," *Frankfurter Allgemeine Zeitung,* February 20, 1995, 9.

285. Eckart Henning and Wolfgang Ribbe, *Handbuch der Genealogie* (Neustadt, Germany: Degener, 1972), v.

286. See Antje Hildebrandt, "Ahnenforschung: Armin Rohde und die Suche nach dem Nazi-Opa," *Die Welt,* April 8, 2008.

287. "Joys of Collecting One's Ancestors," *Guardian,* October 17, 1962, 21.

288. Phebe R. Jacobsen, "'The World Turned Upside Down': Reference Priorities and the State Archives," *American Archivist* 44, no. 4 (1981): 341–345, here 341.

289. Felix Hull, "The Archivist and the Genealogist," *Genealogists' Magazine* 19, no. 10 (1989): 339–345, here 339.

290. Samuel P. Hays, "History and Genealogy: Patterns of Change and Prospects for Cooperation," *Prologue* 7, no. 1 (1975): 39–43, here 39.

291. Sharpe, *Family Matters,* 21.

292. Alison Light, *Common People: The History of an English Family* (London: Fig Tree, 2014), xxvii.

293. Weil, *Family Trees.*

294. Jay P. Anglin, "The Fundamentals of Genealogy: A Neglected but Fertile New Field for Professional Historians?," *Southern Quarterly* 13, no. 2 (1975): 145–150, here 147; Jonathan D. Sarna, review of *From Generation to Generation,* by Arthur Kurzweil, *Commentary* 70, no. 2 (1980): 69.

295. David A. Gerber, "Local and Community History: Some Cautionary Remarks on an Idea Whose Time Has Returned," *History Teacher* 13, no. 1 (1979): 7–30, here 11.

296. Tanya Evans, "How Do Family Historians Work with Memory?," *History Workshop,* February 6, 2019, https://www.historyworkshop.org.uk/how-do-family -historians-work-with-memory/; Tanya Evans, "Genealogy and Family History," in *A Companion to Public History,* ed. David Dean (Hoboken, NJ: Wiley, 2018), 175–185, here 180.

297. Anthony Wagner, *English Genealogy* (Oxford: Clarendon, 1960), 3.

298. See, for instance, Gerber, "Local and Community History," 11–13; Taylor, "Summoning the Wandering Tribes"; and Jacobson, Kunz, and Conlin, "Extended Family Ties."

299. Leo Derrick-Jehu, "Genealogy in Everyday Life," *Family History* 5, no. 28/29 (1968): 117–123, here 122.

300. J. N. Thompson, "Genealogy Counts!," *Genealogists' Magazine* 26, no. 4 (1998): 138–141, here 139.

301. Patrick M. Quinn, "The Surge of Interest in Genealogy Reflects a Populist Strand in Society with Important Implications for Our Culture," *Chronicle of Higher Education,* May 22, 1991, B2.

302. John Rayment, "The Functions of a Family History Society," *Family Tree Magazine* 5, no. 3 (1989): 10–11.

303. Noel Currer-Briggs, ed., *A Handbook of British Family History: A Guide to Methods and Sources* (Flitwick, UK: Family History Services, 1979), 10.

304. A. P. Joseph, "Delights of Genealogy," *British Medical Journal* 283 (December 1981): 1680–1681, here 1681.

305. See Stephanie Coontz, *The Way We Never Were: American Families and the Nostalgia Trap* (New York: Basic Books, 2016).

306. See, for instance, Jacobson, Kunz, and Conlin, "Extended Family Ties."

307. R. D. Lambert, "Reclaiming the Ancestral Past: Narrative, Rhetoric and the 'Convict Stain,'" *Journal of Sociology* 38 (2002): 111–143, here 131.

308. Birmingham and Midland Society for Genealogy and Heraldry, ed., *Personally Speaking: About This Ancestry Business* (Birmingham, UK: Birmingham and Midland Society for Genealogy and Heraldry, 1974 [vol. 1], 1981 [vol. 2]), 1:21, 42, 50, 77, 80, 92, 94, 102, 113, 116; 2:11, 14, 23, 28, 45.

309. See Birmingham and Midland Society for Genealogy and Heraldry, 1:50, 107; 2:49, 50.

310. See Birmingham and Midland Society for Genealogy and Heraldry, 2: 25, 50; 1:5. See also Camp, *Everyone Has Roots,* 9; Wagner, *English Genealogy,* 4; Sharpe, *Family Matters,* 10; and Light, *Common People,* xxii.

311. *The Mass Observation Project: Summer 2008 Directive* (Brighton, UK: Mass Observation Archive, 2008), http://www.massobs.org.uk/images/Directives/Summer_2008 _Directive.pdf. See also Anne-Marie Kramer, "Kinship, Affinity and Connectedness: Exploring the Role of Genealogy in Personal Lives," *Sociology* 45, no. 3 (2011): 379–395.

312. University of Sussex, Mass Observation Archive, Smxoa2/1/83/1/1, A883, A4348, A4127, B3968, S3779. The following references are all of these records.

313. A1706, B4236, B1989.

314. B3968.

315. T1961.

316. W2322.

317. C3513.

318. T1911, W3393.

319. B3968.

320. A4127.

321. R3765.

322. G3752

323. W3994.

324. See Tristram Hunt, "Reality, Identity and Empathy: The Changing Face of Social History Television," *Journal of Social History* 39, no. 3 (2006): 843–858, here 851.

325. Ashley Barnwell, "Telling Social Stories: Family History in the Library," *Australian Library Journal* 64, no.2 (2015): 105–112, here 111.

326. Wendy Bottero, "Who Do You Think They Were? How Family Historians Make Sense of Social Position and Inequality in the Past," *British Journal of Sociology* 63 (2012): 54–74, here 68.

327. Newens, "Family History Societies," 156.

328. Newens, 155.

329. David Hey, *Family History and Local History in England* (London: Longman, 1987), xi.

330. Evans, "How Do Family Historians?," 101.

331. Simon Fowler, "Our Genealogical Forebears," *History Today,* March 2001, 42–43, here 43; similarly Sharpe, *Family Matters,* 1; Newens, "Family History Societies," 159; Titley-Bayes, "Family History in England," 59, 91.

332. Lambert, "Family Historian," 131.

333. Sharpe, *Family Matters,* 25.

334. De Groot, "Genealogy Boom," 28.

335. Ivan Jablonka, *A History of the Grandparents I Never Had* (Stanford, CA: Stanford University Press, 2016); Mark Mazower, *What You Did Not Tell: A Russian Past and the Journey Home* (London: Penguin, 2018).

336. Light, *Common People.* See also Light, "Visit to the Dead."

337. Rymsza-Pawlowska, *History Comes Alive,* 5.

338. Rymsza-Pawlowska, 1.

339. Samuel, *Theatres of Memory,* 18.

Conclusion

1. Dua Lipa, "Future Nostalgia," Genius, https://genius.com/18639027.

2. Brittany Spanos, "Dua Lipa Crafts a Studio 54-Worthy Disco Revival on 'Future Nostalgia,'" *Rolling Stone,* March 26, 2020; Ken Tucker, "With 'Future Nostalgia,' Dua Lipa Reminds Us How to Feel Care-Free," NPR, April 21, 2020, https://text .npr.org/839968207.

3. Quoted in Rhian Daly, "Dua Lipa Releases Pulsating New Single 'Physical'— Listen," NME, January 31, 2020, https://www.nme.com/news/music/dua-lipa-to -release-new-single-physical-next-week-2601049.

4. See, for instance, Tim Wildschut and Constantine Sedikides, "Psychology and Nostalgia: Towards a Functional Approach," in *Intimations of Nostalgia: Multidisciplinary Explorations of an Enduring Emotion,* ed. Michael Hviid Jacobsen (Bristol: Bristol University Press, 2021), 110–128; and Clay Routledge, *Nostalgia: A Psychological Research* (London: Routledge, 2015).

5. Maurice Halbwachs, *On Collective Memory,* ed., trans., and with an introduction by Lewis A. Coser (Chicago: University of Chicago Press, 1992), 17.

6. Simon Reynolds, *Retromania: Pop Culture's Addiction to Its Own Past* (New York: Faber and Faber, 2011), xxiii.

Acknowledgments

I
t all began with a trip—not a trip down memory lane but a family holiday to Devon and Cornwall in 2013, during which we visited countless country houses, heritage centers, and open-air museums, and also rode the occasional steam train. Stopping in London on the way back, I wondered aloud to my colleague and friend Len Platt whether this heritage landscape was not indicative of a certain kind of ingrained British nostalgia. Len responded that this was not exactly an original observation and steered me toward the work of Robert Hewison, David Lowenthal, and Patrick Wright, featured prominently on the preceding pages. When applying for a job at the German Historical Institute London some months later, I decided to propose a project on nostalgia. At the time, I thought this was the sort of niche subject I gravitate toward. I soon realized what a many-headed beast nostalgia was, Brexit and Donald Trump making the use of this term even more ubiquitous, understanding it even more challenging.

I could not have navigated these difficulties without the help of a lot of people. First of all, I would like to thank Andreas Gestrich, the former director of the German Historical Institute London, who saw the potential of this project when I was still uncertain about it myself and supported me in developing it, as well as his successor, Christina von Hodenberg; Paul Nolte, who hosted me in 2020–2021 as a fellow of the Max Weber Foundation at the Freie Universität Berlin, where I completed the manuscript; and Martin Sabrow and Frank Bösch, the former and current directors of the Leibniz Centre for Contemporary History in Potsdam, where I revised it. My thanks also go to all the colleagues at these institutions who read and commented on draft chapters and especially the interns at the German Historical Institute London who assisted in researching it.

The book has profited much from my presenting drafts of chapters at various conferences and talks. I am grateful to inviters and interlocutors at the Universities of Aarhus, Bielefeld, Cambridge, Cologne, Copenhagen, Jena, Konstanz, Leiden, Nottingham, and Oxford; University College London; the Queen's University Belfast; the University of Southern Denmark Odense; the Center for the History of Emotions at the Max Planck Institute for Human Development Berlin; the German Historical Institute Rome; the Institute for Contemporary History Munich; and the Institute of Historical Research London.

I am also indebted to many colleagues and friends. The project benefited early on from a presentation given at the Arbeitskreis Geschichte + Theorie. I am particularly thankful to Alexander C. T. Geppert; Daniel Morat, who helped me get to grips with Chapter 4; and Nina Verheyen. My interest in the subject of memory was sparked by a seminar taught by Karl Borromäus Murr many years ago, and I have continued to profit from our conversations about history, memory, and theory ever since. Major thanks go to Fernando Esposito, who read and commented on Chapter 1 and from whom I learned everything I know about the history temporalities that I did not learn from Achim Landwehr. Many thanks also to Peter Bailey, Martin Baumeister, Maria Framke, Felix Fuhg, Dion Georgiou, Anne Gnausch, Mathias Häußler, Bastian Herbst, Angelika Hoelger, Juliane Hornung, Tom Hulme, Jan-Holger Kirsch, David Linton, Ole Münch, Len Platt, Stefanie Rauch, Emily Richards, Emily Robinson, Klaus Seidl, Olga Sparschuh, Sabine Stach, Martina Steber, Dylan Trigg, Andreas Weiß, Felix Wiedemann, Nicole Wiederroth, and Barbara Wünnenberg.

Without Paul Nolte it would have been impossible to overcome that remnant of medieval torture still practiced at German universities called "Habilitation"; he also provided the required report, as did Willibald Steinmetz—many thanks! Thanks, too, to the two anonymous colleagues who reviewed the manuscript for Harvard University Press.

I also want to thank the people who let me interview them for this book: first and foremost the late David Lowenthal; Robert Hewison, who invited me into his home in South Acton; and Roy Strong, former director of the Victoria and Albert Museum, as well as the countless librarians, archivists, museum workers, and participants at historical reenactments. The artists Peter Kennard and Klaus Staeck allowed me to use their wonderful photo collages. Summer Banks read and corrected the entire manuscript.

Special thanks go to Bernhard Rieger, who not only paved the way for me to become a guest lecturer at University College London but also gave me the courage to send a proposal to Harvard University Press. At Harvard I am grateful to editors Ian Malcolm and Sam Stark as well as Jillian Quigley and Stephanie Vyce; at Westchester Publishing Services to Ashley Moore for her meticulous copyediting.

Finally, I want to thank my family: my parents and Kristina and Josephine, who accompanied me on many trips undertaken for this book following the one on which it all started. When Josie and I shared an office during the first COVID-19 lockdown, she doing her schoolwork, me working on the manuscript, she used to tease me, telling me my book was so boring that nobody would ever read it. I tried my best to prove her wrong! To her and Len, without whom it might not exist, I dedicate this book.

Index